250 YEARS OF
CHILTERN METHODISM

Frogmoor Gardens, High Wycombe, c 1890, with Primitive Methodist Church.

11

250 YEARS
OF
CHILTERN METHODISM

by   BARRY P. SUTCLIFFE and DAVID C. CHURCH

Line-drawings by STANLEY SHERRATT

A celebration of 250 years of
Local Methodism
since the Conversion of
John and Charles Wesley

24th May, 1988.

Published on behalf of the authors by

MOORLEY'S B I & Bookshop Ltd.
L E

23 Park Road, Ilkeston
Derbys. DE7 5DA
Tel: (0602) 320643

ISBN 0 86071 289 3

Copyright © 1988

Barry P. Sutcliffe and David C. Church

Local distribution by the authors:

Barry P. Sutcliffe,   David C. Church,
20, Grimms Meadow,   1, Hobart Close,
Walters Ash,   High Wycombe,
Nr. High Wycombe,   Bucks. HP13 6UF
Bucks. HP14 4UH

Permissions.

Cover map by kind permission of Mr. St. John Thomas,
David & Charles Publishers Plc. from the 19th Century Ordnance
Survey copy, Sheet 71.

The Methodist Church Overseas Division Photo Library, for the
copy of the painting "Fire at Epworth".

Rev. John Banks, M.A. permission to quote from "My Dear Sister"
by Rev. Maldwyn Edwards.

Printed and Bound by Oxford University Press.

ACKNOWLEDGEMENTS

We wish to offer our sincere thanks for the invaluable help and encouragement given us by people - not all Methodists - too numerous to mention individually. To the many people who have contributed articles and often very much more in the way of information, photographs, Circuit Plans and advice, our grateful thanks. We have not been able to use all the material offered and some may be disappointed that their contribution has apparently been ignored. Yet all have been invaluable in shaping the finished product.

In particular our thanks to:

David W. Riley, FLA and Miss Alison Peacock of the Methodist Archives, The John Rylands University of Manchester.

The County Archivist, and staff of the Bucks.County Record Office, Aylesbury.

The Chief Librarian and staff of the Central Reference Library, High Wycombe.

Mr.Ivan Sparkes and staff of the Chair Museum, High Wycombe.

The "Bucks Free Press" and "Bucks Examiner".

Mr.Alan Rose, The Circuit Plan Society.

Rev. Geoffrey Jones and Rev.Tony Barnard, for use of the Circuit archives.

If we may be forgiven for singling out certain individuals - our gratitude to Mrs. Ada Day, Miss Helen Smith, Mr. Norman Keen and Mr. John Moorley for their great interest, help and advice, and to Mrs.Frances Sears and Mr.David Lewis whose collection of Plans, together with our own, gave a virtually unbroken record from 1934 to date.

Our warmest thanks must go to Mr.Stan Sherratt for his splendid line-drawings which often seem to capture a church's inner beauty, lacking in a photograph. We are also indebted to our wives: Mrs.Hilary Sutcliffe who has checked the proofs; and Mrs.Myrtle Church who has been responsible for the photographs and illustrations.

DEDICATION

TO MARGARET

FOREWORD

I warmly commend to all Methodist people and indeed to all who
have an interest in the history of High Wycombe, this book by
two Methodist local preachers, Barry Sutcliffe and David Church.
Here are some of our roots in the past 250 years - and to know
our roots is often to understand our present situation better.
I am sure you will enjoy delving into the past with the two
authors whose labour of love has produced this fascinating
study.

                              (Rev.) Tony Barnard
                              Superintendent Minister
                              High Wycombe Circuit

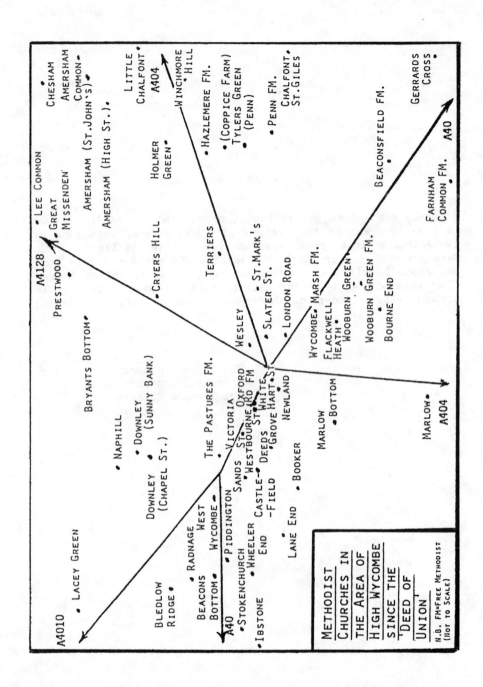

METHODIST
CHURCHES IN
THE AREA OF
HIGH WYCOMBE
SINCE THE
DEED OF
UNION

N.B. FM=FREE METHODIST
(NOT TO SCALE)

CONTENTS

Chapter   Page

CALENDAR OF EVENTS   xi
CALENDAR OF CHAPELS   xiii
INTRODUCTION   xvii

1.   JOHN WESLEY AND THE METHODISTS   1

        Early Methodism in High Wycombe - Hannah Ball

2.   THE WESLEYAN METHODIST CHURCH   19

        High Wycombe Wesleyan Methodist Circuit -
        Ministers - preachers - leaders - trusts

3.   WESLEYAN METHODIST CHURCHES   63

        St.Mary Street - Penn - Marlow - Wooburn Green
        West Wycombe - Stokenchurch etc. (no chapels) -
        Downley (Sunny Bank) - Lane End - Bledlow
        Ridge - Beaconsfield- Holmer Green - Booker -
        Winchmore Hill - Prestwood - Flackwell Heath -
        Wesley - Victoria Street - London Road -
        Terriers - Chesham - Amersham (High Street) -
        Piddington - Bourne End

4.   THE PRIMITIVE METHODIST CHURCH   139

        High Wycombe Primitive Methodist Circuit -
        Rev.James Pole - Ministers and preachers

5.   PRIMITIVE METHODIST CHURCHES   161

        Wooburn Green - Littleworth Common - Speen etc.
        (no chapels) - Lee Common - Penn (Tylers Green) -
        Chalfont St.Giles - Flackwell Heath - Frogmoor
        Gardens - Naphill - Cryers Hill (Great Kings-
        hill) - Lacey Green - Amersham Common -
        Winchmore Hill - Wheeler End - Ibstone -
        Downley (Chapel Street) - Radnage - Great
        Missenden - Stokenchurch - Beacons Bottom -
        Bryants Bottom - Slater Street (North Town) -
        Marlow - White Hart Street - Westbourne Street -
        Sands

Chapter   Page

6.   THE WESLEYAN REFORM UNION   223

        High Wycombe Free Methodist Circuit -
        Ministers and preachers

7.   FREE METHODIST CHURCHES   231

        Penn - Beaconsfield - Wooburn Green - Oxford
        Road - Wycombe Marsh - Hazlemere - Farnham
        Common - Newland - Gerrards Cross - The Pastures

8.   THE UNITED METHODIST CHURCH   247

        Newland

9.   THE METHODIST CHURCH   251

        "Deed of Union" - High Wycombe Methodist
        Circuit - "Supers" - Ministers and preachers -
        Amersham Methodist Circuit

10. METHODIST CHURCHES   303

        Marlow Bottom - Castlefield - Little Chalfont -
        St.Mark's - Amersham (St.John's) - Deeds
        Grove - Tylers Green (Coppice Farm)

11. CHURCH LIFE AND WITNESS   325

        Memories - Meetings - Preaching

12. THE PRESENT AND FUTURE CHURCH   345

        Influence of Methodism - Methodism today -
        Future of Methodism

     MEMORIALS   357

     TABLE and INDEX of CHURCHES   381

     INDEX of PEOPLE   387

CALENDAR OF EVENTS

1738 "Conversion" of John Wesley (Aldersgate Street, London – 24th May)

1739 Wesley's first recorded visit to High Wycombe

1769 First Sunday School founded in High Wycombe by Hannah Ball

1779 First Wesleyan Methodist Chapel opened in High Wycombe at St.Mary Street

1789 Wesley's last service in High Wycombe

1791 Death of John Wesley (aged 87)

1792 Death of Hannah Ball (aged 58)

1815 High Wycombe Wesleyan Methodist Circuit formed out of Oxford Circuit

1835 Rev.James Pole (Primitive Methodist) begins "missionary labours" in area

1836 High Wycombe Primitive Methodist Circuit formed out of Hounslow Circuit

1850 Beaconsfield and Penn secede from Wesleyans to join Wesleyan Reform Union

1867 Richard Nicholls first Minister of Wycombe Free Methodist (WRU) Circuit

1910 Newland secedes from Free Methodists – first United Methodist Church

1934 Wesleyan, Primitive & United Churches join Wycombe Methodist Circuit; Stokenchurch, Beacons Bottom & Ibstone join from Chinnor Prim. Circuit

1937 Chalfont St.Giles, Amersham Common & Winchmore Hill join from Chalfont Circuit

1951 Seven Churches leave Wycombe Circuit to form Chesham & Chalfont Circuit

1962 Chesham & Chalfont Circuit renamed "Amersham Methodist
     Circuit"

1970 Newest Church opens (The Pastures Free Methodist, High
     Wycombe)

1977 Chalfont St.Giles Methodist & U.R.C. Churches become
     Deanway United Church

1988 This book published to celebrate "250 years of Chiltern
     Methodism"

CALENDAR OF CHAPELS

<table>
<tr><th></th><th colspan="4">OPENED</th><th>CLOSED</th></tr>
<tr><th></th><th>WESLEYAN</th><th>PRIMITIVE</th><th>FREE METH.</th><th>METHODIST</th><th></th></tr>
<tr><td>1779</td><td>St.Mary Street</td><td></td><td></td><td></td><td></td></tr>
<tr><td>1808</td><td>Penn</td><td></td><td></td><td></td><td></td></tr>
<tr><td>1810</td><td>Marlow</td><td></td><td></td><td></td><td></td></tr>
<tr><td>1811</td><td>Wooburn Green</td><td></td><td></td><td></td><td></td></tr>
<tr><td>1815</td><td>West Wycombe</td><td></td><td></td><td></td><td></td></tr>
<tr><td>1824</td><td>Downley (Sunny Bank)</td><td></td><td></td><td></td><td></td></tr>
<tr><td>1832</td><td></td><td>Littleworth Common</td><td></td><td></td><td></td></tr>
<tr><td>1832</td><td></td><td>Wooburn Green</td><td></td><td></td><td></td></tr>
<tr><td>1834</td><td>Lane End</td><td></td><td></td><td></td><td></td></tr>
<tr><td>1834</td><td>Bledlow Ridge</td><td></td><td></td><td></td><td></td></tr>
<tr><td>1838</td><td>Beaconsfield</td><td></td><td></td><td></td><td></td></tr>
<tr><td>1839</td><td></td><td>Lee Common</td><td></td><td></td><td></td></tr>
<tr><td>1841</td><td>Holmer Green</td><td></td><td></td><td></td><td></td></tr>
<tr><td>1843</td><td></td><td>Penn (Tylers Green)</td><td></td><td></td><td></td></tr>
<tr><td>1847</td><td>Booker</td><td>Chalfont St.Giles</td><td></td><td></td><td></td></tr>
<tr><td>1848</td><td></td><td>Flackwell Heath</td><td></td><td></td><td></td></tr>
<tr><td>1848</td><td></td><td>Frogmoor Gardens</td><td></td><td></td><td></td></tr>
<tr><td>1850</td><td></td><td></td><td>Penn (ex-Wesleyan)</td><td></td><td></td></tr>
<tr><td>1850</td><td></td><td></td><td>Beaconsfield (ex-Wesleyan)</td><td></td><td></td></tr>
<tr><td>1851</td><td></td><td>Naphill</td><td></td><td></td><td></td></tr>
<tr><td>1852</td><td></td><td>Cryers Hill (Gt.Kingshill)</td><td></td><td></td><td></td></tr>
<tr><td>1855</td><td></td><td>Lacey Green</td><td></td><td></td><td></td></tr>
<tr><td>1859</td><td>Holmer Green (No.2)</td><td></td><td></td><td></td><td></td></tr>
<tr><td>1860</td><td></td><td>Amersham Common</td><td></td><td></td><td></td></tr>
<tr><td>1860</td><td></td><td>Winchmore Hill</td><td></td><td></td><td></td></tr>
<tr><td>1860</td><td></td><td></td><td>Wooburn Green (ex-Primitive)</td><td></td><td></td></tr>
<tr><td>1861</td><td>Winchmore Hill</td><td></td><td></td><td></td><td></td></tr>
<tr><td>1861</td><td></td><td>Wheeler End</td><td></td><td></td><td></td></tr>
<tr><td>1862</td><td></td><td>Ibstone</td><td></td><td></td><td></td></tr>
<tr><td>1863</td><td>Prestwood</td><td></td><td>Oxford Road</td><td></td><td></td></tr>
<tr><td>1864</td><td></td><td>Downley (Chapel Street)</td><td></td><td></td><td></td></tr>
<tr><td>1865</td><td>Flackwell Heath</td><td></td><td></td><td></td><td></td></tr>
<tr><td>1865</td><td></td><td>Radnage</td><td>Wycombe Marsh</td><td></td><td></td></tr>
<tr><td>1866</td><td>Vesley</td><td>Great Missenden</td><td></td><td></td><td>St.Mary St</td></tr>
</table>

WESLEYAN   PRIMITIVE   FREE METH.   METHODIST

1866 Lane End (No.2)
1866   Chalfont St.Giles (No.2)
1867   Farnham Common
1867   Hazlemere
1868   Beacons Bottom
1868   Stokenchurch
1871   Bryants Bottom
1873 Wooburn Green (No.2)
1873   Slater Street
1874   Marlow
1875   White Hart Street   Frogmoor

1877   Fl.Heath PM
1878 Victoria Street
1878   Westbourne Street
1880   Newland
1886 Booker (No.2)
1887 Bledlow Ridge (No.2)
1893 London Road
1894 West Wycombe (No.2)
1895 Terriers
1896   Stokenchurch (No.2)
1896   Wycombe Marsh (No.2)
1897 Chesham
1899 Amersham (High Street)
1900 Marlow (No.2)   Beaconsfield (No.2)

1906 Piddington   Hazlemere (No.2)
1910 Bourne End   Newland United (ex-F.M.)
1911   Oxford Road (No.2)
1912   Sands
1915   Gerrards Cross
1924   Amersham Common (No.2)

1930   Naphill (No.2)
1931 Gerrards Cross (ex-F.M.)
1933 Chesham (No.2)   Marlow PM
1934   Winch.Hl.V
1936   Marlow Bottom
1937   Holmer Green (No.3)

	OPENED			CLOSED
WESLEYAN	PRIMITIVE	FREE METH.	METHODIST	
1938				Wooburn FM
1938				G. Missenden
1951				Wh. Hart St.
1953			Castlefield	
1955				Newland
1955				Slater St
1958			Gerrards Cross (No.2)	
1958				Ibstone
1959			St. Mark's	London Road
1959			Little Chalfont	
1960			Amersham (St. John's)	
1960				Amersham
1961				Westbourne
1963			Deeds Grove	
1965				Downley PM
1966			Castlefield (No.2)	
1966			Chesham (No.3)	
1968			Tylers Green (Coppice)	
1968				Penn/Tylers
1970		The Pastures		Oxford Road
1970				Beacons Bm.
1970				Terriers
1975				Victoria St
1982				Sands
1983				W. Wycombe
1986				Piddington
1987				Wheeler End

INTRODUCTION

For 250 years at least, Methodists have been at work in the South Bucks Chilterns. During those years a multitude of people - of different Methodist traditions - have by their faith, dedication, service and witness had a profound effect upon the life of the society in the area. Some, like John Wesley, Hannah Ball and James Pole, have a place in our national history books and will be long remembered for the work they did. Many more are people who gave service but will be forgotten with the passing of time. Theirs is a service that, though individually lost in the stream of time, combines to make a heritage that benefits all who follow after.

This book attempts to chronicle the history of the Methodist Church in this area. Some of this history is well known and documented. Much is not generally available. Still more is lost in time. We have tried to bring together in one place whatever is available - to show the structure of the Circuit; to record the societies that met together for worship, prayer and service, but above all to give tribute to those who have striven, in whatever way they could, to serve their Lord and to promote His Church. It has become obvious to us that there are large gaps in our knowledge. There may well be inaccuracies in the record. Certainly the story is by no means complete. But it is hoped that now "the ball has been set rolling", there may be additions, corrections and enhancements at a future date.

During these 250 years the world has changed. The structure of society, the mobility of people, modes of communication, health and life expectancy, family life and hopes for the future are all very different from what they were in 1738. What has not changed, is man's need to belong. His search for identity, his desire for peace of mind remain the same. Methodism, as part of the whole Christian Church, has proclaimed that at the heart of a changing world is a changeless God. It has encouraged people to seek Him in a Methodical way. This book deals largely with the physical organisation undertaking this task. The important work however is not in the building of churches nor in the forming of congregations but in the presentation of God as relevant to the people of the present day, whatever day that is.

Fire at Epworth Rectory, 1709.
"Plucked as a brand from the burning"
(Painting by Henry Perlu Parker)

CHAPTER 1.

JOHN WESLEY
AND THE METHODISTS

The old thatched rectory was ablaze. All the family had escaped - except five year-old Jacky. As Samuel Wesley turned to go up the burning stairs once again, they crashed to the ground in flames. The distracted rector knelt in prayer and at that moment his small son, awoken by all the noise and the light of the flames, appeared at a window. There was no ladder but a quick-thinking neighbour jumped on the shoulders of another and rescued the boy, just as the roof fell in. Referring to this incident, John Wesley often described himself as "a brand plucked from the burning". Little did those brave neighbours realise that they were saving the future leader of one of the world's largest Christian organisations!

John was born, the fifteenth of Susanna's 19 children, at Epworth Rectory on 17th June 1703. He was educated at Charterhouse, London, and Christ Church, Oxford, and took holy orders in the Church of England in 1725. At first he served under his father, as a curate in Lincolnshire but in 1729 he became a tutor at Lincoln College, Oxford, where he joined his brother, Charles, in the "Holy Club". Their ordered habits which included rising at 4 o'clock each morning, earned them the nickname of "Methodists". In 1735 he took charge of the Georgian mission in America and on his return joined the Moravians, whose calm faith on the outward voyage had so impressed him, at their chapel in Fetter Lane, London.

On the evening of 24th May 1738, he writes in his journal, "I went very unwilling to a society in Aldersgate Street, where one was reading Luther's preface to the Epistle to the Romans. About a quarter before nine, while he was describing the change which God works in the heart through faith in Christ, I felt my heart strangely warmed. I felt I did trust in Christ, Christ alone, for salvation: and an assurance was given me, that He had taken away my sins, even mine, and saved me from the law of sin and death." In 1739 John Wesley began open-air preaching at Bristol. In 1742 he went to Yorkshire and Newcastle-on-Tyne and his teaching took root everywhere. With his brother and George Whitefield he set up an independent society which met at the Foundery, near Moorfields, London. A noble band of lay preachers gathered round the Wesleys and despite fierce opposition the work grew.

Wesley made Bristol his headquarters and divided his followers into classes, each class being under the direction of a leader. He preached all over the country, travelling about 5000 miles a year, mostly on horseback, and delivering more than 40,000 sermons. He used simple language and was especially successful with poorer people who were less in touch with the established Church than the rich.

It had never been his intention to set up a separate Church but opposition forced him in 1784 to execute the "Deed of Declaration" which effectively meant the start of the Methodist Church. Wesley's Chapel which he had opened in City Road, London, in 1778, became the "Methodist Cathedral". In 1784 also he appointed Dr. Thomas Coke as Superintendent of the work in America. John Wesley wrote many letters and pamphlets and published numerous books which became very popular. He was a social worker too who provided work for the poor and set up dispensaries from which he distributed his own medicines.

He preached his last sermon at Leatherhead on 23rd February 1791. When he died on 2nd March 1791 at his home in City Road, his followers, many of whom were organised into "societies", were reckoned to number 100,000.

EARLY METHODISM IN HIGH WYCOMBE

Nearly every town in the land tells of the visits of John Wesley and of the impact that he and his preachers made on the life of its citizens. His travels throughout the length and breadth of Britain are well documented by him in the journal that he so methodically kept for many years. Generally, his journeys took him from London to Bristol, from there northwards to Newcastle-upon-Tyne and so back to London. From that basic triangle the most frequent diversions were into the West Country through Devon and Cornwall and through Wales, to take ship for Ireland. From London to Bristol he would often take the Great West Road, running to the south of the Chilterns, through Windsor and Maidenhead and Reading. More often than not however he would take the Oxford Road through Beaconsfield, High Wycombe and Stokenchurch, spending the night at Oxford.

So it is, that right from the earliest days, the town of High Wycombe, together with the surrounding villages, has been witness to the great evangelical revival of the eighteenth and nineteenth centuries. The first recorded visit made by John was less than a year after the conversion experience of the two brothers, in March 1739. It is most likely that there was already a small group of Methodists in the town at that time. South Buckinghamshire, with its strong history of dissent and non-conformity, was well prepared to embrace the "enthusiasm" of those who preached a new approach to religion. Certainly by 1765 when Hannah Ball was attracted to the Methodists, there was a small but growing number in the Society. Little is known of these early days except that one of the early band of adherents was Thomas Humphries who supported the Methodist Preachers when they arrived in town, often standing by them as the crowd turned on them with a hail of stones and muck. In 1769 Hannah commenced her Sunday School in High Wycombe.

It is not clear where the Society met for worship in those early days. It may have been that at first John Wesley would have preached in the Parish Church. It is very likely that on a number of occasions he would have preached in the open air. Certainly in 1745 and 1746 that was so but by 1766 the references are to a room and preaching house. It is believed at that time the worship was conducted in a room in Easton Street. The period between 1748 and 1761 contains only a single reference to the district, yet the methodical nature of Wesley's care for the Church is shown most distinctly during the 20 years from 1768 to 1788. Each year he records in mid-

High Wycombe High Street. November 30th 1772.

October, "I begin my little journey into Oxfordshire". That journey invariably included reference to High Wycombe, as well as Oxford and Witney. His comments during these years showed a warm-heartedness for Wycombe and a note of the developing earnestness on the part of the congregation there.

The Circuit system was set up in 1744. Initially there were only seven Circuits covering the whole country. The Bristol Circuit included Somerset, Wiltshire, Gloucestershire, Oxfordshire and Buckinghamshire. So Wycombe and the Chilterns were right on the periphery. From 1765 High Wycombe was a part of the Oxford Circuit. The Circuit Travelling Preachers seem to have been only visitors to the town, until John Murlin came to live there in 1788. The Preachers were, nevertheless, frequently in the town in order to meet with and "examine" the Society there. John Wesley, in a letter to Hannah Ball from Bristol on August 12th 1774 writes: "I hope Mr. Harmer's preaching in the church will have many good effects. He will prepare the way for brother Wolfe, and his two fellow labourers; all alive to God, simple of heart, and of one heart and mind, without any jarring string. And I suppose, by the addition of a third Preacher, you will have a Travelling Preacher every other Sunday."

As the Society grew and the congregation became more settled, it became more necessary for a new and "more commodious" preaching-house to be built. Despite some setbacks and delays, a site was found suitable for erection of a chapel in St. Mary Street. Mr. James Batting, after handsomely subscribing to the building, generously undertook the superintending of the whole work. Wesley recommended that the building be modelled on the new Wesley Chapel just completed in the City Road, London, but to a reduced scale "fifty or sixty by forty feet; according as your ground will allow". This chapel was opened by Wesley himself on November 11th 1779, his text being, "We preach Christ Crucified; unto the Jews a stumbling-block, and unto the Greeks foolishness; but unto them which are called, both Jews and Greeks, Christ the power of God, and the wisdom of God" (I Corinthians 1. 23-24). The Church had a home. It was now established.

WESLEY'S JOURNAL

Friday,2nd March,1739   It was the advice of all our brethren, that I should spend a few days at Oxford, whither I accordingly went on Saturday,3rd. (Dinner was taken at 12.30 at Wickham). [On his return, on Thursday,15th he again had dinner, at 11 o'clock.]

Monday,12th November,1739.   I left London, and in the evening expounded at Wycombe the story of the Pharisee and the Publican.

Wednesday,17th June,1741.   I set out, and rode slowly towards Oxford; but before I came to Wycombe my horse tired. There I hired another, which tired also before I came to Tetsworth. I hired a third here, and reached Oxford in the evening.

Monday,29th June,1741.   I preached in the morning (in London) on, "Ye are saved through faith". In the afternoon I expounded, at Windsor, the story of the Pharisee and Publican.

I spent the evening at Wycombe; and the next morning, Tuesday,30th returned to Oxford.

Thursday,26th May,1743. I had a large congregation at Wycombe; from whence I hastened to London.

Monday,20th June,1743. [On his way to Staffordshire] I set out early in the morning, and after preaching at Wycombe about noon, in the evening came to Oxford.

Friday,24th August,1744. (St.Bartholomew's Day). I left Oxford about noon, preached at Wycombe in the evening, and on Saturday, 25th, returned to London.

Friday,10th May,1745. I preached at High Wycombe, in an open place, to a mixed multitude: some of whom were as rude as they dared to be, having none of the great vulgar to set them on.

Thursday,15th August 1745. At Wycombe. [Riding from Cirencester to London.]

Thursday,25th September,1746. I came to Wycombe. It being the day on which the Mayor was chosen, abundance of rabble, full of strong drink, came to the preaching, on purpose to disturb; but they soon fell out among themselves: so that I finished my sermon in tolerable quiet. Friday, 26th. Mr. B. went to the Mayor and said, "Sir, I come to inform against a common swearer. I believe he swore an hundred oaths last night: but I marked down only twenty." "Sir", said the Mayor, "you do very right in bringing him to justice. What is his name?" He replied "R..... D....." "R.... D.....!" answered the Mayor: "Why, that is my son!" "Yes, Sir." said Mr. B. "So I understand." "Nay, Sir," said he, "I have nothing to say in his defence. If he breaks the law, he must take what follows."

Monday,14th November,1748. I rode to Windsor and after preaching, examined the Members of the Society. The same I did at Reading, in the evening; at Wycombe, on Tuesday; and on Wednesday, at Brentford.

Wednesday,30th March,1757. I rode to a gentleman's near Beaconsfield, and preached at six in the evening, in a large, convenient place, filled with serious hearers, several of whom had come five or six miles. Thurs.31st. I was earnestly importuned to go over to High Wycombe. I went and preached there at noon, on the Parable of the Sower. Perhaps some of the seed which has been sown here for many years, will at length bring forth fruit. At six it seemed as if the whole town of Beaconsfield was assembled together; and I bear them witness, they gave earnest heed, high and low, to the things which were spoken. A large number of them were present in the morning, on Friday, April 1st. Fair beginnings these! But, "he that endureth to the end, the same shall be saved".

<u>Monday, 9th March, 1761.</u>   I set out early, and about noon preached at High Wycombe, where the dry bones began to shake again. In the afternoon I rode on to Oxford, and spent an agreeable evening with Mr, H. His openness and frankness of behaviour were both pleasing and profitable. Such conversation I want; but I do not wonder it is offensive to men of nice ears.

<u>Monday, 16th January, 1764.</u>   I rode to High Wycombe, and preached to a more numerous and serious congregation than ever I saw there before. Shall there be yet another day of visitation to this careless people? A large number was present at five in the morning; but my face and gums were so swelled I could hardly speak. After I took horse, they grew worse and worse till it began to rain. I was then persuaded to put on an oil-case hood, which (the wind being very high) kept rubbing continually on my cheek, till both pain and swelling were gone.

<u>Monday, 7th January, 1765.</u>   In the evening I preached at High Wycombe; and <u>Tuesday, 8th.</u> at Witney. The congregation here, though of so late standing, may be a pattern to all England. When the service was ended no one spoke, either in the evening or morning. All went silently out of the house and yard. Nay, when I followed a large part of them, I did not hear any open their lips, till they came to their own houses. <u>Thursday, 10th.</u>   I preached again at Wycombe, and on Friday returned to London.

<u>Monday, 27th October, 1766.</u>   I rode to Wycombe [from London]. The room was much crowded, and yet could not contain the congregation. In the morning too they flocked together in such a manner as had not been seen here before. In the evening I preached at Witney..... <u>Thursday, 30th.</u> At one I preached at Wattleton, and thence rode with some difficulty, the wind being exceeding high, over the mountain to Wycombe. The congregation was as before, both for number and earnestness. So at length we see the fruit of our labour.

<u>Monday, 24th August, 1767.</u>   (Following the conference with our Assistants, and a select number of Preachers.) Having

finished my work at London for the present, on <u>Monday,24th.</u> I rode to Wycombe, and preached in the evening to a numerous and deeply attentive congregation. <u>Tuesday,25th.</u> In the evening, the multitude that flocked together obliged me to preach abroad. I saw but three or four that seemed unaffected; and those, I suppose, were footmen; a race of men who are commonly lost to all sense of shame, as well as of good and evil. <u>Wednesday,26th.</u> I rode to Ipstone Hall, near Stoken Church, and preached about ten o'clock; and in the evening at Witney.

<u>Monday,7th November,1768.</u>
I set out for Oxfordshire [from Hertford]; preached at Wycombe in the evening, and on Tuesday and Wednesday at Witney. On Thursday, in my return, I was desired to preach at Oxford. The room was thoroughly filled, and not with curious, but deeply serious hearers. Many of these desired that our travelling Preachers would take them in their turn, with which I willingly complied. In the evening I preached in the chapel at Henley, to a considerable number of serious people. One or two of the baser sort made some noise, but I reproved them, and, for once, they were ashamed.

<u>Friday,20th October,1769.</u> I had appointed to be in Oxford at eight (a.m.); so I took horse at two (in the morning), and took chaises from Shipston, which brought me thither at my time. After spending an hour quite agreeably with a few young serious students, I set out for Ipstone, near Stoken Church. But I was obliged, when we came to the bye-road, to quit my chaise, and go as I could, part on horseback, part on foot. The congregation had

waited for me for some time; so I began immediately on, "Fear God, and keep his commandments; for this is the whole of man". In the evening I preached to a lively congregation at High Wycombe, and on Saturday reached London.

Tuesday, 16th October, 1770. I preached at Witney, in the new house, and again on Thursday morning. After service, many crowding with me into the house, I spent some time with them in prayer. It was a happy opportunity; and many praised God for the consolation they had received. We had afterwards a fair and pleasant ride to Wycombe. For many years we had little prospect of doing good here; but now the seed which had been so long dead, springs up into plentiful harvest. Friday, 19th. I conversed particularly with several, who believe God has saved them from sin: and their lives, I find, are suitable thereto, and do in no wise dishonour their profession. Saturday, 20th. I returned to London.

Thursday, 17th October, 1771. About ten I preached at Oxford, in a room well filled with deeply-attentive hearers, on part of the "Sermon on the Mount", the noblest compendium of religion which is to be found even in the oracles of God. In the evening I preached at High Wycombe, the next at Chesham, where, our own room being too small, that friendly man Mr. Spooner, willingly gave me the use of his meeting-house. I found the little Society much alive, many knowing in whom they had believed; several enjoying, and others thirsting after, the whole image of God. On Saturday I had a pleasant journey to London.

Monday, 19th October, 1772. I began my tour through Oxfordshire. Tuesday, 20th. In the evening I preached at Witney to a crowded congregation, and, at present, one of the liveliest in the kingdom. Afterwards I met the Society, much alive to God, and growing both in grace and number. Thursday, 22nd. I found another Society at High Wycombe, almost as earnest as that at Witney. A large congregation was present at five in the morning, many of whom were athirst for full salvation. I talked with twelve of them, who seemed to have experienced it. This is the genuine Christianity! Friday, 23rd. I preached at Chesham, and on Saturday returned to London.

Monday, 18th October, 1773. I began my little journey through Oxfordshire and Buckinghamshire.

<u>Monday,17th October,1774.</u> I set out for Oxfordshire, and preached at Wallingford in the evening. <u>Thursday,20th.</u> I preached at Wattleton, at the front of Mr.Stonehill's house. The whole congregation was seriously attentive. In the evening I preached at High Wycombe, to many more than the room would contain; and I believe not in vain. <u>Friday,21st.</u> I preached in Chesham; and on Saturday returned to London.

<u>Monday,9th October,1775.</u> I preached at Chesham, on, "The straight gate"; and all that heard seemed affected for the present. <u>Tuesday,10th.</u> I went on to Wycombe, and was much refreshed by the earnest attention of the whole congregation. <u>Wednesday,11th.</u> I took a walk to Lord Shelburne's house. What variety, in so small a compass! A beautiful grove, divided by a serpentine walk, conceals the house from the town. At the side runs a transparent river, with a smooth walk on each bank. Beyond this is a level lawn; then the house, with sloping gardens behind. Above these is a lofty hill; near the top of which is a lovely wood, having a grassy walk running along, just within the skirts of it. But can the owner rejoice in this Paradise? No; for his wife is snatched away in the bloom of youth! <u>Thursday,12th.</u> About noon I preached at Wattleton; and in the evening at Oxford.

<u>Monday,24th March,1777.</u> I left Bristol, and preaching at Ramsbury, Witney, Oxford, and High Wycombe, in my way, on Thursday came to London, whence I cannot be long absent while the new chapel is building.

<u>Monday,20th October,1777.</u> I went to High Wycombe; but good Mr.James having procured a drummer to beat his drum at the window of the preaching-house, I only prayed and sung by turns, from six to seven; and many of the people were much comforted. In the rest of the week I visited the Societies at Oxford, Witney, Finstock, and Wallingford, and had reason to believe, that many received the seed in honest and good hearts.

<u>Friday,16th October,1778.</u> I was desired to preach at Thame, on my return to London. I came thither a little after ten. The mob had been so troublesome there, that it was a doubt with the Preachers, whether the place should not be given up. However, I thought it might not be amiss, before this was done, to make one trial myself. But I found it impracticable to preach abroad, the wind being so exceeding sharp. I went therefore into a large building, formerly used by the Presbyterians. It was quickly filled, and more than filled, many being obliged to stand without. Yet there was no breath of

noise; the whole congregation seemed to be "all but their attention dead". We had prayed before, that God would give us a quiet time, and He granted us our request. In the evening I preached at High-Wycombe, and on Saturday returned to London.

Monday 30th October, 1780. I went to High-Wycombe, where the new preaching-house was well filled in the evening.

Monday 15th October, 1781. I set out for Oxfordshire, and spent five days with much satisfaction among the Societies. I found no offences among them at all, but they appeared to walk in love. On Friday, 19th, I returned to London.

Thursday 17th October, 1782. I preached at Thame; this evening and the next at High-Wycomb, and on Saturday returned to London.

Monday 14th July, 1783. I took a little journey into Oxfordshire, and found the good effects of the late storms. The thunder had been uncommonly dreadful; and the lightning had tore up a field near High-Wycomb, and turned the potatoes into ashes.

Thursday 16th October, 1783. I preached at High-Wycomb, and on Friday returned to London.

Tuesday 22nd October, 1784. I preached at High-Wycombe about noon, and in the afternoon went on to London.

Thursday 13th October, 1785. Returning to Oxford, I once more surveyed many of the gardens and delightful walks. What is wanting but the love of God to make this place an earthly paradise? I preached in the evening to a very serious audience; as also the next evening at High-Wycomb. In all this Circuit the work of God appears both to widen and to deepen. Sat. 15th I returned to London.

Monday 15th October, 1787. I began a little tour through Oxfordshire.... Thursday 18th. We went on to High-Wycombe. The work of God is so considerably increased here, that although three galleries are added to the preaching-house, it would scarce contain the people. Even at five in the morning, Friday, the 19th, it was thoroughly filled. Never before was there so fair a prospect of doing good at this place. I dined in London.

Thursday 16th October, 1788. We went on to High-Wycomb. Mr. Murlin's settling there has been of great use. Here is now a steady and understanding people; to whom I preached, as usual, evening and morning, with a good deal of satisfaction.

Friday 30th October, 1789.   In my way to Wycombe, I spent an hour at Mr. Smith's, in Cudsden.   He has ten children, from eighteen to a year or two old, but all under government: so that I met the very picture of my father's family.   What a wretched steward was he,   who influenced Lord H--- to put away such a tenant!   In the evening the house at High-Wycombe, though full, was still as night.   Sat. 31st   We came safe and well to London.

[John Wesley died on 2nd March, 1791 in the 88th year of his age. He was aged 86 when he preached that last service at St. Mary Street chapel in which he held the congregation "still as night".]

HANNAH BALL: FIRST SUNDAY SCHOOL & CHURCH

Wesley's journal tells of the rough or indifferent reception he often experienced at the hands of men.   But women generally responded well to him - and he to them.   Maldwyn Edwards in his book, "My Dear Sister", writes:

> "Women had an extra fascination for him and he wrote three times as much to them as he did to men. He was keenly susceptible to their beauty and more so if it was combined with wit and sparkle. But it is fair to say that most of all he rose instinctively to a woman of unaffected goodness. He wasn't deceived by words but when he saw grace in graciousness, he capitulated.   One might say he admired practical piety if the words were not so hard and angular. If a woman had love for God and man, then for John Wesley, she was lovely!"

Hannah Ball whom he first met on 7th January 1765, was typical of Wesley's women helpers.   But unlike most of them, she kept a diary which also includes the regular correspondence they had.   Born in 1733, she had come in 1759 to Queen's Square, High Wycombe, where she acted as housekeeper to her brother who was a lacemaker.   She had a high opinion of herself and her station in life but was aware that there was something missing.   A violent thunderstorm in 1762 had brought her to understand God's mercy.   She had heard of the Methodists but although curious, she comments: "So great was my aversion to that despised people, I once thought I would soon go to hell as unite with the followers of John Wesley". Her mind however was soon to be changed, spurred on by a book of sermons by Thomas Walsh, a highly gifted Irish preacher who had been stoned by the Wycombe mob. His writings "gave her an insatiable desire to hear a Methodist preach". She records on 8th January 1765:

> "Some time after this, Mr.Wesley came to Wycombe. I had now a conflict between desire and aversion. Desire at length so far prevailed, that though I did not attend the preaching at night, yet I went at five in the morning. I was struck with the venerable appearance of Mr.Wesley; but more deeply affected with the words of his text, which were taken from Matthew 15.28: "O woman, great is thy faith: be it unto thee even as thou wilt".

Hannah Ball is best remembered as the founder of the first Sunday School. Around 1761 she had begun a school for small children, possibly in her brother's house. It was therefore a natural development, following her meeting with Wesley, for her educational activities to focus on the children of the Methodists. In 1769 she began the work with children which became the first Sunday School. On Sundays between 30 and 40 childen met her to "read the scripture, learn the catechism and repeat the collect for the day" before they accompanied her to divine service. Finding that few of them could read, she had a second session on Monday evenings for teaching reading and writing. (This was 11 years before the more famous Robert Raikes began his Sunday School in Gloucester.) Annoyingly she makes little reference to the work in her diary. She writes in 1770: "The children are a wild little bunch but seem willing to be instructed. I labour among them, earnestly desiring to promote the interests of the Church of Christ." In 1782 Wesley wrote to ask what had happened to her "little maidens" some of whom, he hoped, would "bring forth fruits to perfection". If she could gain one in ten for Christ, he said, that would be a good reward. After her death in 1792 at the age of 59, the work was carried on by Hannah's sister, Ann.

In their letters we see how much John Wesley came to rely on Hannah Ball, to promote the work not only in Wycombe, but as far as Watlington and Oxford. In 1768 he confesses a particular love for her and urges her to confide in him all her troubles. Hannah demurely comments, "I bless God for counting me worthy to correspond with so good a man". Later he begs her to use all her gifts and graces in the work at Wycombe. Throughout her life Hannah remained outwardly respectful to Wesley but she had a quiet determination and could be ruthless when necessary. She once confessed, "I do not talk of people's faults behind their backs but prefer doing it in person".

A lot of her work was concerned with the preachers. She was asked by Wesley in 1773 to clear up a misunderstanding between preacher Sanderson and a Mr.Westrup. Preacher Joseph Bradford who could be as forthright as Hannah herself, was to be urged to speak gently, not too fast or loud. Preference for a certain preacher varied then, as now. The one whom Hannah disliked, Mr.Wolfe, was - according to Wesley - a man with great pastoral gifts and should not be treated with such reserve; the one she did like and praised enthusiastically, preacher Valton, had kept only one sixth of his converts, he reminded her. Hannah felt that many preachers were not particularly good and in fact she ensured the dismissal of Joseph Accult in 1781. As for preacher Rhodda, Wesley told her, he must be encouraged to teach "Perfection".

Priory Road Sunday School arrive at Daws Hill Park for their annual festival - about 1895.

So we see the large part the redoubtable Hannah Ball played in organising John Wesley's Methodist people in this area. She knew how to control both congregations and preachers and in 1783 he was commending her to others as an example of standing firm against opposition. She turned down at least two chances of marriage because the men concerned were not of her persuasion, but was deeply affected by the death of Samuel Wells whom she had helped when he came as an assistant in the Oxfordshire Circuit. Some of her later letters did not please Wesley who became rather irritated by her vagueness. In 1786 he asked what exactly was troubling her. "Don't you think I still love you?" he demands. "Use me as a friend, my dear sister!"

Undoubtedly Hannah Ball was the spiritual mother of the many faithful and gifted women who have served God in our local churches ever since. John Wesley was its founder but the rapid spread of Methodism in this area over the next century owes much to Wycombe's own Hannah Ball!

HANNAH BALL'S DIARY

[The first account of Miss Ball was published by Rev.Joseph Cole who was a Minister in the circuit in 1797 and Superintendent in 1803 and 1804.]

June 3rd 1770. Mr.T.Eden's sermons have been rendered not only instructive, but very profitable; and his private conversation no less so, to me and others.

Aug.24th 1770. I have profited much under the ministry of Mr.Henderson and Mr.Rhodes. Mr.Rhodes has been a laborious man, and rendered useful in this Circuit. He has been truly upright in all things. May his usefulness continue and abound.

Letter from John Wesley to Hannah Ball. Bristol, Aug 12th,1774. I hope Mr.HARMER's preaching in the church will have good effects. He will prepare the way for Brother Wolfe, and his two fellow labourers; all live to God, simple of heart, and of one heart and mind, without any jarring string. And I suppose, by the addition of a third Preacher, you will have a Travelling Preacher every other Sunday. You will love sister Wolfe; she is an amiable creature, and has done good to the children here.

April,16th 1775. Lord's-day morning. Mr.Wolfe preached from these words, "If ye then be risen with Christ, seek those things which are above". My faith was strengthened, and I felt encouragement to press towards the mark for the prize; and to believe that Christ would feed His flock. I afterwards commemorated the death of Christ at our parish church, and found it good to be there. I esteem it a privilege to be a member of the Church of England, and desire to be kept in her doctrines faithful unto death.

Letter from John Wesley to Hannah Ball. Bristol March 13th, 1777
My Dear Sister,
It seems the time has come, that you are to have a more commodious preaching house at High Wycomb. I will give you a Plan of the building myself; and employ whom you please to build. But I hope to see you on Wednesday, the 26th instant, and to preach about six in the evening, after preaching at noon in Oxford. Peace be with your spirit!   I am,
Your affectionate brother,
J.WESLEY.

March 24th 1777.   Mr.Valton has been an indefatigable Minister in this Circuit, and rendered useful to many:. his instructions in private, as well as in public, have been much owned of the Lord.   Mrs.Hauks's pious conversation has been made very useful to me. I have great fellowship with that good woman. She has an enlarged soul to serve the interests of her Lord and Master.

Feb.18th 1779.   The little society in this town, having passed through much persecution and great interruption in their public devotions, by a Mr.James's frequently beating a drum during the whole hour of meeting, Providence has at length pointed out a convenient situation for erecting a chapel.   Mr.Batting, after handsomely subscribing to the building, generously undertook the superintending the whole work, till it was completed.   This labour of love will not be unnoticed by the Lord.

Letter from John Wesley to Hannah Ball.   London, Feb 24th, 1779.
My Dear Sister,
I am in great hopes that the manner of your mother's death, together with her dying exhortations, will make a deep and lasting impression on some (at least) of her children. B.T. did well to make a full use of so solemn an occasion.   It is not improbable that, from this very time, a good work may commence, which, if you build a large and commodious chapel, will greatly and swiftly increase.   I advise you, whenever you build, to build exactly on the model of our new chapel; only reducing the dimensions, perhaps, from eighty by sixty, to fifty or sixty by forty feet, according as your ground will allow. Surely He will withhold from us no manner of thing that is good.
I am, my dear sister,
Your affectionate brother,
J.WESLEY.

Officers of Priory-road Methodist Church High Wycombe, at the church centenary celebrations during the weekend, admire a drum said to have been used in 1777 when John Wesley preached in the town. In the group are, left to right, Mr. J. Phillippo and his daughter, Mr. S. Willott, Mr. J. Parkins, the Rev. W. G. B. Ream, Mr. K. T. Fox, the Rev. Eric W. Barker, secretary of the Methodist Conference, and Mrs. J. Goodearl.

Letter from John Wesley to Hannah Ball. London, Oct. 23rd, 1779.

My Dear Sister,

To-morrow night I am to set out for Norwich; and this little tour will take up a fortnight. At my return, I have appointment to visit the classes, which requires a fortnight more. I see no possibility, then, of my opening the House, unless I steal away from them for a few hours. I care not for labour; but I want time. This, then, with God's help, I will do. On Tuesday noon, November 9th, I will steal away to Wycomb, preach at five in the evening, and then return to London. So I can go on with the classes at six on Wednesday morning.

If the Preachers and Leaders strongly exhort the believers to go on to perfection, then the entire work of God will prosper among you: otherwise it will languish.

I am, my dear Hannah,

Your affectionate brother,

J. WESLEY.

Nov.11th 1779.   The Rev. John Wesley opened our new chapel, by preaching on "We preach Christ crucified; unto the Jews a stumbling-block, &c." On this occasion we had a crowded and genteel audience.   My heart's desire and prayer to God is, that this neat and convenient house, erected to Jehovah's glory, may be an everlasting blessing to the town of Wycomb.

Dec.5th 1779.   A letter is come to hand, which informs me of Mr.S.Wells' death; a man for whom I had the highest esteem and regard.   His public labours and private conversation were rendered exceedingly useful to many, and much owned of God to my furtherance in the divine life.   He was near to me as my own soul; but the Lord can preserve in the most painful trials.   I have, in the course of my pilgrimage, derived the best experience from the most painful occurrences.

[Letter from John Wesley dated 17th February, 1780 refers to the death of Mr.Hawes.   In the 1818 Plan a preacher named Haws is listed.]

Feb.25th 1786.   This day I followed to the grave the remains of that faithful friend of truth, Thomas HUMPHRIES, who for many years was an ornament to the Gospel, and the first person that received the Methodist Preachers in Wycomb.   He stood by the pious Mr.WALSH, amidst a shower of stones, whilst he was proclaiming the glad tidings of salvation to a part of the people of the town.   His last moments were triumph.   He spoke with the warmest animation of the love of Christ to him, and that his departure hence would be to dwell with angels.   His last words were, "Dear Jesus, I am coming".

[Aug.16th 1792.   Five minutes after eleven o'clock, the Lord graciously released her from the body of clay and admitted her happy, triumphant spirit to be forever with Himself, according to His gracious promise, "Where I am, there My servants shall be, that they may behold My glory".]

CHAPTER 2.

THE WESLEYAN METHODIST CHURCH

Only four years after his death John Wesley's "People called Methodists" in this country severed their remaining links with the Church of England and in 1795 set up the Wesleyan Methodist Church. The change had been inevitable from the time Wesley sent out his first preachers in 1741 and held his first Conference three years later. With his brother Charles he had drawn up rules of membership and set them out in his sermons: each person must have a "desire to flee from the wrath to come and to be saved from sin". Every Methodist must "avoid evil and do good to all". The Wesleyan doctrines had much in common with the evangelical section of the Church of England.

In 1786 Wesley authorised the use of the Book of Common Prayer in his 359 "preaching houses". His "Deed of Declaration" two years before had set up a governing body of 100 Ministers and after his death this caused considerable unease. However a letter written by Wesley some years earlier and only now made public, reminded the chosen few, "You must never assume superiority over your brethren". This may have reassured the faithful but - as we shall see in following chapters - setting up such an elite was to be the cause of numerous breakaway movements in later years.

Laymen had to wait until 1878 - and women until 1911 - before being admitted to the annual Conference. Each year a new President was elected. The system of church government was broadly the one with which we are familiar today, except that the itinerant Ministers were not normally allowed to stay in one circuit longer than three years. Each church ("society") was administered by stewards and every member was put into a class meeting and given a regular "ticket of membership", reminding him of his commitments. A group of churches formed a circuit under the control of a Superintendent Minister and circuit stewards. A Quarterly Meeting for business was held, while the Synod for the District which was made up of a group of circuits, met twice a year. A quarterly Plan was issued, listing the Churches in a circuit and showing the Ministers and preachers appointed to conduct services each Sunday.

The Wesleyans ran many schools and colleges and organised Guild meetings which covered subjects of general interest, as well as devotional. In 1885 Conference decided to build "central halls" in larger towns. These became well known not only for their bright services but also as centres of social work.

FORMATION OF THE HIGH WYCOMBE WESLEYAN CIRCUIT

High Wycombe remained in the Oxford Circuit for the remainder of the eighteenth century. As the Church grew however it became necessary to form circuits which could be more manageable from the point of view of both pastoral care and the distances that had to be travelled. In 1794 there were four Ministers in the Circuit, including Richard Gower (the third Minister). The following year Newbury Circuit was formed and Oxford then had two Ministers again. In 1805 and 1806 Richard Gower returned to Oxford as the Superintendent. From 1807 there were again three Ministers in the Circuit until 1815 when the High Wycombe Circuit was formed. Henry Anderson, Superintendent in 1814, now became the Superintendent of Wycombe and Richard Gower returned for the third time to lead the smaller Oxford Circuit for three years. Richard Gower later became the High Wycombe Superintendent in 1825-26.

At least five Churches had been built when the High Wycombe Circuit was formed. St.Mary Street was firmly established as the Circuit Church. The Penn church had been built in 1808 followed by Great Marlow (1810), Wooburn Green (1811), and West Wycombe (1815). Of these Penn remains in use as a Methodist Church to this day, being part of the Free Methodists' schoolroom. West Wycombe is now used by the Christadelphians and stands in Church Lane. There seems little doubt that there were other Societies in the Circuit without their own church building. High Wycombe (St.Mary Street) would undoubtedly have been the largest. In 1816 the Circuit membership was reported as 290 which was probably about 170 in High Wycombe with the village churches around 30 each. For the most part the people would meet in cottages for prayer and exhortation. These would be led either by a local preacher or

by a prayer leader or exhorter. There would often be a Sunday
School meeting in the same locality.

PREACHING PLACES (1779 - 1824)

```
          11        1         1         1          1  1
          77        7         8         8          8  8
          78        9         0         1          2  2
          9012345678901234567890123456789012345678901234

High Vycombe.
  St.Mary St   B                                      t  t
Penn                               ρ  B               t  t
Great Marlow                          B              t  t
West Wycombe                             B           t  t
Wooburn Green                         B              t  t
Lane End                                             t  t
Stokenchurch                                         t  t
Winchmore Hill                                       t  t
Downley                                              t  t  B
Amersham                                             t  -
Walters Ash                                          t
Flackwell Heath                                      t
Knotty Green                                         t
Radnage                                              t
Gt.Kingshill                                         t
Workhouse                                            t
```

B = Chapel Built
t = Services (from Plans available)
ρ = Services (from Preachers' Minutes)

    There are only two Plans that we have found, surviving from
this period - for 1818 and 1822-23. Copies of these are to be
found in the vestry of Wesley Church. The Plan of 1818 shows,
in addition to the five Churches mentioned earlier, preaching at
Lane End, Stokenchurch, Winchmore Hill, Downley and Amersham.
Of these, churches were to be built at Downley (1824), Lane End
(1834), Winchmore Hill (1861) and Amersham (1899). Stokenchurch
appears on the 1822-3 Plan but not on the 1838 one. It does
not appear on the Wesleyan Plan again (as far as we know).
Amersham, although missing from the 1822-23 Plan, appears on all
other documents through to 1932 and the "Deed of Union".

250 YEARS OF CHILTERN METHODISM

PREACHING PLACES (1825 - 1870)

```
                   1    1         1         1         1         1
                   8    8         8         8         8         8
                   2    3         4         5         6         7
                   56789012345678901234567890123456789012345678901234567890

High Wycombe.
  St.Mary St          x††            †     †       †   † †
  Wesley                                                          B
Penn                  x††            F
Great Marlow          x††            †     †       †   † †
West Wycombe          x††            †     †       †   † †
Wooburn Green         x††            †     †       †   † †
Lane End           B  x†† E          †     †       †   † †B
Winchmore Hill        x††            †     †      †B   † †
Downley               E††      E     E     †       †   † †
Amersham              x††            †     †       -   † †
Flackwell Heath       x††            †     †       †   † B
Knotty Green          --     ρ       -     -       -   - -
Radnage               x††            †    †C
Saunderton            -†              -     -       -   - -
Bledlow Ridge      B  x††            †     †       †   † †
Beaconsfield          xB†            †F
Holmer Green          x†† B         †R     †       †   † †
Bradenham             x††            †     †       -   - -
Lacey Green           x††            -     -       -   - -
Little Missenden       ††     C      -     -       -   - -
Booker                       ρB      †     †       †   † †
Hazlemere                    ρ                     †   - -
Cadmore End                  ρC
Prestwood                                        †B†
Handy Cross                  C                     † †
Wycombe Marsh                                     †
```

B = Chapel Built
C = Services Ceased
E = Chapel Extended or Additional Buildings e.g. Schoolroom
F = Transferred to the Free Methodists (W.R.U.)
R = Rebuilt or New Building to replace
† = Services (from Plans available)
ρ = Services (from Preachers' Minutes)
x = Classes (from Membership Returns)

Apart from Amersham, the 1822-23 Plan includes all those from 1818 and in addition lists Walters Ash, Flackwell Heath, Knotty Green, Radnage, Great Kingshill and the Workhouse. The only one of these to eventually build a church was Flackwell Heath in 1865. Walters Ash, Knotty Green, Great Kingshill and the Workhouse only appear on this Plan, although the Preachers' Meeting minutes show an attempt to re-establish causes in these places in 1844. (The Workhouse which is possibly the same as the cause referred to as "Saunderton" on the 1838-9 Plan, was an institution maintained at public expense where able-bodied paupers did unpaid work in return for food and accommodation.) Radnage seems to have been a cause with fluctuating fortunes, often only established during the summer months and eventually closing in 1855. (The Primitive Methodists, whose High Wycombe Circuit began in 1836, finally established their chapel there in 1865.)

During the 1830's and 1840's attempts continued to be made to establish Societies in a number of localities. Usually these were to set up class meetings and cottage services. Lacey Green, with a class of 18 in 1837, was on the Plan in 1838 and 1839 but was missing in 1844. Similarly Little Missenden and Bradenham (membership 27 in 1837), both on the Plan in 1838/9, closed or ceased to meet in 1844 and 1856 respectively. Attempts over the years to start causes at Hazlemere, Cadmore End, Handy Cross, Wycombe Marsh and Little Hampden all failed in the long term. More success was achieved at Bledlow Ridge built in 1834 and with the small membership of seven in 1837; Beaconsfield where there were 15 members in two classes in 1837; and Holmer Green, said to have started in 1822 with a cottage meeting, where the six members in 1837 were to increase sufficiently to undertake the building of their first church in 1841. The only other church to become established during this period was Booker, built in 1847.

When division occurred in 1849 and the Wesleyan Reform Union (Free Methodists) broke away from the Wesleyans, it was a major set-back to the growth of the Circuit. Penn and Beaconsfield were two who departed from the Plan. In addition a breakaway group in High Wycombe built the first Oxford Road Free Methodist Chapel in 1863, while new Churches in Wycombe Marsh (1865) and Hazlemere (1867) were also attached to the Free Methodists. In 1851 the number of Churches had dropped from 17 (1838) to 14, a figure which remained until the 1890's. Various places came on or "dropped off" in the 1860's. Prestwood started in 1863 and three years later came the new Wesley. The old chapel in St. Mary Street was now not big enough to hold the growing congregation in the town and so in 1866 a new church was opened in Cemetery Road (now Priory Road). Wesley Sunday School continued to use the old Church until 1871, thus completing the century from Hannah Ball's little class in 1769.

PREACHING PLACES (1871 - 1934)

```
                  1        1        1        1        1      1
                  8        8        8        9        9      9
                  7        8        9        0        1      3
                  12345678901234567890123456789012345678 90  34
High Wycombe.
  Vesley          x †† †       †     † E      †      †     †       M
  Newland Missn   †- -         -     -        -      -     -       -
  Victoria              B      †     †        †    E †             M
  London Road                  S B   †        †      †     M
Great Marlow      x †† †       †     †        †B     †     †       M
Vest Wycombe      x †† †       †     †     B  †      †     †       M
Wooburn Green     x B† †       †     †        †     †E     †       M
Lane End          x †† †       †     †        †      †     †       M
Winchmore Hill    x †† †       †     †        †      †     †       M
Downley           x †† †       †     †        †      †     †       M
Amersham          x †† †       †     †        B      †     †       M
Flackwell Heath   x †† †     E    †           †      †     †       M
Bledlow Ridge     x †† †       † E   †        †      †     †       M
Holmer Green      x †† †       †     †        †      †     †       M
Booker            x †† †       † E   †        †      † E †         M
Prestwood         xE†† †       †     †        †      †     †       M
Handycross        ρ           †
Wycombe Marsh     x †(Tu)
Little Hampden       † †
Chesham                              S B †   †      †     RM
Terriers                               B †   †      †     M
Piddington                                   † B    †     M
Bourne End                                          B     M
```

B = Chapel Built
E = Chapel Extended or Additional Buildings e.g. Schoolroom
M = United in the Methodist Church.
R = Rebuilt or New Building to replace
† = Services (from Plans available)
ρ = Services (from Preachers' Minutes)
S = Services (from other source)
x = Classes   (from Membership Returns)

As the town grew, so did the need for additional churches. In 1877 a new church was built in Victoria Street and 14 years later on the other side of town London Road opened (1893), followed in 1895 by the small tin church at Terriers. The final additions of the century were: Chesham (1897) where Methodism had languished ever since those early days when John Wesley himself had preached from the friendly Church of England pulpit; and Amersham, High Street (1899). So with a little spurt in the closing years, the Plan at the close of the 19th century had grown again to 17 churches, the same number as in 1838, but with congregations that were now established and permanently housed.

The 20th century up to the "Deed of Union" (1932) saw a period of stability in the Circuit unequalled in any other similar span of its history. All the churches that started the century were included in the united Plan of the Methodist Church in 1934. There were two additions – Piddington in 1906 and Bourne End in 1910. The former was not strictly a Wesleyan church as the Circuit felt that Piddington was well served by West Wycombe which was a large church not very far from the village. However, it was included on the Wesleyan Plan.

HIGH WYCOMBE WESLEYAN CIRCUIT : MINISTERS

OXFORD CIRCUIT : 1765-1814

	SUPERINTENDENT	OTHER MINISTERS
1765	Thomas Tobias	
66	William Minethorp	
67	Richard Henderson	
68	Benjamin Rhodes	Martin Rodda
69	: : :	Richard Whatcoat
1770	John Furz	John Duncan
71	Samuel Wells	William Barker
72	: :	William Brammah
73	Hugh Saunderson	John Whittam
74	Francis Wolfe	Joseph Moore / William Tunney
75	Samuel Wells	John Valton / George Shorter
76	John Valton	William Whitaker / John Gouldston
77	James Cotty	William Severn
78	Thomas Carlill	William Tunney
79	George Story	Thomas Newall

	SUPERINTENDENT	OTHER MINISTERS
1780	George Story	John Accut
81	Richard Rodda	Thomas Warwick
82	: : :	John Cole
83	John Broadbent	Simon Day / John Cole
84	Samuel Hodgson	: :
85	Jonathan Cousins	Barnabas Thomas
86	Joseph Harper	Samuel Edwards / John Rowbotham
87	Joseph Pescod	Joseph Entwistle / Richard Reece
88	: : :	Charles Bland / Abraham Moseley
89	William Horner	John Cricket / Richard Reece
1790	William Horner	Joseph Sutcliffe / Jasper Winscom
91	George Baldwin	William Stevens / Thomas Jones
92	: : :	: : : / Edward Gibbons
93	Joseph Algar	Thomas Trethewey / Leonard Ledbrook
94	: :	Jonathan Cousins / Richard Gower
		/ William Moulton
95	Owen Davies	John Dean
96	William Shelmerdine	: :
97	: : : :	Joseph Cole / Stephen Wilson
98	: : : :	George Deverell
99	William Holmes	James Bridgnell
1800	William Holmes	James Bridgnell
01	: : :	Jacob Stanley
02	Jacob Stanley	Thomas Edman
03/04	Joseph Cole	William Hicks
05	Richard Gower	Maximilian Wilson
06	: : :	Robert Gunn
07	Richard Waddy	: : / William Simpson
08	John Aikenhead	Thomas Dowty / Mark Day
09	: : :	: : / William Toogood
1810	Daniel Campbell	John Smith
11	Marmaduke Revell	Thomas Ashton / William Dixon
12	Edward Roberts	: : : / Thomas Key
13	: : :	William Hayman / Thomas Moxon
14	Henry Anderson	: : : / : : :

WYCOMBE CIRCUIT : 1815-1933

1815	Henry Anderson	William Wilson
16/17	James Burley	William Hicks
18	William Pearson	Samuel Robinson
19	: : :	Solomon Whitworth

THE WESLEYAN METHODIST CHURCH

	SUPERINTENDENT	OTHER MINISTERS
1820	George Dermott	George Banwell
21	: : :	Charles Colwell
22	John Furness	: : :
23	: :	John Piggott
24	John Knowles	: :
25/26	Richard Gower	George H.Rowe
27/28	Daniel Campbell	William Harrison
29	William Brocklehurst	William Edwards
1830	William Brocklehurst	William Edwards
31/33	Philip Jameson	Thomas Robinson
34	Thomas Twiddy	James Sydserff
35	James Etchells	Charles Colwell
36/37	John Simmonds	Thomas Jones
38	William Taylor	John Overton
39	Isaac Phenix	: :
1840	Isaac Phenix	George F.Driver
41/42	John Coates	: : :
43	: :	Joseph Lowthian
44	Joseph Lowthian	John T.Barr
45	Richard Cooper	: :
46	Richard Cooper	John Anderson
47	John Booth	: : :
48	: :	William Jewett
49	: :	Thomas Withington
1850/51	James Bartholomew	Thomas Withington
52/54	William Davies	Henry Needle
55	John Bissell	James Eacott
56	: :	John Lewis
57/58	John W.Cotton	Charles B.Ritchie
59	Edward Branston	William Robinson
1860/61	Edward Branston	William Robinson
62/63	Samuel Lucas	Henry Keet
64/66	George Buckley	John Raw
67/68	William Satchell	Joseph Little
69	William Lewis	Robert Broomfield
1870	William Lewis	Robert Broomfield
71	: : :	John Skeratt
72/73	Thomas Jefferies	Francis Barker
74	: : :	William Dunstan
75	Matthew Giles	: : :

	SUPERINTENDENT	OTHER MINISTERS
1876	Joseph M. Browne	William Dunstan
77/78	: : :	W. Wheatley Smith
79	James Taylor	Henry J. Cornish
80/81	James Taylor	William J. Dawson
82	Henry Lewis	: : :
83/84	: :	Clement S. Reader
85/87	Henry J. Quilter	Arthur B. Pinnegar
88/89	S. Wesley Lawton	Charles Thomas
1890	S. Wesley Lawton	William Powell
91	John Hogg	: : :
92/93	: :	Archibald Bayliss
94	Richard Harper	: : : :
95	: : :	Henry J. Brookfield
96	: : :	Ralph Philipson
97/98	William Earl	: : :
99	: :	William Cuthbert
1900/01	Thomas H. Penrith	William Cuthbert
02/03	Hilderic Friend	William Brookhurst
04	Joseph H. Cadman	Robert S. Maynard
05/06	: : :	William Musson
07	Eneas Mosscropp	: : :
08/09	: : :	Alfred W. Coulson
1910	Sebastian De la Mare	Alfred W. Coulson
11/12	: : : :	Ernest Marshall
13	W. Terry Coppin	: : :
14/16	: : :	Arthur T. Dean
17	: : :	Walter Standley
18/19	Walter Seed	F. Percy Gent
1920/21	Walter Seed	F. Percy Gent
22	Henry G. Godwin	: :
23	: : :	H. John Ivens
24	: : :	W. J. Heaton/H. Scares
25	E. J. Bennett Richards	: : / : :
26	: : : :	K. H. Crosby/ : :
27/28	: : : :	: : /E. Penna
29	J. G. Penman	T. Westerdale/W. Cardy
1930	J. G. Penman	T. Westerdale/W. Cardy
31	: :	R. O. Stobbs/ : :
32/33	Ernest Dennis	: : /E. V. Eavis

The Sunday Plan of High Wycombe Circuit.
A. D. 1818-19.

Preach the Word. 2 Timothy iv. 2.

Places and Time of Preaching.		November.					December.				January.					February.				March.				April.			
		1	8	15	22	29	6	13	20	27	3	10	17	24	31	7	14	21	28	7	14	21	28	4	11	18	2[illegible]
High Wycombe	10½	1	2	2	1	1	2	2	1	1	2	2	1	1	2	2	1	1	2	2	1	1	2	2	1	1	2
	2½	2	5	1	3	6	4	3	8	2	3	1	7	2	5	1	3	6	8	3	7	2	3	1	5	2	6
	6	2	2	1	3	2s	2	1	1	2	3	1	1s	2	2	1	3	2	2	1	1	2	3s	1	1	2	2
Penn	10½	9	3	9	4	8	9	8	5	6	8	9	8	9	3	8	5	9	6	9	8	10	5	8	3	9	5
	2½	1	6	2	4	1	7	2	9	1	5	2	6	1	3	2	9	1	4	2	8	1	5	2	9	1	8
	6	1	3	2	4	1	5	2s	5	1	8	2	6	1s	3	2	5	1	4	2s	8	1	5	2	3	1s	5
G. Marlow	10½	4	1	5	2	3	1	7	2	8	1	6	2	5	1	4	2	7	1	8	2	3	1	5	2	6	1
	2½	4	1	5	2	3	1	7	2	8	1	6	2	5	1	4	2	7	1	8	2	3	1	5	2	6	1
	6	1	1	5	2s	3	1	7	2	8	1	6	2	5	1s	4	2	7	1	8	2	3	1	5	2s	6	1
West Wycombe	2½	5	2	8	1	4	2	5	1	3	2	8	1	6	2	5	1	4	2	5	1	8	2	3	1	4	2
	6	5	10	8	1	4	6	5	6	3	2	8	10	6	6	5	1	4	10	5	6	8	2	3	10	4	6
Wooburn	10½	2	4	1	7	2	5	1	4	2	8	1	4	2	7	1	6	2	3	1	4	2	8	1	4	2	9
	6	6	4	10	7	10	7	4	4	9	5	4	4	9	7	10	6	5	3	6	4	9	8	7	4	7	9
Lane End	10½	7	8	6	10	7	8	10	7	4	6	5	10	7	8	7	4	8	5	10	5	6	7	4	6	5	7
	2½	7	8	6	5	7	8	10	7	4	6	5	10	7	8	7	4	8	5	10	5	6	7	4	6	5	7
Stokenchurch	2½	10		7		5		6		10		7		10		6		10		7		5		6		10	
W. Hill	2½	9	3	4	8	8	9	8	5	6	9	10	8	9	4	8	5	9	6	4	9	10	9	8	3	8	5
Downley	6	10		7		5		6		10		7		10		6		10		7		5		6		10	
Amersham	2½	8	7		6	9	10	9	10	5	7			8	9	9	8		7			7	6	9	8		10
	6	8		9		9		9			7	9	8	8	9		8	9		9	9		9	9	8	8	

Preachers.

1 Pearson.
2 Robinson.
3 Holmes.
4 Lawrance.
5 Bird.
6 Daveney.
7 Wright.
8 Hearne.
9 Haws.
10 Wright.

s Sacrament.

Printed by E. W. Morris, Wycombe.

High Wycombe Circuit, 1822 & 1823.

PLAN OF THE PREACHERS AND EXHORTERS ON THE LORD'S DAY.

Places & Time of Preaching.		Oct.		Novemr.				December.					January.				Feb.				March.					Apr.	
		20	27	3	10	17	24	1	8	15	22	29	5	12	19	26	2	9	16	23	2	9	16	23	30	6	13
High Wycombe	10½	F	C	C	F	F	C	C	F	F	C	C	F	F	C	C	F	F	C	C	F	F	C	C	F	F	C
	2½	2	3	4	6	8	5	2	3	8	5	6	8	2	3	4	6	5	7	2	3	4	6	7	8	2	3
	6	F	C	C	F	F	C	C	F	F	C	C	F	F	C	C	F	F	C	C	F	F	C	C	F	F	C
Penn	10½	3	F	4	C	5	F	1	C	7	F	2	C	8	F	5	C	6	F	7	C	8	F	2	C	4	F
	2½	*	2	*	14	1	10	*	13	9	8	*	*	*	10	*	*	*	*	*	*	9	14	*	1	*	*
	6	3	F	4	C	5	F	1	C	7	F	2	C	3	F	5	C	6	F	7	C	8	F	2	C	4	F
Winchmore Hill	2½	3	F	4	C	5	F	*	C	7	F	2	C	3	F	5	C	6	F	7	C	8	F	2	C	4	F
	6	P	P	P	P	P	P	P	P	P	P	P	P	P	P	P	P	P	P	P	P	P	P	P	P	P	P
Great Marlow	10½	C	5	F	2	C	3	F	4	C	6	F	7	C	8	F	2	C	3	F	4	C	5	F	7	C	8
	2½	C	5	F	2	C	3	F	4	C	6	F	7	C	8	F	2	C	3	F	4	C	5	F	7	C	8
	6	C	5	F	2	C	3	F	4	C	6	F	7	C	8	F	2	C	3	F	4	C	5	F	7	C	8
West Wycombe	2½	F	8	C	3	F	4	C	5	F	7	C	15	F	10	C	16	F	4	C	13	F	17	C	15	F	14
	6	9	8	10	3	9	4	12	5	13	7	14	15	7	10	*8	16	2	4	3	13	7	17	4	15	5	14
Wooburn	10½	4	6	8	9	*	11	5	15	2	14	3	12	15	*	20	11	21	1	14	2	3	8	21	13	2	1
	2½	4	C	8	F	*	C	5	F	2	C	2	F	1	C	20	F	21	C	14	F	3	C	21	F	2	C
Lane End	10½	6	18	2	4	17	8	3	6	16	18	17	2	14	9	6	3	7	12	15	18	17	16	6	2	14	18
	2½	6	18	2	4	17	8	3	6	16	18	17	2	14	9	6	3	7	12	15	18	17	16	6	2	14	18
Stoken Church	2½	7	4	3	17	2	6	18	16	17	9	18	16	17	14	12	11	9	2	4	6	18	21	3	4	5	6
Downley	6	18	13	14	11	12	15	7	8	9	2	4	18	10	16	11	14	15	10	[illegible]	3	10	7	9	18	21	16
Walter's Ash	2½	18	13	14	11	12	15	7	8	9	2	4	18	10	16	11	14	15	10	16	3	10	7	9	18	21	16
Flackwell Heath	6	2	19	1	6	3	7	8	9	10	11	12	18	19	20	21	4	3	6	9	10	11	12	[illegible]	2	20	21
Knotty Green	6	5	*	6	*	1	5	19	*	[illegible]	*	14	2	4	19	*	7	*	1	5	16	*	19	*	1	5	*
Radnage	[illegible]	17	4	7	18	16	17	[illegible]	11	18	16	17	9	18	4	3	11	17	16	[illegible]	18	12	15	8	5	6	17
Great Kingshill	6	16	18	9	10	11	12	15	16	8	20	5	19	16	*	7	[illegible]	8	9	16	15	14	*	12	11	7	9
Workhouse	[illegible]	11		12		16		11		15		9		12		14		20		13		13		10		4	

Preachers.

F Furness.
C Colwell.
H Holmes.
1 Laurence.
2 Bird.
3 Daveney.
4 Wright.
5 Hearne.
6 Cole.
7 Beck.
8 Burkitt.

Exhorters.

9 Barney, Ives.
10 Willoughby, C. Holmes.
11 Bidmead, Allen, Chapel.
12 Wooster, Salmon.
13 Miller, H——.
14 West, Barton.
15 Wright, Hill.
16 James Plumridge, Barlow, Folly—*Downley.*
17 J. and James Plumridge—*Lane End.*
18 Butler, Harris.
19 Ravenell, Pottinger.
20 Pymm, Lacinon.
21 Rolfe, Grimsdale.

Sacraments.—Wycombe, Nov. 3, Dec. 15, Jan. 26, March 9; Penn, Jan. 5, March 30; Marlow, Nov. 17, Feb. 23.

Love Feasts.—Wycombe, Dec. 25, March 30; West Wycombe, Feb. 9; Marlow, Dec. 29, April 6.

Missionary Prayer Meetings.—High Wycombe and Wooburn, the first Friday in every Month, at 7; Penn, first Monday, at 7; Marlow and West Wycombe, first Thursday, at 7.

* Penn.

N. B.—C stands for Kingswood and Woodhouse Grove School Collections.—T for Tickets to be given.—The Quarter Day will be on Wednesday, January the 1st, 1823.

(MORRIS, PRINTER, WYCOMBE.)

WESLEYAN METHODIST CHAPELS
in the HIGH WYCOMBE CIRCUIT

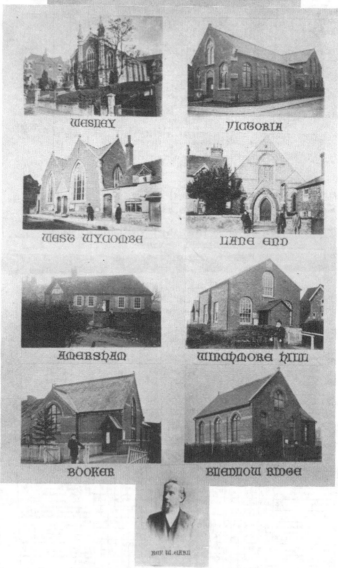

WESLEY

VICTORIA

WEST WYCOMBE

LANE END

AMERSHAM

WINCHMORE HILL

BOOKER

BLEDLOW RIDGE

REV W. CASE

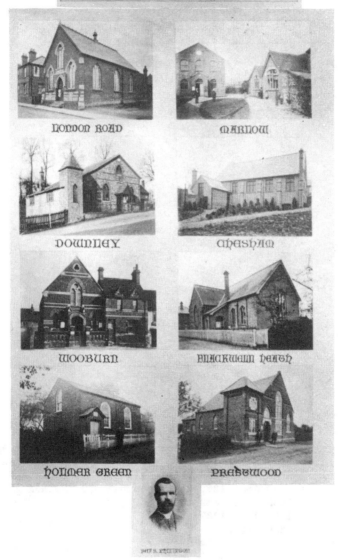

PRESENTED to WESLEY SUNDAY SCHOOL by Mr JOSEPH STONE in commemoration of fifty years connection with the School. Xmas. 1899.

LONDON ROAD

MARLOW

DOWNLEY

CHESHAM

WOOBURN

BLACKWELL HEATH

HOLMER GREEN

PRESTWOOD

HIGH WYCOMBE WESLEYAN CIRCUIT : LOCAL PREACHERS

NAME	1st REF.	ACCR 'TED	LAST REF.	ADDRESS	NOTES
Lawrence	1818		1818		
Bird	1818		1860		d. 18th Oct Age 84
James Daveney	1813	1813	1842		d. 8th Apl Age 54
Weight	1818		1818		
Hearne	1818		1818		
Haws	1818		1818		
Wright	1818		1818		
Cole	1822		1822		
Beck	1822		1850	"Bird in Hand"	LP.Sec.1843.
Burkitt	1822		1822		
Jos.Moorcock	1822	1822	1845	West Wycombe	d. 27th Sep Age 45
Restal	1838		1838		
Revenal	1838		1850	Wooburn	
Wingrove	1838		1838		
J.Hawkins	1838		1889	West Wycombe	
Bird	1838		1860	Lane End	
Hinton	1838		1841		
Pottinger	1838		1838		
Hill	1838		1838		
Weight	1838		1838		
Robert Long	1838		1847		Died 7th July
Woolmer	1838		1838		
Ashton	1838		1850	Burnham	
Thyme	1838		1838	Windsor	
Young	1838		1838	Windsor	
Hester	1838		1838		On Trial only
Wood	1838		1839		
Harris	1839	1839	1850	West Wycombe	
Wright	1839	1839	1862	Flackwell Heath	d. 16th Dec Age 75
William Chapel	1839		1848		Died 2nd Jan.
Aaron Cock	1839	1839	1873	Little Missenden	Died 27th Nov.
Sammons	1839	1839	1860	High Wycombe	d. 20th Aug Age 78
R.White	1839	1839	1889	Lane End	
Croxton	1839	1839	1839		
Wheeler	1839	1839	1839		
Pusey	1838		1854	Great Marlow	
Hawes	1838		1850	West Wycombe	
W.Mead	1838		1876	West Wycombe	
A.Hughes	1838		1889	West Wycombe	

NAME	1st REF.	ACCR 'TED	LAST REF.	ADDRESS	NOTES
	------Dates------				
Daveney Jnr.	1841		1850	High Wycombe	
Snell	1841		1850	Beaconsfield	
Simeon Stone	1842	1842	1873	Flackwell Heath	d. 5th Mar Age 59
Hirst	1840	1842	1849	Candidate for Ministry	
W.Goodearl	1841	1841	1889	Lane End	
M.Tubb	1841		1858	Bledlow Ridge	Name removed
Long	1842		1847		Died
Butcher	1844	1844	1858	Winchmore Hill	Died
Blackwell	1844		1845	Beaconsfield	Resigned
Thomas Howard	1844		1844		On Trial only
Taylor	1845		1855	Great Marlow	Name removed
R.Baker	1848		1876	Loudwater	
Snapes	1844	1845	1847		
Thos Anderson	1846	1846	1854	High Wycombe	
Jas Hussey Sn.	1846	1846	1904	Downley	
Henry Hirst	1846	1846	1850	Beaconsfield	
T.Gill	1847	1847	1888	Lane End	Died
Harman	1845		1845		On Trial only
Edwin Hughes	1847	1847	1865	West Wycombe	
Daniel Smith	1847	1847	1854	West Wycombe	
John Ball	1847	1847	1889	Downley	
Charles Bradbury					
Joseph Abbott					
T.Garland	1850		1851	Penn	Excluded himself
Wheeler	1850		1850	Wooburn	On Trial only
T.E.Dukes	1850		1893	Great Marlow	d. 25th Nov Age 81
Andrew	1850		1850	Wooburn	Exhorter
Ashton	1850		1868	High Wycombe	Resigned.
Turner	1854		1854	High Wycombe	
Dudley	1853	1853	1853	West Wycombe	
Styles	1853	1853	1853	Great Marlow	Trans.to Wantage
Bavin	1853	1853	1853		
Crutch	1853	1853	1859	Loudwater	Trans.to Windsor
J.Child	1853	1853	1898	High Wycombe	Died
Henry Collins	1854		1877	Downley	d. 29th Jan Age 44
S.Weller	1856	1856	1904	High Wycombe	
Oxlade	1857	1857	1863	Downley	Died
W.Smith	1859	1859	1871	Flackwell Heath	To America
B.North	1850	1860	1875	West Wycombe	Died
H.Johnson	1860	1860	1875	Lane End	Died
J.Beck	1860	1860	1874	Beaconsfield	To Uxbridge
B.Howland	1860	1861	1884	High Wycombe	
J.Steevens	1860	1861	1904	High Wycombe	

NAME	1st REF.	ACCR 'TED	LAST REF.	ADDRESS	NOTES
Male	1861		1865	High Wycombe	From Wantage
H.Senior	1860	1861	1904	High Wycombe	
James Collins	1860	1861	1889	Downley	
J.Woodbridge	1860	1861	1884	Downley	
W.Almond	1860	1863	1876	Great Marlow	
John Hussey Jr	1862	1863	1884	High Wycombe	
John Busby JP	1862	1863	1904	High Wycombe	
Alb't Saunders	1862	1863	1866	Lane End	Resigned
R.Goodearl JP	1862	1863	1931	High Wycombe	Died
J.Randall	1863	1863	1876	Holmer Green	
R.Wheeler	1863		1884	Wooburn	Trans.in
Lanham	1860	1863	1867	High Wycombe	Resigned
James Brown	1864		1884	Lane End	Trans.from Thame
A.Gray	1863	1864	1904	Lane End	
D.James	1863	1864	1901	West Wycombe	Died
C.West	1863	1864	1903	West Wycombe	Died
J.Nash	1863	1864	1921	High Wycombe	
W.Bartlett	1863	1864	1916	High Wycombe	Died
Porter	1865	1865	1865	Flackwell Heath	Trans.in
Loveland	1867		1868		Resigned
J.R.Dring	1873		1915	High Wycombe	Died
C.Hawes	1864	1867	1876	West Wycombe	
B.North Jr.JP	1864	1867	1921	West Wycombe	
James Bates	1865	1867	1902	West Wycombe	Died
Henry Pearce	1865	1867	1876	West Wycombe	
Derrick	1867	1867	1867		
Thomas Mead	1865	1867	1867		To Middlesboro'
William Hughes	1865	1868	1868		
Joshua Wheeler	1869	1869	1873	Wooburn	Left the circuit
Woods	1869		1869		From Newbury
Boot	1869		1869		On Trial only
P.Harman	1868	1869	1869	Great Marlow	Left the circuit
Abel Cutler	1871		1873		Left the circuit
J.Money	1871	1872	1876	High Wycombe	
James Brooker	1871		1889	Lane End	
Henry J. Plumridge	1871	1873	1904	Lane End	
Edwin Hussey	1872	1873	1876	High Wycombe	
S.Pilcher	1873		1874	Loudwater	From Gravesend.
R.Lane	1871	1873	1904	Booker	
F.G.Dukes	1872	1873	1928	Great Marlow	Died
C.W.Deacon	1873	1874	1903	High Wycombe	
D.Stone	1873	1874	1931	Flackwell Heath	To Portslade,Sx.

THE WESLEYAN METHODIST CHURCH

NAME	------Dates------			ADDRESS	NOTES
	1st REF.	ACCR 'TED	LAST REF.		
Alfred Hawes	1873	1873	1874	High Wycombe	
Geo. Looseley	1873	1873	1876	Great Marlow	
A. W. Baddeley	1876		1876	High Wycombe	
S. Baldock	1873		1874	High Wycombe	Resigned health
A. Moore	1874		1874	Prestwood	On Trial only
V. Millburn	1874		1876	High Wycombe	
E. Hatton	1876		1904	Great Marlow	
C. Jennings	1875		1901	Prestwood	Died
J. Platt	1884		1889	Wooburn	
Thomas Coles	1884		1884	High Wycombe	
George Seymour	1878		1934	Booker	See Methodist list
W. J. Cook	1881	1881	1934	Lane End	See Methodist list
A. Edwards	1882	1882	1934	Amersham	See Methodist list
J. Burnham	1884		1899	High Wycombe	
G. Gray	1884		1916	High Wycombe	Died
G. A. Darwent	1884		1884	Great Marlow	
Isaac Brearley	1886	1886	1934	Lane End	See Methodist list
F. J. Sharp	1884		1889	High Wycombe	
J. Oxlade	1889		1904	Downley	
W. Wright	1889		1904	Prestwood	
W. White	1889		1921	Wooburn	
Jas. Hussey Jr.	1873		1889	High Wycombe	
G. Stephenson	1889		1889	High Wycombe	
E. Nash	1889		1889	High Wycombe	
H. Bishop	1889		1921	Lane End	
J. Cheshire	1889		1889	High Wycombe	
F. Britnell	1889		1889	High Wycombe	On Trial only
G. Nash	1889		1889	High Wycombe	On Trial only
F. W. Davis	1888	1888	1933	Marlow	Died
G. Ellis	1889		1904	Lane End	
A. Dadswell	1889		1903	High Wycombe	
G. Ireland	1889		1889	High Wycombe	On Trial only
T. W. Apps	1890	1890	1934	High Wycombe	See Methodist list
C. Bunce	1891	1891	1934	High Wycombe	See Methodist list
John Deacon	1892		1898	High Wycombe	Died
John Hussey	1892		1894		Resigned
G. Church	1897		1897	Chesham	Top name on Plan.
J. Woodbridge	1899		1904	High Wycombe	
T. Barfield	1899		1904	High Wycombe	
C. J. Cutler	1892	1892	1934	Lane End	See Methodist list
Benj. Burton	1894		1904	Marlow	From Thame
E. Bartlett	1899		1904	Loudwater	
W. Youens JP	1892	1892	1934	Downley	See Methodist list

NAME	1st REF.	ACCR 'TED	LAST REF.	ADDRESS	NOTES
H. Woodward	1893	1894	1934	High Wycombe	See Methodist list
F. Sherwin	1899		1904	High Wycombe	
W. A. Steevens	1896	1896	1934	High Wycombe	See Methodist list
C. Parker	1899		1904	Chesham	
G. Burnham	1899		1921	Flackwell Heath	
B. Hornby	1899		1904	Great Missenden	
J. Fletcher	1899		1904	Chesham/Chenies	
E. Johnson	1898	1898	1902	Chesham	
C. Swann	1898	1898	1900	Amersham	
V. Elgar	1899	1899	1901	High Wycombe	
T. Markham	1899	1899	1902	Chesham	
A. Higgs	1898	1898	1934	Southall	See Methodist list
A. Purdue	1898	1898	1934	High Wycombe	See Methodist list
J. Shirley	1898	1900	1934	Flackwell Heath	See Methodist list
R. Nancarrow	1901	1901	1934	Great Missenden	See Methodist list
Thomas Ayres	1901	1901	1904	Amersham	
E. A. Murrells	1903	1903	1904	High Wycombe	
James Bedford	1901	1903	1904	Chesham	
George Goddard	1902	1903	1921	Flackwell Heath	
Henry Collins	1901	1903	1934	Flackwell Heath	See Methodist list
V. H. Knowles	1903	1903	1904	High Wycombe	
George Brown	1903	1903	1934	High Wycombe	See Methodist list
V. G. Ellis	1904		1904	High Wycombe	
A. P. Ploughman	1904		1904	High Wycombe	
John Line	1904		1904	Lane End	
W. Markham	1904	1904	1934	High Wycombe	See Methodist list
W. Evans	1904		1904	High Wycombe	On Trial only
T. Weston	1904	1905	1934	High Wycombe	See Methodist list
H. D. Bishop	1905	1905	1934	High Wycombe	See Methodist list
George Pratt	1905	1905	1934	Amersham	See Methodist list
J. Chilton	1904		1904	Flackwell Heath	On Trial only
Albert Pearce	1906	1906	1934	High Wycombe	See Methodist list
W. V. Hearn	1906	1906	1934	Lane End	See Methodist list
Walt. Goodearl	1906	1906	1934	High Wycombe	See Methodist list
John Howard	1906	1906	1934	High Wycombe	Died
P. Lee	1919		1929	Hazlemere	Died
A. H. Nixby	1919		1919	Moor End	Died
A. Edwards	1919		1937	Amersham	
O. Bailey	1919		1928	High Wycombe	
C. H. Dyche	1919		1921	Flackwell Heath	
E. Leeson	1919		1921	West Wycombe	
J. H. Binns	1919		1921	Holmer Green	To Southark
V. E. Garlick	1909	1909	1934	Chesham	See Methodist list

THE VESLEYAN METHODIST CHURCH

NAME	1st REF.	ACCR 'TED	LAST REF.	ADDRESS	NOTES
S.Carr	1910	1910	1934	Lane End	See Methodist list
T.H.Weatherall	1912	1912	1934	Chesham	Ex Dunstable 1919 See Methodist list
G.A.Puzey	1913	1913	1919		To Skipton
W.Saunders	1915	1915	1934	High Wycombe	See Methodist list
Stephen Edge	1916	1916	1934	Flackwell Heath	See Methodist list
W.G.Cooper	1919	1919	1934	Bourne End	See Methodist list
T.Smith	1920	1920	1934	High Wycombe	See Methodist list
E.Weller	1920	1920	1934	High Wycombe	See Methodist list
V.J.Parkins	1920	1920	1934	High Wycombe	See Methodist list
H.A.Goodearl	1921	1921	1934	Bourne End	See Methodist list
Williamson	1921		1921		On Trial only
T.Bird	1921		1921		On Trial only
James Jarvis	1921		1921	Flackwell Heath	
Major E.H.Dean	1921		1921	High Wycombe	
Lt.-Cmd Withell	1928		1928	Lane End	
H.A.Coleman	1928		1928	Flackwell Heath	
F.Batts	1925	1925	1934	Downley	See Methodist list
Miss.D.Browning	1928		1928	Chesham Bois	
J.N.Foster	1928		1928	High Wycombe	
W.A.Peet	1928		1928	Chesham	
A.Ewart Steevens	1927	1927	1934	High Wycombe	See Methodist list
A.W.Cluett	1928		1928	Cadmore End	
Charles Cooper	1928		1928	High Wycombe	
Alfred Potter	1928		1931	West Wycombe	
Albert Hester	1930	1930	1934	High Wycombe	See Methodist list
Frank Collins	1930	1930	1934	High Wycombe	See Methodist list
Wilf.Osborne	1930	1930	1934	Marlow	See Methodist list
W.J.Cook	1931		1931	Lane End	
Percy Willott	1931		1932	High Wycombe	
Miss Davis	1930		1932	Marlow	
H.D.Bishop	1932	1932	1932	High Wycombe	
E.W.Bunce	1932	1932	1934	High Wycombe	See Methodist list
Fred Howard Jr	1932	1932	1934	Flackwell Heath	See Methodist list
G.W.Sheppard	1932	1932	1934	High Wycombe	See Methodist list
M.G.Evans	1932	1933	1934	High Wycombe	See Methodist list
Miss N.Ives	1933	1933	1934	Marlow	See Methodist list
F.Welford	1933	1933	1934	High Wycombe	See Methodist list
L.J.Goodway	1932		1934	Marlow	See Methodist list
S.Howard	1934		1934	High Wycombe	See Methodist list
W.Myers	1934		1934	Chesham	See Methodist list

The above list was compiled mainly from circuit Plans augmented by imformation extracted from the minute books. It is therefore incomplete. Plans used for reference are for the years 1818, 1822, 1838/9(2), 1850, 1854, 1860, 1863, 1865, 1873/5(7), 1876, 1884, 1889, 1897/1904(31), 1928, 1931 and the first combined Plan of 1934.

An analysis of the attendance at the preachers' quarterly meeting during the decade 1841-1850 shows the following:

* Mr.Sammons was the only preacher with 100% attendance at the meetings. Others with a good record include Brothers Hawkins, A.Hughes, Snell, Hirst, Daveney Junior, Hawes, Mead, Beck, Cock, Hussey and Anderson.

* Average attendance was 12, ranging from 5 in 1842 to 21 in 1850

LOCAL PREACHERS' MEETINGS: MINUTES (1844-1870)

Jan.1844   a. Three services at West Wycombe.
b. Evening service to be continued at Lane End.
c. There being no prospect of usefulness at Little Missenden, it was thought best that it should be left off the Plan.

Aug.1844   That on the next Plan Knotty Green have preaching at 6 o'clock.

Dec.1844   Any new places to be brought on the Plan? Yes. Brother Cooper's house (Cadmore End) and also at Hazlemere – at both places once a fortnight in the evening.

Jun.1846   That Handy Cross and Cadmore End be given up.

Mar.1847   Booker to have preaching every Sunday night.

Dec.1847   Holmer Green to have service afternoon and evening.

Dec.1851   The Brethren desire to record their grateful thanksgiving to God for that Spirit of His harmony which has pervaded this meeting. Notwithstanding some painful but necessary acts of discipline performed during the past quarter, they cannot but rejoice in those special tokens of the Divine presence with which they have been favoured. Great fidelity was manifested by the brothers towards each other – but the truth was spoken in love. A kind feeling was evinced towards Bro.Snell and a disposition to receive him back on the frank acknowledgement of his error in the recent agitation.   The meeting was one long to be remembered.

Sep. 1851 That a deputation consisting of Bros. White, Turner, Hawkins, Butcher, Smith, E.Hughes, wait upon the Penn Society to ascertain their present sentiments respecting the late unhappy division and whether now willing, as reported, to this meeting, to make any just and reasonable concession, and to comply with Methodistic rules and usage.

Sep. 1854 That Radnage be put off the Plan.

Mar. 1860 That Bros. Child, Weller and H.Collins be appointed to ascertain if there is an opening for preaching at Penn and Hazlemere.

Jun. 1860. That there be service at Hazlemere at half past 2 o'clock on Sunday afternoons.
That a committee of the Superintendent and Bros.White, Hussey and H.Collins wait upon Mr.Bovington of Winchmore Hill respecting a new chapel there.

Oct. 1860 That Amersham come again on the Plan in its former place.

Apr. 1861 That there be preaching at Hazlemere both in the afternoon and evening.

Mar. 1862 That there be service at Handycross to commence at 2 o'clock in the afternoon.

Mar. 1863 Resolved that a Brother who may leave this Circuit, on his return to it shall retain his former status, but a stranger shall have his name placed at the foot of the Plan.

Sep. 1863 The local preachers at West Wycombe to be Planned at Bledlow Ridge once a month on a Thursday evening.

Jun. 1864 That there be services at Penn afternoon and evening.
That Beaconsfield be put on the Plan.

Sep. 1864 That Penn be left off the Plan and Marsh be put on.

Jul. 1867 That a public collection be made through the Circuit to form a fund for local preachers' horse hire; and that the brethren Robt.White, Jas.Hussey and Jas.Beck constitute a committee for dispensing the fund.

Dec. 1867 The meeting suggested the propriety of the Rev. V.Satchell visiting Chesham and to exercise his discretion as to placing any of the local preachers residing there on the next Plan.

Mar. 1868 Walters Ash to be put on the Plan. Two services on the Sabbath, afternoon half past 2 and evening at 6 o'clock.

Sep. 1868 Walters Ash to be left off the next Plan.

Sep. 1869 That in consideration of the distance of many places in the circuit and the necessity of more vigorous action in their cultivation it is desirable that there should be a fund to defray the necessary expenses of travelling to them. It is therefore respectfully suggested that there be one collection in the course of the year in every place in the circuit for this object.

Mar. 1870 Resolved that a sub-committee comprising Brethren Howland, Johnson and Woodbridge, hold interview with the Town Sabbath School Committee to arrange for rendering the library available to the local Brethren throughout the Circuit.

Wycombe Marsh to have service every Sabbath afternoon.

Jun. 1870 That Wycombe Marsh have preaching in the evening as well as in the afternoon.

HIGH WYCOMBE WESLEYAN CIRCUIT MEMBERSHIP

Church	1837	1840	1850	1860	1870	1880
High Wycombe						
– Wesley	156	126	129	139	183	230
– Victoria St.	–	–	–	–	–	21
West Wycombe	38	33	56	62	58	22
Penn	38	27	43	–	–	–
Winchmore Hill	12	23	16	13	9	11
Great Marlow	67	76	83	64	50	36
Wooburn Green	9	9	18	17	10	16
Flackwell Heath	13	15	28	13	19	20
Radnage	8	–	8	–	–	–
Lane End	27	29	50	67	78	51
Downley	16	13	38	53	78	47
Beaconsfield	15	33	24	–	–	–
Holmer Green	6	13	7	26	13	10
Amersham	28	41	25	11	9	12
Bradenham	27	23	15	–	–	–
Bledlow Ridge	7	–	13	12	20	22
Lacey Green	18	5	–	–	–	–
Booker	–	–	20	34	33	19
Prestwood	–	–	–	–	26	23
Wycombe Marsh	–	–	–	–	7	–
	485	466	573	511	593	540

A PLAN OF THE WESLEYAN PREACHERS IN THE HIGH WYCOMBE CIRCUIT, 1839.

PLACES	Hours.	MARCH. 3 10 17 24 31	APRIL. 7 14 21 28	MAY. 5 12 19 26	JUNE. 2 9 16 23 30	PREACHERS, &c.
HIGH WYCOMBE - -	10& 6	1 o,t t,t t o,q o	t t,8 o o	t t,s o o	t t,t o,q o tt	t Taylor
	2&| 6	1 11 2 12	10 8 9 5	1 24 22 2	1 11 9 8 10	o Overton
Thursday - - -	7	o 1 o	o t o	o t t o	t o o	
WEST WYCOMBE - -	2&| 18	9 24 25 o,L	1 16 8 11	5 8 o 10	2 1 6 21 7	1 Daveny
	6	6	9 24 22.q 7	1 t 8 11	5 8 6 10	2 1 6,q 23 7	2 Beck
Tuesday - - -	7	o t o	o t t	o t	t o o	3 Moorcock
PENN	10& 6	9 o,11	5 t.q 11	o 1 t.9 6	o 2 8 7 o.24 10.23 t.L 11 13	4 Revenal
Tuesday - - -	6&	t	o t	t o t	t o t	5 Vingrove
WINCHMORE HILL -	2&	11	o.t 4 10 23	24 12 5 20 o.L 19 27 22 o.t	4 2 18 12	6 Hawkins
	6	11	32 4 10.q 23	24 12 5 20 32 19 -28 22	23 4 2.q 18 12	7 Hinton
Tuesday - - -	6&	o	t o	t o	o t o	8 Bird
GREAT MARLOW - -	10& 2&	t 2,22	o 6 13o18,26	o 1 t19,22 o 10	t13.2 7.q14,25 t 15	9 Pottinger
	6	t . 2 o.t	6 tt 8	o 11 tt 9 o 22	tt 13 o 14 t.t 11	10 Weight
Thursday - - -	6&	t	o t	o o t	o 2 t t	11 Long
WOOBURN - - - -	10& 2	23	4 22 13 15q	2 24 10,t 7	4 11 5 13	15 26 16q 9,o 25	12 Woolner
Wednesday - -	6&		o t	t o t	t o t	13 Ashton
FLACKWELL HEATH	2& 6	4	7 23 t.18 2q	20 15 22 10	7 29 13	11 20 25,11 o,4 17 26	14 Thyne
Wednesday - -	5&	o	t o	o t	o t t o	15 Young
RADNAGE - - - -	2& 6	24	27 6 23 9.q	29 t.30 24 16	6 20 21 27	10 9.q 24 28 5.o	16 Harris
LANE END - - - -	10& 2&|	6 7 8 t.q	27 22 2 8	13 1 t 9	5 o.q 23 2 o	17 Wright
	6	31	8 21 31 8	28 25 21 8	26 1 31 9	8 22 21 16 29	18 Chapel
Tuesday- - - -	6&|	t o	t o t	t o	o t tt	19 Cock
DOWNLEY - - - -	2& 6	2	23 16 5 6,q	9 10 17 o,24 11	9 4 6	16 8,q 29 20 t,31	20 Sammons
Monday - - - -	6&| t	t o	t o t	t o	t o t	21 White
BEACONSFIELD - -	2& 6	10	15 13 11 4 o,q	2 23 13 10 22 11 15	7 13 12,q 6 11	22 Croxton
Wednesday - -	6&|	t t	o 117 t	o t	t o tt	23 Wheeler
HOMER GREEN - -	2& 6	20	29 34,19 32 10q	23 18 4 17	20 5 24 29,23	32 17,19 11 27 23	
			o tt	o t		t o t	ON TRIAL
AMERSHAM - - - -	10&	In	12 1 In In 11n,q	9 12 2 In In In	1n 11 In In,q 1 1n	24 Wood
	6		o,s 1	6 t 2	1 o	1 1	25 Pusey
Monday - - - -	6&|	o	o t	t o	t tt	26 Haves
BRACKENHAM - - -	2&	o	19 2 22,q 16	6 11 o 9	24 17 23 5	4 t 21 22 8	27 Head
	6	18	o 2 25 28	6 11 16 9	24 17 23 5	4 18 20 25 8	28 Hughes
Wednesday - -	6&	t	t o	t o	t o t	29 Daveny & Peace
LACEY GREEN - -	10& 2&| 27	28 9 24 20,q	16 21 27 28	2 23 18 24	9 6,q 8 10 20	
	5	30	35 33 35 30	35 33 35 30	35 33 35 30	35 33 35 30 35	PRAYER LEADERS
Friday - - - -	6&|	o	t o	o t	t o tt	
BLEDLOW RIDGE -	2& 6	16	24 28 9,q 27	30 20 6 29	16 21 9 8	6,q 28 17 24 27	30 West Wycombe
							31 Lane End
LITTLE MISSENDEN	2&| 19	30 20 23,q 19	5 19 20 23	19 18 32 23	19 29 5,q 34 32	32 Penn
							33 Bradenham
SAUNDERTON LEE -	6	28	27 24	28 27	6 28	16 33	34 Flackwell Heath
							35 Lacey Green

The Quarterly Meeting will be held on Monday, April 8th,; the Local Preachers to meet at 11 o'Clock

REFERENCES.- q Quarterly Collection, t Tickets, s Sacrament, L Lovefeast.

HIGH WYCOMBE WESLEYAN CIRCUIT CLASS LEADERS − 1837

	Members			Members	
HIGH WYCOMBE (St. Mary St.)			**FLACKWELL HEATH**		
G. Ives	19		John Wright	13	
Wm. Brown	19				
" (Marsh)	10				
Wm. Willoughby	15		**HOMER GREEN**		
Thos. Daveney	31		Wm. Chappell	6	
Thos. Allnutt	11				
Mary Simmons	13		**BEACONSFIELD**		
John Priest	18		Joseph Lipscombe	7	
Preachers	10		Eleanor Lipscombe	8	(15)
Elizh. King	10	(156)			
			PENN		
GREAT MARLOW			John Tilbury	15	
Wm. Pusey	8		Chas. Garland	8	
John Moore	6		" (2nd)	15	(38)
Sush. White	13				
E. Wheeler	18		**BRADENHAM**		
Jas. Hinton	20	(65)	Robt. Harman	27	
WEST WYCOMBE			**LANE END**		
Jas. Plumridge	15		Jas. Plumridge	13	
Thos. Harris	8		John Mead	14	(27)
Josh. Hawkins	15	(38)			
			LACEY GREEN		
WOOBURN			Robt. Harman	18	
John Revenell	9				
			BLEDLOW RIDGE	7	
AMERSHAM					
Thos. N. Gray	10		**DOWNLEY**		
Elizh. Gray	18	(28)	Jas. Treacher	16	
WINCHMORE HILL			**RADNAGE**		
Thos. Bovington	12		Jas. Plumridge	8	

Total 483

HIGH WYCOMBE WESLEYAN CIRCUIT CLASS LEADERS - 1847

HIGH WYCOMBE (St.Mary Street)
R.Cooper
Bro.Priest
" Willoughby
" Anderson
Sister Anderson
Bro.Brown

GREAT MARLOW
Bro.Pusey
" Dukes
" Gills
" Taylor (2 Classes)

LANE END
Bro.White
" Plumridge
" Goodearl

WEST WYCOMBE
Bro.Harris
" Plumridge
" Butler
" Mead

DOWNLEY
Bro.Barlow
" Oxlade

WINCHMORE HILL
Bro.Bovington
" Butcher
Sister West

MARSH Class
Bro.Allnutt
" Martin
" Ives
Sister King

AMERSHAM
Bro.Gray
Sister Gray
" Rogers

PENN
Bro.J.Garland
" Ancock
" T.Garland

HOLMER GREEN *
Bros.Tilbury
" Garland

BEACONSFIELD
Bro.Hearn
" Snell
" Snapes

WOOBURN GREEN
Bro.Long

FLACKWELL HEATH
Bro.Wright
" Baker

BRADENHAM *
Bro.Butler

BLEDLOW RIDGE
Bro.Tubb

RADNAGE *
Bro.Plumridge

BOOKER #
Bro.Smith

= Taken from the 1845 list
* = Taken from the 1846 list

HIGH WYCOMBE WESLEYAN CIRCUIT CLASS LEADERS 1871

Ministers - Revs.William Henry Lewis & John Skerratt
Stewards - Wm. Almond & Stephen Weller

WYCOMBE
Bro.	John Abbott	22
"	James Hussey	20
"	Joseph Child	28
"	Stephen Weller	
	Sunday	12
	Wednesday	15
"	Robert White	37
"	Henry Senior	12
"	W.H.Lewis	18
"	John Skerratt	
	Male	23
	Female	19 (206)

MARLOW
Bro.	W.Almond	8
"	F.E.Dukes	14
"	Thos.Wellicombe	15
Sis.	Mary Loosely	10 (47)

WEST WYCOMBE
Bro.	Fryer	18
"	Wm.Mead	7
"	Alfred Hughes	19
"	Daniel Lanes	6 (50)

WINCHMORE HILL   8

BLEDLOW RIDGE   23

PRESTWOOD   20

LANE END
Bro.	W.Gill	12
"	James Plumridge	8
"	Ginger	7
"	Henry Plumridge	6
"	Wm.Evans	10
"	James Brooker	9
"	Abraham Gray	15 (67)

DOWNLEY
Bro.	Henry Collins	20
"	Wm.Allen	18
"	Jas. Goodchild	17
"	" "	12
Sister	Ann Keen	7 (74)

AMERSHAM
Sister Avis	9

WOOBURN   12

FLACKWELL HEATH   20

BOOKER
Bro.	Fryer	26
"	Hy. Goldswain	7 (33)

HOLMER GREEN   15

WYCOMBE MARSH   12

Total 596

HIGH WYCOMBE WESLEYAN CIRCUIT : TRUSTS

WESLEYAN CHAPELS

	Year Built	Cost	Legally Owned	1860/61 Trust Treasurer
High Wycombe – St. Mary Street	1779	N/K	Yes	Robert White
Great Marlow	1810	N/K	Yes	Thomas Dukes
Wooburn Green	1811	N/K	Yes	A. Healey
	1872	£350	Yes	
West Wycombe	1815	£233	Yes	Alfred Hughes
Downley	1824	N/K	Yes	Henry Collins
Lane End	1834	£150	Yes	Mr. Meed/
– School	1866	£180		Mr. Elliott
Bledlow Ridge	1834	£140	No	Mr. Almond
Holmer Green	1841	£160	Yes	J. Randel
Booker	1847	£145½	Yes	E. Hughes
Amersham	1860		Private Property	1872 Rented from Society
	1896	£570	Yes	of Friends
Winchmore Hill	1861	£160	Yes	Mr. Shrimpton
Prestwood	1863	£226	O.M.D.	[On Model Deed?]
Flackwell Heath	1864	£276	Yes	Had been private property
– School		£104	Yes	before 1864
Victoria Street (HW)	1877	£160	Yes	Estimated cost
London Road (HW)	1891	£230	Yes	
Terriers (HW)	1895	£175	Yes	
Chesham	1897	£1,300	Yes	
Bourne End	1910	£900	Yes	

WESLEYAN TRUSTEES (1885)

HIGH WYCOMBE
Date of Deed May 30th 1866.
Saml.Shrimpton* Winchmore Hill
Thos. E. Dukes   Great Marlow
James Hussey   High Wycombe
Joseph Child   "   "
Stephen Weller   "   "
Robert White   "   "
Thos. Wellicome   Great Marlow
William Almond   "   "
Edwin Hughes   West Wycombe
William Mead*   "   "
Henry Collins*   Downley
Peter Crusoe MaleHigh Wycombe
A.R. Turney   "   "
John Abbott   "   "

GREAT MARLOW
July 10th 1868 order of
        Charity Commissioners.
Thos.E. Dukes   Great Marlow
Thos. Wellicome   "   "
Wm. Almond
Alfred Gibb*
Joseph Bird   Lane End
Wm. Plumridge   "   "
Alfd. Davis   Great Marlow
Henry Hathaway
John Wellicome
Joseph Woodbridge*High Wycombe
Edmund Pierce*   "   "
Benj. Howland   "   "

WEST WYCOMBE
Joshua West
Joseph Hawkins
Alf. Hughes
Edwin Hughes
Dan James
Chas. West
Thos. Constable
Jas. Bates
Chas. Hawes
Benj. North
Wm. Mead

DOWNLEY   1868 Appointed by
        Charity Commissioners
Henry Collins   Original Trustee
William Allen   "   "
Charles Spriggs   "   "
Alfred Hughes   "   "
Wm. Mead   "   "
James Collins   New Trustee
Richard Barlow   "   "
Fred. Barlow   "   "
James Hussey   "   "
Robert White   "   "
Joseph Child   "   "
John Rd. Dring   "   "

WINCHMORE HILL
Saml.Shrimpton* Winchmore Hill
William Ware   Holmer Green
Charles Spriggs Downley
James Hussey   Chepping Wycombe
Joseph Child   "   "
Stephen Weller   "   "
Joseph Pointing*   "   "
Robert White   "   "
Benjamin Howland   "   "
William Mead*   West Wycombe
Edwin Hughes   "   "
Henry Collins*   Downley
John Ball   "
Edward Branston Chepping Wycombe

WOOBURN
John Revenell   Wooburn Green
Richard Baker*   High Wycombe
Percival Healey Wooburn Green
Joshua Wheeler   Wooburn Mooor
John Dring   High Wycombe
Benjn Howland   "   "
James Hussey   "   "
John Hussey   "   "
Edmund Pierce*   "   "
Joseph Steevens   "   "
Stephen Weller   "   "
Joseph Wooster
        Woodbridge*   "   "

FLACKWELL HEATH
Deed Dated July 3rd 1863
Enrolled July 28th 1863
William Smith   Gone to America
William Burnham Flackwell Heath
William Nichols   "   "
John Tilbury   Loudwater
Benjamin Howland Wycombe
Stephen Weller   "
Joseph Child   "
James Hussey   "
Joseph Pointing*   "
Joseph W. Woodbridge "
Joseph Steevens   "
Henry Edgerley   "
John Devening* Wooburn Green

FLACKWELL HEATH SCHOOL
Thos. Wm. Pocock Virginia Water
Robert Walker   Maidenhead
Henry Collins   Downley
James Hussey   Wycombe
Stephen Weller   "
Thomas Wheeler   "
Benjamin Howland   "
Wm. Smith   Flackwell Heath
Ambrose R. Turney High Wycombe
Joseph Woodbridge   "   "
Joseph Steevens   "   "
Joseph Pointing*   "   "
Henry Edgerley   "   "
Rev. G. Buckley   "   "
Appointed Apl. 10 1867.

FLACKWELL HEATH CHAPEL
(Additional Land)
Deed dated Jany. 3rd 1884
Enrolled Jany. 8th 1884

The Trustees are the same as
above minus Joseph Pointing
who was deceased prior to the
additional land being acquired.

PRESTWOOD   Date of Deeds
1st Deed Dated Apl. 15th 1863
Enrolled July 10th 1863
Deed of addl. Land conveyed to
same   persons dated October 31st
1872.   (Not Enrolled)
James Hussey   Chepping Wycombe
Stephen Weller   "   "
Benjamin Howland   "   "
Peter C. Male   "   "
Joseph Pointing*   "   "
John Hussey   "   "
Robert White   "   "
Joseph Child   "   "
Edmund Pierce*   "   "
Henry Collins* West Wycombe
William Ware   Holmer Green
Benjamin Hildreth Prestwood
Benjamin Cartwright now of Mendy
    Street, High Wycombe
Samuel Lucas   Chepping Wycombe

BOOKER
Edwin Hughes§ West Wycombe
Samuel Hawes*   "   "
Daniel Smith   "   "
William Mead*   "   "
Jonathan Fryer*   "   "
William Daveny* Chepping Wycombe
James Hussey   "   "
Thomas Anderson§   "   "
John Ball   Downley
Henry Ball*   "
James Oxlade*   "
Samuel Beasley Booker

LANE END SCHOOL

Foundation Deed   June 18th, 1834.   Enrolled 30th Jany. 1862
New Deed dated October 4th 1872.   Both Deeds are copies of the
Court Roll of the Manor of West Wycombe.   N.B. The part Deed is
not Enrolled.

Wm. Plumridge	Lane End
Robert White	High Wycombe
Joseph Hawkins	" "
Joseph Jarvis*	" "
Joseph N. Harris	" "
Wm. Evans	High Wycombe
Jas. Goldswain	" "
Reuben Cutler	Lane End
Joseph Bird	" "
Henry J. Plumridge	" "
Thomas Juggins*	" "

VICTORIA STREET

Alfred T. Babb	Wycombe Marsh
William Bartlett	High Wycombe
John Busby	" "
Thomas Coles	" "
Charles V. Deacon	" "
John R. Dring	" "
Henry Edgerley	" "
W. Charles Gibbons	" "
Daniel Glenister	" "
Thomas Glenister	" "
Henry Goldswain	Booker
Henry Goodearl	High Wycombe
Richard Goodearl	" "
Benjamin Howland	" "
Edwin Hussey	" "
John Hussey	" "
John Money	" "
Benjamin North Jr.	West Wycombe
Henry Pierce*	" " Died March 2nd 1879
Edmund Pierce*	" "
Joseph Steevens	" "
Stephen Weller Jr.	" "
Joseph Woodbridge*	" "

DOWNLEY SCHOOL

Deed dated Aug. 1st 1862.
Enrolled Oct. 15th 1862.

William Collins*	
Henry Collins*	
William Allen*	
Charles Spriggs	Downley
Alfred Hughes	West Wycombe
William Mead*	
Peter Crusoe	Male

* = Deceased
§ = Resigned

THE WESLEYAN METHODIST CHURCH

WESLEY Chapel   The only liability is £100. residue of Loan by General Chapel Committee being repaid in Annual (½ yearly £12.10s.0d.) payments of £25.

      N.B. A new Organ has been introduced into the Chapel at a cost of £160. Internal Renovation and decorations done at a cost of £184.17s.9d. Total £344.17s.9d.

      Manse No Debt.   The whole has been raised & paid.

VICTORIA   This Chapel has cost £794.1s.1d. The only debt is residue of a loan of £50 due to the Gen. Chapel Committee, repayable in 10 years at £5 per annum.

GREAT MARLOW   No debt on Chapel property.
Additional Land and New School Buildings.
      A site with property (to be reconstructed at a probable cost of £300) on it has been purchased at a cost of £450 free from Land Tax. A right of way of 12ft. wide being reserved by the vendors from A to B as shown on the block plan Draft Deed of Conveyance has been sent to Gen.Chap. Sec.for approval.

WEST WYCOMBE   Trust Premises are entirely free from debt.

LANE END Chapel No debt except residue of loan £30 due to Gen.Chap. Committee.

DOWNLEY   No debt except about £30 on Current Acct.arising from recent alterations etc.

AMERSHAM   No Trust property. A committee has been formed with a view to purchasing a site and erecting a New Chapel.

WINCHMORE HILL Alterations and enlargements have been effected costing about £140. A year's extension of time has been granted. The case must be reported to next May District Meeting and about £30 is required to be raised before that time.

WOOBURN   No debt on the property. Mr. P.Healey is willing to sell adjoining house and garden for

£200.   This   matter   will   require   immediate
attention.

FLACKWELL HEATH The old debt of £40 was paid 2½ years ago.   The
Chapel has since then been re-constructed and
enlarged (by 120 additional sittings) at a cost
of £521.4s.6d.   When the grant from Extension
Fund is received there will only be a temporary
debt of £130 to be paid off in 10 years.

BOOKER Chapel   There is no debt on existing property.   The
Trust is now being renewed by an order of the
Charity Commissioners which will take effect in
a month after date hereof.

Additional Land This has been secured, but is not conveyed.   It
is to be conveyed to the New Trustees but on the
Model Deed absolutely.   Nearly £100 is invested
in Savings Bank as a nucleus for a New Chapel
and Sunday School.   This case requires and
deserves immediate attention.

BLEDLOW RIDGE   This Chapel has never been settled on any Trust.
A new School Room is needed, and Lord Carrington
is willing to grant a long lease on nominal
terms.   Mr.S.Weller and Mr.Dring will act with
you in this matter.

HOLMER GREEN
     Chapel   No debt on Trust property.
     Land   ditto

PRESTWOOD   This Chapel has been enlarged and renovated at a
cost of £284.7s.7d.   When the grant of £35 has
been received from Extension Fund there will be
a temporary debt of £60 to be paid in 10 years.

LANE END
     Day School This school has been enlarged by addition of New
Class Room etc. at a cost of £110.   A temporary
debt is allowed of £25 to be paid in 10 years.
It is likely to be cleared during this year.

DOWNLEY
     S.School   This Trust requires renewal.

Sept.2nd 1885   HENRY LEWIS
                                       Supt. Minister.

MINUTES OF WESLEYAN UNITED TRUSTEES' MEETINGS(*)
and QUARTERLY MEETINGS: 1896-1934

*2-3-1896   LANE END should increase fire insurance by £50.
             LANE END should have the same trustees for school
             and chapel.
             DOWNLEY should increase subscription to Quarter
             Board.
             WOOBURN should increase fire insurance by £50.

*1-3-1897   WINCHMORE HILL to be visited to see what repairs are
             needed.

*7-3-1898   WESLEY has not received a capitation grant for the
             Militia.
             CIRCUIT: Manse fire insurance to be increased from
             £400 to £500.

*6-3-1899   WESLEY to ask Town Council to continue footpath from
             Dr.Reynolds' premises to railway bridge.
             LONDON ROAD congratulated on clearing debt of £110.
             HOLMER GREEN should pay contribution to Quarter
             Board.
             BLEDLOW RIDGE should look at the state of its
             building.

*4-3-1901   WINCHMORE HILL to be asked about Mr.J.T.Harris'
             account repairs.
             BLEDLOW RIDGE to be asked about sum of £3 paid to
             Mr.J.R.Dring.
             HOLMER GREEN urged to sell piece of land.
             PRESTWOOD should contribute to Quarter Board.

*3-3-1902   LANE END and FLACKWELL HEATH should increase fire
             insurance.
             BLEDLOW RIDGE should pay £3 still owing to Mr.Dring.
             PRESTWOOD should keep proper accounts.

*2-3-1903   FLACKWELL HEATH should increase fire insurance to
             £800.
             VICTORIA STREET should insure house next to chapel.
             LONDON ROAD should attend to matters of seat-rents,
             fencing their land and erecting a notice-board.
             BOURNE END has secured site for schoolroom and
             chapel.

*8-3-1904   TERRIERS: G.E.Stephenson must complete schedule.

*6-3-1905   WESLEY should attend to draughts from ventilations
in chapel roof and to providing ventilation in
lower schoolroom.
LONDON ROAD value should be increased to £900.
PRESTWOOD should attend to matter of seat-rents.

*3-3-1906   BOURNE END should be transferred to Maidenhead
Circuit.
TERRIERS: Meeting to be held on spot to look at
unsatisfactory state of property.
DOWNLEY should contribute to Quarter Board.
AMERSHAM finances to be put in a more satisfactory
state.
PRESTWOOD should purchase extra land.

*25-2-1907   WESLEY should insure its chapel-keeper.
VICTORIA STREET should invest its balance-in-hand.
LONDON ROAD should purchase extra land.

*2-3-1908   TERRIERS: Mr.Clark to be asked if any lighting,
heating or cleaning costs.
BLEDLOW RIDGE should be renovated.

*8-3-1909   DOWNLEY does not wish to purchase extra land.
PRESTWOOD: value to be increased to £450.
HOLMER GREEN: value to be increased to £300.

27-12-1911   CIRCUIT: Deficit £94.
CIRCUIT: Membership 701 (on trial 124)
VICTORIA STREET to have organ.

*4-3-1912   VICTORIA STREET should insure caretaker and increase
fire insurance.

25-3-1912   LANE END: Day School average attendance 29.
CIRCUIT: 1761 scholars in Sunday Schools; 197
members of Wesley Guild.
CHESHAM: Home Missions have given £50 grant.
CIRCUIT: Lay-Agent Mr.Bullock has worn out bicycle;
£3 to be granted from Horse Hire Fund to purchase
new one.

23-9-1912   CIRCUIT: Wesley League of Abstainers formed.
LONDON ROAD to erect new classroom.

10-3-1913   AMERSHAM has paid nothing towards fire insurance for
three years.

25-3-1913   CIRCUIT: Membership 680 (on trial 111).
CIRCUIT: Deficit £8 but £100 has been raised to clear Circuit debt.

22-9-1913   CIRCUIT: Village churches should have proper fonts and uniform services.

29-12-1913 CIRCUIT: Mission Band to be formed to grow local preachers; approval for Circuit magazine.

*9-3-1914   WESLEY to consider pew-rents.

23-3-1914   CIRCUIT: Membership 624 of whom 284 pay nothing; Rev. W. T. Coppin consents to stay, only if he is allowed to take practical steps to remedy this.
AMERSHAM: Mr. Bullock to give special attention during winter; also Missioner appointed.
CHESHAM offers to host next Quarterly Meeting. Offer declined - too far away.

27-6-1914   WINCHMORE HILL: Mrs. Walker presented with marble timepiece, Bible and tune-book for devoted work for cause, by Mr. R. Goodearl, the oldest preacher.

26-9-1914   CIRCUIT: Rev. W. T. Coppin reports on soldiers at the front and the National Relief Fund.
CIRCUIT: Mr. Bullock offered rise in salary but declines; Mr. A. Plowman appointed treasurer of Worn-out Ministers' Fund.

28-12-1914 CIRCUIT: During stay of soldiers in town monthly services should be held in villages instead of fortnightly.
CIRCUIT: Weekly envelope system to be tried for a year.

*8-3-1915   FLACKWELL HEATH advised not to erect new schoolroom due to increased cost of building through present crisis.

22-3-1915   CIRCUIT: Balance £7.

26-6-1915   CIRCUIT: Membership 645.
CIRCUIT: Horse Hire Fund to receive annual collection; friends given opportunity to help reduce Circuit debt and a wave of enthusiasm, such as is

rarely seen in a meeting, almost clears Circuit of its burden.

25-9-1915   CHESHAM: George Bullock, lay agent, presented with £8.
CIRCUIT: "Come to Church" campaign to be carried out.

28-12-1915   CHESHAM (£100 debt) and AMERSHAM (no debt) should be transferred to Watford Circuit because of better railway facilities.
WINCHMORE HILL to remain in Wycombe Circuit.

3-3-1916   LONDON ROAD asked to cultivate plot adjoining chapel.
FLACKWELL HEATH congratulated on renovating chapel.

25-3-1916   CIRCUIT: Membership 659; deficit £29.
BOURNE END: Collection to be made throughout Circuit.

26-6-1916   CIRCUIT: Decided not to petition for Total Prohibition during War and for six months after.

28-12-1916   CHESHAM: Deputation (Messrs. W.E.Garlick, J.Moon and G.T.Tebby) explains affairs; Probationer Minister to be sought.

*15-3-1917   BOURNE END: £215 debt remaining; Circuit asked to raise £75.
TERRIERS: Effort to be made to clear £50 debt.

24-3-1917   CIRCUIT: Membership 622; deficit £28; Synod to be asked to transfer Wycombe to 2nd London District.
CIRCUIT: £9 deficit in Horse Hire Fund. Maximum allowance to be 4s.6d.(22½p.) for residents in Borough and 7s.6d.(37½p.) outside, if distance is five miles or more.

16-6-1917   CIRCUIT: 900 eggs received for wounded soldiers (statement received with applause); collections on 28th October to assist Ministers and their families who giving their services for their country, are at great financial disadvantage; letters of sympathy to be sent to Mr.F.Woodward, Mr.J.Harris and Mrs.F.Sherwin on death of sons serving in Forces.

17-12-1917 CIRCUIT: Mr.Haines congratulated   on promotion
            to mayoral chair.
            BOURNE END: Debt now £200.
            MARLOW over-assessed - reduced to £9.
            CHESHAM: Private Charles H.Newland recommended as
            candidate for Ministry.

*11-3-1918 TERRIERS to be given   priority in disposal of
            District Extension Fund.
            WINCHMORE HILL: Mrs.Walker to be advised to invest
            substantial   balance-in-hand   in   War   Savings
            Certificates.

23-3-1918   CIRCUIT: Membership 625.

24-6-1918   CIRCUIT: £36 balance.
            CHESHAM should be transferred to Aylesbury Circuit.

30-9-1918   CIRCUIT: Members pledge themselves to earnest
            prayer for God's blessing on Circuit; stipend of
            Rev.W.Seed to be raised from £170 to £190 per annum.

21-12-1918 CHESHAM: Supernumary Minister to be   appointed
            at stipend of £108.

*3-3-1919   TERRIERS,   AMERSHAM and FLACKWELL HEATH   should
            provide lavatories.

24-3-1919   CIRCUIT: £14 balance;   membership 614;   1561
            Sunday School scholars (decrease of 150), 277 over-
            15's (decrease 106).
            CIRCUIT: Names of those who fell in War throughout
            Circuit to be inscribed on tablet to be placed in
            Wesley Chapel.

15-12-1919 WESLEY: Ladies' Sewing Meeting contributes £10
            to Circuit.
            WINCHMORE HILL: Mrs.Walker moving (after 36 years'
            service) to Holmer Green.

13-3-1920   CIRCUIT: Membership 623.
            VICTORIA STREET can sell cottages.
            WESLEY has New Organ Fund.

12-6-1920   CIRCUIT: £41 balance;   Rev.W.Seed speaks of
            necessity of opening up work in villages; arranging
            for evangelistic mission.

13-9-1920   CIRCUIT: Super's   stipend   increased   to   £300;
possibility of starting Circuit magazine; sympathy
for aims of Save the Children Fund expressed.

13-12-1920 CHESHAM: Harrow Circuit to be urged to take over.

*7-3-1921   FLACKWELL HEATH: Repairs carried out but no details
supplied.

12-3-1921   CIRCUIT: Rev.W.Seed's letter conveys deep sorrow at
enforced   absence   and   heartfelt   thanks   for   help
during illness; Mr. W.J.Cook, Circuit Steward, has
met with serious accident.
CIRCUIT: Membership 613; meeting to be held to
consider Methodist Union.

10-9-1921   CIRCUIT: Rev.W.Seed expresses great pleasure at
being present.

12-12-1921 CIRCUIT: Mr.W.J.Cook speaks of benefit if Watch
Night services could be held at each chapel.

11-3-1922   CIRCUIT: Membership 622; only 125 members of Wesley
Guild; Mr.O.T.Goodearl presents Temperance returns
which are not at all flattering.
CIRCUIT: Application for grant from Connexional
Fund   for   Rev.W.Seed   in   his   special   affliction
unanimously supported.

10-6-1922   CIRCUIT: Earnest conversation on evangelistic work,
chiefly among young people; £135 sent to National
Children's Home.

16-9-1922   WOOBURN: Tribute paid to Mr.W.Eccles J.P. (died 21-
6-22, aged 79) who occupied every position in
Church.   His activities were bewildering in their
multiplicity.
CIRCUIT: Assessments range from £92 (Wesley) to £2
(Terriers and London Road).

16-12-1922 AMERSHAM: As services are held for present on Sunday
evenings and necessary repairs have been carried
out, Mrs Wright agreed to withdraw her resignation.
CIRCUIT: Discussion on providing motor conveyance
for preachers.
CIRCUIT: Methodist Union: 33 for, 18 against, 3
neutral. "Is time opportune?": 27 yes, 27 no, one

neutral. "Does Meeting accept scheme?": 26 yes,
22 no, one neutral. All in Circuit to be asked
their opinion.

18-6-1923   VICTORIA STREET given permission to alter premises
and remove organ (cost of work £550).
CIRCUIT: Week's special Temperance campaign; river
trip on 30th June; £42 sent to War Memorial
Hospital.

15-9-1923   WEST WYCOMBE: Cliff College student to be employed,
paid for by Mr.B.S.North
CIRCUIT: Interchange of pulpits between Methodist
Churches; no guessing games to be allowed on
Methodist premises.

15-12-1923 VICTORIA STREET: Special mission to be conducted by
Rev.Sadler Reece.
CIRCUIT: Horse Hire Fund has income of £15,
expenditure £18.

*7-3-1924   VICTORIA STREET revalued at £2500 (from £1250).

15-3-1924   WEST WYCOMBE: Owen W.Smith, lay evangelist,
nominated as candidate for Ministry.
CIRCUIT: Rev.H.J.Ivens invited to stay but declines
as he desires fuller opportunity for spiritual work;
possibility of Circuit magazine considered.

28-6-1924   CIRCUIT: Membership 665; deficit £64 - to be wiped
out by river trip to Windsor; £35 paid to Foreign
Missions; Rev.H.J.Ivens accepts invitation to stay.

13-9-1924   CIRCUIT: Appreciation expressed for Rev.H.J.Ivens'
open-air work; Week of Prayer to be held.
PRESTWOOD given permission to enlarge schoolroom
(£300).

15-12-1924 CIRCUIT: Methodist Union (speeches limited to three
minutes) 46 for. 11 against, 2 neutral.
CIRCUIT: Mr.D.Lord unwilling to be secretary of
Sunday School Council owing to lack of attention
given over past year by Quarterly Meeting to Sunday
School affairs; Schools' report to be taken as first
item at next meeting; Mr. Lord withdraws
resignation.

*27-2-1925 LONDON ROAD should have piece of land adjoining chapel fenced in without delay as present state is very unsightly.

14-3-1925 FLACKWELL HEATH: Death of George Burnham is great loss.
WOOBURN GREEN congratulated on clearing debt of £200.
CIRCUIT: Membership 712; 1271 Sunday School scholars (62 decrease; Mr.Lord thanked for his efforts); evangelistic efforts have had excellent results; Harold Goodearl reports increase of two in number of Bands of Hope (total membership 473).

*26-2-1926 PRESTWOOD has incurred debt of £300 in connection with alterations; no details sent to Super.

*25-2-1927 CIRCUIT: Debts paid off during year: Wesley House £150; Prestwood £150; Lane End £47; Victoria Street £143. New debt of £1183 on 154 West Wycombe Road (second Minister's home in place of Wesley House).

*2-3-1928 CIRCUIT: Wesley House sold for £1050.

12-12-1928 CIRCUIT: Mr.S.R.H.Edge, nominated as Circuit Steward, says he believes in getting a move on.

16-3-1929 CIRCUIT: Membership of 779; £86 deficit; collection for Miners' Fund £40; Mr.J.N.Foster candidate for Ministry.
WINCHMORE HILL in need; possibility of open-air work in summer.

15-6-1929 CIRCUIT: No discussion on "Work of God".
LONDON ROAD: Opening ceremony 10th July by Valentine M.Millbourn, preacher Rev.A.Burnham; £125 needed to clear debt.

14-9-1929 WESLEY: After sundry remarks about the attendance generally and that of Sunday School scholars at morning services in particular, Mr.R.Goodearl urges importance of prayer meeting.
HOLMER GREEN: Mr.Wingrove pleads case for new chapel.

15-3-1930 CIRCUIT: Membership 793; deficit £187; Rev.J.G.Penman offers to collect sum equal to debt.

14-6-1930   CIRCUIT: £196 deficit but Mr.Penman has collected £202; he is thanked and meeting sings Doxology; Mr.A.E.Steevens tenders resignation as Temperance secretary - not accepted.
CIRCUIT: Mr.R.Goodearl brings message of goodwill from Vicar of Penn; subsequent remarks about the Work in the Circuit are construed by Rev.T.L.B.Westerdale as an attack on the Ministers and repudiated in very outspoken language; feelings run high for short time.

13-9-1930   CHESHAM: Time not yet ripe for married Minister.

10-12-1930   CIRCUIT: Death of Richard Goodearl great loss.
HOLMER GREEN: Steps to be taken as soon as possible to provide new chapel; Christmas Sale to be held.

*6-3-1931   WEST WYCOMBE: Land purchased for £20; electric light installation for £47.
PRESTWOOD: Fire insurance to be increased from £1400 (inadequate).

14-3-1931   CHESHAM: Miss Browning appointed Deaconess - expenses to be paid by Chesham.

6-6-1931   CIRCUIT: Membership 808; balance £1.

4-3-1932   PRESTWOOD should increase fire insurance to £2000.

12-3-1932   LONDON ROAD has largest Sunday School (162 on roll).
LANE END has received ten members into full membership from Junior Society Class.
WESLEY: Young people want tennis court at Epworth Manse; committee appointed.
CIRCUIT: Rev.J.G.Penman speaks of many young men coming forward to take work on preaching plan; opposition to building of new public house in town.
PRESTWOOD: Mr.Nancarrow reports good work being done, services well attended.

11-6-1932   MARLOW BOTTOM: Rev.R.Oswald Stobbs speaks of special work being carried on by Marlow friends; hopes to go and watch further developments;
CIRCUIT: Reduction of 46 licensees in High Wycombe noted with approval; Mr. W.H.Stephenson appeals for special help for relief of members in special need - turned down.

10-9-1932   BLEDLOW RIDGE: Death of Mr.Maunder, oldest member;
CIRCUIT: Protest against dog-racing in Wycombe.
CIRCUIT: "Nomination & General Purposes Committee"
formed to study matters of Methodist Union; Circuit
to remain "Wesley Circuit" and Primitive Circuit to
remain "White Hart Street Circuit".

14-12-1932 CIRCUIT: Circuit plans to be combined in one
booklet; envelope scheme to be considered.
WINCHMORE HILL: Services to be held in two
Methodist chapels alternately.

*3-3-1933   LONDON ROAD over-insured - reduced to £2500.
CIRCUIT: All Churches to keep baptismal records.

11-3-1933   DOWNLEY: Death of Mrs. Batts and Miss Beard.
MARLOW: Two Methodist Churches to be united.
CHESHAM: Methodist Church and United Free Church to
be united; meeting does not agree to Rev.Walter
Wynne (U.F.C) being guaranteed preaching work.
WESLEY: Better attendance at prayer meeting and
quickened interest in spiritual things.
CIRCUIT: Membership 793; balance 11s.10d. [59p.];
Mr.G.W.Shepherd candidate for Ministry.

10-6-1933   WEST WYCOMBE asks to remain in Wesley section.
CIRCUIT: Unanimous agreement to formation of new
High Wycombe Methodist Circuit out of existing
Wesleyan, Primitive and United Circuits.

9-9-1933   CHESHAM manse to be furnished at cost not exceeding
£180.
WINCHMORE HILL to be transferred to Chalfont
Circuit, leaving it to members of the two Churches
which Church shall be closed.

13-12-1933 NEWLAND (United Methodist) pulpit to be supplied in
return for two thirds of assessment coming to this
Circuit (rest to White Hart Street Circuit).
CHESHAM, AMERSHAM and HOLMER GREEN should be
brought into London Mission area.
CIRCUIT: Membership 855.

10-3-1934   STOKENCHURCH, BEACONS BOTTOM and IBSTONE to join new
             High Wycombe Circuit from Chinnor Primitive
             Methodist Circuit.
             CIRCUIT: Strong appeal by Mr. A. E. Steevens for
             definite Temperance teaching as Bands of Hope are
             practically non-existent.

9-6-1934   CIRCUIT: Support for Government in restricting
             betting and gambling; Union Committee to consider
             compiling a book on the history of Methodist
             Churches in this area, to commemorate amalgamation
             of Circuits.

WESLEYAN TWENTIETH CENTURY FUND

The purpose of the fund was set out in a letter dated November
22nd 1898 to all Methodist Circuits signed by Albert Clayton.
An appeal was made to all Methodists, to promise to give a
guinea (£1.05) each so that "One Million Subscribers to the fund
of one million guineas can be obtained".

Churches taking part were:-
        Vesley   Wesley Sunday School
        London Road   Great Marlow
        West Wycombe   Wooburn Green
        Flackwell Heath   Victoria Street
        Holmer Green   Downley
        Booker   Lane End
        Prestwood   Chesham

The typed roll shows the subscription of each individual
contributing. A number of the gifts are "in memoriam". Most
are for a guinea. Each contributor received a certificate.
There is no total of the sum collected.

Church Lane, West Wycombe. c.1900

CHAPTER 3

WESLEYAN METHODIST CHURCHES

ST. MARY STREET (1779)

John Wesley's chapel has disappeared and the area is vastly changed. Nowadays we turn from the High Street into Paul's Row past the Guildhall (and the paved area where once the cattle market was held), cross the narrow bridge over the River Wye and are confronted by the High Wycombe inner relief road. (Its construction caused the demolition of the Nicholls and Janes' factory of which the chapel had become part.) To our left is the British Legion Hall from where St. Mary Street used to continue on its way to the junction with Marlow Hill at the entrance gates of Wycombe Abbey. It is difficult for us to imagine  the turn of that century in which Wycombe's first Methodist chapel was built. There were frequent balls in the Guildhall; the New Theatre was presenting plays by the Windsor Company under the patronage of the Royal Military College; the many furniture factories worked late into the evening; and people might be making their careful way over the wet cobblestones. The street was well-known for its floods right up to recent times and even more for its many pubs - like the "Little Red Lion", "Black Horse", "Horse and Jockey" and "Admiral Napier".

In the middle of all this activity stood "Wesley". The Methodist society had at first used a room in Easton Street, next door to Mr. James who had employed a drummer to beat his drum outside the window. With the growth of the society there was a need for larger premises and in 1777 they undertook to build a chapel on the Borough boundary in St. Mary Street. It was opened on 11th November 1779 by John Wesley himself. He came on horseback, preached, opened the chapel and then rode back to take classes in London that same evening. He was 76 at the time! Two of the first members were Hannah Ball, the first Sunday School teacher in Britain, who had played a considerable part in its building, and James Batting who to a large extent financed and superintended the work. He continued to support the cause after his death under the terms of his will.

JAMES BATTING'S LEGACY

"In the first place, during such time as the Chapel and Preaching House thereto adjoining situate in St. Mary Street in the Borough of Chepping Wycombe aforesaid shall be kept for the use of the Arminian Society called Methodist in the late Revd. JOHN WESLEY's Connection uphold and keep the same Chapel and House and the Offices and appurtenances thereto respectively belonging and also the Furniture in or belonging to the said House in sufficient repair and condition and also Insure and keep Insured the said Chapel House, Offices and Appurtenances and the Furniture against loss or damage by Fire and in the next place pay year by year the several annual sums herein after mentioned in manner following namely the annual sum of one Pound one Shilling to the Collection made for the support of Kingswood School at Bristol.

"The like annual sum of one Pound one Shilling to the annual Collection made for the support of the Society called Arminian Methodist in the late Revd. JOHN WESLEY's Connection. The like annual sum of one Pound and one Shilling to the annual Collection made for the support of the Missionary Society and also the annual sum of one Pound and one Shilling to the Subscription called the Aged Preachers' Fund and in the next place and lastly do and shall once in every half year pay one Moeity or equal half part of the surplus of the said Interest dividends and annual produce which shall then be in their or his hands and which shall remain after answering the purposes aforesaid to the Preachers and Stewards who compose the Quarterly Meeting of the High Wycombe Circuit in order to enable the said Preachers and Stewards to pay the Quarterly Expenses incurred by providing for the Preachers in such Circuit and do and shall pay the other Moeity of the said Surplus to the Preachers Steward and Leaders to pay for the Board and accommodation of such Preachers."

In 1779 the itinerant - or "travelling" - preachers (that is, paid Ministers in contrast to "local" unpaid preachers) in charge of the Oxford Circuit to which Wycombe belonged, were Revs.George Story and Thomas Newall.   Rev.Joseph Cole who was a Minister in 1797 and Superintendent in 1803, wrote the first edition of Hannah Ball's Memorials.   Another   was Rev.John Murlin who came to live in Wycombe in 1788 after his health had broken down, and continued here as a local preacher.   He was a "primitive Methodist, a man of great integrity, sincerity and simplicity" (Minutes of Wesleyan Conference 1799) and his sermons are said to have been of such converting power and emotion that he was called "The Weeping Prophet".

I Charles Harman — Superintendent Registrar of the District of Wycombe — in the Counties of Buckingham and Oxford do hereby certify, That the Building named The Wesleyan Chapel situated at Saint Mary's Street in the Parish of Brough of Wycombe in the County of Buckingham, having been duly certified as a place of Public Religious Worship, was registered for the Solemnization of Marriage therein, on the fourteenth — day of February — in the Year of our Lord One thousand eight hundred and forty eight.

Witness, my hand this fourteenth — day of February — in the Year of our Lord, One thousand eight hundred and forty eight.

Superintendent Registrar.

The first entry in a REGISTER OF BAPTISMS records that he baptised John, son of Francis & Sarah Shrimpton, on 15th January 1792 in the presence of John Brickill, Sarah Dancer and others. Other entries are as follows:

11th entry: Thomas, son of John & Mary Langley of High Wycombe. Baptized Novr. 21st 1801 by Wm. Holmes.

15th entry: Mary, the daughter of Thos. & Mary Langley of High Wycombe.   Bapt. Dec.16th 1803 by Josh.Cole.

16th entry: Ann, daughter of Thos. & Mary Langley of High Wycombe born 9th September 1806, baptized 19th Oct. 1806 by Rich. Gower.

18th entry: Elizabeth, daughter of Richard & Mary Gower, born in Worcester,   July 21st 1805 was baptized in High Wycombe March 29th, 1807 by me, Thomas Coke.

19th entry: Sarah, daughter of Richard & Mary Gower, born in High Wycombe Feb. 20th, 1807 was baptized in the same place on March 29th, 1807 by me, Thomas Coke.

On 22nd June 1830 eight children of Thomas & Sarah Fowler, Farmer of Penn, were baptized. The eldest was 19 years old and the youngest was 6 months old.

Names of some of the children Baptized:
Abbott, Abrahams, Allin, Avery, Barlow, Bristow, Darville, Fowler, Floyd, Gower, Graveney, Grove, Handcock, Harris (West Wycombe), Hawes, Hearn (Farmer of Penn), Heningham, Hulls, Ives, Keen, Langley, Lawrence, Lee, Lewis (Lane End), Line, Lipscombe, Mealing, Pierce, Plumridge, Shrimpton, Sikenhead, Slade, Sparkes (Marlow), Stallwood, Stone, Walker, Wardle, West, Wingrove, Woodbridge (Penn), Wooster, Worley, Wright, Youens.

By 1823 the Sunday School alone numbered 200 and its growth is illustrated by the following tables:

SUNDAY SCHOOL - MEMBERSHIP & ATTENDANCE

| | PRESENT | | ABSENT | | |
	B	G	B	G	TOTAL
4/5/1823					
Morning	68	88	25	18	199
Afternoon	63	85	30	21	199
11/5/1823					
Morning	70	66	23	40	199
Afternoon	75	76	18	30	199
6/7/1823					
Morning	57	74	34	35	200
Afternoon	60	79	31	30	200
29/6/1828					
Morning	62	88	61	40	251
Afternoon	66	76	57	52	251
4/5/1834					
Morning	120	148	40	22	330
Afternoon	123	137	37	33	330
11/5/1834					
Morning	113	139	48	32	332
Afternoon	121	147	40	24	332

WESLEYAN METHODIST CHURCHES

<u>SUNDAY SCHOOL MEETING OF MANAGERS & TEACHERS - 9th April 1827</u>

Miss Ellen West, Miss Eh. Howse and Miss Eh. Hunt Appointed Teachers in the Sunday School.

The following order of Teaching will be observed.

Class	Morning	Afternoon
9th Boys	W. Pickit/C. Abbott	W. Chapple
8th Boys	W. Bird	Jn. Money
7th Boys	Josh.& Geo. Hunt	Thos. Venable
6th Boys	Saml. Abraham	Alexr. Tibbury
5th Boys	Elis. Howse/Josiah Lipscomb	Saml. Salmons Sn.
4th Boys	Thos. Abraham/Thos. Bird	Jas. & W. Salmons
3rd Boys	Jno. Wooster	Saml. Powsey
2nd Boys	Jos. Goodchild	Saml. Church
1st Boys	Monitors Saml. Salmons Assistant to the Senior Sec.	Monitors
10th Girls	N. Willis	Eliz. Venable
9th Girls	H. Brickwell	C. Johnson
8th Girls	N. Dixey	N. Henningham N. Clark
7th Girls	E. & N. A. Collins E. Hunt	Miss. Gowen
6th Girls	T. Chapple/Mary Abbott	E. Coltman
5th Girls	E. Fastnage/M. Miller	M. Smith/E. House
4th Girls	Eliza Hedges/E. Willoughby and Ellen West	R. White S. Willis
3rd Girls	Mary Cox/C. Wingrove	C. Wiginton/C. Ives
2nd Girls	M. Tranter/Johnson	S. Chapple/Ellen Venable
1st Girls	Ann Barrett	Monitors

ANNUAL MEETING OF MANAGERS & TEACHERS - December 1830
(at Brother J.Weight's house)

The Reverend Wm.Brocklehurst President.
The Rev'd.Wm.Edwards   Vice President.

The undermentioned were balloted to serve in their several offices for the year ensuing:

Joseph Hunt	Treasurer for the year
Charles Abbott	Superintendent - morning
Michl.Youens	Superintendent - afternoon
George Abbott	Secretary - morning
George Hunt	Sub.Secretary - morning
George Ives	Sub.Sec. - afternoon
John Weight	Assist.Sec. - afternoon
Joseph Bird	Librarian - morning
Charlotte Ives	Librarian Assist. - afternoon
Samuel Allen	Inspector - morning
Betsy Venable	Inspector - afternoon

TEACHERS - October 1838

Class	Morning	Afternoon
1st	Mr.Willoughby	Jno.Mills/Josh.Straw
2nd	Mr.Foley/Mr.Sammons	Fras.Abrams/Jno.Foley
3rd	George Venable	George Venable
4th	Jno.Weight/Wm. Rogers	Heny.Grange
5th	Josh.Money/Jno.Smith	Josh.Money/Jas.Smith
6th	Edmd.Hutchinson	H.Ringsall
7th	Geo.Ringsall	Ricd.Brinkswell
8th	Jas.Nobbs	Jno.Howells
9th	W.Martin/Josh.Abbott	Ricd.Pearce
10th	Jno.Varley	Wm.Varney
11th	Josh.Smith	Isaac/Jas.McDermot
12th	Saml.Abrams/Alfred Edmunds	Bird/Monitors

WESLEYAN METHODIST CHURCHES

The Rev. Jas. Coats in the chair.

Members present.

The Rev. Mr. Driver	Wm. Daveny
Mr. Josh. Hunt	Thos. Allnut
Chas. Abbott	Thos. Jones
Geo. Ives	Jno. Howells
Michl. Youens	Jas. Avery
Geo. Abbott	Wm. Willoughby
Jas. Smith	Josh. Money
Geo. Ringsell	Jas. Hobbs
Edmd. Hutchinson	

It was proposed by Joseph Money and seconded by John Mills, that those Managers, Teachers and Monitors & children who were present at a dinner held in opposition to the decision of the majority of the Teachers etc. etc. in this place, be no more considered as belonging to the said Sunday School. viz:

Teachers etc. etc.

Geo. Venable	Charlotte Samonds	Jas. Lovegrove
Saml. Samonds	Catherine Samonds	Maria Samonds
Henry Grange	Mary Lovegrove	Ann Pearce
Chas. Cross	Sarah Peters	Joseph Pearce
Saml. Holland	Louisa Wooster	-------------
Jas. Williams		
George Williams		Scholars etc.

In the WESLEYAN METHODIST MAGAZINE we read the obituaries of three people who attended the St. Mary Street Chapel.

JAMES DAVENEY (1788-1842)

James Daveney died on 8th April 1842 at the age of 54. He joined the Wesleyan society in High Wycombe in August 1808 and soon after obtained a sense of the divine favour. He became a local preacher in 1813. Considering his humble circumstances, few men have been more highly esteemed. The last words he articulated were, "Christ is precious".

J.C.

WILLIAM CHAPPEL (1770-1848)

William Chappel died on 2nd January 1848 at the age of 77.
During youth he was more than ordinarily sedate and kept aloof
from gay company. At the age of 18, business caused him to
leave High Wycombe. In January 1796 he was convinced of sin.
He returned in 1826 and was happy to be employed in any way in
the promotion of religion. For some years he was a local
preacher His last affliction commenced in July 1845. A short
time before his death a fire accidentally occurred in his room.
The bed on which he lay helpless was consumed; but he was
mercifully preserved. At the time the flames surrounded him and
immediate destruction seemed inevitable, he was greatly
supported by that passage, the last from which he preached, "My
grace is sufficient for thee: for my strength is made perfect
in weakness". The shock then sustained greatly increased his
weakness. He survived but a few weeks. Four days before his
death he attempted to sing, "My God, the Spring of all my joys".
JOHN ANDERSON

WILLIAM BRIDGNELL (1800-1858)

Rev. William Bridgnell was born in High Wycombe on 17th
September 1800, his father, Rev James Bridgnell being minister
in the town. He was converted at the age of ten in Bristol
having heard Rev.William Bramwell preach. After the service
something was offered him to eat but he declined to receive it;
as his soul was so richly feeding on the heavenly manna that for
some time he had no relish for earthly food. On his way home
his father inquired why he had declined to eat; when he said,
"Is it not written, Man shall not live on bread alone but by
every word that proceedeth out of the mouth of God?" (There
was, throughout his life, an inclination to take texts of this
kind in their literal signification, which sometimes led him
into perplexity and brought on anguish of spirit, the intensity
of which has not often been surpassed.) In 1812 he was one of
the first boys at Woodhouse-Grove School. At 16 he was employed
by a surgeon at St.Helen's and then with a chemist at
Warrington. However, he later became apprentice to a Bookbinder
at Burslem.

He was received as a local preacher in Chester at the age
of 20 and was proposed as a candidate for the Ministry. In 1822
he was appointed to Sandhurst. He offered himself for the
Overseas work following a missionary meeting held in Canterbury.
Despite strong opposition from his parents, his mother in

particular, the Conference of 1823 appointed him to Ceylon. Sailing on the "Thames" from Gravesend, he landed at Colombo on 30th June,1824 just ten years after Dr. Thomas Coke had founded the mission there. His service lasted for 25 years in Ceylon and he saw service at a variety of stations. During that period he was ably assisted by his wife, a Miss Weerman, whom he had married on 21st March,1827. She died in 1841 at Galle.

Returning home to England in 1849 with his daughter, Mrs.Miller and family, he resided in Birmingham for a time as a Supernumary, due to ill health. He recovered sufficiently to return to the full work for a period of three years at Bridlington but on removal to Gateshead in 1855 he again became unwell and was unable to continue in the work. He died at his daughter's home in Edinburgh on 12th April, 1858.

(Rev.) R.SPENCE HARDY

By the middle of the nineteenth century despite the addition of galleries the building was no longer adequate for the number of Wesleyans in the town. On 3rd October 1865 they therefore assembled for prayer and processed to Cemetry (Priory) Road where the foundation stone of the new Wesley Chapel was laid. By July 1866 the old chapel was closed.

Apart from John Wesley himself the name which bridges the gap between the two Churches best is that of Rev.John Murlin. He died in 1799 at the age of 77 and was interred in Wesley's vault. He left the income from an investment of £300 for the support of the Methodist chapel and the poor of the society. "Murlin's Charity" was later administered by the Wesley Trust. The entries below, all concerned with the one man, take us in a broad sweep of history from 1722 to 1977.

JOHN MURLIN'S EARLY LIFE

He was born in the parish of St.Stephen, Cornwall, in the year 1722. Employed in farming to the age of 12, he then (Michaelmas 1735) became apprentice to a carpenter. Seven years later, when the apprenticeship expired, he started work with another master for three or four years. By day he worked as a carpenter and in the evening learned writing and accounts. Occasional concern for his soul and a conviction of sin were in these years soon stifled. He was prone to "cursing and swearing, soon adding gaming and soon after drunkenness". In February,1749 he heard the Methodist preachers and was brought under a deep conviction of sin. In April, he heard Mr.Downes preach, "My burden was taken away". Some time after this Mr.William Roberts, then the travelling preacher in the circuit, told him "he must take care of the little class" near where he lived. He was struck with fear, saying he could not do it. Mr.Roberts insisted and at last he complied, "and yet with fear and trembling, as I thought there were some in the class whose abilities were far superior to mine". This soon lead to his call as a local preacher. A letter from John Wesley asking if he was willing to become a travelling preacher, was answered by objections, but a second letter answered these and "accordingly, on October 12th 1754 I took my horse, and without delay rode away into the west of Cornwall". His ministry took him to many parts of England, to Ireland and the Isle of Man. From August 1767 to August 1768 he was in the Bristol Circuit and during that year there was "a very remarkable increase of the work of God in Kingswood". He writes, "Yet how much longer I shall be able to travel, I cannot tell, as I have a settled Rheumatism in my knee and thigh, and am far past the meridian of life"

ARMINIAN MAGAZINE (1st August,1779)

JOHN MURLIN'S LEGACY - AN INQUIRY

JOHN MURLIN by a codicil to his will dated 15th February, 1799 gave unto his executors WILLIAM CLULOW and HENRY WALKLATE MORTIMER the sum of £300 to be appropriated by them at interest on Government or Mortgage security or in the purchase of land as they should think best in their names and he directed that the interest and proceeds should be paid over and applied by his said trustees for the support of the Methodist Chapel and the poor of the Society and Congregation thereof in High Wycombe in such manner as his Wife during her life should direct and after her decease that the same should be paid and applied to and for the same purposes equally according to the direction of his Trustees and in case of the death of either of the said Trustees the survivor do elect another unto whom with himself the property should be transferred for the same purposes and so in like manner as often as such decease should happen.

By subsequent Codicils the Testator appointed JOHN PORSON a co-Trustee of the above Legacy and desired that the number of three Trustees should be always kept up, and that the Legacy should be paid within one month after his death over and above all stamps and duties which should be paid out of his estate, and he also directed that the interest of the Legacy should be paid to his wife during her life. The Testator died about 30 years ago [1799] and his wife has also been dead some time. WILLIAM CLULOW survived his co-Trustee and died about eight years ago having made a Will and appointed Mr.EDWARD ORME of Fitzroy Square one of his Executors. Nothing has been received in respect of this Charity. A Methodist Chapel and a Society of that denomination have existed in High Wycombe from the death of the Testator up to the present time.

Mr. SUTCLIFFE as solicitor for the parties interested in the donation made application to Mr. W. CLULOW during his lifetime to invest the money in the names of Trustees for their benefit according to the terms of the codicil. Mr. CLULOW neglected to do so alleging in reply to this demand that he considered it necessary previously to obtain the opinion of counsel as to whether the gift was void under the Mortmain Act. Mr.EDWARD ORME attended at our office and admitted that he and his co-Trustees held a sum of £367.8s.5d.[£367.42] now invested in mortgage in Trust for this Charity on which the sum on arrear of interest at the rate of four per cent was also due amounting to about £100. He stated that the £300 was on mortgage at Mr. CLULOW'S death but it was paid off and he received on 2nd July 1826 £367.8s.5d. for principal and interest which was reinvested on mortgage.

He further stated that during Mrs. MURLIN'S life the interest had been by her divided into three parts, one of which was received by the Minister of the Chapel, another was expended in repairs thereof and a third distributed amongst the poor of the congregation attending the same. Mr. ORME consented to pay the interest of the sum of £460 at four per cent to such parties as we might consider entitled to receive the same. It appears to us that the application adopted during Mrs.MURLIN'S life is a very proper one and might safely be followed by the executors who should invest the above mentioned principal sum in their own names on Trusts declared accordingly.

CHARITY ACCOUNT BOOK

N.B. It appears that the WM. CLULOW mentioned was the solicitor who witnessed the will of JOHN WESLEY dated 20th February,1789.

THE WESLEY (MURLIN) TRUST

Recovered in the year 1870. £307.5s.7d. Consols The residue of the sum of £570.8s.5d. like stock.

Trustees Revd.W.H.Lewis, Robert White, John Abbott

RECEIVERS.

1908	Stephen Weller	1911	Allan H.Plowman
1920	A.C.Boorman	1936	Edwin Weller
1938	George Foster	1941	A.C.Boorman
1951	Walter W.Webb	1963	Sidney Arthur Day
1968	Mr.Boorman		

TRUST TREASURERS OR STEWARDS

1894	J.Busby	1909	N.Dring
1910	J.I.Harris	1924	W.A.Steevens
1942	S.C.Willott	1974	Denys Hood
1975	R.Ing		

POOR STEWARDS

1889	J.Varney	1891	S.Weller Junr.
1894	B.Woodbridge	1897	J.Busby
1902	C.Lord	1904	A.Willott
1906	F.Turner	1909	A.C./E.Boorman
1910	Henry Green	1912	I.Lord
1917	A.C.Boorman	1923	J.Wright
1925	S.C.Willott	1933	Geo.Evans
1935	L.J.Stephenson	1950	A.J.Goodearl
1953	A.E.Jones	1954	S.C.Willott
1957	K.C.Hinton	1965	D.S.Hart
1971	E.Hitchman	1974	Leonard Mills.

CHURCH TREASURER

1977 J.Higginbottom

WESLEYAN METHODIST CHURCHES

PENN (1808)

NORMAN STRETTON writes:

In 1805 - just 14 years after John Wesley's death - the Wingrove family along with Richard Hunt, Richard Henningham and John Brown, purchased a piece of land in Penn from Baroness Howe. A church was built on the other side of the road to Penn Church and opened for worship in 1808. One of the first trustees in 1812 was John Birkenhead, "a Minister of the persuasion of Rev.John Wesley". The earliest register dates back to 1817 when five members were enrolled.

One of the earliest members was Mary Garland who at the age of 15 relates in her diary: "26th February (1825): Admitted on trial in the Methodist society by Rev.G.Rowe. May the Lord enable me to walk according to the promise which I now make." Later she records: "October 1828: Went to High Wycombe to hear Mr.Henningham's funeral sermon preached by Mr.Campbell. 1000 people were present. Mr.H. was the principle prop in our circuit. He has been a member more than 40 years." Mary herself died in 1836 at the age of 26. The earliest entry in the baptismal register is that of Mary Anne Laurence (1838). In 1850 the members decided to join the Wesleyan Reform Union (Free Methodists).

MARLOW (1810)

The first Wesleyan chapel in Marlow was opened in 1810. It was replaced in 1900 by the present church which lies behind the shops in Spittal Street, up a narrow court. It is a strikingly handsome building. The membership has grown steadily over recent years and it is now one of the largest Methodist Churches in the area. Marlow is described in the Shell Guide as the "happiest town in Buckinghamshire". But there was much anxiety in August 1916 when Rev.W.T.Coppin wrote in the Wesleyan Methodist Circuit Magazine:

"From different scenes we are all getting our unstamped correspondence today; and some of our brave fellows at the front are taking full advantage of the privilege to send home letters without stamps. Says Private Cyril Wellicome: 'Yes, you are quite right. This is the only chance I have to get anything out of the Post Office and I assure you I am going it hot and,' he adds, 'of course mother comes first. It doesn't matter where I am, in or out of the trenches, I always manage to write home.' He continues, 'We rarely have a Sunday off. Sunday out here is the busiest day of the week. So it is lovely to have a service out here and how I do enjoy them! Tell the men,' he concludes, 'who come to your parade services, to put their heart and soul into the service and try and help in the chapel. If so, they will come out to France, knowing that they are straight with God before it is too late.'"

AUDREY BRUNSDON writes:

Mary Webley can remember the 1920's when her Sunday School teacher was an elderly, bearded gentleman called Mr.Davis who got them to read the Lord's Prayer printed on the back of a farthing! Morning School preceded the service which children were expected to attend, at least up to the sermon. Sunday Schools in the town used to visit one another on Anniversary Days. Treats were often held at Burnham Beeches, the children travelling in Jack White's lorries and parents and friends coming later by charabanc. Miss Mabel Wellicome was Sunday School Superintendent and trained the children for the Scripture Exam. In 1933 when the Wesleyans and Primitives amalgamated, it was decided to use the Wesleyan chapel. The Primitive chapel was sold and from the proceeds a pipe organ was purchased, the console at first being below the pulpit. Mr.Harvey from the Primitives became Sunday School Superintendent. His daughter Marjorie became a Deaconess but later returned here as Mrs.Pike. She was a popular preacher and also led the Women's Fellowship.

My own first impressions when I came here in 1966, were: "What a beautiful building and how friendly everybody is!" It wasn't long before I was working in the Sunday School and singing in the choir. Over the years the School has been led by Keith Lewis, John Lee, Arthur Tapping, Mrs.Edith Lee, Mrs.Ann Dennis and (most recently) Mrs.Elizabeth Holmes who was renamed

"Junior Church Co-ordinator". 20 years ago two enormous round coke boilers used to stand in the chapel, halfway down the aisles. They were handy as bases for harvest decorations, having been kept cold for the occasion. The Minister during this period was Rev.Haldane Adams whom I remember meeting in Marlow High Street on one occasion, dressed in a khaki safari jacket and shorts. He was putting the shopping in his knapsack. I also came to know Mr. and Mrs.Denton and learned from Jimmy that he had taught most of the men in Marlow. During the Second World War Jimmy used to go to the church very early on Sunday mornings to light the boilers, the coke for which had to be brought from the gasworks. Two other faithful members were Mr. and Mrs.Harold Plumridge. He always sat in the back pew near the door and refused to move.

The original schoolroom and vestry at the rear of the church had been demolished and rebuilt after the war. Now in 1977 we thought it necessary to "raise the roof" and build an upper room. The work started during Rev.Harold Ward's ministry and was dedicated in 1978 by his successor, Rev.Alan Baxter. John Lee always said that he longed to see some of the congregation sitting in the gallery because there was no room in the main body of the chapel. He did live to see this happen on some special days; nowadays it is used every Sunday morning! Marlow Methodist Church is now 88 years old and has seen many changes. It is a "baby" compared to many churches but - like all healthy babies - it has kept growing. We needed more rooms; our old schoolroom was falling apart. Money had been spent on repairs but the time had come to demolish it and build a modern hall in its place. In March 1987 under the guidance of Rev.Mark Booth we launched our "Challenge '87". It has been good to see so many people working hard, raising funds and enjoying fellowship together, so that in future years we would have the use of improved premises.

There are many more faithful people whom I have not mentioned. They will always be remembered with affection by those who knew them. Thanks be to God!

CHRISTMAS AT MARLOW - 1983

18th December   10.30 a.m. Junior Church Nativity
                4.30 p.m. Candle-lit Carol Service
                            (both followed by coffee and mince pies)

During the week before Christmas a brief service will be held each morning at 11 in the upper room at the rear of the church. We shall pray for some of those in need in our society and world and the work of particular organisations as follows:

Monday	The National Children's Home and all families in distress
Tuesday	Shelter and the homeless
Wednesday	Methodist Homes for the Aged and all elderly people at risk
Thursday	Christian Aid and the underprivileged across the world
Friday	World peace

Christmas Eve	11.30 p.m.	Holy Communion
Christmas Day	10.30 a.m.	Family Service
New Year's Eve	11.30 p.m.	Watch Night Service

CIRCUIT NEWS

WOOBURN GREEN (1811)

JOHN ASH writes:

The present church was opened in 1873 but the story of Methodism in Wooburn Green begins earlier in that century. A tenement was leased for use as a chapel to a Wesleyan Methodist Trust in 1811. Rev.R.B.Ashley, Vicar of Wooburn from 1847 to 1884, records a contest between the Methodist Minister (referred to as "The Independent") and the Mormons. One of their number used to preach long and loud at a signpost between the Parish Church and the vicarage and disturb the Communion. The Methodist Minister challenged him to a public discussion on the Green where platforms were erected. Alas, he was a novice in debate and the four Mormon preachers from London "had a happy hit" for everything. Subsequently two houses were opened on the Green for Mormon preaching weekdays and Sundays. Ashley now called his own meeting at one of the nearby mills and by the light of candles set in half-potatoes, lectured on the history of Mormonism. His audience listened with quiet interest, interrupted only by "gasps of sensation and the scratching of Mormon pens". This did not altogether quell the Mormons however, as one of Joseph Smith's wives who had settled on the Green, continued with her troublesome preaching.

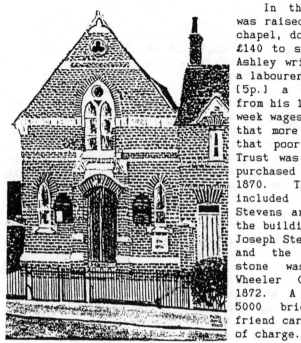

In the 1860's over £300 was raised for a new Wesleyan chapel, donations ranging from £140 to sixpence [2½p.]. Mr. Ashley writes that he knew of a labourer who gave a shilling [5p.] a week to his chapel from his 13 shillings [65p.] a week wages. He exclaims: "Oh that more churchmen were like that poor Wesleyan!" A new Trust was formed in 1868 and purchased the present site in 1870. The 16 trustees who included Messrs. Dring, Stevens and Howland, accepted the building tender of £298 by Joseph Stevens of High Wycombe and the single foundation-stone was laid by Thomas Wheeler (T.W.) on 9th July 1872. A well-wisher donated 5000 bricks which another friend carted to the site free of charge.

Writing 100 years later, Neville Marsland says: "The opening day was 1st January 1873. Posters (one still hangs in the chapel) announced that Rev.G.T.Perks. the secretary of the Wesleyan Methodist Conference, would conduct two services. On each of the following three Sundays three services would be held. Now on 7th January 1973 our Centenary services are to be conducted by Rev.Dr.Kenneth G.Greet, secretary of the Methodist Conference. Mr.Perks' text 100 years ago is still relevant to us today: 'I am He that liveth and was dead; and behold I am alive for evermore' (Revelation 1.18)." Such was our ancestors' faith by the way that it took them three years to insure the building with the Wesleyan Fire Office!

In 1901 the Trust purchased the house adjoining the chapel and in 1903 land at the rear for a schoolroom. About 90 scholars had been meeting twice each Sunday in a "shanty" but now, on 3rd May 1905 30 foundation-stones were "well and truly laid" for a building which was to be used in the First World War by troops en-route for embarkation to France, and in the Second World War by evacuees from London and for food storage.

Every church has its saints and I choose Fred Slade simply because I remember him from my early boyhood when he was the village blacksmith and Sunday School superintendent. Fred was built on traditional blacksmith's lines - tall, broad and muscular - and in company with other lads of the village, I stood in awe and fascination at the half-door of his blacksmith's shop watching him, wreathed in steam and smoke, his forge glowing in the background as he fashioned the horseshoes and fixed them on the huge shire-horses which had been brought in from the neighbouring farms. Nothing short of perfection was good enough for Fred: each shoe was made with exactness; each shoe rasped to a nicety. Looking back, I feel that he had in mind the same care that his Master applied long ago in fashioning the yokes and collars for the beasts of burden which were brought to Him.

At an opportune moment Fred would pause in his work, smile and enquire if we went to Sunday School. If the answer was "no", then we would be invited to his Sunday School, but if the answer was "yes", he would say: "That's all right then, boy". I learned many years afterwards that all males, whether they were eight or 80, were addressed as "boy"! I learned also that Fred was an uncompromising Methodist: black was black and white was white and grey was not allowed. He was also a shrewd judge of character and if we took issue with him over certain matters, he would usually close the conversation by saying: "You do what you think best then, boy", knowing full well that we would wrestle with our consciences and usually come round to his way of thinking in the end. After Fred lost his wife who had supported him faithfully in all his Christian works, he lived quietly on his own, continuing to praise the Lord and proclaim the Gospel to the end of his days, even to those who cared for him in hospital during his final illness. I do not think Fred was unique in his way of life; the Christian faith has been sustained down the ages by folk like him.

Now we are faced with major structural repairs to our church and hall. £75,000 is needed to restore both buildings to a state which will require only routine maintenance by the next two or three generations. Some may wonder if we are justified in spending such a sum in view of our small congregation. Surely to do otherwise and allow our church to fall into further decay, would be a betrayal of those who have borne loyal witness to their faith at the church on the Green for the past 115 years.

WEST WYCOMBE (1815)

ANDREW HUGHES writes:

The first Methodist chapel in the picturesque Dashwood (now National Trust) village of West Wycombe was built at the lower end of Church Lane in 1815 near the 15th century Church Loft which bridges the lane. Many names of the first trustees – Treacher, Hughes, Mead, West, Miller, Weight, Tebbles, Hearn, Belson, Harris and Bird – recur well into this century. At the Centenary Thanksgiving the chairman, Edwin Weller, remarked that most Methodist chapels were "barn-like, forbidding-looking structures and their vestries a sort of glorified 'holes of Calcutta'!" Mr.W.Mead recalled the "narrow, high-backed pews of the first chapel, the dim religious light which emanated from the tallow-dips, the frequency of the Sunday services, the first of which commenced at 7 a.m., and the spiritual fervour which characterised the worship". Rev.V.Terry mentioned that the first lamp was used in 1845, although candles continued in use until 1873.

REV.JOHN T.BARR (1845) writes:

Joseph Moorcock died on 27th September 1845 at the age of 45. In 1818 he attended for the first time the Wesleyan chapel at Wokingham and under Rev.John Waterhouse's sermon he was

deeply affected and later obtained a knowledge of salvation by
the remission of sins. He removed to Reading in 1821 where he
obtained a situation in a grocer's shop. The following year he
was admitted on the circuit plan as a local preacher. In 1825
he was employed by Mr.Jarvis at Lane End. Here he formed an
acquaintance with a pious female; and with the anticipation of
enjoying much domestic happiness from an alliance with one who,
he had reason to believe, was truly converted to God, he entered
into the matrimonial state. He laboured abundantly for the good
of souls and as a result was made the instrument of promoting a
revival of pure religion in several places in the neighbourhood.

On leaving the service of Mr.Jarvis he engaged himself to
Mr.Harris of West Wycombe, principally as a traveller. The same
zeal formed the distinguishing features of his character; in
addition to which his amiable disposition and pious conversation
soon gained him the esteem of the society at West Wycombe. He
was a zealous advocate for the doctrine of universal
redemption. This exposed him to the animadversions of those
whose views differed from his own. In 1844 he was invited to
preach their Anniversary sermons by the Wesleyan Methodist
Sunday-school at Haddenham. His text was: "For the promise is
to all that are afar off" (Acts 2.39). A gentleman who had
entered the chapel during his sermon for the purpose of taking
tea, began to dispute the correctness of the sentiments advanced
by Mr.Moorcock who obtained a signal triumph over his
antagonist. He later wrote him a manuscript containing upwards
of 100 pages, closely written on folio paper.

I met him in 1844 and in looking over his little library,
was surprised to find a copy of the Scriptures in Hebrew. He
frequently visited me for the purpose of looking over my books
and conversing on religious topics. He possessed a natural
genius and notwithstanding the deficiency of his education, he
had a strong and capacious mind. His sermons were generally
practical and delivered with such deep earnestness that many
persons were awakened to a sense of their sin. During the last
summer he moved with his family to High Wycombe, having obtained
a situation in the employment of Mr.Skull. Here he was soon, in
consequence of a severe attack of illness, confined to his room.
His death, according to Mr.Barnes at whose house he died, was
caused by water in the heart.

ANDREW HUGHES continues:

By the 1890's the Church was looking for larger premises.
In 1894 some 17th century cottages in the High Street were

demolished to make way for a new chapel - an act of desecration according to my father's cousin, Ella Giles. Most of the wood panelling and furniture in the church came from North's of Piddington. Amongst the locals it was sometimes referred to as "Benny North's chapel"! The following years were the heyday of Methodism. In 1910 Mr.B.S.North was treasurer, steward, organist and choirmaster; Edwin Weller was secretary; and Messrs. Cutler, Giles, Robertson, Harman and Lee were pew stewards for both sides of the church - and the gallery which after the First World War was not needed again. Will Giles also had the office of "collector of seat rents"!

In 1912 the Church was registered for the solemnization of marriages. Bernard Robertson and Mabel Cutler were the first couple after this to be married and were presented with a Bible. The schoolroom was made available for cookery classes at a charge - including fuel and caretaker - of six shillings [30p.] per day. By 1914 there were complaints about poor heating in the chapel - a problem which was never properly solved! At the outbreak of war the only other matter of moment was the introduction of umbrella holders which were to be fixed to the pews! In the absence of those who had joined the armed services, Alfred Hughes now became a pew steward. During the war united services were held with the Congregational Church, but later when Methodist Church Union was considered, West Wycombe voted by a proportion of three to one against!

In 1928 the schoolroom started to be used by the recently formed Village Club, the first of many organisations to use this "acting" village hall. The "genuine article" did not appear for another 30 years! In 1932 Ernest Robertson became a chapel steward. The next year adoption of the Envelope Scheme was suggested - to be taken up 23 years later! In 1936 funds were needed for renovation and an invitation was given to hold a garden-party at the Bolton-Kings' home, "Windyhaugh", on top of West Wycombe Hill. West Wycombe Brass Band appeared - along with the Rainbow Rhythm Boys' Band. David Hughes became organist and choirmaster, assisted by Leslie Vernon.

During the Second World War Reg and Ethel Potter were the joint leaders of the Sunday School. After the war tubular heating was installed in the chapel and schoolroom and Seat Rent abolished. In 1947 came the tragic death of Bernard Robertson in whose memory a seat was erected on West Wycombe Hill two years later, to commemorate his work in arranging the Pleasant Sunday Afternoons (P.S.A.). The Church was given a boost in the early 1950's by the visit of two Cliff College evangelists.

Chapel and schoolroom were both filled with people from the village and other churches. Fred Chilton, the sub-postmaster, and his wife were active in work among young people. Toilets were installed in 1955. A mixed youth club was started by Dennis Bates in 1958 but failed in its objective to bring members within the Church fellowship.

S.SHERRATT 1987   WEST WYCOMBE.

Insufficient heating and caretaking problems prompted the installation of overhead heaters in the schoolroom. Proper maintenance of the premises became an increasing problem throughout the 1960's. This and the declining membership – due to members leaving the area, young people going away to college, the deaths of elderly members and the general unconcern of the majority of village folk from whom leadership might have come – led to the decision to close the premises in 1977. Services were resumed in 1978 at St.Paul's Church, not least so that the Sunday School led by Mrs.Sheila Bell might continue. In 1980 the six remaining society members became a "Wesley class". Problems with heating and small numbers led to final closure in 1983, although the Women's Meeting continued to meet in the Church Room. Thus ended 168 years of Methodist witness in West Wycombe. The first church is now used by the Christadelphians: the second was converted into offices.

SOCIETIES WITHOUT CHAPELS (from 1818)

Groups of Wesleyan Methodists would often meet in a cottage or barn at first, and only when they were sufficiently established did they think of erecting their own chapel. Some used a building which later passed into other use, like the Wesleyans at STOKENCHURCH who are listed in the 1818 plan as holding services. They met on the future site of the village infants' school. The society appears on the 1822 Plan but not the 1838 one. In 1822 also there were societies at GREAT KINGSHILL (Cryers Hill), KNOTTY GREEN and WALTERS ASH but despite later efforts these seem to have disappeared by 1838. The paupers at SAUNDERTON WORKHOUSE were enjoying Wesleyan services as early as 1822 and possibly for the next two decades. RADNAGE struggled on - mostly in summer months - from the same time until 1855.

LACEY GREEN had a class meeting of 18 people in 1837 but this appears to have ceased within a few years. BRADENHAM had 27 members in 1837 and survived until 1856. Wesleyans at LITTLE MISSENDEN met from 1838 to 1844, the year when the society at CADMORE END was meeting, although this soon closed. There were services in 1844 at HAZLEMERE which appears for the last time in the 1860 Plan. We know that Wesleyan groups were meeting at HANDY CROSS in 1863 (efforts here earlier in the century had failed), WYCOMBE MARSH in 1865 and LITTLE HAMPDEN in 1874 but like the others in this section, they did not exist long enough to build their own chapels.

DOWNLEY - SUNNY BANK (1824)

STAN SHERRATT writes:

When I stood for the first time in the Moor Lane pulpit, I was very conscious of the building's 160-year history. I asked the congregation to picture the people arriving all those years ago - on foot, on horseback or (if any were rich enough) in a pony and trap. It was before the days of policemen, trains, cars, fish-fingers or potato crisps. The chapel would have been full and the centre of everybody's life.

HENRY COLLINS. (1832-1877)

A painful impression was produced throughout the West Wycombe parish on Monday 29th January 1877 by a report which unfortunately proved too true, that our respected neighbour, Mr.Henry Collins of Downley, who had proceeded to London by the first train that morning, had suddenly expired while hurrying to catch a train at the St.Pancras Railway Station. It appeared that as he was entering the archway of the Grand Hotel which leads to the arrival platform, he found he was late and started off running, in order, if possible, to save the train. He had not gone many yards when he was seen to stagger and fall. He was picked up insensible and Dr.Brenton of Euston Road who lives opposite the station, was sent for, who pronounced life to be extinct. The deceased's friends were immediately telegraphed for and in the meantime the body was removed to the St.Pancras mortuary where during the afternoon it was identified by one of the deceased's sons. An inquest was held on the following day.

Mr.Collins was one of the largest chair-manufacturers in the neighbourhood and was also largely engaged in the timber trade. He was Chairman of our School Board, Surveyor of Highways and a leading member of the Wesleyan body, being a class-leader and local preacher and also for many years Superintendent of the Downley Wesleyan Sunday School. Mr.Collins was a strong advocate for the education of the young and was one of the founders of the Wesleyan Day School at Downley and one of its most energetic supporters until it merged into the Board School in which also he took the greatest interest. By the high integrity of his character and the suavity of his manners he gained the confidence and friendship of all with whom he had business dealings, while in his social relations he was widely esteemed. His loss is felt in the West Wycombe parish as a public calamity and universal sympathy is felt for his widow and family, thus suddenly deprived of an affectionate husband and father. His workpeople have lost a kind master and the poor a sincere friend.

"BUCKS FREE PRESS" (2/2/1877)

ROY TAYLOR writes:

Beryl and I joined Sunny Bank in 1967, two years after the other Downley Methodist Church (Chapel Street) which was situated on the other side of the common, had at last closed - 35 years after the "Deed of Union". Sunny Bank was Wesleyan and Chapel Street Primitive and over the years there had been a degree of enmity beween them.

WESLEYAN METHODIST CHURCHES

Sunny Bank is the oldest chapel still in use in the High Wycombe Methodist Circuit, having been erected in 1824 when there were only 30 houses in Downley. James Treacher of West Wycombe had started cottage services six years earlier. John Wright, a local preacher, lent the money. The chapel was widened in 1838, giving it the appearance of a lean-to. The choir had a special pew, painted white. The congregation sat on forms and lighting was provided by candles in tins. Scarcely anyone could read so the preacher would read out the hymn two or three lines at a time and deliver a sermon between the sections. The singing was led by violins. In 1847 a third part was added to the chapel, of different height from either of the other two. Worshippers had to avoid the joins in the roofs when it rained! In 1850 the walls were raised and the present chapel emerged.

A small harmonium was bought in 1860 for £10. The schoolroom which was erected the following year, was used as a day school as well as by some of the 22 Sunday School classes which before that time had all met in the chapel. It was a rule of the Sunday School at this time to impose fines on its teachers (1p. for absence and ½p. for lateness) but in 1885 this resolution was passed: "In future all female teachers shall be exempted from fines for the first half-hour in the morning, provided they have the secretary's consent and arrive in time to sit with the scholars during the service". The pulpit and gallery were erected in 1864 and the choir seats and harmonium were moved to the front in 1888. The present schoolroom was built to commemorate the centenary in 1924, when Willoughby Youens J.P. and George Batts were the superintendents.

When Chapel Street closed in 1965, the remaining members came to Sunny Bank. Before that time the two Churches had had little connection - apart from Sunday School Anniversaries when one Sunday School would vist the other. Attendance at "the other chapel" was unusual, unless one had fallen out with one's own Church! An exception was Connie Webster who came to Downley at the age of 17. She was welcomed at Sunny Bank by Harold Ford who invited her to join the choir. (Her mother always referred to the pipe-organ as "Mr.Ford's organ.") But her offer to help in the Sunday School was turned down (volunteering, especially by newcomers, was not encouraged) and so she went to Chapel Street. Connie continued in membership at Sunny Bank and was regarded as somewhat weird for her involvement in the two "rival" Churches!

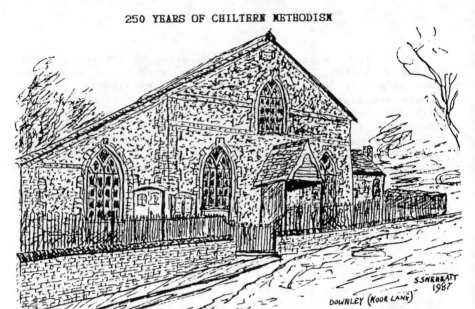

DOWNLEY (MOOR LANE)

S.SHERRATT
1987

It took a German "buzz-bomb" (flying bomb) on the common in 1944, to blow out Joe Meakes' windows; a circuit "thunderbolt" in 1965, to bring the two chapels together at Sunny Bank; and the sudden appearance (another 21 years later) of Rev. Roy Jackson in 1986, to forge stimulating links with the St. Mark's section. The oldest chapel in the circuit awaits the year 2007 with keen expectation!

A WARTIME TREAT

The children of the Sunday School had their annual treat on Monday, July 3rd, 1916 in Mr. Jackson's meadow. The procession started from the school at 1.30 p.m. and marched to the meadow. Here the children had a good time at games, sports and at the stall (in charge of the Lady Teachers). These were kept busy supplying the youngsters with squeakers, whistles, fancies etc. The public tea was well patronised. We were pleased to have our Superintendent Minister with us. As there was a difficulty with regard to securing a band this year, we decided to do without one; and make it up to the children by giving everyone a present. All went away delighted, having had a good time in lovely weather. A gramophone was in evidence during the evening, superintended by Mr. Hotston. The whole proceedings were quite satisfactory, 29/- [£1.45] being handed over to the School treasurer from the stall.

WESLEYAN METHODIST CHURCHES

Anniversary services were repeated on Sunday, July 16th
when Rev. A. T. Dean was the preacher for the day. His remarks in
the morning were based on "Feed my Lambs" after speaking to the
children about "the little captive maid". The afternoon address
on the "Pencil" was very interesting. The text at night was:
"Is the young man Absalom safe?" Special hymns were sung under
the conductorship of Mr. Jackson. The choir also rendered two
anthems: "O taste and see" and "Gratitude". The collections
for the day realised 27/9 [£1.39]. The following children
recited: Edwin Mines, Beryl Plumridge, Jack Tapping, Rupert
Youens, Winnie Hotston, Winnie Plumridge, Dorothy Cross, Mary
Youens, Doris Mines.

WESLEYAN CHURCH RECORD

LANE END (1834)

DAVID LEVIS writes

It stands at the top of the hill at the centre of the
village. Why, I ask myself, is it there at all? A Church is
not a building but a group of Christian people. Our forebears
knew this as well as we do. Why then that material building in
flint-faced brick? We cannot know the thoughts and dreams of
our founders; I do not know the thoughts of my fellows today!
However all our roots go back to Christ Whose deeds and dreams
were one.

What have been the deeds of the Lane End Methodist Church
over its 153 years? The record states:

1820 Services in cottage in Marlow Road started by Mr. Ramsay.
1823 Lane End Methodists linked with Wycombe Wesleyan Circuit;
     James Bird, William Goodearl and James Plumridge prominent.
1834 First Methodist church erected near Weir Pond.
1841 Church enlarged by raising roof and adding gallery.
1866 Present Methodist Church opened on 23rd April.
1867 Old church became Methodist day school;   opened 7th June;
     39 scholars paid about twopence [1p.] per week;   school
     aided by Methodist funds;   received Government grant
     depending on standard of teaching and regular
     upkeep of register; schoolmistress Mary Ann Davey;   total
     outlay about £100 per year.
1880 School enlarged with further classrooms.

1889 School now had 120 scholars;   schoolmistress Mary Crouch
     paid £40 per year; Government grant £60.47; "school pence"
     £32.63.
1896 Vestry added to church in memory of wife of James Elliot.
1900 Gospel hymns of Americans Moody and Sankey provided much
     inspiration.
1902 Electric light in church - first in circuit.
1908 Schoolmaster Mr.H.J.Davies resigned after 14 years;
     became headmaster of Wheeler End Council School.
1915 Day school closed; scholars transferred to Wheeler End
     Council School.
1932 Union of Wesleyan and Primitive Methodist Churches.
1940 New Osmond pipe organ installed in church.
1954 Billy Graham's Greater London Crusade brought breath of
     life.
1979 Old school building sold.
1981 Church renovated; new rooms provided; organ overhauled.
1984 Red carpet laid.
1985 Turquoise upholstered seats replaced most of pews.

     In the early days the whole of Sunday was taken up with
services. Today we run two with difficulty. What has affected
the faith of our Church? In 1871 Charles Darwin declared that
man came from a primeval slime via the monkeys and that our
development results from the survival of the fittest. We sang,
"My faith looks up to Thee, Thou Lamb of Calvary". In the
1950's Bertrand Russell was extolling the power of man's
intellect. We sang, "If there is aught of worth in me, it comes
from Thee alone". In 1961 Yuri Gagarin ushered in the Space
Age. Science Fiction brought home the idea of hostile aliens
with super intelligence. We sang, "Jesus! the name high over
all, in hell or earth or sky". In 1988 the affluence of south-
east England fills our minds with thoughts of cars, travel, food
and drink, home extensions, furnishings and   continuous
entertainment. We sing, "O come to my heart, Lord Jesus; there
is room in my heart for Thee."

     What are our dreams of future deeds? Many believe that all
Christian churches should combine. Should our Lord's garden
contain only one flower? A church that believes in "salvation
full and free" has grass roots in a rugged independence of
spirit. John and Charles Wesley had both been ordained for ten
years before they were saved! I pray, "Lord, you have shown us
the Divine in three forms. Let us not waste Your time, trying
to unify the variety in your Church! Lord, give Your churches a
common task that can engage their full powers and make them
forget their differences!"

The Lord replies, "You are the light of the world. A church that is set upon a hill, cannot be hid." So that is why it is there!

NEWS FROM THE FRONT (1916)

All our men at the front seem to be aware of special protection. Here is an incident recorded by Private Tom Bird: "When I was leaving the trenches one night, being tired out and the bullets making my head split, coming along to some ruins to rest, I said a short prayer beneath my breath. As I was panting away and we took up our loads to go along the road, not a bullet passed for quite two miles distance; and yet other nights there had been about 200 cross the road, as I knew the road well." The latest from Tom is himself in a steel helmet! When he returns - please God he may! - we shall want a speech in foreign costume from him. In another place he says: "Things are going well with us out here but no-one can imagine the difficulties and hardships one passes through, in the course of a day. The danger, yet so far, yet so near - then in the spell of silence you say (only surprised at your own words), 'I am safe!' 'Thank God!' I have breathed out. It is like a Zepp raid lasting for days, not an hour. Still we work our guns."

(Rev) W. TERRY COPPIN

Stewards - Past and Present - May 1935.

| Tom. | John | Walter | Albert | John |
| Wright | Line | Hearne | Harris | House |

| William | George | William | Fred. |
| Judge | Thorne | Pollard | Fletcher |

THE STORY OF LANE END

When Lane End Village was but small
    One hundred years ago,
A man named Ramsey preached the word,
    As the old records show.

In course of time he wished to leave
    The work in other hands
And some of those who came to help,
    Were Wesleyan praying bands.

The cottage where the friends first met,
    Was close by the roadside
That leads to Marlow from Lane End,
    And still it does abide.

One local preacher on the spot
    (His name was Mr.Bird)
And other men of humble lot
    Came there to preach the word.

In eighteen hundred thirty four
    The chapel walls were raised.
There many souls were born again
    And God's dear name was praised.

We can't forget the big square pew
    Nor yet the candlestick;
For there are living still a few
    That heard the snuffers click.

As time rolled on, the place (so dear)
    For worship was too small;
The School and Church it grew so large,
    There was not room for all.

So steps were taken to secure
    Another piece of ground
On which the present church was built,
    Where ample room is found.

HENRY PLUMRIDGE (1920)

A LANE END SUNDAY

At 5 a.m. we met to pray
  And then again at 7,
Commencing well the sabbath day,
  To us the type of heaven.

At 9 we went to Sunday School,
  To sing and pray and teach,
And after that before 'twas noon,
  We heard God's servant preach.

To school again when we had dined,
  At 1.15 we went;
To feed once more the youthful mind,
  It was our best intent.

At 2.15 the school was closed
  And this was none too soon
For preaching service that was held
  On Sunday afternoon.

At 6 o'clock the chapel door
  Again was opened wide,
That all who chose, might come and hear
  Of Christ the crucified.

But this was not the closing up
  Of every sabbath day:
Before we journeyed home to sup,
  We stayed behind to pray."

                    HENRY PLUMRIDGE

WESLEYAN METHODIST CHURCHES

WHERE HAVE ALL THE PEOPLE GONE?

Since those days we have seen much change
  And not all for the best.
New people came and others left
  But where are all the rest?
For only twenty years ago
  I have been told it's true
These pews down here were quite full up
  And those up there were too.

Where did those other people go?
  Explain it to me please.
Whose fault was it? Could it be ours?
  Should we be on our knees?
Let's not lose heart: God's on our side
  How could we ask for more?
When we are weak, then He is strong;
  His love is always sure.

GEOFFREY LEWIS (1981)

Lane End's 150th Anniversary Celebrations - 1985

BLEDLOW RIDGE (1834)

S.SHERRATT NOV. 1987   BLEDLOW RIDGE.

REX ROGERS writes:

Bledlow Ridge Chapel was built in 1834 on ground given by the Marquis of Lincolnshire and consisted at first of a single room. The chapel was rebuilt in 1877. I knew an old man who as a ploughboy had helped bring the bricks by horse and cart from Lane End. This larger two-roomed building with gallery, kitchen and outside toilets was built to a wider plan and extended on to an additional narrow strip of land which was held leasehold. By the time I became steward and later trustee and treasurer, all knowledge of this had vanished although someone did remember "a ground-rent of one shilling [5p] per year". A few years ago we tried to find out the actual size of the ground from the County archives. No such records existed but we did discover that the lease had only two years to run! However Lord Carrington who had inherited the Marquis' land, kindly gave us the small strip of land - although it still cost £866 in legal fees for a Deed of Gift!

In 1964 Messrs W.A.Steevens extensively renovated the chapel. The gallery was sealed off into a small upstairs room. New flush-toilets were built, also a new kitchen with piped water - in place of the rainwater trough which had been the previous supply. The long pews were replaced by chairs and the high pulpit taken away. Electric lights replaced oil-lamps and electric heaters the coke-burning tortoise stoves. A new pulpit - given in memory of my eldest son who had been involved in a fatal accident -, Communion table and rail, organ screen and seat were fitted. All of these were made from the wood of sycamore trees grown by my father, a chapel steward for 50 years. The timber had been cut and stored by Mr. Steevens for 22 years. A certain amount of carpeting was also done and the ceiling lowered in the schoolroom where once, it is said, lace-making classes had been held. An account of all these renovations appeared not only in the "Bucks Free Press" but also in a B.B.C. programme. Rev. L.O. Brooker conducted the rededication service at which Wycombe's Member of Parliament, John Hall, was present.

The Loosley family was responsible for the music for the first 64 years of my life. James played the organ with his sons accompanying him on their violins. Harold took over until 1964 when he died. The chapel was in such a chaotic state that it couldn't be used for his funeral but later a thanksgiving service was held there. Since that time Francis Cross has served us at the organ.

We always had a large Sunday School (50 or more children at any one time). Hardly a child living in Bledlow Ridge had not attended at some time. A "Bucks Free Press" report in December 1910 states: "On Saturday last the Sunday School scholars connected with this place of worship enjoyed a free tea in the Schoolroom, a good muster being in attendance. After tea, time was made to fly all too quickly by a number of games in which such favourites as General Post, Turn the Trencher, and Minister's Cat took a prominent place. The teachers and friends in attendance must have been repaid for their labours when viewing the very evident enjoyment of the youthful band." Diminishing numbers in recent years have at least brought the bonus of closer co-operation with St. Paul's Church and occasional united services.

Preachers sometimes smile when I assure them, "The water in the pulpit is fresh!" This dates back to the time when one of our preachers (long forgotten), claimed that the water in one of our chapels (also long forgotten) had green algae on the top of it and another preacher had threatened to put a small fish in it!   Of course we hill-folk did have a reputation for drinking pond-water. Not many churches can claim to have an animal on their roll. Our chapel used to have railings around it and the grass was grazed by a local donkey. Alas, railings, donkey and a good many humans too have long since disappeared.

BEACONSFIELD (1838)

This Church was in existence in 1838 and a chapel was situated in Queen's Terrace, Windsor End. In about 1850 it joined the Wesleyan Reform Union (Free Methodists).

HOLMER GREEN (1841)

Rebuilt 1859. Demolished 1937

MARGARET MORRIS writes:

Methodism in Holmer Green began in 1822 when services were held in a cottage. When this became too small, part of our present site was purchased in 1841 for £7 and a small chapel was built for £53. Most people at that time were engaged in farming, chair-making, straw plaiting or tambour beading. Some

were busy making tennis racquets! Adjacent land was purchased
for £15 in 1859 and the chapel rebuilt. The first harmonium
appeared in 1881.

Ralph Stevens who was born in 1888, recalled being carried
to Church by his father who started the Sunday School in 1890.
School lasted two hours in the morning; one hour in the
afternoon before the service. A building fund was started and
people saved as little as one penny each week. Our present hall
was built in 1912 and cost £310. It opened free of debt. At
this time Holmer Green was made up of about 65 scattered houses
and a single shop. Gypsies were constantly driven away but one
family of tinkers was allowed to remain as they sold pots and
pans. Earl Howe had his land enclosed. Once in the First World
War a German airship passed over Holmer Green.

There were no buses in the 1920's so preachers walked or
cycled. Evening services usually attracted about 60 people.
Ralph Stevens, Albert James and Will Pursey accompanied the
harmonium with their violins and Jack Pursey played the cello.
The village orchestra practised in the church and violins were
supplied to the children at ten shillings [50p.] each. A local
farm stored the removable stage. Once when it was needed, the
farmer had just had a ton of hay delivered on top of it! Water
came from a local well.

From 1870 seats could be rented but this was superseded by the envelope scheme in 1932. In 1928 the trustees decided to subscribe five shillings [25p.] annually to the "Worn-out Ministers' Fund"! Some had to sign with a cross. The new Methodist Hymn Book was bought for use in 1934.

By the 1930's the church was in poor condition and much too small. The ventilation was so poor that on a hot Sunday afternoon an exasperated elderly man put his foot through a window-pane! A new church (much larger but still compact) was finally opened after several years of fund-raising, in 1937. Mr.Wingrove's daughter's wedding was the first in the new church; Colin Haddock was the first baby to be baptised.

This lament for the old orchestra was written in 1937:

The old organ's finished; the new one's in place;
    The chapel has now got a different face.
The new one, complete with its power and might,
    Will now give to many both joy and delight.
But to some, like Will Pursey, old Ralph and the rest,
    The old one will somehow still seem to be best.
For sabbath by sabbath - for years, don't you know? -
    They've sat by the old one with fiddle and bow,
Helping in this way to swell the great chorus
    With many and many who've gone on before us.
We shall all miss the strains of their fiddles no doubt,
    As we realise now they will have to sit out.
But we thank them sincerely for the help they have been
    In fiddling for Jesus at beloved Holmer Green.

A Church choir was formed in 1950 and a new organ was bought for £2000 in 1956. The cradle roll commenced in 1958 with nine children. A Women's Meeting was also formed. The trustee's list for 1954 includes many well known names:

Frank Howland	Horace William Wright
Norman William Charles Bayliss	Arthur John Peatey
Norman Gardiner	Ralph Stevens
Bert Saunders	Henry Wingrove
Alfred Richard Coppock	Ronald Daniel Nicholls
Arthur Nicholls	Sidney Frank James
Albert James	William Parker
William Leonard James	William George Pursey
Florence Howland	Freda Payne
Eva Lawrence	Connie Bayliss

A building fund was started for new classrooms. After many gift days, bazaars and concerts the extensions were completed in 1967.

Life in Holmer Green has changed greatly over recent years. Many new houses have been built. From the period of the wartime evacuees the population has tended to "float" and is no longer so close-knit. This has had a bad effect on the life of the Church in some ways but it has also inspired new activities for young people. A pre-school playgroup began in 1967. Youth clubs have been started and in 1972 a Boys' Brigade Company was inaugurated. The old pulpit has been removed and the Communion area (with a smaller movable pulpit) opened up. At family services many of the children have to be squeezed into this space. In 1987 Holmer Green Girl Guides started to meet in our hall. Only future generations will be able to judge how far we have succeeded in our desire to serve God and the community.

BOOKER (1847)

In 1845 Jonathan Fryer and Daniel Smith held an open-air service on Booker Common and after several such meetings they began to use a cottage. In 1847 Mr.Giles gave a plot of land adjoining the common and on this the church was built. The first trustees were Jonathan Fryer, Samuel Giles, Daniel Smith and Samuel Hawes and the cost was £78.

REMINISCENCES OF GEORGE SEYMOUR (1844-1939)

I was born at Booker, when Booker was then and for some time after, a benighted place. There was no school, no Church, no Chapel. The common was the arena where they fought out their quarrels. I have a vivid recollection of seeing a bunch of men coming across the common. When they got to a certain place they stopped, and two of them stripped off their shirts and fought. This sort of thing was often seen at Booker, so much so, one man said if any one came to Booker he must expect to fight or run.

If the children went to Sunday School they had to go to West Wycombe Church. Then about this time Methodism came in and began to hold services in a cottage near the present Chapel, occupied by Samuel Beasley, the village shoe-maker. Soon after this, in the year 1847, a small Chapel was built mostly of flint

collected by the people for the purpose, and was opened in 1848.
A society was formed, but there was no one in the place to lead
the class, so a man from West Wycombe walked up every Sunday
morning to lead it. A Sunday School was started. As I was now
four years old, I was one of the earliest scholars. The first
thing I can remember about it is a rap on my finger with a cane
which caused a gathering on my poor little finger. The next
thing I can remember is being lifted on to a table to give a
recitation at the Sunday School anniversary for which I received
a Bible as a reward, in which the date is written May 1852.

As my birthday came in November, I was then seven years
old. I then went to work minding the pigs in the stubble
field, for one shilling a week. I had to go on Sundays for
which I received dinner. That took me away from Sunday School
for a time. When I returned, my teacher said I got worse in my
reading. I then went to another farm as shepherd boy for four
years. Still I went to the Sunday School, but in those days,
out in the field alone, I was lonely and hungry. The day seemed
as long as a week. I often ate all before 10 o'clock in the
morning. I formed bad habits and was a bad boy, but I had a
good mother - she was a Christian according to the light and
knowledge that she possessed - poor, but honest as steel. She
would deny herself to the outside limit to pay for what she had.
When I was quite a child, I stole a farthing. Going into my

sister's house as I often did, being next house, I saw a farthing on the table. I took it and ran out unto the common to the sweet shop. I got my sweets and was coming out when I saw my mother coming to meet me with one hand behind her. She had a little stick in her hand to teach me a lesson that "it is a sin to steal a pin, much more a bigger thing". Whatever may be thought of it, I honour my mother for that lesson which I have never forgotten. My father used to go to West Wycombe Church on Sunday morning, and mother used to go for the afternoon service. My father wanted me to be confirmed, but as he did not press it, I never went to confirmation.

After my four years as shepherd boy, my brother who had joined the society in the cottage before the chapel was built, had already got in to the chair-making, so he took me with him to the chair-making, so that I continued in the Sunday School. I was now twelve years old, and was able to attend Sunday School more regular. Mr.Wane, a farmer, rendered some help in the school at the time. He was a Baptist, and drove down to Wycombe on Sunday mornings for the service at the Baptist Church, but he rented a pew in the Booker Chapel, and attended some of the services. Mr. Joseph Blackwell, another farmer, also rented a pew and attended the services. For some years they lived at Clay Lane Farm, and the family attended the services at the chapel until they left the farm.

Mr.Henry Goldswain and his wife now lived in the cottage where the services were first held, and as they were ardent Methodists, they took a great interest in the cause. Mr. Goldswain was Chapel Steward for many years, and they took the preacher to tea almost every Sunday for a long time, and were among the chief regular supporters. Mrs. Goldswain was a very great help in the prayer meetings. She had a remarkable gift for public prayer, and for praying with the sick and dying. Her pleading with them and for them seemed almost compelling in its power with God. She prayed and wrestled with God like Jacob when he said "I will not let Thee go except thou bless me". Although she was not strong herself, if she was told that some one was very ill, or likely to die, she would if possible go at any time night or day. Truly it would be said of her, "As you did it to one of the least of these my brethren ye did it unto me. Enter Thou into the joy of thy Lord".

I was now 14 years old, and it was arranged to hold some special services to try and bring in some of the elder scholars to give their hearts to God and live the Christian life. These services were somewhat successful. William Batson, a farm labourer used to attend. He then lived at Handy Cross. He was a very earnest and powerful man in a prayer meeting. He had voice in singing, and brought life and power into meetings. The boys and girls were so affected that they decided to give their hearts to God and live for Jesus. It was at this time that I with some others was persuaded to join the class and become members of society as it was then called. Having obtained help of the Lord, I continued until this day still holding my membership in the Methodist Church in the High Wycombe circuit. "By the grace of God I am what I am."

At this time there was a very notable conversion took place. A man about 30 years old, a big rugged strong man possessing physical strength of two ordinary men, he was a hard drinker and a great fighter, but he gave up the drink, and I don't think he ever tasted it again all his life. Instead of fighting, he became a little child and went into the Sunday School and sat with the children in the infants class to learn the A.B.C. James Smith, for that was his name, became one of the most devoted members of the little chapel, a great help in the Sunday School and in the weekly prayer meetings. He always took part both in prayer and in singing with a voice that could be heard out on the common. He could give out his verse of hymn from memory:

> "Oh that I could for ever sit
> With Mary at the Master's feet!
> Be this my happy choice,
> My only care, delight and bliss,
> My joy, my heaven on earth be this-
> To hear the Bridegroom's voice".

At the anniversary, I and another boy was chosen for a dialogue for which I received as a reward a copy of Bunyan's "Pilgrims Progress" the reading of which impressed me very much. I could not understand it, but it made me want to know more about the writer of that book, so that I never missed reading anything that came in my way about John Bunyan. Some time after this, a man came round to the shop where I was working, to try and sell the works of John Bunyan in one shilling [5p.] numbers, so I said I would take them, 32 numbers I got bound in one large volume. Coming home from work one evening I met Mrs Goldswain; she looked at the book and said "So then you are going to be the pilgrim". I have always regarded John Bunyan as one of the most remarkable men that God ever raised up and to preach, and the greatest help to me in my Christian life and preaching. Out of the darkness of Bedford gaol there came forth one of the most wonderful books that was ever written, "The Pilgrims Progress".

WESLEYAN METHODIST CHURCHES

In those early days of Methodism at Booker, the poor singing was a great draw-back to the services. There was no one in the place that knew anything about music. Someone would start a tune and pitch it too high and have to give it up. Very often a hymn was given out that they had no tune for, and so another hymn had to be chosen. James Seymour was the most dependable man to pitch the tunes. He got someone that he worked with to learn him some tunes while at work, so that in time he could sing a good number of them. By getting some of the eldest boys and girls to sit with him in a corner pew to help him in the services, he brought about some improvement in the matter of the singing.

About this time the chapel was enlarged and a gallery was added. I don't know the date, I think it was about ten years after the chapel was built, 1857 or 1858. Now that we had got into the gallery we began to think we should like to bring some instrumental music into our singing, but this must need take time, because no one around us had any knowledge of music, so one and another began to learn the A.B.C. of music. One or two tried the violin, another the flute, and so after a time we managed to get a violin to lead the singing. Eventually some more instruments came along, but our singing was all treble, we had no bass, and no one attempted to sing bass, so that if bass is the foundation of music, then our singing was without foundation. In order to get some bass into the singing of the hymns, I bought a cello. I got some instructions from Mr Samuel Collins of Downley who wrote me out a scale for fingering, and stuck it under the strings of the cello, so that I could see where to place the fingers to make the notes. He invited me to his home and gave me some lessons. After some long time I was able to bring a little, though very imperfect, bass into the singing. John Parker, a lawyer of High Wycombe, owned property at Booker, and contributed ten shillings [50p.] a year to the Sunday School funds. When his daughter came of age, he gave the children of the school a tea out among the trees on the common. I took my cello out to help in some singing, and so I got a lesson from John Parker. He played the double bass at the Congregational Church at High Wycombe.

I was now about 16 years old, and while I was yet a scholar in the Bible Class, the teachers' meeting appointed me to be one of the teachers of the same class, not that I was at all competent, but it just goes to show the lack of workers at that time. I now began to feel the need of self-improvement in reading. My time was fully occupied, so that I found it difficult to find time for all that was needed to be done. I

took the "Christian World" weekly paper, read a fine sermon in
it every week, and got a dictionary to study the words that were
beyond me. Then I had to practice the cello, and as we had but
one copy of many of our tunes, I had to copy out one for my own
use, which took me some considerable time to accomplish. I took
in the "Sunday School Times" to help me in the teaching in the
Sunday School class. So with a game of cricket now and again on
the common, my time was fully taken up. We had Sunday morning
class meeting at half past nine, Sunday School at half past ten,
and half past one in the afternoon. Sunday public services at
half past two in the afternoon, and 6 o'clock in the evening.
We had Prayer Meeting every Monday evening, and preaching
service Tuesday evening once a fortnight when we had one of the
Ministers appointed.

I used to have a very great respect for the Local Preachers
that came Sunday after Sunday to preach the gospel to the
people. I thought it must be a very great honour to occupy such
a position. I never dreamed at that time that I should ever be
a Local Preacher to occupy such a lofty position, and to do as
these men were now doing. In the class meeting on Sunday
morning we used always to pray for the preacher that was coming
to preach, that God would give him both matter and wisdom, seals
for his ministry and souls for his hire, such as would be the
crown of His rejoicing.

Having occupied the gallery for some time now, we were
able to get a few young women to join a small choir and occupy
the front seat. We were able to buy a couple of what was called
"The Union Tune Book" for our use in the chapel. Some time
after, we got some copies of hymn tunes composed by Cornelius
Ward of Speen. We struggled on, but did not attain to anything
like proficiency in the musical part of our services. As we got
some little help from Lane End and Downley, we were able to get
up some special singing for the Sunday School Anniversary every
year from this time. Some time after this, Mr. W. Youens of
High Wycombe composed some simple anthems for village choirs,
which after some little time we were able to bring into our
Sunday services. I was now about 19, and had been appointed one
of the Superintendents of the Sunday School.

What I have written will give some idea of the beginning
and development of Methodism at Booker, and the class of people
who did the work. Before any important house is to be built, a
great deal of work has to be done in clearing the ground and
digging the earth away for the foundation. This is hard work,
it is not done by skilled workmen, but by labourers. Men with

hard hands, heavy boots and coarse clothing, using pick and spade, shovel and wheelbarrow, work that is out of sight. Because it is not seen, the work is often forgotten or thought little of. But it is very important work hidden under the noble building that has been built upon it. It is not noticed or thought of by those who look upon that which is now built upon it and under which it is now buried out of sight. But the Architect and the Master-builder knows how very important the foundation work must always be, because there can be no substantial building without a good foundation. So much of the hard work in connection with the Church of God in this world has been done by humble men and women whose names have never been known beyond their own surrounding, because their work did not stand out to public view. But the great Architect and Master-builder of His own church Who has a perfect knowledge of all the work that has been done, will not forget the humble men and women who have been working unnoticed and unknown, loved and prized by God alone. He will not forget their work of faith and labour of love, and although their work may now be lost sight of, the great Master-builder knows the importance of the work they have done. It shall certainly be said of all such "Well done thou good and faithful servant, enter thou into the joy of thy Lord".

We had about 60 children in the Sunday School at this time, and used to give them their annual treat on Wycombe Fair day as that was the farm labourers' annual holiday, and everybody went to the Fair. It was thought it would keep the elder scholars from going to the Fair. Each child had to bring a cup in which to have its tea. Then, in order to meet the expense of the chapel, at Whitsun a monster tea meeting was arranged, as that was one of the chair-makers' holidays. Three to four hundred people were served with tea in Mr. Goldswain's orchard. A large quantity of cups and saucers were bought for the purpose, each cup having a picture of John Wesley on it. This crockery was supplied by the late Mr. T. E. Dukes of Marlow, who was at that time one of our local preachers. You can very well fancy that there was some work to be done on such an occasion. It would be no small undertaking to get provisions and provide accommodation for say three hundred. We never knew how many would come along, so it meant work for all the volunteers we could get for the full day from early morning - women for cutting up the bread and butter, the men for fitting up the tables and seats in the orchard. How to get good water for the tea was a difficult matter. The men would have to go with buckets and yokes three times in the morning, good part of a mile to get water. But all this was a work of love, so we lost the duty in the joy because it was set to music, sometimes to singing, but all the time to the music of the heart so that we enjoyed our happy toil that day as much as the young people of the present day enjoy their games of different sorts.

As one of the Superintendents of the Sunday School, I often had to give the address to the children and sometimes in the afternoon service. In the absence of the violin I had to start the tunes with the cello. So under such conditions the development of the Methodist cause at Booker must of necessity be very slow. As there was no increase in the population, no houses being built in the village, and as the children passed through the Sunday School they had to get away to find employment. The work at the little chapel seemed to be almost at a standstill, just holding enough of the elder boys and girls to carry on the school, notably the young people of the Sherwood family, the Crook family, the Piercey family and a few others.

November 24th. 1865 I was 21 years old. April 2nd. 1866 I was married to Elizabeth Fane who had been with me in the Sunday School and in the singing in the services from the beginning. We continued to live at Booker for about four years after we were married, and then moved to High Wycombe. I had been a member of the society at Booker eleven years, and now I transferred my membership to the Wesley Society, High Wycombe. I often went to Booker on the Sunday to help in the school and play the cello in the services. I continued to do this for about four or five years. Then Henry Crook brought the small harmonium into the services which he and his brother James Crook had learned to play. The harmonium now took the place of the cello which was no longer needed, so I retired from my so far lifelong connection with the Booker Sunday School. But not to forget - no not as long as I live - because I feel that all that is best in my life I owe to the fact that by the grace of God, the Lord Jesus Christ was brought into my life when I was 14 years old, very largely by the prayers and efforts of the humble men and women who were pioneers of Booker Methodism.

My friends at Booker had for some time wanted me to preach, but I had hitherto held back from that work. Now as I had got a little more time on my hands, somehow or other I was persuaded to try. They got me to take a service at Booker chapel. At the next Local Preachers' Meeting my name was brought up. I received a note from the Superintendent Minister asking me to preach. That was the December Quarterly Meeting in 1877, the Rev. J.W. Browne was then the Superintendent Minister of the circuit. When the next Plan came out, I had a Plan given to me with a note from the Super which read: "Please go to Lane End with Mr.Woodbridge such a date, please go with Mr.Hussey to Victoria such a date, please go to Bledlow Ridge with Mr. Nash such a date".   At the next Local Preachers' Meeting it was decided that my name should come on the next Plan.   That was April 1878, my name appeared "ON TRIAL"   My first appointment was at Prestwood.

FRANK PEARCE writes:

For the present church a bazaar was held in the Wesley schoolroom.   The sum of £175.13s.3d. raised. The stone-laying took place on Easter Tuesday 1886 when a further £94.10s.0d. was raised.   In 1907 the schoolroom was added.   Booker was now part of the High Wycombe Circuit. The church became the main meeting place for the village and I remember many families who rendered valuable service, such as the Sherwood, Silvey, Dean, Piercey, Burnham, Pearce, Saunders, Seymour, Wheeler and Stevens families.   William Murcott conducted the choir and orchestra and taught many of its members the violin.   Another memory is the purchase of a new pipe organ for which a special committee under Fred Welford (chairman) and Mrs.J.Saunders (treasurer) was formed in 1948.   The target was   £7000.   After Whit Monday fetes and other efforts we were able to install it in 1953.

Over the years the Church has passed through good periods – and bad when it looked as if it would have to close.   For the past eight years it has been a happy, successful Church with sound finances.   Membership has grown from seven to 22.   Sunday services now have an average attendance of 30 and on special occasions the chapel is full.   This is due not least to the welcome given for many years by Ron and Jean Stevens.   Charlie Ager keeps the church garden looking beautiful; Violet Wheeler organises coffee mornings; the Booker Flower Club supplies and arranges flowers for every Sunday; the Sunday School which had to close due to a lack of scholars and teachers, has been reopened by Ken and Rosemarie Acton.   From 1980 to 1987 we enjoyed the services and help of our Minister, Rev.Keith Phipps, and his wife, Lynda, who have now moved to Sunderland.   I hope they will have many happy memories of Booker!

WINCHMORE HILL (1861)

METHODIST CHURCH WINCHMORE HILL   1988 S.SHERRATT

The Wesleyan society here first met in 1818. By 1860 there was urgent need for a chapel. The "Bucks Free Press" reported: "The society in Winchmore Hill has enjoyed the privileges and blessings of a preached gospel; but the time has come in which it is necessary for the convenience of the families and community in that neighbourhood to have another place for the enjoyment of their religious privileges; and the very liberal offer of Mr. E. Bovington of a suitable and eligible site, has induced the friends in the place and the High Wycombe circuit to resolve on the erection of a new Wesleyan Chapel. Last Monday 20th August 1860 was fixed upon for the first meeting to envisage means by which the above object should be accomplished. The weather was exceedingly propitious. The friends from nearly all parts of the circuit manifested their attachment and concern by their numerous attendance and liberal contributions to the good cause. About 400 partook of tea in Mrs. Butcher's two large barns, well fitted up for the occasion, after which the chapel committee repaired to the site to take the plan and dimensions of the ground. That being done, the public meeting was held in the largest barn in which was erected a spacious platform for the speakers and where the listening crowd manifested their earnest attention to the appropriate addresses all of which were

of an animating and congratulatory character, and it was
manifest to all that "the people had a mind to work", as the
donations and collection amounted to about £65, being the first
effort to present the Winchmore Hill Society and the Wesleyan
Conference with a new sanctuary free of financial incumbrance."
The chapel opened in 1861. After the "Deed of Union" (1932)
services were held in this chapel and the Primitive chapel on
alternate Sundays. It was left to the members to decide which
should be closed. The lot fell on this one and it was sold to
the Church of England. It is now disused and in a sadly
neglected state.

PRESTWOOD (1863)

ANNIE GIBBS writes:

     In 1861 a few Methodists met together in a private house.
Later they obtained the use of a skittle alley in the old
"Traveller's Rest" inn where they held meetings. After a time
they decided to build a chapel. Mr.W.Cartwright of Flint
Cottage, grandfather of Mr.W.O.Haines of Peterley Wood, gave a
piece of land for a site in the High Street. The conveyance of

this land is dated 15th April 1863. Much willing help went into the building but no proper foundation was laid. The shell was made of bricks and stones many of which were gathered by the women from local fields. The cost was £130 and it was licensed as a Wesleyan place of worship on 8th September 1863. At first there was no flooring, pews or pulpit. Straw was spread on the earth and people sat on forms borrowed from the local inn. Flooring was added in 1865 along with pews and pulpit at a cost of £60. Alterations were made in 1869 when a gallery was built, the ironwork for the front of which was made by Benjamin Hildreth, and a larger pulpit replaced the original one. On 18th September 1872 a foundation stone for a schoolroom was laid by Mr.Glenister. The collection at the evening meeting amounted to £42. The cause grew and as the site was felt to be restricted, an extra piece of land was purchased for £35 the conveyance for which is dated 31st December 1907.

Music is a valuable aid to Methodist worship and in the early days several members led the singing on violins. The first harmonium was bought in 1892 for £5 and a choir was started, rendering a service of song, "Bells across the snow", on Christmas Day 1902 - with 50 people sitting down to a good tea afterwards! Many choirmasters carried on the work until the Second World War. Our last three organists have given a total of 70 years' service. The present organ, opened on 1st January 1920, was a memorial to the men of Prestwood who died in the First World War. By the close of the service £142 had been raised towards the £150 needed. On 12th October 1926 the opening ceremony for the new schoolroom took place. Rev.E.J.Bennett-Richards, the Superintendent Minister, Rev.E.D.Green, Chairman of the District, and Mr.R. Goodearl took part. The cost was £600 most of which was raised by Miss L. Addison, sister of Lord Addison. Several missions were held and many conversions took place. But the old ex-Primitive chapel in Great Missenden fell on hard times and closed in 1938. Four members transferred to Prestwood.

In 1951 a new circuit hived off from High Wycombe, was formed - to be known as the "Chesham & Chalfonts Circuit" and including Prestwood. Centenary celebrations took place in 1963 when the ex-President of Conference, Rev. Maldwyn Edwards, conducted services for crowded congregations. As Prestwood was rapidly ceasing to be a small village, it was felt that a new hall should be built on adjoining ground for Church and community use. A fund was started in 1965. Before he left Prestwood, our Minister had helped to raise £5000 which enabled us to go forward with the project. The foundation stone was laid by Mrs.F.Clarke on 11th November 1972.

The new hall was opened on 9th June 1973 and was free of debt. Mr.R.Daykin, the former treasurer, performed the opening ceremony and the sermon was given by Rev.Tony Bullock who had done so much to help. The cost was £18,500 and many now felt that a new church building also was needed in view of the decaying state of the present one and to accommodate the growing congregation. But costs were rising rapidly and a decision was shelved. Work was finally carried out in 1977 to alter the building and make a new structure, including a new staircase and chancel. The old pulpit was remodelled and the total cost was £23,000. The old schoolroom was decorated by volunteers. The church was reopened on 16th July 1977 when over 200 people attended and Rev.R.L.J.Kaye, former Superintendent Minister of the High Wycombe Circuit and now Chairman of the District, gave the address. So Prestwood has been enabled to continue its mission of serving God and its neighbours.

FLACKWELL HEATH (1865)

DEREK WALKER writes:

A Wesleyan society first met in Flackwell Heath in 1822. In 1832 Mr.Wright of Swains Lane built a room for them to use on Sundays and for a school during the week. Preachers' horses were stabled in a farm on the common behind "The Three Horseshoes". The tune-pitcher - this was before the days of the organ - ensured the hymn did not go beyond the congregation's vocal range, while the candle-snuffer kept the lighting under control. The church moved to its present site at the junction of Heath End Road in 1865 and could accommodate 100 worshippers. The cost was £276 and there were 18 members. The new chapel had a gallery with a vestry underneath and a pulpit opposite. A harmonium and paraffin lamps were installed.

By 1883 the membership had grown to 50 out of a circuit total of 633 and on 20th March 1884 an extended building, seating 200, was opened at a cost of £521.22 towards which the Duke of Westminster subscribed £10. Families could pay an annual "seat-rent" to ensure pews for their families every Sunday. The Sunday School met in the church, the boys in the gallery flicking holly berries at Christmas on to the girls below. The teacher faced his class who sat on pews, and delivered a prepared talk. Ernest Whopshott was the most popular because of his wealth of stories which he told in an imaginative way. Outings were to Burnham Beeches or West Wycombe Hill. When going to the former, the horses and their drivers would be thirsty by the time they reached the bottom of White Hill where there was a convenient hostelry. George Bryant who had a shop opposite the church, used to set up a stall at the Beeches selling sweets and novelties. A "scramble" of sticky boiled sweets was invariably won by the boys! At West Wycombe which meant an exciting rail journey from Loudwater, sledging and donkey rides were the main attractions.

In 1923 a schoolroom was built and accommodated (among others) a Bible Class of 40. Children loved sitting next to George Burnham, a huge man both in stature and character, because he always carried a good supply of peppermints! His daughter, Louie Collins, was the organist in whose memory a stained glass window was placed in 1952. George's son, Rev.Alfred Burnham, who had been a missionary, lived in Fennels Way and was a beloved supernumary Minister who - as the brass plate in his memory says - "went about doing good". As a memorial to his daughter, Joan, who died at the age of 27, the church hall was extended in 1948. By the time of his own death in 1959 an electric lighting and heating sytem had been fitted, also a sloping floor and blue tip-up seats. Later the gallery was blocked off. Youth work was now expanding rapidly and it was obvious that better premises were urgently needed. In 1980 it was decided to follow the same pattern that had been used at Stokenchurch Methodist Church where a big church had been converted into a small chapel and large hall. Huge efforts were made to raise £50,000, including the sale of 10,930 bars of chocolate! Significant rot problems (of buildings, not teeth!) and a leaning wall increased the cost to £84,000 but by the time of the dedication on 17th November 1984 the shortfall was only £4000. 12 kneelers were embroidered and upholstered by members of the congregation. The balcony is now opened up again and an intimate sanctuary seats 60 worshippers in semi-circles round a table. No longer is the preacher greeted in the pulpit which now stands to one side, by the old notice requesting him to complete the service by noon!

Ours is a "family" church, catering for all ages but with a particular emphasis on the young among whom there is a continuing evangelical work. A feature is the "Church Weekend Away" where we get to know one another better. The family is far flung and includes a former church steward, 25 year-old Roger Pettit, who is working as a missionary in Tanzania. In days past Anglican clergy used to use our church to robe up, before walking in procession to their own church. No longer an Anglican dressing-room, we work with them in more significant ways to extend God's kingdom at old "Frackell".

WESLEY, HIGH WYCOMBE (1866)

The Wesleyans had outgrown John Wesley's chapel in St. Mary Street. By the mid-nineteenth century, despite the addition of galleries, this building was no longer adequate for them. By negotiation with Lord Carrington a new site was acquired in Cemetery (Priory) Road in exchange for £400 cash, the chapel, a detached schoolroom, a house and two cottages. And thus at 11 a.m. on 3rd October 1865 a considerable company assembled at the chapel and processed solemnly to the site of the new church. The following year, under the direction of the builder (Mr.Edmund Pierce), for the sum of £5000 the church took shape to the plans of Wilson and Wilcox of Bath and was ready for Rev.William Shaw, President of Conference, to open for worship on 12th July 1866. Later Sunday School buildings were added and in 1893 enlarged, thus completing the work of construction.

LAYING THE FOUNDATION STONE - Tuesday October 3rd, 1865

Friends to meet in the Wesleyan Chapel, St.Mary's Street, at Eleven o'clock; procession to be formed at half-past Eleven as follows, viz:

1   The Worshipful the Mayor of the Borough
2   The Superintendent Minister and his Colleague
3   The Reverend the Ex-President of the Conference and the Chairman of the District
4   Other Ministers, two and two
5   Architect and Contractor
6   Friends specially invited, two and two
7   Both Circuit Stewards
8   Trustees, two and two
9   Society Stewards, two and two
10 Leaders and Local Preachers
11 Choir, two and two
12 Sunday School Conductors
13 Sunday School Teachers, two and two, with their Classes
14 Other Friends generally, two and two
15 On reaching the Site to form a segment of a circle, the Stone to be laid forming the centre
16 The Superintendent Minister to give out the 1st, 2nd, 3rd and 6th verses of the 526th Hymn, to be sung, Mr.F.Hill acting as Precentor
17 The Reverend the Chairman of the District to offer Prayer
18 The 737th Hymn to be sung
19 Appropriate Scripture by Rev.J.F.Raw
20 THE STONE TO BE LAID by THE RIGHT HONOURABLE LORD CARINGTON (sic) Lord Lieutenant of the County
21 The Reverend Ex-President of the Conference to address the assembly, followed by W.McArthur, Esq.
22 Opportunity given for anyone to lay Contributions on the Stone
23 The Benediction to be pronounced
24 "Praise God from whom all blessings flow" to be sung
25 Audience to be dismissed
26 Ministers and gentlemen will speak at the close of the Collation
    Public Tea at Five o'clock
    Public Meeting in the evening, to be presided over by the Worshipful the Mayor of the Borough. Friends are earnestly requested to come to our help.

GEORGE BUCKLEY, Superintendent Minister,
St.Mary's Street, September 30th, 1865
P.S. - Prayer Meeting at 8 a.m. in St.Mary's Street Chapel

OPENING SERVICES & EARLY DAYS

The opening services commenced on 12th July 1866 with a morning prayer meeting in the old building, followed by an afternoon service at Wesley at which the choir sang a Dedication Ode, specially written for the occasion by Miss Rachel Moorcock and set to music by Mr. William Youens. The sermon was preached by Rev. William Shaw, President of the Conference, whose text was Micah 6.8. There was a large gathering for tea in the Guildhall and in the evening Dr. Osborn preached from the text, "Other men laboured and ye are entered into their labours". About £50 was realized by the services of the day which concluded with a prayer meeting. In continuation of the series special services were conducted on the following Sunday by Rev. Richard Ray, Chairman of the Oxford District, and on Tuesday July 18th by Rev. Gervase Smith.

DEDICATION.

AN ODE,

TO BE SUNG AT THE OPENING OF THE

New Wesleyan Chapel,

HIGH WYCOMBE,

July 12th, 1866

O THOU, before whose throne
  The angels bow with reverential awe,
Shall we ! poor sinful worms, presume to draw
    Thy blessing down ?

Wilt Thou in very deed,
Thou whom the heaven of heavens cannot contain,
    Dwell with us here ?
Thou wilt. O not in vain
    With Thee we plead:

This temple, made with hands,
    We dedicate to Thee,—
A monument of grace it stands,
    O let us here Thy glory see ;
And when within these hallowed walls we meet,
Let the Shekinah beam above the mercy seat.

    Oft as we worship here,
When from this sacred altar shall arise
The morning or the evening sacrifice,
    Incline Thine ear.
And when Thou hearest, O do Thou forgive ;
Beneath Thy benediction may we live.

RACHEL MOORCOCK.

The temporary palisading which at first enclosed the grounds, gave place later to the present dwarf wall, iron fence etc. the plans for which were prepared by Messrs. Hutchinson and Son, and the cost of the work was almost entirely defrayed by the Ladies' Sewing Meeting. The Sunday School met initially in the old chapel, then in the Guildhall and later in the Wesley Chapel galleries until the school buildings behind the church, built to designs by Mr. Arthur Vernon, were completed and occupied. The font which stands within the communion enclosure, was presented by the Ladies' Sewing Meeting, in commemoration of the centenary of Wesley's death (1891). Alterations and renovations have been executed at various times, notably in 1904 when £800 was expended on floor, walls and roof, the whole cost being met by means of an eminently successful bazaar in the Town

Hall in 1905. Again early in 1916 certain parts of the stone work have had to be renewed.

During the past 50 years we have been favoured with the services of 43 Ministers, all proclaiming the same gospel and seeking to extend the kingdom of God. There have been seasons of dearth and decrease; again there have been times of refreshing from the Lord, as for instance during the ministry of Rev. Joseph Little in the church's early days. At a Sunday School meeting the Superintendent was inspired with a very forceful message to the younger teachers and monitors which made a deep impression on the minds of many. During the week two of these young men agreed to accept the Minister's invitation the coming Sunday evening to publicly declare their desire for salvation. The compact was kept and upwards of 20 young men and women followed their example at the service. The work continued and effected the attachment of a large number to the membership of the church. The anniversary of that movement was celebrated regularly for more than 30 years and scarcely ever without manifest tokens of God's presence and saving power.

Again towards the close of 1871, an accident having disabled Rev. John Skerratt, Rev. Ralph Green was sent to supply and God greatly blessed his work among us. Not only here at Wesley but throughout the Circuit signs and wonders were wrought and scores gave themselves to the Lord. Would to God such a movement might mark the commencement of the second half-century in this House of Prayer!

EDWIN WELLER (1916)

JUBILEE CELEBRATION (1916)

The Jubilee of Wesley Church, Priory Road, was celebrated with fitting appropriateness on Wednesday July 12th. There was a service in the afternoon when Rev. R. C. Gillie M. A. (of Marylebone Presbyterian Church and Moderator of the North London Presbytery) preached an eloquent sermon from the text, "As far as the East is from the West, so far hath He removed our transgressions from us". Tea for visitors was provided in the schoolroom. A public meeting was held in the evening under the presidency of Sir John Thomas J. P. , supported by Revs. R. C. Gillie and H. J. Quilter, W. Terry Coppin and A. T. Dean (Circuit Ministers). Before addressing the meeting himself, Sir John Thomas called upon Rev. H. J. Quilter who had to leave early to catch a train.

Rev.H.J.Quilter who was a minister in the Wycombe Circuit in 1885-7, began by alluding to changes which had taken place in his family after leaving this circuit to take charge of the Woking Circuit. He was pleased to renew acquaintance with his friends in Wycombe. From all parts of the Circuit he had been pleased to meet his friends and to receive their hearty handshake. Referring to the work of the Church, Mr.Quilter remarked that what he felt they wanted more than ever was the living Christ - that full dedication of heart and soul to Jesus Christ their Saviour and a greater interest in the work of God.

Rev.W.T.Coppin explained that although some of the former Ministers of the circuit could not be present that day, they had sent their kindliest greetings. In making the arrangements for that celebration, they had not forgotten that the late Lord Carrington laid the foundation of their Church, and they wrote to the Marquis of Lincolnshire, inviting him to be present. His Lordship was detained in London by Parliamentary duties but he sent his best wishes to the congregation and friends at Wesley in their great work. Mr.Coppin quoted extracts from Dr.W.J.Dawson, a Minister of the Circuit from 1880-2, who wrote from Newark, New Jersey and expressed his hearty congratulations upon the Jubilee Celebration.

The Chairman said he put this question to himself: "What ought to be the influence of the erection of a building like this in any town or place?" Such a building was not simply an ornament to the neighbourhood or a place in which to meet, but it was a Christian Church. It was a centre for work, for blessing and responsibility. No-one of them could live in a neighbourhood where there was a centre for Christian work without feeling that they had a responsibility in that work. Let them go home that night, feeling intensely thankful for the blessings of the past but let them resolve to go on with the work because there was still much work to be done as the world had not yet been won for Christ. Rev.R.C.Gillie took as his theme "Lessons of the past" which throbbed with encouragement and our duty to the future which demanded our highest faith and service. It was a noble address. It was a sermon for preachers and for everyone bearing Christ's name.

(Rev.)A.T.DEAN

PETER FOX writes:

During more than two centuries of its existence - in St.Mary Street and Priory Road - Wesley has seen as many changes in its congregation as in its buildings. In the early days those who claimed to be Methodists were considered "enthusiasts" of no great consequence, to be treated with contempt or ridicule. By the end of the 19th century Wesley was a "fashionable" Church, supported by pillars of local society. One former member had the following to say about its character in the early years of this century: "We arrived in High Wycombe just after Easter 1916. Father had been there several weeks, staying with a local preacher, William Saunders, and his wife in West End Road. They introduced us to Wesley. It was an elite Church in those days as a number of chair factory owners and their wives were members, together with other well-known people in the town. Most of Priory Road and Priory Avenue went there and this was the monied area at the time. The membership was nearly all local and Wesley was the in-place. It was not particularly friendly until YOU had made the effort to get to know people. My parents went for three weeks without being spoken to, so my mother took the matter into her own hands and spoke to several folk. From then on it was easier. The Minister was Rev.W.T.Coppin but he was at the top and not very approachable - it took time!

"There was a very large Sunday School which filled the upper hall. It was very proud to be known as the first Sunday School and the Anniversary was the crown of the year, always having a crowded congregation for the three services and the Monday concert. There used to be an annual bazaar which was opened by a bevy of Sunday School scholars who had to pay 2/6d.[12½p.] each for the privilege; I was never one of them as we couldn't afford it. Another special day was the Treat which took place in Loakes Park. It began with a parade through the town with a band and our banners flying. On Sunday mornings the Sunday School filled the gallery - boys on one side and girls on the other. The organ which was pumped by hand, was in the back of the gallery, played by William Crook or his son Hubert. The choir sat in front of them and membership was by invitation and an annual subscription of 2/6d [12½p.]."

Other older members have also commented on the social character of the Church at this time. One remarked that on Sunday evenings the gallery was full of the furniture firms' employees who were present for two reasons; it was important to be seen at church by one's employer; also the fire at home could be extinguished in the afternoon and fuel saved, as one sang hymns in a warm chapel! Wesley played an important part in the social life of the town. In 1929 the Springtime Bazaar used the entire facilities of the Town Hall for two days and involved the Scouts as parcel carriers throughout the locality.

The Church also ran many celebrity concerts in the same building. There was an active tennis club with courts behind the church and in Priory Avenue. A small group formed a concert party known as "The Goslings", which gave performances throughout the area. As one reads the programmes, one wonders whether Wesley's social life tended to obscure its original evangelical objectives.

As we look forward to a transformation of our old buildings ready for the needs of the 21st century, perhaps we are nearer now in purpose to those who began the society. Over recent years the combination of natural decay and arson has focused attention on whether we still need a Methodist witness in the centre of the town. If John Wesley's call to discipleship and his message of salvation remains relevant, it will need to find new expression related to the needs of the present age. On the 250th anniversary of his conversion experience it must be our prayer that we will be alive to the Holy Spirit and sensitive to God's guidance in bringing the message of His Son to High Wycombe.

THE ORGAN

1876   Organist - Jonathan Plumridge

1885   Organ purchased from Ossett (Yorks.) Methodist Church for £120; Rev.Clement S.Reader gave opening recital.

1896   Organist - B.Woodbridge

1907   Organist - W.E.Crook

1922   Organ rebuilt. Plaque reads:
"This organ was erected to the Glory of God and in memory of those who fell in the Great War, 1914-1918.

George J.Ball	Arthur J.Bass
Frederick J.Coombes	Frank W.Elliott
Henry Eccles	Clifford J.P.Goodearl
Joseph B.Eccles	Rupert V.Goodearl
William C.Harman	Eric Hodgkinson
Stanley W.Powell	C.Frederick Rose
Walter J.Smith	F.Harry Turner
Joseph H.Varney	George W.Venables"

1942   Organist - Kenneth T.Fox

1948 and 1965   Organ improved.

1978   Organ rebuilt and added to (ten stops of original instrument retained); cost borne by Mr.W.O.Haines as memorial to his wife. Plaque reads:
"In gratitude to God for the life of ETHEL ROSE HAINES this organ was restored in 1978. Born in this town, schoolteacher, Christian leader of women, a Mayoress of the Borough, closely connected with the chair trade, in life she was serene and gentle, yet a most determined person. She died 4th May 1976, aged 74, and at death was sorely missed by her husband, two daughters, their families and an exceptional company of friends."

1985 Organist - David G.Cambridge

VICTORIA STREET (1878)

CLARICE RUMBLE writes:

When Bethany Gospel Hall took over our chapel, they had all the Methodist memorial stones cemented over, no doubt wishing to make a completely new start. But the memory of a century of work and witness in that tightly-knit High Wycombe community will surely never perish. Built originally in 1878 the church took on its present appearance in 1904.

Our own memories (Millicent Brooker's and mine) start in the Sunday School and end many years later in the choir. The upper schoolroom was crowded twice every Sunday and there one would hear well-known Wycombe names, like Valentine Millbourn, Caleb Bunce, Owen Haines and the Whartons (coal-merchants of Desborough Street). Mrs. Edith Goodearl ran the Primary for many years, followed by Miss Connie Bunce. Tom Goodearl, Len Silvey and James Brooker were teachers too. What Treats we had, led by the Salvation Army Band, in Daws Hill Park! Newland closed in 1955 and many of their members joined us, including Alf Cant who became a steward and class leader. Some of their children joined our Sunday School. Sunday 8th July, 1956 was the first anniversary of the union, when the preachers were Sister Elsie Maynard and Rev. A. W. Curtis. The lesson was read by Mr. W. J. Perfect.

There was always so much going on at Victoria Street; we almost lived there when we were young! There were the Sunday Bible classes; the Friday evening class meeting; Band of Hope which we had to sign the temperance pledge to join; Wesley Guild on Mondays; Busy Bee meetings for the young girls who did lots of sewing and fancy work for the bazaars (which always had "grand openings" by local dignitaries); the Women's Meeting (first presidents - Mrs. Owen Haines and Mrs. William Haines); the youth clubs; uniformed organisations; and many other activities. Almost inevitably our turn came to close. The people were too few; the bills too many. At that last evening service in June 1975 we were joined by many old friends and members. We thanked the Lord for our memories, sang a very emotional Doxology and journeyed on to Deeds Grove.

LONDON ROAD (1893)

The London Road, High Wycombe, Church was opened at the junction with Gordon Road in 1893 by the Wesleyan Methodists after a series of services held in the Cricket Club pavilion opposite. In 1929, owing to extensive work amongst young people, a new schoolroom was added plus two classrooms and at the same time pews were installed in the church. There was no debt on this work. In July 1955 the Slater Street Society united with London Road and services, together with other activities continued on these premises which were solemnised for marriages for the first time on 19th March 1957. The united Society moved into the new Church of St. Mark's in 1959. The London Road chapel was sold by auction on 6th March 1959 for use as a furniture warehouse.

PRIVATE HARRY FRY (1916)

Private Harry Fry is still "poultice walloping" in and around Salonika. In his last message he describes a whirlwind attack upon his bivouac. "The dust went round and round and ascended like a thick volume of black smoke. It was very dark and the sky was lit up by sheet lightning. At about 1.30 in the morning it grew much fiercer and we were awakened by a strong volume of dust sweeping into our bivouac and nearly blinding us. It did not stop at that but blew the back of our bivouac down. It was amusing groping our way about in the dark for our belongings and it all appeared to be a huge joke. But it was really very serious and thankful we ought to be to God for carrying us safely through these dangers." The copy of the "Balkan News" - an English production - which he encloses, is very interesting and must be to the men out yonder a boon indeed. By the way, that he is "poultice walloping" is not strictly correct for the moment, for at present he is acting as messenger between Brigade Headquarters and the Ambulance.

CHURCH RECORD OF WESLEYAN CIRCUITS

CLEM WHITE writes:

The first time I went to London Road, it was to please my wife. (But I think really I was pleasing the Lord Jesus.) It was wartime and the blackout. We got off the bus at the Cricket Ground and made our way over the London Road into Gordon Road. Up the three steps, into the porch, then the chapel. "Lumme!" I thought, "this place is crowded - big dark pews all packed together, large harmonium and everybody getting in everybody else's way as they came in. It was noisy too with the passing traffic. Lena was Cub Mistress - never had fewer than 30 Cubs.

She used to take one disabled boy home in a taxi. No parade services - nowhere to parade! The hall wasn't big but they never broke any windows - well, not deliberately! The Scouts were run by Harry Fry who was Group Scoutmaster, and the Guides and Brownies by Alice Youers.

The people were nice - came from the Park Street area mainly. I remember Rev. Tony Wells - very tall and very young. Old Albert Pearce used to help my wife with the chairs but he would help anybody. He used to shout "Hallelujah" in the services. Mrs. Fry was a marvellous worker, absolutely devoted to the work. I remember the tea parties - what a squash! "Were they sad when it closed?" you ask. Not really! I think they were glad to be going to St. Mark's where there was more space and more people to run things!

TERRIERS (1895)

MARY COLLIER writes:

When Terriers Wesleyan Chapel opened in 1895 in Amersham Road, High Wycombe, there was little traffic or indeed any other noise, to disturb the worship. Opposite was the toll house behind which the original narrow Totteridge Lane wound its devious route to Totteridge Common. How different from its last days in 1970 with the constant roar of traffic at the nearby crossroads!

The little "tin tabernacle" never made the headlines. It just went quietly about its business of pointing people to Jesus. There never was a "Terriers Problem" for the circuit to discuss, never any demands for money. Perhaps our self-effacement was our downfall because when we did need help with repairs - the "ship-halfpennies" we had been collecting so zealously, proved to be inadequate - none was forthcoming and as St. Mark's was "just down the road", we could quite as well go there! But Brian Ridgley who ran the Sunday School with Keith Lawrence, had family connections with Bryants Bottom so we went there instead (and some of us still do).

Terriers was a warm, friendly chapel, none more so than the Meeks who lived in the house next door and did the caretaking. Mr. Meeks was tall and thin and always seemed to have a bag of sweets in his pocket. No wonder the children loved him! Every year there was a Christmas party. A "Bucks Free Press" report from 1913 records that the scholars of Terriers had a prizegiving and tea on 31st December. The chairmen were Mr. Howard-Smith and Rev. W. Terry Coppin. "The School secretary, Miss O. Jupe, gave the report," it concludes. I remember the happy Anniversary services in more recent times and especially Mother's Day when the children brought home their flowers. It was a sad day when our little chapel was sold to the High Wycombe Deaf Church and Social Club (for £3650).

CHESHAM (1897)

ERNIE WOODSTOCK writes:

John Wesley records in his journal that on his first visit to Chesham in 1769 there was "a great number of hearers who were very attentive". Again in 1775 he writes, "All that heard, seemed affected for the present". More than a century passed and in 1895 Rev. Richard Harper, Superintendent Minister of the High Wycombe Wesleyan Methodist Circuit, wrote in the "Methodist Recorder" that he had "discovered a township of 8000 people, only 25 miles from London, with no provision for Methodism"!

Soon he formed a small society which met in Townsend Road School and preachers came from Wycombe, mostly on foot. A year later a schoolroom was built in Broad Street for £1000 and put in the charge of Mr.G.Church, a lay pastor.

The work was soon lagging : there were too many churches (including four Baptist alone) in Chesham already! The "Chesham Problem" became a regular feature of the Synod agenda and most agreed, "There is no room for Methodism in Chesham". From 1917 to 1927 the work was carried on by four supernumary Ministers, the first being the 80 years-old Rev.C.W.L.Christian, and for the next five years by two probationers - all with apparent lack of success. Then in 1932 a number of Methodists from Waterloo Road, London, became members and at last the work began to prosper. New premises were urgently sought by the untiring Minister, Rev.E.W.Eavis. In 1907 Rev.Walter Wynne and a large part of the congregation had broken away from Broadway Baptist Church to start a United Free Church in Bellingdon Road. A brilliant lecturer, his ministry was sensationally successful. But by 1933 he was beginning to lose ground and the building - complete with tip-up cinema seats - was bought for £4637 by the Methodists who also inherited the remaining United members. By the mid-century Chesham's population had grown to 20,000. The ministry of several able men was enhanced by music under the inspired direction of Charles York. Performances of great oratorios for which the town had been famous, were resumed and people crowded in. The need for larger and more varied accommodation, added to the ravages of woodworm in the old building, inspired the erection of the present church which was opened in 1966. While the new building was being erected, morning services were held at the Emmanuel Church, Broad Street.

In the past 20 years the work, aided by an influx of newcomers from the London suburbs, has grown excitingly and by 1987 there were about 150 members. The present emphasis is on youth activity and the new Wesley Hall - with three youth clubs and various uniformed organisations - is always in demand and seldom available for outside bookings. The Local Ecumenical Project (L.E.P.) includes the Methodist Church. "Under God's guidance," wrote Mr.W.E.Garlick in an article on which much of the present article has been based, "the past paves the way to a glorious future". We believe this still to be true.

DEATH OF TWO STALWARTS

The passing to higher service of W.E.GARLICK of Chesham reminds us to give thanks to God for a tremendous life of service in the Circuit through many decades. Wherever one goes, the name of Mr.Garlick is spoken of with respect and affection as a caring, far-seeing and generous leader of men. The whole Circuit owes him a great debt and we salute the memory of a fine servant of God.

We salute also the memory of one of our good Circuit servants, CHARLES YORK, called to Higher Service at the age of 94. For 37 years he gave magnificent witness to his Lord in this Circuit and had a lifetime of devotion to music - even to having Sir Malcolm Sargent in his choir when the great conductor was a young man. Mr.York was active to the last and was actually planning a concert in aid of Church funds for April - a concert which will now be held as a memorial to him. We are proud to have so distinguished a servant of God on the Circuit's Roll of Honour.

(Rev.) WALLACE JENKINS (1972)

WESLEYAN METHODIST CHURCHES

AMERSHAM - HIGH STREET (1899)

"BUCKS FREE PRESS" (25/8/1860)

The Wesleyan Society at Amersham which has long been favoured with the good counsel and liberal efforts of T.N.Gray Esq., is to be soon deprived of that gentleman's judicious services and oversight, as he is about to remove to the neighbourhood of London and will therefore dispose of the property in which the society has enjoyed for so many years its religious privileges. But we are somewhat relieved in being able to inform our Wesleyan friends that in future divine service will be conducted by the Wesleyan preachers on the Lord's-day in the Friends' Meeting House, Amersham.

"BUCKS EXAMINER" (8/7/1949)

The Wesleyans later transferred to the (now demolished) row of cottages in the High Street. It was this group who were responsible for the building of the Methodist church opposite the Swan Inn in the High Street. Erected in 1899 this compact red brick church was designed by Mr.C.E.Moxham of High Wycombe and constructed by the local builders, F.P.Williams. The numerous inscriptions that enabled its construction, are commemorated by a number of stone tablets set into its walls.

JOAN STRATFULL writes:

So the present church was built in 1899 at a cost of £350 on the site of the old cottages which had become a rubbish dump. It is still the most modern building in the High Street! Now the Wesleyan worshippers had their own chapel with no tempting orchard for the children to gaze at, like the one behind the Quaker Meeting House in Whielden Street! Originally there was no water supply, lighting was by gas brackets and heating probably came at first from an open fire but later from a big donkey stove. There were no vestries. At the north end of the church was a rostrum style pulpit seating five persons. Outside the building were spiked iron railings across the whole front of the pavement.

Twenty years later Alice Wright, a society steward, recorded a membership of eight. The cost of the building debt was so crippling at one time that the Church came near to being closed. But by 1930 the membership had grown to 26 and the finances had improved. Vestries, supposedly temporary, had been added; they are still in use! The old stove was removed and the central heating system was purchased from the old post office and installed with a coal boiler. During the 1960's this was replaced by a gas boiler and additional pipes were added. The sash windows, now rotten, were replaced and single chairs from the old Woodside Road Church were installed. The iron railings were removed and the forecourt was paved. The rostrum pulpit was also removed. The present panelling and pulpit had formerly been in the Memorial Chapel at Park Lane Church, Wembley, and came as a gift from Stanley Comben. The brick pillars and iron gates were added in the 1970's to the memory of Miss. K. Mason. The society which began in 1818, had in 1987 a membership of 18; the Sunday School had 25 members.

PIDDINGTON (1906)

LEILA ING writes:

In April 1986 public worship at Piddington was discontinued and the site of the church sold for residential development. My own memories date from the 1930's but I learned much from my father, George Lee, who was living in the village when the mission hall was built, and remained closely connected with it throughout his life. The "death" of the chapel came soon after his own.

WESLEYAN METHODIST CHURCHES

In 1904 there were about 28 houses in Piddington and
religious services were held in the home of two Primitive
Methodists. After a time they thought there was a need for a
church building. The High Wycombe Wesleyan Circuit was
approached but with a large Church in West Wycombe already,
another in Piddington was thought unnecessary. Undeterred the
villagers went ahead and the mission hall, a prefabricated
wooden and corrugated iron building, was erected in 1906. at
the corner of King Street and Queen Street.

The main use of the hall was "for Protestant worship", so
it was an early ecumenical venture! But it also served as a
meeting place for the village. An independent chapel, it came
under the general care of the Wycombe Circuit who supplied
preachers. In 1942 an actual Methodist society was formed.
Until that time the Methodists among the worshippers had held
their membership at West Wycombe. In 1971 the mission hall was
offered to the Methodist Connexion and at last became a fully-
fledged Methodist Church! To the children of my generation the
mission hall was the centre of our life. There we met our
Sunday School friends and had fun on social evenings. At that
time there were several concert parties, such as "The Goslings",
in the circuit, willing to go round entertaining. The Women's
Meeting's annual socials were also eagerly awaited, especially
the amateur dramatics.

The Sunday School was started in 1907. Early records list
"six Bibles purchased for five shillings [25p.]" Joint outings
with West Wycombe were organised to Bisham, Velvet Lawn and
Taplow Court and in later years to the south coast. In the late
1960's Wheeler End teachers and scholars formed a combined
Sunday School with ours at Piddington. One of our members when
the Church closed, had been a Sunday School scholar in 1907 and
two others in 1910. Our Sunday School Anniversaries would seem
old-fashioned now but they served their purpose. Children were
keen to participate and many visitors came from the village and
other churches. A circuit fellowship, so important to the small
village church, was fostered also in the Women's Meeting
Rallies. Christmas parties too were lively village events. For
many years young children were invited with their parents as
guests. This made for noisy parties but helped the Church to
keep in touch with the village. A Christmas carol party always
used to go round the village, singing and collecting money for
the National Children's Home. Some years ago however, as our
singers were getting older, a concert was held instead with the
West Wycombe Band in the new village hall. These concerts have

been very popular and we hope to continue them as a Christian witness to the village.

When Piddington Chapel closed, the few remaining members transferred to Stokenchurch or Wheeler End (where services ceased in 1987 and members transferred to Lane End) and the remnant of the Women's Meeting joined with the West Wycombe group which had continued to meet after the society there closed. Methodism struggles in this rural area but the future of the Christian Church as a whole could be exciting. We pray for guidance.

PIDDINGTON FACES UP TO SOME QUESTIONS

In December 1973 the village of Piddington came under the religious microscope of Rev. Norman Burrows and a team of 23 Methodists. They knocked on the doors of 150 houses and conducted 62 interviews. The results were as follows:

Do you belong to a church?		Yes	-	41
		No	-	21

How often do you attend church services?		Frequently	-	10
		Seldom	-	31
		Never	-	21

Who is Jesus according to your belief?	Son of God	-	35
	Good man, leader, teacher	-	9
	Founder of Christian Church	-	4
	Mythical person	-	2
	Don't know/other answer	-	12

How does a person become a Christian?	Brought up as a Christian	-	13
	Believe in Christ as Saviour	-	5
	Live a good life	-	29
	Believe in God	-	3
	Join a church	-	3
	Don't know/other answer	-	9

Do you have a satisfying purpose in life?		Yes	-	46
		No	-	10
		Don't know	-	6

What will happen when you die?	Reincarnation	- 1
	Cease to exist	- 16
	Afterlife (unspecified)	- 9
	Heaven/eternal life	- 20
	Don't know	- 16

Do you believe in God?	Yes	- 43
	No	- 5
	Don't know	- 14

If you could know God personally, would you be interested?	Yes	- 43
	No	- 11
	Don't know	- 8

CONCLUSION: Piddington is neither godless nor Christian!

BOURNE END (1910)

ALAN GOODEARL writes:

Shirts and ponies (among other things) figure in the history of Bourne End Methodist Church! The shirts were made by a group of women who included Mrs.Purcell, Mrs.Cordery,

Mrs. Gray, Mrs. Shirley and Mrs. Woodbridge, and were sold to raise money for the erection of the chapel in 1910 in Furlong Road. On the day of the stonelaying ceremony a stone was laid by Mrs. Woodbridge to represent the raising of £75 from the sale of the shirts at 4/6d [22½p.] each.

Services had been held for many years before this in the home of Mr. and Mrs. John Shirley in Recreation Road and then in the day-school. Messrs. Weathered, Dean and Goff were among the members of the Bible Class. The "guiding force" behind the many meetings held to plan the building was Joseph Woodbridge while practical help came from Mr. W. A. Steevens and Richard Goodearl J. P. of High Wycombe. Mr. Spry, a local solicitor, provided the legal advice. So the new chapel was opened, the rostrum and seats coming from the old Wesleyan chapel (now the Stanley Spencer Art Gallery) at Cookham. It is interesting to note that the building was erected as a Sunday School hall "to be used also as the church until such time as a separate church building can be erected on the adjoining land". The average weekly collections in the first few weeks were only 4/6d [22½p.] and the church accounts reveal occasional expenditure of 1/6d [7½p.] for "oats for the visiting preacher's pony", a pony and trap being the usual mode of travel from High Wycombe in those pre-bus days. More than one preacher however used "shanks's pony" for the journey, thinking nothing of the six-mile walk each way!

Gas lighting was used until 1956 when electricity was installed. Heating at first was by a form of central heating but this method was quickly replaced by coke stoves, following an explosion! These stoves, while providing adequate warmth for those sitting near them, were never really effective for others and have now been superseded by modern gas heaters which provide a more even heat distribution. A Sunday School was formed, led by Mr. Woodbridge, Mr. Gray and Mr. Shirley, and an early outing was to West Wycombe Hill by train. Week night magic lantern shows were presented by Mr. Brown, a local Rechabite secretary, and a "threepence-a-week" thrift club was supported by chapel and non-chapel folk alike. The Church has always enjoyed a good team spirit. Mention must be made of one stalwart (among many) - John Shirley, a loveable and humble man of God, who was School superintendent, society steward and a local preacher. Often in pain from the result of an accident at work, he continued to witness for his Lord until his death during the Second World War.

The postwar years have seen great changes both for Bourne End village and the Methodist Church. Large housing estates from the Little Marlow Road almost up to Flackwell Heath made the members wonder whether a new church development should take place there. Eventually in 1982 the vacant site next to the chapel was sold for the building of flats. On the other side another block of flats, Alfred Court, has been erected following demolition of the original village school, providing sheltered accommodation for a number of senior citizens, some of whom have become regular worshippers at the chapel. After a period of decline the chapel has recently shown a marked up-turn. Attendance at morning service now averages nearly 30 and the members are looking to the future with quiet, prayerful confidence, led by Rev.Arthur F.Royall, their very active Supernumary Minister.

"METHODISM WAS BORN IN SONG"

In 1737 John Wesley produced a "Collection of Psalms and Hymns" which was followed in 1753 by "Hymns and Spiritual songs". "Wesley's Hymns" (1780) contained 525 hymns of which 515 were written by his family, notably Charles. It lasted over a century and contained "no doggerel, botches, creeping or cant"! Hugh Bourne produced an evangelistic hymn-book for the Primitive Methodists in 1825. Another followed in 1886. The first "Methodist Hymn Book" was published by the Wesleyans in 1904 and while thoroughly Methodist, drew on many other sources. With the "Deed of Union" came the 1933 "Methodist Hymn Book". The preface states: "A hymn is only a hymn if in it men speak to the Most High and He to them". "Hymns and Psalms" was published in 1983 in order to include Methodist traditions in a contribution to the universal Church. All these hymn-books show (in the words of the 1933 preface) - "Methodism was born in song".

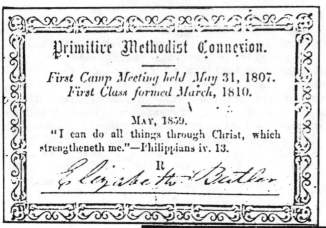

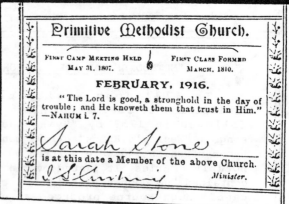

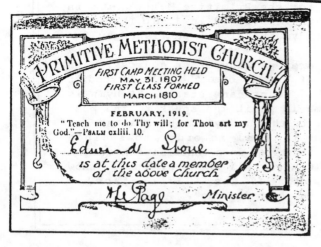

CHAPTER 4

THE PRIMITIVE METHODIST CHURCH

The best known of the many groups which broke away from the Wesleyan Methodist Church departed partly from a desire to conduct worship in a less ordered way, and partly from a dislike of ministerial authority. It was to give laymen a much higher status.

Primitive Methodism started at the beginning of the 19th century. Hugh Bourne joined the Wesleyan Methodist Church in the summer of 1799. Eight years later (1807) he and William Clowes held the first "Camp Meeting" which followed the American Negro tradition, at Mow Cop in Staffordshire. Open-air revival meetings followed - both against the express orders of the Wesleyan Methodist Conference. As a result they were expelled in 1812 when the Primitive Methodist Church was formed with a membership of about 200. At first local to Burslem and the Potteries, it spread through Cheshire and Lancashire and by its first Conference in 1820 there were eight circuits, 48 "travelling preachers" (Ministers), 277 local preachers and 7842 members. (The previous year there had been only three circuits until the Hull Branch of the Nottingham Circuit became the fourth.)

As its name suggests, the "Prims." wanted to revive the old fervour of the early Methodists under Wesley. Even today there are those who remember their Primitive origins with pride. Younger folk too, who have never heard the title, have been known to raise their hands in prayer, murmur the occasional "Praise the Lord!" and prefer "Mission Praise" to "Hymns and Psalms" (both published in 1983)! So the feeling, if not the name, still persists.

The "Prims." suffered much persecution from the Wesleyans and some of their preachers were beaten or imprisoned. Nevertheless (or perhaps as a result?) their numbers quickly increased and they spread throughout most of the country and even to America. Their services, which included hearty singing and revivalist exhortation, appealed to those who disliked the more dignified Wesleyan worship. Even small villages often had two Methodist chapels, one for each denomination and both full on Sundays! Despite the rivalry however it was commonplace on important occasions, such as Anniversaries, for the Minister "from the other Church" to be invited to preach. The "Prims." had a strong sympathy for social outcasts and in 1880 Thomas Jackson set up a home for "friendless and orphan lads". The Primitive Methodists remained estranged from the Wesleyan Church until the "Deed of Union" in 1932.

FORMATION OF THE HIGH WYCOMBE PRIMITIVE CIRCUIT

The Primitive movement spread only slowly to London and the south east. In the early 1830's missions were extended to the central southern counties of Buckinghamshire, Berkshire and Hampshire. The whole of the south east was included in the Norwich District. High Wycombe came into that district as part of the Hounslow Circuit when that was formed in 1832 with about 70 members. In 1835 Rev. James Pole, Superintendent of the Hounslow Circuit, was commissioned to mission High Wycombe. So on 8th April, having walked the twenty miles to get there, he "fixed his standard in a spacious area in the centre of the town, known as Queens Square". His preaching in the town, at Downley, Naphill, Lacey Green, Speen and Penn was effective and in 1836 the High Wycombe Circuit was formed with 160 members. These increased in 1837 to 200, and in 1838 to 260. It is obvious that some of the members were transferred from the Wesleyans. Then came a period of reversals. In 1841 and 1842 the area was a Branch of the Reading Circuit in the Brinkworth District with the membership still about 250.

The earliest reference to a church was to a "small plain Chapel" built about 1832 at Littleworth Common (although there was probably one at Wooburn Green as well). The cause had struggled for some years and had been down to a single member at one time. In 1842 it was just about "ticking over". Churches were built at Lee Common (1839) and Penn (1843). The congregation in High Wycombe had met in the cottage of Mr. Pierce in Frogmoor for a number of years but as the numbers grew it became necessary to build in order to accommodate the numbers. Frogmoor Gardens was opened in 1848 in the same year as the chapel at Flackwell Heath. The next 30 years saw a good period of growth and expansion; in the fifties Naphill (1851), Great Kingshill (1852) and Lacey Green (1855) were erected; in the

sixties, Wheeler End (1861), Downley Chapel Street (1864),
Radnage (1865) and Great Missenden (1866) all appeared; then the
seventies saw Bryants Bottom (1871), Slater Street (1873), White
Hart Street - to replace Frogmoor Gardens - (1875) and
Westbourne Street (1878). Thereafter, right up to the "Deed of
Union" in 1932, the only addition was the Church in Sands (Road)
built in 1912. The membership had grown to about 500 in 1875
and stayed at 500 to 600 through the next fifty years. At Union
there were 14 Churches, 2 Ministers and 38 local preachers who
joined in the new High Wycombe Methodist Circuit.

JAMES POLE'S JOURNAL (1835)

(Rev. James Pole, ex-Superintendent Minister of the Hounslow
Primitive Methodist Circuit, wrote from Wisbech on Feb.24,1837
in the PRIMITIVE METHODIST MAGAZINE: "Hounslow Circuit wished
these extracts to be sent months ago; but a long fit of illness
prevented it. But having since received a request to that
effect from the quarter-board of that circuit, I have sent them,
hoping their insertion in our excellent miscellany, will oblige
the friends of the gospel. Yours in the Lord, JAMES POLE.")

<u>Monday, March 9,1835</u>   Attended the quarter day at
Hatton. It was a good day. I have been in this circuit about
nine months, have laboured hard, and have had to encounter many
hardships, and have seen but little fruit. The circuit was very
low both in temporals and spirituals. We were more than fifteen
pounds short in our salaries; the circuit not having, till
lately, brought in money enough to support one married man; and
we are two of us, myself married and the other single. At this
quarter day it was agreed for me to open a mission on entire new
ground in the county of Buckinghamshire.

<u>Wednesday, April 8,1835</u>   I commenced my missionary
labours at HIGH WYCOMB. This day I walked twenty miles; and on
my arrival at H.Wycomb, I fixed my standard about the middle of
the town, in a spacious place, called Queen's square. Hundreds
gathered round me, and good attention was paid. After service I
was kindly received by several, though an entire stranger.

<u>Friday 10</u>   I preached at Dounly, a new
place. A friend who had heard of my coming, had prepared a

wheelwright's shop, and it was crowded with people of all classes. Here seemed a good opening.

Saturday 11   Visiting and praying with the people. Dounly is an obscure village; but it has a chair manufactory, which employs near forty hands.

Sunday, April 12   Preached three times at Lacey Green. Three or four professed to find liberty. And on Monday several cried for mercy, and found liberty.

Tuesday 14   At Dounly; visited several families. At dinner time held a prayer meeting in the open air: there were more than a hundred people, and God was working. At night the wheelwright's shop was crammed, and many could not get in. Several wept, and some found peace with God.

Wednesday 15   Visited at Dounly, and at noon held an open-air prayer meeting; and much interest was excited. At night preached to a large congregation in the market house at H. Wycomb. At the close I shook hands with the people, and a respectable female left two-pence in my hand; and a man, one of the greatest reprobates in the town, perceiving I had a cold, kindly asked me to go and take something.

Thursday 16   Preached at Penn. Much tempted; met with discouragement from some professors who laboured to shut up our way. But others encouraged me; and it being cold they provided a place for me to preach in. Next day held a prayer meeting in the forenoon; and one soul appeared in good earnest for salvation. At night preached in the open-air at Penn street; and was annoyed by a drunken man, but we got the victory.

Sunday, April 19   P. meeting at Dounly, and then class, the first ever held by the P. Methodists in this county. Eight joined, and this may be said to be a foundation stone of P. Methodism in this vicinity. I pray God it may rise to glorious structure. Went to Lacey Green, and preached to a large congregation. In the afternoon at Napple Common. Hundreds came to hear, and a mighty Unction attended the word. At night at H. Wycomb, to a large concourse of people in the open air.

Monday 20   It being Easter Monday, we held a meeting on Dounly Common. Several lately converted engaged in prayer; this made a move, and stimulated others to prayer. The scene was both delightful and affecting: some praising God for deliverance, and praying him to keep them in future - others crying for mercy. At night preached at Lacey Green: at the prayer meeting after, several wept on account of sin; one found the Lord.

Tuesday 21   Family visiting. Dined with the constable; who observed he had not before witnessed such an Easter; for every Easter since he had been constable, he had been called out to keep peace; but this time there was no need of it, for most of the people were praying, and at the worship on the Common.

Wednesday 22   At H.Wycomb, in the open air: large attendance, good attention, great prospect, and good was done. Held a prayer meeting after, and formed a society of six members. Here is another stone put into the building of P.Methodism in this county.

Sunday, April 26, 1835   Preached four times, twice at Penn, then at Penn Street, and at H.Wycomb. At H.Wycomb many were deeply affected under the word. Held a prayer meeting and good was done.

Monday 27   At Lacey Green. More than two hundred. It being cold, a person gave us liberty to go into a cart house. Tears flowed on every hand. Oh! what a spirit of hearing! The fields are already white to the harvest. Oh! that our circuit were strong enough to send another labourer forth!

Tuesday 28   At Dounly in the open air. A large congregation, a mighty influence prevailed, and a powerful conversion took place.

Wednesday 29   At H.Wycomb. Here souls are coming to God.

Sunday, May 3   Preached three times in the open air. At night at H.Wycomb. It was thought a thousand people attended; and I think I never witnessed a better spirit of hearing.

Monday 4   Family visiting. At night preached at Dounly. In the P.meeting after, several were crying for mercy, and some were brought into liberty.

Wednesday, Thursday, Friday   At   Bladlon,   Longwick   and Risborough.   These places appear to be very dark; and at present no particular spirit of hearing is manifested.   May the Lord undertake for us.

Sunday, May 10   Attended   a   Camp   meeting   at Littleworth, within the circuit.   A great many attended from the mission places.   A great cry for pardon was heard; a mighty power rested on the services of the day; and many who came with a load of sin and guilt, went home rejoicing in God their Saviour.   (We have two or three local preachers on the plan, who were brought to God at this meeting.)   I left the mission and laboured some time on the circuit.

Sunday, May 24   At Hatton Camp meeting.   In the lovefeast some wanderers professed to be restored to the favour of God.

Sunday, May 31,1835   Camp meeting at Marlow.   Many attended from the mission places, and the forenoon services were very powerful.   In the afternoon the rain hindered.   But a powerful influence prevailed in-doors, and much good was done. In the lovefeast the people spoke in quick succession and the power of God rested.   Before we began prayer meeting I spoke a little on present salvation; and showed that Satan would tempt the mourners, and the persons praying for them.   I spoke of what I had experienced in praying for mourners, and endeavoured to show the conflict kept up by the powers of darkness; and that we should hold out and not give up, although we might feel at times as if our strength was gone, and all our faith was lost. Several of the people appeared to enter into it.   We began to pray and the kingdom of Satan soon began to shake: and in a short time seven or eight professed to receive salvation through the blood of the Lamb.   Young and old were crying for mercy.

Monday, June 1, Tuesday 2   At Dounly and H.Wycomb; being now returned to the mission; and am happy to find the work of God going on well.   Sister Smith, one of our local preachers, has laboured in my absence, and I am happy to say, God has made her a blessing to many.   The new societies are increasing daily, and the converting work is going on.

Monday, June 8   Quarter-day.   The best we have witnessed in the circuit.   The mission brought in more than six pounds; and many souls have been converted.   And now, for the first time we had money to meet all demands.

THE PRIMITIVE METHODIST CHURCH

Sunday, July 19   Camp meeting at Woburn. Much opposition from professors and profane. The congregation was large, and at the lovefeast two souls professed to find liberty.

Sunday, August 2   Camp meeting at Penn. It was thought there were fifteen hundred present. Many were pricked in their hearts; and at the lovefeast the people spoke with freedom. At this place we have suffered most from professors; but still we go on and have a rising society.

Monday 3   Preached at Spien, a new place. The cause of my preaching here was this: two men were fighting, and one killed the other; and some thought that to visit it at such a time, would do good. It is only a small village, but people flocked from different places, until it was thought there were more than four hundred present. I spoke from Romans v. 21, "That as sin hath reigned unto death, even so might grace reign through righteousness unto eternal life by Jesus Christ our Lord". The scene was different from what appeared a few days ago. Now many, I think scores, were weeping under the word. And since that time, we have had a house opened, and a society formed. It is shocking to say that within the last six months, no less than three wretched beings have been hurried into eternity, within five miles of this place, by this wretched fighting. And the brother of the one killed at Speen, killed one of the others, and is now in prison. Oh! what a blot upon human nature!

Sunday, September 6   A Camp meeting at Lacey Green. Here we had the happiness to hear many who, a short time ago, were strangers to religion, now lifting up their hearts in prayer and praise to God, and speaking of his wondrous grace to their fellow creatures. It was a time which will be remembered in eternity with joy by many.

Monday, Sep. 7   Quarter-day. The cause appeared to be rising in a general way, and the local brethren are much encouraged to go forth afresh in the good work. At the close we held a watch night; some cried for mercy, others were made happy in God.

Sunday, Oct. 11   In the open air at Penn Street. Here on account of not having a house to preach in, it has for weeks been thought that it must be given up. But I prevailed to keep it on, hoping that God would open the way, there being no place of worship near; and some of the people were getting much good to their souls.

Friday, Nov.13   At Penn Street again. It was a
cold wet day, and no place to preach in. I sometimes thought it
would be no good to go, it being not only dark, but too wet to
stand out.   I, however, did go, thinking it would be fully
settled one way or other. And so it proved, for a master baker
took me into his bakehouse to preach. Thank God, the way was
open: and when I came again I preached in his kitchen.   And
this is now our preaching house. His wife is a member of
society; his house is a home for the preachers; and himself, I
believe, a lover of God's cause. O may God bless his soul with
all his pardoning mercy.

Friday, November 20   Somewhat afflicted in body, and
greatly depressed in mind. I don't know when I felt such an
inward conflict as I have this week. Sometimes my mind has been
so harassed that I have felt as if my nerves were unstrung; I
cannot fully describe my feelings.
                           At night I and Bro.D.Clarke, one
of our local preachers, accompanied by several friends from
H.Wycomb, went to Heazlemere, about two miles, to hold a
meeting. He spoke first with a good feeling. I spoke next, and
felt the Lord to be present. We held a P.meeting, and sinners
began to cry for mercy. And a woman from H.Wycomb, who had been
seeking the Lord for some weeks, appeared to be in the deepest
distress.   Several prayed with and for her; still her sorrows
increased, and the enemy of souls took advantage of her
convictions. She would often cry out, "O Lord, what have I done
that thou wilt not pardon me? Am I too great a sinner? Must I
go without pardon and perish?"   At other times she would
apparently rise into a hope of pardon, and then again sink into
deep distress. Thus we continued for more than an hour, and
then the enemy appeared to have got the mastery, for nearly all
were shut up. One and another would say, "You must believe; if
you believe, God will save you." She would reply, "I do try to
believe; but something keeps me back. Oh! what a load! Oh!
what hard work to bear this!"
                           It was strongly applied to my
mind, "You must pray, and remove this darkness which hangs over
her."   It appeared as though we were surrounded by all the
powers of hell.   Indeed it appeared to me as though the
invisible world was opened: and I addressed the people as
follows: "My friends, we are surrounded by thousands of evil
spirits, and they are trying to ruin this soul. You that can
now believe, must come forth by your united faith and oppose
Satan. It is no good (it will not avail) to tell her to
believe. She cannot at present, because of the powers of hell
which surround us. If we pray and believe, and (by so doing)

remove these spiritual foes, she will come into liberty
directly. Come then, enter into the conflict with her, and we
shall conquer."

We kneeled down again; but
before I had prayed one minute, I was completely shut up, and
for a time, could not utter a word. I felt as though something
would tear my soul, or faculties to pieces. I could only groan
to God for strength. But in about one minute I felt these awful
clouds of darkness begin to fly. Satan was completely spoiled
of his fortress; the woman received liberty in a minute, yea, in
an instant. Her soul was filled with glory, and she could give
a clear account of what God had done for her.

This person was afterwards a
subject of severe conflicts with Satan. But when I left the
circuit in June, 1836, she was a steady member in society; and
her husband has since become a local preacher. In the course of
my ministry I have prayed with hundreds of mourners for
salvation, but never witnessed such a scene as this. O Jesus,
ride on!

<u>December quarter-day, 1835</u>   Our income more than met our
outgo; a third preacher was called out; and the work went on.

<u>March quarter-day, 1836</u>   I was ill, and had been quite
laid up for one month. On this account there had been several
disappointments. Yet there was a great many brought to God in
this quarter. The first fortnight of my illness I was much
comforted with the accounts of the work. One would come and
say, "There were two souls brought in yesternight. God was
there though we could not have you there." Another day, another
would come and say, "We had a blessed time last night; we had
God with us, and one soul brought in." This was the case
several days.

<u>June quarter-day, 1836</u>   I was ill nearly all the
quarter, and on this account we, to human appearance, suffered
much; but still there was an increase of money and of members.
I had now been in the circuit two years, and had neither house
nor furniture; but this quarter something was done about it.
High Wycomb was made the circuit town; and another mission was
opened, called Chesham mission of High Wycomb circuit. When I
left this circuit it was approaching to two hundred members.
Brother William Hardwick succeeded me. And I have been very
thankful to hear that Brother and Sister Hardwick have been made
a great blessing to the circuit.   Thus this once shattered,
wasted circuit is now, I trust, rising into a good one. All the
glory shall be the Lord's, for ever and ever. Amen.

PREACHING PLACES (1830-1870)

```
                      1         1         1         1         1
                      8         8         8         8         8
                      3         4         5         6         7
                      01234567890123456789012345678901234567890
Frogmoor Gardens      S             B             E           †
Naphill                    S             B                    †
Lacey Green           S                     B                 †
Penn/Tylers Gn        S         B                             †
Gt.Kingshill          S                   B      ρ          E †
Lee Common                 B                                  †
Gt.Missenden                          ρ                     B †
Flackwell Heath                   B                           †
Wheeler End                                         B         †
Radnage                                                    B  †
Downley               S                                    B  †
Wooburn Green      B
Bledlow Ridge         S
Hazlemere             S
Penn Street           S
Speen                 S
Seer Green                  S
Wooburn Moor                                              ρ †
Moor's Town                                               S †
```

CHALFONT ST.GILES BRANCH.

```
Chal.St.Giles         S             B       ρ             B †
Littleworth        B                                         †
Beaconsfield                               S                 †
Winchmoor Hill                             S    B           †
West Hyde                                                    †
Chorley Wood                                                †
Amersham Common                                 B           †
Fulmer                                                      †
```

B = Chapel Built
E = Chapel Extended or Additional Buildings e.g. Schoolroom
† = Services (from available Plan)
ρ = Services (from Preachers' Minutes)
S = Services (from other sources)

THE PRIMITIVE METHODIST CHURCH

HIGH WYCOMBE PRIMITIVE CIRCUIT (1837-1867)

PRIMITIVE METHODIST MAGAZINE

Membership of Wycombe Circuit in 1837: 200; local preachers: 26. As regards temporal matters we are rather low, about £6 short in the preachers' salaries. But we expect to be clear by midsummer and our preachers seem resolved not to leave the circuit in debt. The cause of our deficiency is this: we in our zeal stretched our lines too far. Being unwilling to give up any places which we had missioned, we took out a fourth preacher rather too soon. But we were beat out of some of the places by the inclemency of the season, having no houses to preach in at some of the missioned places, which places did not open as we expected. Another matter is the poverty of the times, together with the great pressure of affliction. This country seems to rather sink in temporal things during the winter; but rises in the summer. The travelling and some of the local preachers have had short attacks of affliction, apparently to our disadvantage. But now we have full work for four preachers. The country and the summer are before us and we intend to open a mission on new ground. We have had a blessed revival at Wycomb and its neighbourhood, sinners have been converted, backsliders restored and believers sanctified by the Holy Ghost. NORWICH DISTRICT REPORT

260 members in 1838 in High Wycomb. We have had persecution in some places but through Divine help we have got on hitherto. NORWICH DISTRICT REPORT

We rejoice to say that the High Wycomb Branch of Reading Circuit is in a rising state. During 1841 we have had some powerful conversions; our places of worship are better attended and our prospects are brightening. We have had to encounter a great deal of persecution and have had severe trials through the fall of two official characters: 20 have left society, ten have fallen and two have died in peace. But the Lord has been with us; our deficiency is filled up and we have an increase of 29 members. Our present number is 250. We have three Sunday schools which are doing well. The travelling and local preachers have laboured hard and successfully; the praying-labourers are rising in faith and holiness and usefulness; and the members generally are growing in grace. We have held some powerful revival meetings and lovefeasts at which the Lord has poured out His Spirit, and a great deal of good has been done. BRINKWORTH DISTRICT REPORT

I came to the Wycombe Branch of Reading Circuit in July 1842; and when I first went round it, I found the cause generally rather low and so it continued for some time. At the September quarter-day we found that we had decreased in the number of our members and sunk in our quarterly finances. O, how grievous! At the December quarter-day we had increased two members; but were more behind in finances than we had been at the close of the preceding quarter. This led to the following inquiries: "What is the cause of the deficiency and what can be done to prevent its recurrence?" One of the brethren said he thought we should unitedly covenant to pray that we might have a specified number of souls during the ensuing quarter. Immediately it was proposed that we should unite to pray for 50, and the proposition was adopted. At night we held a salvation meeting in the chapel which was much crowded; and the speaking was effectual. The power of God arrested the people; so that some cried for mercy, and some shouted "Glory!" Others stood amazed and said, "O what a confusion!" In the confusion however five or six souls were converted. Halleluia! A good work has taken place at Wycombe which has secured an increase of members. Our place of worship is now much too small; therefore we are using means to get a new chapel. May God open our way.

Some of the brethren from the country who were at the salvation meeting, caught the heavenly fire, then carried it into some of the country places and kindled up a revival blaze, the result of which has been glorious; for at the renewal of the February tickets we found the increase for the quarter to be about 100 souls. To God's name be all the glory.

(Rev.) JOHN STROUD

I forward you a short account of the work of God in High Wycombe Circuit in 1855. At one place the heavenly influence has fallen on the people like the gentle refreshing dew, quickening believers and melting the impenitent heart, and about ten souls have emerged out of darkness into God's marvellous light. At another place where the chapel was enlarged last summer, the Lord has caused songs of deliverance to burst forth from about 15 blood washed souls. At another place where a new chapel was erected during last summer, the tone of piety in the society was low; but the friends of truth rallied round the cross and sinners were awakened and saved; and already about 20 have been plucked as brands from the burning. Other societies have likewise received some additions; so that after filling up all vacancies caused by deaths, removals and withdrawals, we shall be able to report an increase for the year. To the great Head of the church be all the praise! (Rev.) DENNIS KENDALL

PREACHING PLACES (1870-1910).

```
                   1         1         1         1         1
                   8         8         8         9         9
                   7         8         9         0         1
                   01234567890123456789012345678901234567890
Frogmoor Gardens   C
White Hart St.     B †       †              †         †
Slater St.        B †       †              †         †
Westbourne St.      B       †              †         †
Naphill             †       †              †         †
Lacey Green         †       †              †         †
Penn/Tylers Gn.     †       †              †         †
Gt.Kingshill        †       †              †         †
Lee Common          †       †              †         †
Gt.Missenden        †       †              †         †
Flackwell Heath     †
Wheeler End         †       †              †         †
Radnage             †       †              †         †
Downley             †       †              †         †
Bryants Bottom   B  †       †              †         †
Scrubwood           †
Little Hampden      †
Sands Road                                 S         †
```

CHALFONT ST.GILES BRANCH.

```
Chal.St.Giles          T
Littleworth            T
Beaconsfield           T
Winchmoor Hill         T
West Hyde              T
Chorley Wood           T
Amersham Cm.          T
Fulmer                T
```

CHINNOR CIRCUIT

```
Stokenchurch                               B
```

B = Chapel Built
C = Chapel Closed
T = Transferred to Chalfont St. Giles Circuit
† = Services (from available Plans)
ρ = Services (from Preachers' Minutes)
S = Services (from other sources)

At the March 1867 quarterly meeting of the High Wycombe Circuit it was resolved to report to the next conference that our station is prosperous in every respect; and for our prosperity we thank God and take courage. After having filled up numerous vacancies occasioned by deaths, removals etc., we report 24 members as increase. We have sent a greater proportion of missionary money to the general treasurer than has been sent in any previous year, and higher salaries have been paid to our travelling preachers than have been paid heretofore. We have an increase in the number of Sabbath-schools, teachers and scholars, also a considerable increase in our Sunday-school financial matters.

(Rev.) WILLIAM BIRKS

PRIMITIVE METHODIST CHAPELS - 1875.

Chapel Name	Year Built	No. of Members	No. S.S. Scholars	Atten- dance	Popu- lation	Original Cost
Frogmoor Gardens	1848	–	247			
White Hart Street	1875	171	–	500	11,000	£3,662
Slater Street	1873	28	93	100	600	£585
Naphill	1851	63	69	100	1,000	£122
Lacey Green	1855	39	90	180	1,000	£182
Penn	1843	8	20	50	1,000	£174
Great Kingshill	1852	41	106	240	650	£123
Lee Common	1839	64	123	200	900	£116
Great Missenden	1866	14	–	60	2,000	£203
Flackwell Heath	1848	6	32	40	500	£86
Wheeler End	1861	37	113	200	600	£140
Radnage	1865	30	82	100	600	£125
Bryants Bottom	1871	6	45	100	600	£151
Downley	1864	25	33	50	800	£135
		532#	1,053			

Circuit Return states membership as 482.

Westbourne Street	1878	59(1884)		100	600	£416

(20 members when opened with average attendance of 50)

Sands	1912					£800

HIGH WYCOMBE PRIMITIVE CIRCUIT (LAST DAYS)

FRED ROLLS writes:

I am glad to be counted with a diminishing number who remember the Primitive Methodist tradition in our town. My memories start with Westbourne Street Sunday School at the age of three. In my teens our Minister was Rev.F.G.Saville who used to hold me spellbound with his beautiful messages interspersed with anecdotes which had us rocking with laughter. The organists too knew their congregations and were ever ready with the "last verse again, brothers!" call. Worship in those days had a reality and not only in town chapels but also in the little rural Bethels such as Ibstone, Radnage and Lacey Green where love for the Lord Jesus sent the echo of the "joyful news" reverberating along the Chiltern Hills and through the valleys.

Joey Rackstraw, my grandfather, was a true Victorian "Prim." He loved his Church and liked nothing better than being occupied in His Lord's service. On Sundays he and others would journey out to Wheeler End, Naphill, Tylers Green, Ballinger or The Lee. "Holy" Joe Rogers used to come from North Bucks. on an old motor-bike, his wife sitting in the sidecar. Who of my age will ever forget Bill Line? His simple but effective Gospel message led many to Christ and the fellowship of the Church. His face shone for Jesus Who had wonderfully saved him from a dissolute life at the age of 18, at a camp meeting on Wheeler End Common. "Give me a long life, Lord," he said, "and every remaining day of my life shall be lived for You." God kept His side of the bargain - Bill lived into his 80's - and I am sure Bill kept his. Most preachers were unlettered and simply educated but they knew their Bibles and were able simply but forthrightly to give reason for their faith. None had any doubt as to the way of salvation.

Membership in those days meant you had to attend class meetings and "ceased to meet" was a judgement to be avoided at any cost. Old Jim Plested was "as deaf as a post" but he hated to miss any of the sermon so - when necessary - "I caan't 'ear 'ee - speak up!" was the peremptory cry to many a discomfited preacher. (Electronic hearing-aids had not yet reached the pew.)

I recall many great servants of God and His Church in the 1920's. They seemed still to be in touch with the influence of the Primitive Methodist Revival, led by Hugh Bourne and William

Clowes; Mow Cop was still a living reality to them. In spite of Darwin and the emergence of the "higher criticism" of the Scriptures, their faith held. Despite the terrifying days of the 1914-18 War they could not be shaken. The effect of these onslaughts would not be felt until the next generation – ours – and this was to be evidenced in the "falling away" of the 1930's onwards. But personally I would still rather hear Bill Line's simple Gospel truths than "higher criticism"!

Our many activities reflected the happy friendly fellowship of the "Old Prims." whose lives were based on the love of a Saviour God in Whom all believed without any shadow of doubt. They even prayed for sunshine on Sunday School Treat day – and got it!

PREACHING PLACES. (1910-1934)

```
                           1           1         1   1
                           9           9         9   9
                           1           2         3   3
                           01234567890123456789001234
```

White Hart Street	†	† M
Slater Street	†	† M
Westbourne Street	†	† M
Naphill	†	E † M
Lacey Green	†	† M
Penn/Tylers Green	†	† M
Gt.Kingshill	†	† M
Lee Common	†	† M
Great Missenden	†	† M
Wheeler End	†	† M
Radnage	†	† M
Downley	†	† M
Bryants Bottom	†	† M
Sands Road	† B	† M

B = Chapel Built
E = Chapel Extended or Additional Buildings e.g. Schoolroom
M = United in the Methodist Church
† = Services (from available Plans)

HIGH WYCOMBE PRIMITIVE CIRCUIT - MINISTERS

	SUPERINTENDENT	SECOND MINISTER
1832	James Pole	John Oscroft
33/34	: :	William Grant
35	: :	George Stacey
36	William Hardwick	James Varne
37	William Tomkins	: :
38/39	: : :	
1840	George Gingell	
41	John Guy	
42/43	John Stroud	
44	John Grey	Charles Lock
45/46	Joseph Willimott	: :
47	Thomas Williams	
48	C.Robbins	
49	: :	Samuel Wilshaw
1850/51	Edward Tocock	
52	T.Jackson	
53	: :	John Friller
54/55	Dennis Kendall	James Mules
56	: : :	R.V.Monkman
57	James Symonds	: :
58/59	: : :	
1860/63	M.Wilson	
64/65	Elijah Jackson	Joseph Toulson
66	William Birks	
67	: : :	J.T.Kearns
68	: : :	
69	P.Coates	
1870	P.Coates	
71	: :	J.Spooner
72	: :	
73/74	Robert R.Connell	
75/76	: : :	Robert Andrews
77	Charles Jupe	: : :
78	: :	John H.Atkinson
79	: :	George R.D.Austin
1880/81	Josiah Turley	George R.D.Austin
82	: : :	Samuel T.Wallis

	SUPERINTENDENT	SECOND MINISTER
1883/84	Samuel T. Wallis	Thomas McKenzie
85	Robert Andrews	: : :
86/88	: : :	Charles Higgins
89	: : :	George Stanyer
1890	Dennis Kendall	Geo. Stanyer/Geo. Ellis
91	: : :	John Cope/Wm. Hindes
92	Henry J. Beckhurst	John Milner/ : :
93	: : : :	: : /Chas. Carter
94/95	Edwin Millichamp	Jos. Everingham/R. Burnett
96	: : :	: : : /J. Barnes
97	Charles Jupe	Frederick W. Atkin
98	: :	A. Walsham/Geo. Turburfield
99	: :	: : /Abijah Heaton
1900	Charles Jupe	J. White/Abijah Heaton
01	Thomas Peatfield	James Naisbit/Chas. Jupe
02/04	: : :	: : :
05	: : :	Walter Curtis/Harold Pope
06	John Smith	: : : / : :
07	John Richardson	: : : / : :
08	: : :	: : :
09	: : :	John Holmes
1910/11	John Holmes	Daniel Dunn
12/13	John G. Cushing	: :
14/16	: : :	William Booth
17/18	William Booth	William D. Turner
19/22	Thomas L. Page	Frederick G. Saville
1923/24	Ernest G. French	: : : :
25/27	: : :	Walter C. Healdfell
28	Frank E. Yeomans	: : : :
29/30	: : :	Samuel Walpole
1931/32	Wilfred S. Hinchcliffe	: : :
33	: : :	F. C. Searle

HIGH WYCOMBE PRIMITIVE CIRCUIT: LOCAL PREACHERS

NAME	FIRST REF.	LAST REF.	ADDRESS	NOTES
Sister Smith	1835	1835		
J.Clarke	1836	1836	Marlow	
S.Foley	1841	1883	Downley	
Sister Tomkins (nee Dell)	1841	1841	Downley	
Dell	1841	1841	Downley	
J.Pierce	1867	1883	Frogmoor Gardens	Died
T.Pierce	1867	1883	Frogmoor Gardens	
W.Woodley	1867	1877	Paradise Row	
C.Beeson	1867	1867	Lee	
W.Plumridge	1867	1896	West Wycombe	
Thomas Lloyd Robinson	1867	1883	Frogmoor Gardens	Died
J.Hunt	1867	1867	Frogmoor Gardens	
J.Pratt (Sup)	1867	1877	Lee Common	
J.Fryer	1867	1877	West Wycombe Road	
J.Stone (Sup)	1867	1883	Bridge Street	
J.Worley	1867	1883	Oxford Road	
W.Johnson	1867	1905	West End	
W.Dean	1867	1910	North Town	
Jas.Nash (Sup)	1867	1883	White Horse, Little Kingshill	
W.Avery	1867	1867	Newland	
G.Worley	1867	1867	Temple End	
T.Anderson	1867	1867	Denmark Street	
Joseph Bailey	1861	1924	Wheeler End	Died 18th Mar
S.Plumridge	1867	1905	High Wycombe	
E.Coker (Sup)	1867	1905	Oxford Street	
W.Page	1867	1910	Great Kingshill (1877) Hyde Farm, Gt.Missenden (1896) Widmer Farm, Lacey Green (1905)	
J.King	1867	1877	Lee Common	
T.Manders (Sup)	1867	1877	Denmark Street	
R.Youens	1867	1877	Oxford Street	
W.Neville	1867	1905	Mendy Street	
E.J.Darke	1867	1867	Frogmoor Gardens	
F.Blackwell	1867	1867	Lee Common	
Alfred W.Hunt	1862	1910	Naphill	Died 28th Feb
J.Lane	1867	1877	Newland	
L.Batchelor (Sup)	1867	1867	Lee Common	
W.Wheeler (Sup)	1867	1867	Penn	
A.Taylor	1877	1877	Newland	
E.Pewsey	1877	1877	Hunt's Green, Lee	

NAME	FIRST REF.	LAST REF.	ADDRESS	NOTES
W. Pewsey	1877	1877	Hunt's Green, Lee	
J. Holland	1877	1896	Lacey Green	
D. Sargeant	1896	1910	Castle Street	
J. Bristow	1877	1877	Great Kingshill	
T. Lee	1877	1896	Naphill	
J. Strange	1877	1877	Wheeler End	
G. Bailey	1877	1910	Remington Terrace	
W. Cheese	1877	1883	St. Mary Street	
D. Chandler	1877	1905	Lee	Died
J. Ratliffe	1877	1877	Lee	
J. Page	1877	1877	Great Kingshill	
J. Anderson	1877	1910	Great Kingshill	
P. Hunt	1877	1883	High Wycombe	
T. Croxford	1883	1883	Westbourne Street	
W. Hawkins	1877	1910	Bridge Street	
J. K. Filbee	1877	1903	West Wycombe	
T. Savin	1877	1883	Egham Lee	
J. Batchelor	1877	1877	Lee	
C. Hudson	1877	1877	High Wycombe	
W. Pierce	1877	1883	Ward's Row	
F. Pierce	1877	1883	Oxford Road	
G. B. Lacey	1877	1932	Naphill	
W. Holland Sen.	1877	1932	The Lee	
H. Rackstraw	1877	1877	Oxford Road	
C. Wilbin	1883	1883	Totteridge Road	
C. Hawes	1883	1903	Gordon Road	
W. Line	1877	1934	West End Road	See Meth. list
A. Stone	1883	1905	Totteridge	
H. Monk	1883	1910	Ballinger Lee	
S. Hathaway	1883	1910	Totteridge Road	
E. H. Coker	1883	1883	Westbourne Street	
W. Vickers	1883	1883	Flackwell Heath	
F. Nash	1883	1883	Great Kingshill	
J. Stallwood	1883	1883	Westbourne Street	
H. James	1883	1883	Naphill	
F. Rentall	1883	1883	White Hart Street	
J. Williams	1883	1883	West Wycombe	
W. B. Gibson	1896	1903	Slater Street	
J. Evans	1896	1910	West End Road	
H. Abram	1896	1910	Lane End	
G. Darvell	1885	1934	Oak Mead	See Meth. list
F. Hunt	1885	1934	Baker Street	See Meth. list
H. Haddow	1896	1932	Oxford Road	
W. Bates	1896	1896	West End Road	

THE PRIMITIVE METHODIST CHURCH

NAME	1ST REF.	LAST REF.	ADDRESS	NOTES
G.Castle	1888	1934	Castle Hill	See Meth.list
G.H.Taylor	1896	1934	Oxford Road	See Meth.list
W.Worley	1896	1910	42,Brook Street	
J.Brooks	1896	1896	Bledlow Ridge	
J.Busby	1896	1910	5,York Place	
E.A.Stevens	1896	1896	Desborough Avenue	
E.J.Dormer	1892	1934	Radnage	See Meth.list
E.J.Gray	1896	1934	75,Desborough Road	See Meth.list
J.Plested	1896	1934	208,Desborough Road	See Meth.list
A.W.Nash	1896	1905	Hughenden Road	
C.T.Mold	1896	1903	Bridge Street	
W.Youens	1896	1903	Downley	
W.Shorto	1896	1896	Remington Terrace	
G.Shaw	1892	1934	Naphill	See Meth.list
Jno.Bailey	1903	1903	Wooburn Green	
J.Holland	1897	1934	94,West Wycombe Road	See Meth.list
A.Witney	1903	1905	Lacey Green	
J.Bristow	1903	1910	Cryers Hill	
H.James	1903	1934	Totteridge Road	See Meth.list
D.Sargeant	1898	1934	60,Totteridge Road	See Meth.list
J.Sargeant	1898	1934	105,Gordon Road	See Meth.list
T.H.Evans	1903	1905	Sands Road	
J.Copeland	1903	1910	Roberts Road	
Gibbs	1903	1903	Amersham Hill	
A.Richings	1903	1903	Hughenden Road	
A.Evans	1903	1905	Green Street	
J.Seymour	1903	1903	114,Desborough Road	
J.Hussey	1903	1910	High Wycombe	
E.Craft	1905	1905	High Wycombe	
E.Coker	1905	1910	Hughenden Valley	
J.Lacey	1904	1934	Suffield Road	See Meth.list
A.Sargeant	1904	1934	131,West End Road	See Meth.list
F.G.Berry	1904	1934	39,Abercrombie Ave.	See Meth.list
W.Hill	1905	1905	High Wycombe	
T.G.Castle	1904	1934	Bassetsbury Lane	See Meth.list
A.Hook	1905	1905	High Wycombe	
A.Randall	1905	1934	The Lee	See Meth.list
H.Bignell	1907	1934	The Lee	See Meth.list
F.Rixon	1908	1934	Lacey Green	See Meth.list
S.Goodearl	1908	1934	Kitchener Road	See Meth.list
H.T.Turnbull	1909	1934	Bassetsbury Lane	See Meth.list
T.Barnett	1910	1934	85,Oakridge Road	See Meth.list

NAME	FIRST REF.	LAST REF.	ADDRESS	NOTES
A. Farr	1910	1910	Newland	
R. Burge	1910	1910	West Wycombe Road	
W. Smith	1913	1934	Winch Bottom,	See Meth. list
F. Randall	1913	1934	Ballinger	See Meth. list
G. W. Darvill	1916	1934	34, Slater Street	See Meth. list
J. Symes	1932	1934	11, Temple End	See Meth. list
J. Leaver	1932	1932	10, Oxford Street	
W. Coker	1932	1934	Station Road	See Meth. list
R. Jupe	1932	1934	Widmer End	See Meth. list
W. R. Bates	1921	1934	159, Abercrombie Ave.	See Meth. list
H. Marrett	1932	1934	Priory Road	See Meth. list
E. Barlow	1932	1934	Oakridge Wood	See Meth. list
G. H. Jones	1926	1934	Ashfield, Naphill	See Meth. list
E. Castle	1926	1934	118, Oakridge Road	See Meth. list
W. Smith (2)	1930	1934	Bryants Bottom	See Meth. list
J. H. Ayres	1932	1932	15, Coronation Place	
Miss E. Shipham	1934	1934		See Meth. list
C. Brake	1933	1934		See Meth. list

Names were taken from available Plans. Apparent disorder of
dates results from references in other sources, but Plan order
has been preserved indicating seniority.

(Sup.) = Supernumerary.

CHAPTER 5

PRIMITIVE METHODIST CHURCHES

WOOBURN GREEN (1832)

Baptismal records exist from 1832 to 1836 for a Primitive chapel which stood at the bottom of Windsor Hill. Rev.James Pole held a camp meeting at Wooburn in 1835 and despite opposition saw two conversions. In his "Account of the work of God in the High Wycombe Branch of Reading Circuit" (1842) Rev. John Guy states that the chapel was due to be sold in 1839.

He continues: "It was 25 pounds (two years' interest) behind. The society was low and the congregation small. In 1840 Brother G.Grigg was stationed at this branch. He begged for the chapel £6.17s.10d. [£6.89] which, with the anniversary, paid the interest for the current year. The Golden System was introduced and at the anniversary of 1841 £31.5s.0d.[£31.25] was paid off which cleared all up to that time. A few of the friends from this place attended the Conference Camp meeting at Reading June 13, 1841, got quickened in their souls and have been doing better ever since. In their low state a few laboured hard to keep up their sabbath school; and they believe it is on that account the Lord is smiling on them again."

In 1857 the Primitive Methodist Magazine reported that the members at Wooburn had been revived and "two souls converted". There is no further mention of the cause which we believe was taken over in about 1860 by the Wesleyan Reform Union (Free Methodists).

LITTLEWORTH COMMON (1832)

The village nowadays nestles round a rough wooded common and consists of a few cottages, a pub ("The Jolly Woodman"), a school and the small flint church of St.Anne's (built 1866). When Lord Granville gave the Methodists permission in 1832 to build a chapel on the common-ground, the area was even more heavily wooded. (At one time Burnham Beeches extended as far as Wooburn.) Into this forest area in 1835 came the evangelist, Rev.James Pole, and his camp meeting produced great results, including the conversion of two or three future preachers. But in 1842 Rev.John Guy reported that the "plain chapel" still owed £45 to his Lordship. He continues: "The chapel got embarrassed. There was but one member for six or seven years. But we held revival and other extra meetings. A few have been added, the congregation has increased and the chapel is paying its way." Today - alas! - there is no trace of one of the earliest Primitive chapels.

SOCIETIES WITHOUT CHAPELS (from 1835)

Like the Wesleyans, groups of Primitive Methodists often met in a cottage or barn at first but in some villages they did not last long enough to build their own chapel. Some were evangelised by Rev.James Pole in 1835.

SPEEN (1835): Two men in the village had been fighting and one had been killed. His brother had killed another man and was in prison. During a period of six months within five miles of Speen three others had been killed fighting. Into this dread area came James Pole - and a crowd of 400 to listen! The visit was so successful that soon afterwards a Methodist society was formed and a preaching house opened. But it does not seem to have lasted many years.

PENN STREET (1835) : James Pole preached here in the open air but was almost beaten by the cold wet weather. At last a baker allowed him to use his bakehouse which "became our preaching house". The society continued until at least 1859 as the following obituaries from the Primitive Methodist Magazine show:

"Died at Penn-street on 19th October 1857, aged 25, Elizabeth Pierce. About eight years ago she was awakened to her sinful state by reading a book called 'Early Piety'. We having a little society at the place, the members of which were ready to take their neighbours by the hand and lead them to Jesus, one of the number, William Flexman, invited her to go to a public meeting at Wycombe; and at that meeting she found peace with Jesus and went home rejoicing. Her mother informed me that she has known her frequently sit up to read her Bible till 4 o'clock

in the morning. She was also very fond of singing and being
regular at the means of grace, was a great help in the singing
part of the service. She was an example to young females in the
village; and often when returning home, she would make the woods
ring as she sang of the love of her blessed Redeemer.   Her
sufferings at last were very great. A few days before she died,
her mother said, 'My dear, you will soon be in heaven;' and in a
moment with her eyes turned upwards she said, 'There I shall see
William Davey' and a few brethren that she knew who had died.
Then she wished to see Rev.J.Mules.   'I shall see him in
heaven,' she said."

T.PIERCE

"Sarah Moorcroft was born at Winchmoire Hill, High Wycomb
Circuit, and died at Penn Street on 28th January 1859 at the age
of 62. In her early life she was strictly moral and often seen
at the house of prayer. She however lived a stranger to the
saving grace of God until after her marriage in 1836. At length
she became deeply concerned for the salvation of her soul and
great was her distress of mind.   Previous to this she had
attended religious ordinances among the Baptists; but living
neighbour to one of our female members who had a class-meeting
conducted in her house, she was induced to attend and soon found
peace in her troubled conscience. From that time she cast in
her lot among our people and remained a consistent member to the
time of her death."

EPHRAIM BOVINGTON

HAZLEMERE (1835):   Rev.James Pole's evangelistic campaign
reached this village too and a woman had a dramatic conversion
at one of his meetings. In his journal he speaks of a society
existing here in 1836.

BLEDLOW RIDGE (1835):   James Pole preached in "Bladlon"
(Bledlow) which appeared "to be very dark". A society was
formed in nearby Bledlow Ridge but Rev.George Gyngell,
Superintendent of the High Wycombe Circuit in 1840, writes in
the Primitive Methodist Magazine:
"A train of circumstances which I shall not intrude on the
attention of the reader, caused the preaching to be withheld
from Bledlow Ridge, which was the subject of much trial to the
writer of these lines."

SEER GREEN (1840):   Rev.John Guy, Superintendent of the High
Wycombe Circuit in 1841, writes in the same Magazine:
"The work of God was low here till about Michaelmas 1841.
I preached in the open-air one moonlight evening, in the

harvest, just as the people were coming from their labour. I
spoke on judgement and several were powerfully wrought on: and
sometime after, when I was family visiting round the Green, I
was told by several that they had not forgotten the night I
preached by moonlight on "A time to die" (Ecclesiastes 3.2).
Brother Watson began to be anxiously concerned for the salvation
of sinners in the place. We counted up the inhabitants and
found that not one in ten belonged to any Christian society. He
called a meeting of the members and showed the necessity of
making more exertions to turn the people to the Lord. They
resolved to wrestle in faith and prayer until God converted a
tenth part of the people and they became members. As soon as
the society began in earnest, more hearers attended and some of
the most ungodly began to seek the Lord. Ten persons joined who
can testify that their sins are forgiven; and an old man who had
been a year or two in the society, died in peace. A short time
before he died, he said, 'The farther I go, the brighter it
gets'. And our people are going on for another tenth; or, as
they express it, are tithing them over again. 'Sing ye to the
Lord for He hath triumphed gloriously' (Exodus 15.21)."

BEACONSFIELD (1856): Rev. R. W. Monkman, second Minister in the
High Wycombe Circuit in 1856/7, writes in the Primitive
Methodist Magazine:
    "On Sunday 26th October 1856 a revival meeting was held at
Beaconsfield when the hearts of Brother Symonds and others were
cheered by hearing nine persons profess to have found the Lord."

WOOBURN MOOR (1866): Rev. William Birks, Superintendent of the
High Wycombe Circuit in 1866/8, writes in the same Magazine:
    "At Wooburn Moor after preaching in the open air during a
portion of the season in 1866, we obtained a cottage in which to
hold our regular services, and we are happy to say we have
formed a small society and our congregations are pretty good on
the whole. May heaven clear our way and bless us speedily with
a more commodious place in which to worship God; and may this
station soon be honoured with a greater outpouring of the Holy
Spirit than it has hitherto experienced."

MOOR'S TOWN (1866): No-one seems to know where this place was!
"Town" traditionally means "an enclosed place" (that is, not
necessarily a densely populated urban area) but we do not know
of which Moor it was part. It clearly was not Wooburn Moor
which is listed as a separate place on the 1866 plan. We
wondered if it was Moor Common - near Lane End - but local

historians assure us that there have only ever been an Anglican church - which was transferred stone by stone to Cadmore End before this time - and a Brethren's (later Elim Pentecostal) chapel there. But it certainly existed! Rev.William Birks records (note the change of spelling):

"At Moore's Town the Lord has graciously cleared our way. We missioned this place during the end of summer 1866 and in October took a chapel at an annual rental of £5, which was opened for Divine service on Lord's day 14th October 1866 when the writer preached two sermons to large congregations, and our congregations continue to be good, the chapel being generally full at our regular services. Here we have raised a Sabbath-school which is doing well and likely to be made a great blessing to the neighbourhood."

The "Bucks Free Press" also reports on 4th May 1867:

"The 1st Anniversary of the Sunday School was held at Moore's Town. Mr.T.P.Robinson (of High Wycombe) presided and addresses were given by Mr.E.J.Darke and Rev.W.Birks."

CHORLEY WOOD, FULMER & WEST HYDE (1867) appear in the circuit plan of that year in the "Chalfont St.Giles Branch" section. We have no record of any chapels.

LITTLE HAMPDEN & SCRUBWOOD (1877), like the others in this group, apparently had "no earthly tabernacle". Little Hampden already had a Wesleyan society (1874); perhaps the people transferred from one to the other. As with Moor's Town, we do not even know where Scrubwood was!

LEE COMMON (1839)

THE NEW CHAPEL (1841)

Our chapel here is 30 feet long and 18 feet wide. It was opened about midsummer 1839. It cost £114 and about £14 was collected. There are no pews. It is fitted up with rail-backed seats and benches. The seats let well and more than pay the interest. At the anniversary, 18th July 1841, we introduced the Golden System and £8 5s.0d.[£8.25] was promised for the next year. I came here in July 1840 and found there was something wanting; namely a sabbath school. I laid the matter before the quarterly meeting; and being planned here on Sunday 4th October

1840, on that day the school was opened; and since then two of
the boys have been removed to the paradise of God. The school
has increased to about 50 scholars and has been a blessing to
the society and congregation. O Lord, watch over it and make it
a blessing as long as the sun and moon endure.

On Sunday 17th October 1841 a protracted meeting was
commenced at Lee. The services were powerful through the day.
On Monday afternoon we held a tea meeting on behalf of the
chapel. We thought of speaking while the friends were taking
tea; but it was a trial of faith to begin. As the brethren
wished me to speak first, I began and succeeded better than I
expected. Brothers Isaac Hedges and George Adey followed; and
meanwhile there was a glorious outpouring of the Holy Spirit.
Some of our friends who had heard me speak of Mr.Hugh Bourne
preaching at Burghfield in May 1840 while the friends were
taking tea, wished to see it so themselves; and on this occasion
we found it practicable to take food, drink tea and shout
"glory" between times. We had also a very powerful service
after tea; two souls were converted and the whole of the society
began to rise by faith into the power of God.

Tuesday morning there was much power in prayer. In the
evening the anxiety of the members for the salvation of sinners
much increased and the hearers were much affected. Wednesday
morning, a conflict. In the evening there was great solemnity
among the people under the preaching. Afterwards I led a class,
desiring the mourners to stay. Two stayed and both were set at
liberty. Thursday morning and evening, good times. Friday
evening, a fellowship meeting. Some spoke of having neglected
to warn sinners when they had opportunity; but were minded not
to let sin go unreproved. Others spoke of instances wherein the
fear of man had brought them into a snare. At the opening I
desired them to give an account of their experience for the last
fortnight. Several spoke of strong inward conflicts and
heaviness through manifold temptations. A few had had great
manifestations of glory and of God. On the whole it was a very
profitable meeting to many souls. Near the close, I told the
members that the unconverted had heard their vows and
determinations to be faithful with them. And I told the
unconverted that it was a great mercy for them that there was a
Primitive Methodist chapel to come to, and a society that cared
for their souls. The work of God has been deepening since. We
have 45 members and the chapel is usually crowded.

(Rev.) JOHN GUY

PRIMITIVE METHODIST CHURCHES

PROGRESS (1850)

On behalf of our chapel at Lee Common three sermons were preached on 15th September 1850 by brother E.Tocock and we had large congregations and encouraging collections. On the following day about 120 persons sat down to an excellent tea. Here several of our friends for years have felt a deep interest in their chapel matters; consequently the trust-debt has been considerably reduced. In the evening we received a handsome sum, collected on the golden system, by Mrs.E.Batchlor, Mrs.Beeson and Mrs.Mereden. An interesting public meeting was then held, well supplied with speakers, for we had just closed the business of our quarterly meeting. Two of our members had died in the Lord during the quarter but several persons had joined our societies; and though the expenditure was greater than the preceding one, yet after paying all demands, we had a balance in hand of £1 4s.9d.[£1.24]. This happy state of things incited us to "thank God and take courage".

(Rev.) C.ROBBINS

17th ANNIVERSARY (1856)

On 5th October 1856 the anniversary of Lee Chapel was held when three sermons were preached by R.W.Monkman. The congregations were good and a blessed influence pervaded the assemblies. On the following day about 70 persons sat down to a tea given by a few friends. A public meeting was held in the evening. The proceeds of this anniversary were considerably in advance of those of the preceding year.

(Rev.) R.W.MONKMAN

REVIVAL (1866)

At Lee Common special efforts have been made in 1866 to promote a revival of God's work and some souls have been saved and our chapel debt reduced £11.10s.0d. [£11.50], leaving only £74 debt on the school and chapel premises.

(Rev.) WILLIAM BIRKS

A LIVELY SERVICE (1867)

In April there was a tea at Lee Common Primitive Methodist Chapel, followed by a service, conducted in a lively manner by Miss Stedman.

"BUCKS FREE PRESS"

CHRISTMAS DAY (1876)

Christmas Day was celebrated by a Christmas tree and a tea at 4 o'clock. Evening entertainment was provided by members of the Tonic Sol-Fa Class (under Sunday School Superintendent Mr.Stiles). The room was packed and £10 was realized for School funds.

"BUCKS FREE PRESS"

VIOLET GHORST writes:

Lee Common Chapel, like many other buildings in this area, was constructed out of bricks and flints. The 1878 minute-book records a Sunday School membership of 100 most of whom came to both sessions. There were three services each Sunday. Preachers came from High Wycombe - on foot or bicycle or in the circuit pony and trap. Primitives loved open-air services and I can remember the camp meetings of my childhood days when Mr.Rixon, Mr.Jarrett and William Line would conduct services in an orchard behind the church, a farm cart serving as pulpit. Centenary celebrations in 1939 lasted three days and drew many visitors who had been connected with the Church in the past. A commemorative vestry was built. At first a member of the Wycombe Circuit, Lee Common moved to the newly formed Chesham and Chalfont (later Amersham) Circuit in 1951. Church Anniversaries have always been celebrated with enthusiasm at Lee Common and attract notable preachers and good congregations.

Over the years many repairs and renovations have taken place. The gallery was removed in 1962. As village life changed, so did the life of the Church and by the 1980's the membership had dropped to a handful. The building had deteriorated so badly that a Circuit Consultation was called to consider possible closure. Otherwise extensive repairs would be needed. Renovations were in fact carried out in 1985-6 and the church refurbished. Rotten wood was removed and the building was made damp-proof, warm and comfortable. £9000 was raised - partly from local efforts and partly from the Circuit and churches of other denominations. We now have a beautiful church with a deeply spiritual atmosphere and a friendly welcome. It is used for interdenominational study, quiet days, conferences and for Methodist Sunday afternoon services. Membership is increasing, as we continue to worship and bear witness to the glory of God.

PRIMITIVE METHODIST CHURCHES

1987 PILGRIMAGE

The village consists of several old flint and brick cottages and the chapel itself is set back from the main road. Since its modernisation it has been used by several different organisations. The interior is bright and attractive, combining old pews with modern comfortable chairs. The carved lectern is on loan from Prestwood

Methodist Church and the pew behind the organ came from the chapel in Great Missenden when it closed in 1938. Each piece of the tea-set, which is still in regular use, is stamped 1899. The church is used as a retreat and is a place of peace for all.

MYRTLE CHURCH

PENN - TYLERS GREEN (1843)

After Rev.James Pole's meetings at one of which 1500 people were present, a society was established at Penn. Despite opposition from other churches the numbers increased sufficiently for a chapel to be built in Church Road. Rev.William Birks wrote in 1866 that the debt had been reduced by £10. He remarks: "Although the interest here is somewhat feeble, yet the Lord is with us and we are praying for better days".

REV.EDMUND HANCOCK (1817-1883)

Born at Penn in the year 1817, he was brought as a young man to God through the preaching of our people in his native village. It was at an open-air service that he was convinced of sin, and in his father's house, while earnestly praying for pardon, where he obtained forgiveness and peace. He was called into the ministry by the Missionary Committee in 1843 and commenced his labours in the Tredegar Station where he laboured with much success; and for 31 years he continued to labour earnestly and successfully on some of the most extensive circuits in the Connexion. He was known as a good sound preacher, as a man of deep-toned piety and with a burning desire for the salvation of souls. Through failing health he became superannuated in 1875. In 1879 he came to reside at Penn where with unabated zeal he continued to work in the Sunday School and in visiting the sick until the time of his death. He was indeed a good man and loved by all who knew him. After some weeks of severe affliction his happy spirit passed away on 14th April 1883. His last words were: "I have the victory". May it be ours to triumph so when all our warfare is past.

CIRCUIT PLAN (1883)

MARION HOWARTH writes:

Penn Chapel was bought by the John Metcalfe (Christian Publishing) Trust in 1968 when the remaining members transferred to the new Coppice Farm Methodist Church. Memories go back to the coke boiler which provided heating in the chapel, and the open fire in the schoolroom. Water was carried from nearby houses for chapel teas. The Women's Own meetings – with hymns from Sankey's "Sacred Songs and Solos" – were very popular. The wiry Mrs.Grenstreet was quite a character and the mainstay of the chapel for many years. When it was sold, she continued the Sunday School in a caravan in her garden next door to the chapel. As there wasn't room for a piano, she learned to play the zither! Tragically, she was killed by a lorry in the narrow road close to her beloved chapel.

CHALFONT ST.GILES – DEANWAY UNITED (1847)

WILFRID NEVILLE writes:

Two Primitive Methodist evangelists from High Wycombe, Joseph and Thomas Pierce, conducted open-air meetings at Chalfont St.Giles in 1832. A little society was formed and a small room rented. Among the first members were Lowing Tripp, the blacksmith (remembered for his loving welcome), and Isaac Pratt, a yeoman. In 1847 a plot of land, measuring seven poles, between Three Households and Chalfont St.Giles, was purchased for £11. A chapel was built – a "neat connexional building" – at a cost of £120 and the first Minister was Rev.James Horberry.

PRIMITIVE METHODIST MAGAZINE

At Three Households in 1856 several were converted. The
anniversary of the chapel was held on 12th and 13th October when
three sermons were preached by Rev.J.Symonds to large and
attentive congregations. On the following day about 200 persons
sat down to tea. A public meeting was held in the evening when
addresses were delivered by Messrs. Hunt, Smith, Worley,
Robinson, Pierce, Gamble, Monkman and Symonds. The collections
were more than those of last year. One who does not wish his
"left hand to know what his right hand doeth", gave liberally to
the chapel funds. At the close of the sabbath services one
penitent found the "pearl of great price" and went home
rejoicing. Another who was in distress, obtained some comfort.
On 26th October two or three souls were in great distress and
requested to be prayed for; and could we have but commanded more
strength in the prayer meeting, I doubt not but that they would

have been brought into liberty. We feel thankful to God for these signs of future good.

(Rev.) R.W.MONKMAN

WILFRID NEVILLE continues:

The Church became part of the Wycombe Circuit in 1863. The foundation stone for a larger church was laid on 28th May 1865 when 400 people enjoyed tea in Mr.Hill's orchard. The "Bucks. Free Press" reported that it was hoped to call the building the "John Milton Memorial Chapel". (The poet's cottage is on the other side of Dean Way.) It was opened on Christmas Day when despite heavy falls of snow a service, tea and public meeting were held. Payments to Northcroft, the builder, amounted to £500, while lamps for the new chapel cost £1.13s.1d. [£1.65½.] The baptismal register reveals that most men at that time were labourers, farmers, gardeners or chairmakers. One was a brickmaker, another a horsekeeper - and a third gave his occupation as "gentleman"! Later iron moulders, engine drivers and police officers joined the list. The chapel opening was celebrated each Christmas. In 1870 the singers were asked to "get up a concert and limit themselves to a selection of sacred music"! Mrs.Carter, the chapel keeper, was requested to "boil water at tea meetings and wash up". For these services she received £3 a year.

The growing importance of the work led in 1876 to the formation of the Chalfont St.Giles Circuit with three other societies: Winchmore Hill, Amersham Common and Chorley Wood. The "Bucks. Free Press" in 1877 reported: "The Primitive Methodist Chapel held special services on Sunday 28th January when the preachers were Rev.Jupe and Rev.W.Hobling (Gold Hill). The annual Missionary Meeting was held on Tuesday 30th January when the preacher was Rev.J.Rackham." A new harmonium was purchased in 1882 for £15.15s.0d.[£15.75] and an organ in 1901 for £46.8s.0d.[£46.40]. In 1897 Danesbury House, next door to the chapel, was bought as a Minister's house and continued in use until 1951. A new schoolroom was built for £243 in 1905, followed by the complete renovation of the chapel which now included a brick and stone porch, a new rostrum with a "beautiful green plush pulpit cover" and a Communion rail. Much of the £400 cost came from churches of other denominations. It reopened in 1907 and one of Rev.F.Stone's first tasks was to chase up those members who had wandered away during the year's closure.

PRIMITIVE METHODIST CHURCHES

In the inter-war years Chalfont St.Giles took a special interest in the Epileptic Colony where Sunday afternoon services were held, and in more recent times Ponds Spastics' Home at Seer Green. By 1937 the financial burden had become so heavy that the circuit rejoined the High Wycombe Circuit. In 1951 the new Chesham and Chalfont St.Giles (later Amersham) Circuit was formed. Centenary celebrations were held in 1966. Further celebrations on 10th September 1977 - to mark the union of the Methodist and United Reformed Churches into "Deanway United" Church - were led by Rev.R.L.J.Kaye, Chairman of London North-West District, and Rev.R.J.Hall, Moderator of North Thames Province. The Methodist chapel was retained as the new Church. Chalfont St.Giles is notable for the families who have served the Church long and faithfully, such as Tripp, Lofty, Neville, Stone, Carden, Kirby, Wellings and Axe, some to the present day. They were glad to do God's will. We thank God and pray that there may be many more to follow in their footsteps.

THE WORK GOES ON!

We offer our warmest congratulations to Stuart Cato on his acceptance as a candidate for the Methodist Ministry. He and his wife Lene will be moving up to begin training in Manchester. We thank them both for their ministries among us and pray God's blessing upon them in the future. Martin Wellings also is offering himself as a candidate for the Ministry during this coming year.

CIRCUIT PLAN (1987)

FLACKWELL HEATH (1848)

A group of Primitive Methodists met at first in Chopsticks Alley where there was much heckling and general pandemonium. The "Ranters" - as the "Prims." were commonly known - opened their chapel in 1848. The Primitive Methodist Magazine reported that a missionary meeting was held on 8th February 1866, presided over by Rev.W.Birks. Sermons were given by Revs.J.Phillips (London) and W.J.Bullivant. Thereafter the voice of Primitive Methodism in Flackwell Heath appears to have been silenced.

FROGMOOR GARDENS (1848)

Unlike the Wesleyans whose first chapel in this area was in Wycombe itself (in St.Mary Street), the first Primitive chapels were in the villages outside the town: note the number which have preceded Frogmoor in this chapter. Following Rev.James Pole's evangelistic campaign which started in Queen's Square, a group of Primitives had in fact been meeting in Mr.Pierce's cottage at Frogmoor since 1835, and now at last in 1848 a chapel was built in the borough itself. But although it was extended in 1860, it was never really big enough for the large numbers who flocked there, and by 1875 it had been replaced by the much larger White Hart Street chapel. The Frogmoor church was taken over in 1882 by the Salvation Army who were beginning to make their noisy presence felt at this time. In 1909 they moved over the road to their present citadel - and a greater acceptance by the townsfolk! The chapel then became the Palace Cinema before that too moved to the other side of Frogmoor.

Picture the Wycombe of 1848 in company with Henry Kingston who wrote:

"The beech-clad hills of Bucks. which spontaneously adorn and beautify the Hundreds of Desborough, encompass not a more picturesque valley than it does the place where stands my Native Town. Sequestered little spot! Adorned by nature with many delightful varieties of hill and dale, it seems to afford security for retirement; and those who love to watch the sparkling brook and gaze with delight on the verdure and fertility of the surrounding pasture, in preference to luxury; or repose in the shade of secluded woods, rather than seek the honours of princes or the equinoctial hurricanes of political notoriety, may dwell for a time in Wycombe and 'babble o' green fields'."

Many of our older readers will recall the Frogmoor of the pre-1939 War era - especially the old fountain which James Griffits had given to the town in 1875 when he presented the island site for use as a public meeting place. Its main basin was usually full of rain water and general refuse but it was so solidly constructed that it never seemed to get vandalised! (It was removed "to help in the War Effort"!) But when the Primitive chapel opened in the middle of the last century, Frogmoor (or Frogmore) Gardens was an enclosed private place to which the Methodists had no access. The streets were dimly lit by gas and the Borough ended just up the road at Temple End. In its later years proceedings were sometimes interrupted by the thunder of hooves outside as the horses dashed from their normal bus duties between West Wycombe and Loudwater, to haul the fire-engine which was kept in a small house at the end of Frogmoor.

The following extracts from the PRIMITIVE METHODIST MAGAZINE give us a flavour of this busy chapel:

EARLY DAYS (1842)

In the town of High Wycomb the society is more alive to God and lately a few have been converted.

(Rev.) JOHN GUY

CHAPEL OPENING (1848)

A new Connexional chapel was opened in High Wycombe on 3rd September 1848 when sermons were preached by Messrs. J.Hayden (Independent) and T.Hobson. On the 4th a tea meeting was held in the Town Hall; upwards of 300 persons were present and several effectual addresses were given by Messrs. Foizey, Hobson and several ministers and gentlemen of the town: and on the 10th we had the pleasure of hearing sermons from Mr.T.Hobson (Baptist) and brother Foizey. A good influence was felt at all the services and upwards of £50 was realized. The chapel stands on the most eligible freehold site in the town; it is 22 feet by 40 inside, 20 feet from the floor to the ceiling, is well ventilated under the floor, has four Gothic windows in front, and four plain ones in the back, all openable at the top. It has a front gallery, as well as several good pews and rail-backed forms, and is well

lighted with gas and is enclosed in front by iron palisading. In its erection there has been expended about £500 towards which the noble sum of about £200 has been raised by subscriptions, donations and collections; and we have promises that a good amount shall be brought next Christmas. The trustees and friends intend raising £100 for the first anniversary, leaving a debt of only £200 on the erection. The former are thankful that God has enabled them, with the aid of their friends, to rear this place of worship which is deemed the cheapest and neatest in the town. To all the friends (especially J. Hunt Esq. who sold us the premises at great sacrifice and has otherwise nobly assisted us) we tender our sincere thanks and pray that they may be amply rewarded and that God's work may revive here and throughout the Connexion.

(Rev.) THOMAS WILLIAMS

FIRST ANNIVERSARY (1849)

The first anniversary services of the chapel at High Wycombe were held on 2nd and 3rd September 1849. On the former day two heart-searching sermons were preached by brother H. Pope from Luton; and we had an able discourse from Rev. W. Roberts (Independent). An excellent tea-meeting was held in the Town Hall on the 3rd when our respected friend, Joseph Hunt Esq., presided in his usually interesting manner; and spirited addresses were delivered by Rev. J. Hobson (Baptist), T. N. Baker Esq. from London and Messrs. Pope, Foizey, Wigley and Bendle. The tea was furnished gratis; and the collections and subscriptions amounted to £23.4s.8½d. [£23.24]. The chapel has already proved the birthplace of many souls; the society and congregation are doing well and we have an excellent prospect of future improvement.

(Rev.) C. ROBBINS

SUNDAY SCHOOL TREAT (1850)

On the morning of 25th June 1850, the children of our Sunday School assembled in our chapel and proceeded thence in four waggons lent by J. Hunt Esq. to his residence at Cressex Farm, singing as they proceeded. Here 200 teachers and children dined on beef and plum-pudding; in addition to which Mr. Hunt presented them with a fat sheep. After an appropriate interval suitable addresses were delivered to the children by brothers Bishop and Wilshaw from Reading. Next about 600 persons partook of tea; and the people who had increased to about 1000, were addressed by the forenamed brethren, H. Cassham Esq. and Messrs. Dobinson, Briggs, Herbert, Buckland and Herridge. In the name of the teachers a very elegantly bound octavo edition of Bagsters' Polyglot Bible was presented by Mr.Hunt to Mr.D.Mossop who is about leaving Wycombe for Hawkesbury. The cover of the Bible bears the following inscription in gold letters: "Presented to the Rev.D.Mossop, by the teachers of the Primitive Methodist Sunday-school, High Wycomb, on 25th June 1850". The day's proceedings were conducted with religious propriety and to the satisfaction and profit of those who had the happiness of being participators therein.

(Rev.) SAMUEL WILSHAW

SUNDAY SCHOOL FESTIVAL (1851)

The annual festival of this flourishing institution was celebrated on Tuesday 8th July 1851. Prior to this time many prayers were offered to the Most High that He would honour the services in connection with the occasion with a large measure of heavenly influence. The place appointed for the occasion was Cressex, the residence of J.Hunt Esq., who is deeply interested in promoting the wellbeing of the rising race and who, in connection with the noble band of zealous and devoted teachers, thinks no trouble or sacrifices too great, so that this end may be accomplished.

At eleven o'clock a.m. the teachers and children met at the chapel; nearly an hour was spent in singing and prayer and making preparations for starting; a procession was then formed, headed by two of our ministers and several local preachers, and followed by a goodly company of friends from the country. It proceeded through the town in Primitive Methodistic style, singing the 17th hymn in our small hymn-book. In the course of an hour the destined spot was reached and soon afterwards the little ones did ample justice to the good old English fare, "beef and plum-pudding", a sufficient supply of which was provided by the teachers. Next followed the tea-meeting at which about 200 persons sat down.

The public meeting in the evening was one of deep interest. The speaking was not confined exclusively to the subject of sabbath school instruction but a variety of subjects were discussed by the different speakers. Brother J.Pierce (the oldest local preacher on our plan) was called to the chair and after making a few appropriate remarks, was followed by Messrs. Sharman, Hancock, Hunt, Pierce, Rose; and Robbins - our late respected superintendent - who on this occasion took his farewell of the friends, being about to remove to the Maidenhead

Circuit. In the course of the evening the chairman, in the name of his local brethren, presented Mr.Robbins with a copy of the English version of the Polyglot Bible, bearing the following inscription: "Presented to the Rev.Charles Robbins, by the Primitive Methodist Local Preachers of the High Wycombe Circuit, as a token of their esteem, July 5th,1851".

In regard to the school I may just observe that it is prospering; the number of scholars is about 200; the number of teachers is 45 and most of them are pious members of our Society. Several children have been admitted as scholars during the past year; also additional teachers have been received. Some of the little ones have begun to love Jesus and a Juvenile Class has been formed for some of the girls, which is also prospering. To God be all the praise.

EDWARD BALL (1821-1851)

Edward Ball died, aged 30, on 29th October 1851. He had been a member of our society about 14 months; but before his union with us he was strictly moral and a punctual teacher in our sabbath school and the leader of the singing in our chapel. He became an earnest seeker of salvation and to his unspeakable joy he found the Lord. The church has lost a devoted member, his mother a dutiful son and his two orphans a tender father.

ELIZA PIERCE (d.1852)

Died at High Wycombe 15th May 1852 Eliza, wife of Joseph Pierce, senior local preacher of this circuit. She lived in the family of a Wesleyan minister 14 years, during the third of which she was brought to God. She joined the Wesleyan Methodist Society in connection with which she adorned the doctrine of Christ her Saviour until three years ago when she was married to brother Pierce, and then she united with us, continuing to be a devoted follower of Jesus. The affliction which terminated her earthly career, was a consumption.

(Rev.) EDWARD TOCOCK

CHAPEL ANNIVERSARY (1852)

The Anniversary Sermons for High Wycombe chapel were preached by Mr.J.Fuller and Mr.W.Butler (Independent) on 5th December 1852, in connection with our protracted meeting which commenced at the same time; and truly the Lord was amongst us. The tea-meeting and the public service afterwards were well supported. Several of our local preachers and the itinerant preachers delivered interesting and stirring addresses. Many hearts were warmed and God was glorified. The collections were liberal and the donations and the sums collected on the golden system considerably exceeded those of last year. Our gallery has lately been enlarged by making it two pews deeper, and our congregations are good, especially on Sabbath evenings.

During our protracted meeting which lasted nearly a fortnight, many believers were baptized anew with the Holy Spirit, and several sinners were converted to God. One whose life had been very profligate, through the influence of one of our members was prevailed upon to attend one of our services. When under the word his mind was powerfully impressed, and at prayer his guilty and burdened spirit obtained pardon and peace. The lovefeast was most interesting. Oh, how did our hearts burn within us while the members of the Church were talking of Jesus and His work! We take fresh courage and go forth to the help of the Lord.

A few extra services have grown out of this protracted meeting, prayer meetings being appointed to be held in different parts of the town purposely to bring sinners who may have felt reluctant to attend services at the chapel, under the sound of the word; and already we have beheld signs of good work being done. Last Sabbath evening another sinner stepped into liberty; also at the morning's prayer meeting another professed to lose his guilty burden. Praise God for all His mercies!

(Rev.) T.JACKSON

MATILDA YOUENS (1810-1854)

Mrs.Matilda Youens of High Wycombe fell asleep in Jesus 17th June 1854, aged 44. In early life she was humble and truly devoted to her widowed mother. More than 20 years ago she obtained true religion and identified herself with the Wesleyans. The graces of the Spirit abounded in her. About three years ago she united with our people. Her rich, deep-toned experience and aspirations were very refreshing to her classmates. She had no spiritual helper at home but she pressed on against wind and tide, like a majestic steam ship, until she reached the harbour in safety; and now, we doubt not, she enjoys repose. Her affliction was brief; she died as she lived, calm, peaceful and happy.

(Rev.) JAMES MULES

SPECIAL CAMPAIGN (1858)

A few weeks ago several of our official and private members in Wycombe began to feel "jealous for the Lord of Hosts" and increasingly anxious about the prosperity of Zion. We arranged to hold a society meeting and have a little friendly conversation on the subject. We did so; several spoke; some thought the society was not so healthy as was desirable; others pointed out certain evils which ought to be removed; but all was done in a Christian spirit. After which we passed the following resolutions:

(1) That it is the opinion of this meeting that there are evils in the Church which are to be lamented as being detrimental to the cause of Christ.

(2) That we resolve to put away from among us those evils, whatever they may be.

(3) That we consecrate ourselves afresh to God and seek a fuller baptism of the Holy Ghost.

(4) That we engage to pray for the conversion of souls and do what we can, to promote a revival.

The meeting closed under the blessing of heaven. Many felt it good to be there. Since then we have been progressing and the result has been a quickening of the Church and the conversion of souls.

On Sunday 17th January 1858 we commenced a protracted meeting at Wycombe when three souls found peace; some degree of power rested on us during the week and another soul was saved. On Sunday the 24th a woman was made happy and declared she had never felt so much enjoyment in all her life. Having been encouraged with these few drops, the brethren determined to continue the services another week; and in the prayer meeting following the evening service on Sunday 31st January ten souls professed to find the Lord. On Tuesday 2nd February four more were made happy. One case is worthy of special notice. A man whose wife had got made happy, was much enraged because she would go to the chapel, and declared that if she still persisted in going, he would "kill her". In this matter she resolved to obey God rather than man. He came to the chapel on Tuesday last, when an arrow, winged by the Spirit of God, stuck fast in his soul. He bowed down at the mercy-seat and God, for Christ's sake, pardoned his sins.

(Revs.) JAMES SYMONDS & R.W.MONKMAN

PRIMITIVE METHODIST CHURCHES

CHURCH EXTENSION (1860)

Under the Divine blessing we have completed the enlargement
of our chapel and the erection of the schoolrooms, involving an
outlay of nearly £300. Our reopening sermons were preached on
Sabbath 18th November 1860 by Revs. J. Hayden and E. Foizey. On
Monday 19th November a public meeting was convened in the
chapel; J. Hunt Esq. was in the chair; addresses were delivered
by Revs. J. Hayden, T. H. Browne, D. Pledge, E. Foizey and D. Kendall
and the circuit preachers. The collections amounted to
£8.3s.0d. (£8.15). It is gratifying to state that our Wycombe
Sunday-school teachers have unitedly promised the splendid sum
of £50. By general subscriptions we have raised £40. Among our
friends who have liberally responded to our call, we may
mention: Sir George Dashwood M.P. (£5); Martin T. Smith Esq.
M.P. (£5); T. Wheeler Esq. (£5). In furtherance of our object we
held a tea and public meeting in the Town Hall on Wednesday 26th
September 1860 when the trays were furnished gratuitously and
the sum of £13 was realized. Thus we have already raised £111
and hope shortly by special effort to raise £50 more. May we
have enlarged prosperity.

(Rev.) M. WILSON

CHAPEL ANNIVERSARY (1865)

On 5th and 6th November 1865 our chapel anniversary
services were held. On the Sabbath W. Birks preached in the
morning and in the afternoon Rev. J. F. Raw (Wesleyan) officiated
and in the evening John Rutty Esq. occupied the pulpit. The
congregations were good; and on the day following a public tea
meeting was held in the chapel and schoolroom when a goodly
number of persons was present. Several trays were furnished by
the friends and in the evening a public meeting was held in the
chapel, ably presided over by our well-tried friend, Mr. James
Smith. The meeting was addressed by J. Hunt Esq., D. Clarke Esq.,
W. Woodley and Revs. T. H. Brown (Independent), W. Norris and
William Birks. The proceeds of this anniversary, including
profits of tea, golden system money and collections, amounted to
about £35. We hope to pay off this year £28 of the present debt
on the chapel and we are happy to say that providing we can pay
off £80 more next year, we have £40 promised towards it for the
next anniversary and our trustees and friends are resolved to
try.

CHAPEL DEBT (1866)

At High Wycombe praiseworthy efforts have been made during 1866 to reduce our chapel debt. Our seat-rents' income has been in advance of several years previous and although our chapel anniversary collections were but £1.3s.9d. [£1.19] in advance of last year, yet by special efforts, donations and subscriptions we raised £68.4s.5½d. [£68.22], including a donation of £10 from the Hon.C.Carrington Esq. M.P.; also a donation from D.Clarke Esq. of £10. Thus we have been able to reduce our chapel debt £80 and we propose shortly to enlarge and greatly improve our chapel accommodation at this place.

(Rev.) WILLIAM BIRKS

FESTIVAL OF SONG (1875)

On Monday evening last a Festival of Song was held in the Town Hall, the proceeds being for the Building Fund of the large new chapel in White Hart Street. Miss Skull was at the piano, aided by Miss Nash (harmonium), Mr.Winch (flute), Mr.Gill (violin), Master M.Youens (corn-a-piston) and the Misses Emma Youens, Howland and Fanny Pierce (soloists). The conductor was Mr.John Youens and the proceedings were under the charge of Rev.R.R.Connell, the Superintendent Minister.

DEATH OF TWO FROGMOOR STALWARTS

JOSEPH HUNT fell asleep in Jesus on 23rd March 1877 at the age of 70. As a child he had a love for books and wished to study for the medical profession. This was not granted and he was apprenticed to the grocery trade in High Wycombe and for some time was also engaged in farming. He loved Nature and exhibited at many floral shows. He was also an amateur musician. He was brought up in the Wesleyan Methodist Church where he became Sunday School superintendent in 1833, although painfully conscious of his own need of salvation. After his first wife's death in 1836 he was stirred by the spiritual discourses of Rev.Jones, a Wesleyan minister, and as a result made a full consecration to God. At the time of the Reform agitation he joined the Primitive Methodist Society with his second wife and family. In 1837 he was elected a councillor for the borough of Wycombe and served in that capacity until 1862 when he was appointed Alderman. He was four times Mayor. He was one of the Guardians of the Parish and one of the Trustees of the town Charities and a member of the first School Board for the parish. Above all he was a Christian. The house of prayer was the home of his soul and he particularly valued the Sacrament of the Lord's Supper. As a local preacher he was well gifted and for many years was superintendent of the Sabbath-school. In 1873 when the society established a mission near to his residence, he took charge of the school. He was a benevolent man; not that he gave princely sums but he gave continuously. He laid the foundation stone of the first Primitive Methodist Chapel in the town and in many of the surrounding villages. He represented the London District in Conference and was once the General Missionary Treasurer. In 1876 he was paralyzed. Notwithstanding his weakness his efforts to attend the means of grace were marvellous. He once said to the writer, "I feel I am more mellow than I used to be". The last meeting he attended was the quarterly meeting of the circuit but the exertion was too much for him and he never after rallied. The last Sabbath he lived, he requested his beloved wife to play and sing the hymn, "Safe in the arms of Jesus". The funeral was a public one and was attended by the Corporation, the Board of Guardians, the majority of the members of the Primitive Methodist Societies of the town and many friends. Funeral sermons were preached in each of the town chapels by the writer.

THOMAS LLOYD ROBINSON, one of the firstfruits of Primitive Methodism in High Wycombe, has passed away into the general assembly and Church of the firstborn. He was born on the Bay of Biscay, March 3rd, 1806. His early life was spent in sin. So great was his pugilistic tendency that he was a terror to the neighbourhood. The preaching and earnest efforts of the pioneers of the Connexion attracted his attention. He was led to attend a service held in the cottage of Mr.Pierce in Frogmoor Gardens, in the year 1836, and became deeply impressed whilst listening to a sermon by J.Clarke, a local preacher, of Marlow, and eventually yielded himself to Christ. Although 30 years of age he was ignorant of the alphabet, but desiring to read the Scriptures, he applied himself to knowledge. The Bible became his daily delight. He read through it 22 times, and was engaged in repeating his loved study up till the time of his death. He was a man brimful of quaint humour, and this manifested itself in society, religious exercises, and in his pulpit ministrations. His originality and racy speech always attracted for him a congregation who felt their preacher was not straight-laced by conventionalities. His affliction was brief and painful, but was borne patiently. His trust was in Jesus only. His last words were - "I am going to be with Christ: all of you meet me there". Enquiring during his last week on earth what was the day, he said, when told, "Next Sunday, when the Church bells are ringing, I shall be spending my first Sunday with the Saviour," and so it fell out to him, for at 9.30 a.m. on Sunday, June 18th 1882, he was welcomed home.

(Rev.) ROBERT ANDREWS

NAPHILL (1851)

1835: FIRST MEETING (by Rev. James Pole)

April 19: In the afternoon at Napple Common. Hundreds came to hear and a mighty Unction attended the word.

1841: FIRST SOCIETY (by Rev. John Guy)

Naphill had been preached at several summers; but no house being opened, the preaching was withdrawn in the winters. Sept. 28, 1840, a Camp meeting being held at Downley, a mile distant, the preachers and members rose into mighty faith and looked for better days. Persecution soon rose and through this we were at a loss for a place for evening services. We waited on the Lord; and a person residing at Naphill opened his house, and in November 1840 we commenced preaching. A large congregation assembled which still keeps up. An account kept by Brother Joseph Ives, speaks as follows: "This winter my soul has been stirred up within me, and my soul much oppressed on account of the low state of religion in this neighbourhood. Every effort appeared to fail till Feb.14,1841, when I commenced a class at Naphill with myself, an old member and a new one. This was lower than I expected, and it bowed me down so that when I got home, I could only groan and sigh out my wishes to the Lord. The burden remained until the evening when I had another struggle, put my cause into the Lord's hand, and light sprang into my soul.

"February 21, added three members: the prospects brighten. Saturday evening, March 27, went after one I knew to be under conviction; but whom Satan had led off again: this person was rescued. On Saturday I went with Brother Gyngell about four miles in the snow from Wycomb to Naphill, to get an appointment supplied; and while talking to Brother Ives, a local preacher, my mind was impressed to say something to a young man present. He appeared to feel what was said, and on the following morning attended preaching. His so doing raised a little surprise; and Brother Ives thought much good might be done by conversing on the subject of their salvation with all to whom we have access. In February Brother D.Lewis talked with Brother S.Folly, local preacher of Downley, on living near to God and caring for the perishing souls in that neighbourhood. The Lord blessed what he said; Brother F. began to be more in earnest; the society was stirred up to diligence and each member began to pray and believe for a revival. The work went on at Naphill and Downley began to rise and they joined two new members: but we had many trials of faith. We however made a firm stand against the enemy and the Lord carried on His work. Brother F. proposed a protracted meeting for Easter-week to be carried on between Downley and Naphill. On Easter Sunday the services were well attended; believers were strengthened and sinners appeared to be greatly concerned. Monday, a little Camp meeting. Brothers Roberts and Watson, and Sister Gray spoke with power; and there was great power in prayer. Several were in tears during the afternoon. In the evening we had a band or fellowship meeting and one soul found the Lord."

Tuesday morning at Naphill. A refreshing time. Some wept. Faith rose; we cast our burden on the Lord and He sustained us. Wednesday evening, Brothers Roberts and Thomas Pierce preached in the Spirit. We wrestled very hard in prayer and two souls were set at liberty. Thursday morning, Folly, Woodley and others preached with great earnestness. Some young men came to persecute. There was a mighty struggle in prayer; convictions were wrought and good was done. On Friday evening the lovefeast was a good meeting. And this closed the protracted meeting; a meeting which was owned of God to the reviving of religion in these parts. To God be all the glory. Just before this meeting the brethren at Naphill counted the number of unconverted persons in the neighbourhood, as correctly as they could. They then portioned out to each member a share. To those they judged strongest in grace, they assigned the largest shares. These the members were to pray and believe for and never to give them up until they became converted. There was soon a great excitement among the people: and after they had been praying a week or two, I and A.West visited the people and we found that some who had not as yet been to our meetings, were under conviction of sin. Also friend Gyngell states that in visiting he found many under a concern about their souls.

April 18,1841: four joined at Naphill; Sunday May 2: two joined and on the 9th two more were added; Sunday May 23: the ungodly disturbed the class; but the Lord was with the people and three joined. There has been a great improvement in the morals of the people in the neighbourhood. Other societies have shared of the fruits of our labours. But we have raised a new society of 20 at Naphill. Jesus Christ is the same yesterday, today and for ever. To Him be glory, world without end. Amen.

1851: FIRST CHAPEL (by Michael Webb)

The first Methodist chapel was built in 1851 in Chapel Lane from flints which women and children gathered in their aprons and petticoats from the common and the surrounding area. What an opening it was! Villagers and others packed the church and the throng stretched back as far as the common. On a cold night in January 1877 (we learn from the "Bucks Free Press") a Christmas tree was planted "to the accompaniment of Sankey's hymns (Mr.G.Free at the harmonium)".

The Sunday School was very popular for it gave each child £1 for a year's good attendance (Naphill has always been a rich area!). At the Christmas party tea was provided for 300 people and crockery had to be borrowed from Bryants Bottom - for a 1s.0d.[5p.] donation. At the Treats in a farmer's field Speen

Band or the Gospel Mission Band played items. Goods for the stalls cost the church 15s.0d.[75p.] Adults had to pay 2d. [1p.] admission and children 1d. [½p.] and the profits went to the Sunday School Union and the Orphanage Fund. Hannah Ball, the founder of Sunday Schools, who is said to have lived at Coombe Farm as a child, would have been proud of our present-day scholars who, in 1986, on their first attempt at the Scripture Examination won the challenge shield. They repeated their success the following year.

1930: SECOND CHAPEL (by Michael Webb)

Architect - MR. T. THURLOW   Builder - MR. G. SHAW

Primitive Methodist Church, Naphill

OPENING *of*
New Church

Saturday and Sunday
November 1st and 2nd, 1930

SOUVENIR   PRICE 3d.

The present church was built in 1930 by Mr.G.Shaw, a local builder. The stone-laying was performed by Major Disraeli before a large crowd who later enjoyed a tea in the village hall. Others who took part included the ex-Mayor of High Wycombe, Richard Goodearl, a local preacher for 70 years. At an evening meeting Alderman W.O.Haines presided, George Pearce (of Booker) sang two solos and Brusher Parslow conducted the choir. The new building allowed many weeknight meetings to take place, including Christian Endeavour and Band of Hope, a temperance movement whose signature tune was: "Dare to be a Daniel; dare to stand alone!" Rev.Daniel Dunne once said in our pulpit that he had been brought up in a pub where they dispensed alcohol, but now "I am a dispenser of the water of life which is free!" Church Anniversaries brought people from Speen and Downley, many with their musical instruments.

We have many memories. An old local preacher, Mr.G.B.Lacey, grew so annoyed with a preacher whose words he struggled in vain to hear, that when he remarked it was his first visit, Mr. Lacey replied that he didn't mind if it was his last! A certain gentleman used to come straight from his duties with the cows to play the violin. He was always puzzled why the choir gave him a wide berth! The choir was in full voice on one occasion when Norman Mead tapped his baton and said, "I would like a sweet choir, not a squeaking gate!" A sad memory is of Mrs. Ethel Anderson collapsing at the organ and being tended by the preacher, Dr. Geoffrey Rose. (She died the next day.) The most recent memory is of our Open Day exhibition which 200 people visited, on 31st October 1987. Members had donated trustees' books, Sunday School registers and many photographs. Some of the exhibits dated back to the opening of the first chapel. Mrs. Connie White, the oldest member, who had recently moved to South Africa, had donated the mallet which her mother, Mrs. King, used to lay a stone at the building of the present chapel. The following day the 136th Church Anniversary was held and good numbers of people, including from the neighbouring Churches of Bryants Bottom and Lacey Green, joined in the services at the conclusion of which a cake was cut.

Our Church today tries to carry out a caring outreach work in the village, especially among those who are sick or in distress. We have regular united services with Hughenden Church. We give thanks to God "for all that is past and trust Him for all that's to come".

CRYERS HILL - GREAT KINGSHILL (1852)

MABEL EVANS writes:

After a mission in Great Kingshill in 1835 a few converts met together for fellowship. Numbers increased, land was secured and a Primitive chapel was erected at a cost of £120. It was opened on 21st November 1852 and by the end of that chilly autumn day gifts received amounted to £35.9s.3d. [£35.46]. The balance was soon cleared - despite the low wages of that time. "Chapel Anniversary sermons were preached on Tuesday 26th October 1856", records the Primitive Methodist Magazine, "by brother J. Symonds and Mr. Meeking (Wesleyan) of London. The congregations were large, the meetings good and the collections liberal. On the following day a tea and public meeting were held. Addresses were given by Messrs. Hunt, Meeking, Symonds and several others." A later report says: "At Great Kingshill in 1866 we have purchased an additional piece of ground joining our

chapel property for the sum of £8. We have also enlarged the
chapel about 12 feet in length and erected a good vestry on one
side of the chapel. Here we have a good work of soul saving
going on and many have been added to our ranks and this society
is one of the best on station."

My own memories go back to the beginning of the century and
for many years I observed events from my regular back seat. One
of the first was of the oil-lamps hanging from the ceiling and
the tortoise stove ("slow but sure") smelling more than usual
after one of the boys had placed a rubber ring on top of it!
I'll never know how I've managed to live so long, considering
how many gallons of water I've drunk, drawn up by bucket from
the well and containing many interesting specimens of insect
life! The pond at the corner of the main road had a fence round
it and children would queue from here to the chapel on
Anniversary days. Many would never get in but they were not
forgotten: the collection plate was taken out to them! Our
annual Treats were to nearby Lisley's field, led by the Speen
Brass Band. I remember the preachers arriving in the circuit
trap en route for Great Missenden and Lee Common. They wore
high black straw hats and were usually singing. If they had the
magic lantern on board, it was sometimes left at Cryers Hill, to
lighten the pony's load - and to the delight of us children. I
recall the words of two saints and still try to live by them:
Miss Feesey, my Sunday School teacher, who wore a high bonnet,

made us repeat each Sunday, "It's as much a sin to steal a pin as it is to steal a greater thing!"; and one of our regular preachers, George Shaw, who always instilled into us the need for "good books, good companions and good language".

At the centenary celebrations in 1952 a window was dedicated to the memory of Rev.C.Jupe. In 1954 the trustees were: Frank Burrows, Ernest Putnam, Phyllis Newell, Marion Lawrence, Eva Putnam, Doris Stratford, Edith Mason, Kenneth Newell, Irene Bristow, James Copeland, Gwendoline Brittin and Wilfred Turnbull. When the new organ was consecrated in 1962, Sandy Macpherson and Hazel of the B.B.C.'s "Chapel in the Valley" series delighted two packed congregations. To celebrate the Queen's Silver Jubilee in 1977 two trees were planted by Mr.F.Burrows and Mr.G.Batts and to mark the chapel's 125th Anniversary in the same year, a wrought-iron arch was erected over the gateway. The church has become well known in recent years for its Old Scholars' Reunions and Cherry Pie Suppers. Christmas is always an hospitable time. For example in 1983 folk were invited to: "Christmas Dinner on 17th December (tickets £1.75);   Carols round the Christmas Tree on 24th December. (Mince pies too!)" In 1986 a new porch was built, covering the entrances to both chapel and schoolroom.

The name "Cryers Hill" seems an odd one for what many preachers (who sit with the children in the schoolroom before the morning service: what happened to that vestry?) tell us is one of the happiest churches anywhere. Certainly I have few unpleasant memories. Some say the women used to cry under the weight of the shopping which they had to carry from Wycombe, others that the cries of wounded soldiers in the Civil War which raged through the valley below, gave us our name. We may be "Cryers" but we are full of joy as we continue with our founders' work, engraved in the stone: "We preach Christ crucified".

LACEY GREEN (1855)

DENNIS CLAYDON writes:

Lacey Green's earliest connection with Methodism stems from the Hounslow Primitive Methodist Circuit in 1835. Rev.James Pole, the Superintendent Minister, began "missionary operations" around Wycombe. Services were mostly held in the open air. He made several visits to Lacey Green and on one occasion more than 200 people gathered. As the weather was cold, the assembled crowd was given (we read in his journal) "liberty to go into a cart house". After the service "tears flowed on every hand." "Oh! what a spirit of hearing!" he cries. "The fields are already white unto the harvest." Due to the ardent endeavours of Mr.Pole a society was founded at Lacey Green. Little is known of its progress during its early days. An early meeting place may have been situated to the rear of the "Black Horse", adjacent to the buildings formerly known as "Floyds Farm". One of the first members was Elizabeth Buckingham who died at the age of 36 on 13th December 1836 at Redlands End. The Primitive Methodist Magazine records: "In 1835 curiosity induced her to hear the P.M. missionaries and she became deeply convinced of her lost state; and at the after prayer meeting she was made happy and went home rejoicing. She joined the society and was an example to all. Her husband being out of the way, her trials were great; and she lived two miles from the means of grace, yet she constantly attended when health would permit."

In 1841 the work is described as "low" and in that year Ann Britnell of Bledlow Ridge died. We are told "she was convinced of sin under the preaching of Sister Dell (now Tomkins). After the preaching was withdrawn from Bledlow Ridge, she joined the society at Lacey Green which was three miles from her home. Far as she had to go to her class and the means of grace, she was never known to neglect them, except when compelled by ill health or family duties." The Sunday School was growing however and the Baptists kindly allowed the Primitives to hold Sunday School Anniversary services on their premises in 1854. Next day a large tea meeting was held, when addresses were given by the Baptist Minister and his "lay brethren". This ecumenical gathering was described as "one of the good signs of the times". In 1855 the Minister, Rev.James Mules, wrote that for many years the society's progress had been retarded for the need of a "larger sanctuary". This would certainly indicate the use of an earlier building. Although poor, the. people had nobly persevered until £40 had been raised towards a new building. In the spring of 1855 after "experiencing some repulses and other annoyances", a plot of land in Main Road was secured for £5. Construction work began immediately and the building was completed by September at a total cost of £175. The account book records these items: "10 loads of stones for the foundations - £1; turnpike toll gate for 1 load of bricks - 4½d.[2p.]; begging cards - 3s.[15p.]".

The opening services on Sunday 23rd September 1855 were conducted by Rev. Edward Bishop (of London) and the Minister. An account records: "The day was very beautiful; the chapel was densely crowded and scores could not gain admittance. Mr. Bishop's original, powerful and earnest discourses were calculated to do much good." On the following day a public tea meeting was held with nearly 300 persons present who enjoyed themselves exceedingly. Imagine catering for such a number without the aid of mains water, electricity, bottled milk, teabags or sliced bread! The first anniversary was celebrated on 21st September 1856 when Rev. R. W. Monkman reports: "Three sermons were preached by brother J. Fuller of the Maidenhead Circuit. A tea and public meeting were held on the following day. The collections were good and the Master of assemblies was present to bless. We here record our gratitude to the friends who have shown their attachment to the voluntary principle by giving liberally to support the work of the chapel." In 1866 Rev. William Birks was able to announce that the chapel debt had been "entirely swept away. Arrangements are being made for improving the chapel by wainscoting etc. Our society has also experienced a quickening." The chapel was lit by candles until 1869, the cost being met by a special collection which varied from 8s. 0d. [40p.] to £1, every year.

PRIMITIVE METHODIST CHURCHES

Since that time the praise and prayers of village congregations have never ceased. From the beginning the church has enjoyed the services of many Ministers and Deaconesses. The contribution made by countless local preachers too, has always been appreciated. In early days preaching in a rural area meant leaving home early in the morning. Sometimes it was not only the preacher who needed hospitality: his horse had to be fed too! The end of the nineteenth century saw much poverty. State benefits were unknown and there was often need for financial help at a time of crisis. During this period the Sunday School ran a Sick Club and a Clothing Club for its members. Methodism was reputedly "born in song". The congregations of Lacey Green have long been renowned for making a "joyful noise". In addition to the organ a variety of musical instruments has been used over the years, to accompany the singing. In very early times the singing may have been led by an orchestra only, for the minute book records the resolution "that the violins be asked to play properly"! The Sunday School lost many of its former scholars in the Great War and memorial gates were erected in their honour.

To mark the chapel's centenary in 1955, the premises were enlarged and other improvements, including the addition of a kitchen, were made as a memorial to the Tomkins family who had served the church for over a century. Unusually for the south of England, the church has its own cemetery which is neatly kept and contains the remains of many of its stalwarts. In 1987 extensive repairs to the chapel were carried out. Worshippers for over 130 years were greeted by words from Psalm 100, painted above the pulpit: "Serve the Lord with gladness". This the early founders certainly did, as indeed have those who have continued the work to the present day. In our renovated chapel text and large pulpit have gone but we hope to carry on serving Him.

AMERSHAM COMMON (1860)

HELEN SMITH writes:

In the middle of the last century a few Methodists of the Primitive persuasion felt the need to worship in the Amersham Common district. They had little money and therefore small hope of building a chapel. Mr.and Mrs.Grover of Loudhams Farm in Burtons Lane, had a bit of room to spare and generously invited

the little group of Methodists to meet once a month in one of
their rooms or barns. It is said there was always a good tea
after the service so obviously the Methodists, then as now,
rejoiced in a dual nourishment of the inner man! The Beckley
brothers of Chesham attended the farm services, Charles no doubt
in his capacity as local preacher.

When at length the little society felt led to move to the
Chesham side of Amersham Common, they made what was for them a
great step of faith: they built a chapel in 1860 at the end of
Chestnut Lane on ground supplied by Sir William and Lady
Elderton. Rev.James Horberry was the Minister. There are
several people still in Amersham who remember that chapel. Miss
Winifred Bryant, a local preacher, told us that the brethren at
Chestnut Lane were mighty men of prayer and she recalled the
great draught which would sweep through the chapel when old
Mr.Woodbridge would fling wide the door just before the sermon -
in case there should be "a sinner wandering without at
eventide"! Miss Bryant also remembered the aspidistra which
graced the little table and came to end its days in the vestry
of the church built in 1924 at Woodside Road, near Blackhorse
Bridge.

Numerous were the trials of the faithful in their new home.
The little society was loaded with debt and magnificent were the
"efforts" held to cancel it. The collection of a "mile of
pennies" was undertaken, there were fetes on the ground behind
the church and countless were the sausage suppers demolished in
the "cause". The stoke-hole flooded, the stove emitted
suffocating smoke, the roof began to spread and the walls
started to crack. But through it all we had our text written
across a wall of glorious blue: "The love of Christ
constraineth us". The Church was replaced in 1960 by the fine
new St.John's Church further up Woodside Road.

WINCHMORE HILL (1860)

THE OPENING

Tuesday 21st August 1860 was a joyous day for Primitive
Methodism in this much-neglected neighbourhood, it being the day
selected for laying the first stone of a new chapel at Winchmore
Hill. The ceremony commenced soon after two o'clock in the
presence of a large assemblage. Appropriate hymns were sung and

prayer offered, when Rev.Murray Wilson with characteristic ability and fervour delivered a preliminary address. Having remarked that they were met to witness an interesting ceremony in connection with the tenth chapel in this circuit, nine chapels being already raised at a cost of £1437, he proceeded to show that the promise given to the ancient Church was addresed to the present: "In all places where I record My name, I will come unto thee and bless thee".

He then in terms of eulogy and respect introduced Thomas Wheeler Esq. who proceeded at once to lay the stone, to the evident satisfaction of the gazing crowd. Mr.Wheeler spoke with more than usual pathos and power and with his wonted catholicity of spirit congratulated the Primitives upon their success and prospects, assured them of his heartfelt sympathy and expressed the sincere pleasure he felt in serving them. Prayer and praise terminated the afternoon service when the people retired to a booth in Mr.Woodbridge's orchards where upwards of 350 took tea. After tea the evening meeting, a most enthusiastic one, was held, the chair being taken by Mr.James Smith. Earnest and appropriate addresses were delivered by Revs.M.Wilson and G.H.Fowler, to which the people responded by a liberal collection. The sum of £36 was announced as already received, with promised donations that form a total of more than £50. The Wycombe choir very creditably performed several select pieces.

"BUCKS FREE PRESS"

GLADYS STRATFULL writes:

In early days two Methodist chapels existed in Winchmore Hill - one Wesleyan and one Primitive. In 1856 services took place in a small room in Glory Farm and later in a cottage. Mr. E.Bovington who had given the ground for the Wesleyan chapel to be built, was also involved in the Primitive chapel where he was Sunday School superintendent until 1880. It opened in 1860 and improvements for which he was responsible included a small schoolroom and coalshed. The church was originally heated by a coal fire from which a tin chimney went up through the roof. Lighting was by paraffin lamps. All the water was drawn from a tub and boiled in a copper.

A new youth hall was opened in 1953. Thanks to the efforts of people like Mrs. Bilbey who collected threepenny and sixpenny pieces for ten years, it was free of debt. The original front door of the chapel was altered in time for the chapel's centenary in 1960, when a choir formed some years before by

Leonard Stratfull, led the singing. The Sunday School at that
time had 60 scholars. In 1966 extensive renovation took place.
The platform and pulpit were removed and a new pulpit and organ
installed. The Communion rail was dedicated to the memory of
Mrs. Elizabeth Hatch and the table and chairs were given in
memory of other faithful workers. The Winchmore Hill chapel was
independent until 1876 when it joined the Chalfont St. Giles
Circuit, which in turn joined the Wycombe Circuit in 1937,
finally becoming part of the new Chesham and Chalfont (later
Amersham) Circuit in 1951. The Bible given by Reginald
Nancarrow is still to be found in the pulpit.

"WE WILL REMEMBER THEM"

Remembrance Sunday - and the usual November bleak greyness.
Turning off the main road, we ascended The Hill and made our way
for the first time into the sanctuary at Winchmore Hill. We
looked at the memorial plaques, then at the members of the
congregation some of whom were related to those commemorated.
We stared through the window at the lines of gravestones behind
the chapel. All the time we were drinking in the silence which
envelops this most peaceful of country churches. We were deeply
aware of "all those saints". One of the young girls smiled at
us and in that moment we knew that this society, so deeply
rooted in the past, has got to have a future too. There is
after all no other church in the village.

WHEELER END (1861)

FREDERICK G. WEBB writes:

The smallest chapel in the Wycombe Circuit (just the one
room) opened as a Primitive Methodist cause in 1861. On 6th
February 1866 it was hosting a missionary meeting, chaired by
Rev. W. Birks and addressed by Rev. J. Phillips (of London),
Rev. W. J. Bullivant and Mr. S. Plumridge. It closed on 23rd August
1987, the saddest day of their lives to the few remaining
members. (Some had only recently been transferred from
Piddington). In its first year Wheeler End made a profit of
19/1½ [95½p.]. In the last years it couldn't keep up with the
financial demands.

PRIMITIVE METHODIST CHURCHES

I became treasurer in 1920 and continued to the end.
Mr.J.Ing was the Sunday School superintendent in those days.
There were 60 children whose parents always took an interest,
especially at harvest festivals when the chapel was packed to
overflowing, right out to the common sometimes. The lighting at
that time was hanging paraffin lamps, supplemented by candles in
the darkest corners. Heating came from slow combustion tortoise
stoves fed by coke from the Wycombe Gas Company. Sunday started
at 10.30 with the Sunday School, which met again at 2 o'clock
before the afternoon service, and finished with the 6 o'clock
service. All were well attended by the villagers. Special
mention must be made of the devotion shown by Ministers,
preachers and organists. An electric organ was purchased in
1954 for £210. Since my son Russell's departure in 1986, there
has been no regular organist. I feel that the change in the
appointment of trustees was a blow to small chapels like ours.
They came from various churches and took a real interest in
keeping the chapel open. The present anonymous trustees are a
poor substitute!

My memories range from Phoebe Bates paying her seat rent -
1s.1d. [5½p.] per quarter (trespassers, beware!) - through the
chapel orchestra (violins, cellos and cornets); regular
entertainments for the old folk; and stalwarts like Ledru Burr

who built the platform, and Leslie Murgatroyd who on cold
Sundays used to make sure the preacher's cushion was warm; down
to the last concert in June 1987 by the Chiltern Ladies' Choir.
In earlier years there was a magnificent spirit of co-operation
within the chapel and the village. In its last years the Thrift
Club was paying out £1000 at Christmas. In recent years village
and chapel went their own ways. The only place of Christian
witness is now closed.

JOSEPH BAILEY (1842-1924)

The passing of Mr. Joseph Bailey on 18th March 1924 has made
a great gap in the High Wycombe Circuit. He had attained the
ripe age of 81. He was born of humble parents at Wheeler End,
near High Wycombe. His parents worshipped with the Wesleyans in
a neighbouring village but on the opening of a cause at Wheeler
End by our people, became members there. Joseph worked with his
father in his early years but subsequently was apprenticed to
chairmaking. It was the custom in those days when an apprentice
had finished his term, to take his shop-mates to a public house
and "pay his footing". But Joseph refused to be bound by such
an evil custom, much to the chagrin of the drinkers of his day,
and he continued an earnest advocate of Temperance principles
throughout his life. He became a local preacher in 1861 and
continued for 63 years. No weather or minor difficulties
prevented him from filling his appointments, however distant,
and he often walked 30 miles on a Sunday to preach the Gospel.
He filled with credit all the pulpits of his own and many
neighbouring circuits for he was an able and acceptable
preacher. In his early days he was urged to join the ministry
but circumstances stood in the way. He was circuit steward and
represented the circuit several times at the District Meeting
and was twice sent to Conference.

He represented the town on the Borough Council and the
Board of Guardians. In the business world he was a chair
manufacturer and employed a number of people. He was a man of
strict integrity and made great sacrifices to honour his
Christian profession. His domestic life was associated with
much sorrow and affliction but he bore it bravely and with
Christian resignation. He leaves behind a large family of sons
and daughters. His widow lived but a few weeks after his
decease. A large and reverent congregation gathered for the
memorial service conducted by Rev. E. S. French.

PRIMITIVE METHODIST CHURCHES

IBSTONE (1862)

Opened in 1862, this church joined the High Wycombe Methodist Circuit from Chinnor Primitive Methodist Circuit along with Stokenchurch and Beacons Bottom in 1934. John Wesley preached here in the open air. The evangelist, Herbert Silverwood, conducted a campaign in the chapel. It was kept going in its later years by Thomas Judge and George Bradbury despite the small numbers attending. It closed in 1958 and was converted into a house, on a wall of which is inscribed: "Here stood the Ibstone Methodist Chapel 1862-1963".

DOWNLEY - CHAPEL STREET (1864)

REV.JAMES POLE'S JOURNAL (1835)

April 10: Preached at Dounly, a new place. Wheelwright's shop crowded. A good opening.

April 11: An obscure village. Chair maunufactory employs 40. Prayed with people.

April 14: Prayer meeting in open air - more than 100 people.

April 15: Several cried for mercy.

April 19: Class meeting - first in this County. Eight joined and this may be said to be foundation stone of Primitive Methodism in this vicinity.

April 20: Meeting on Dounly Common. Several engaged in prayer. Some praised God for deliverance, others cried for mercy.

April 28: Powerful conversion took place.

May 4: Several cried for mercy and some were brought into liberty.

REV.JOHN GUY'S REPORT (1841)

Sept.28,1840, a Camp meeting was held at Downley. In 1841 Downley began to rise and they joined two new members. Brother F. proposed a protracted meeting for Easter-week, to be carried on between Downley and Naphill. On Easter Sunday the services were well attended; believers were strengthened and sinners appeared to be greatly concerned. Monday, a little Camp meeting. There had usually been a fair, or revel, as on this day; but our meeting put the most of it aside.

On Tuesday evening Bro.Folly and Sisters Tomkins and Dell preached. We had a good deal of prayer. Faith rose high. Some were in distress: one cried out for mercy and soon obtained pardon; prayed that the Lord would keep her faithful, and gave out, "Behold the Saviour of mankind" etc. And when we came to, "'Tis done! the precious ransom's paid", a divine power came down and several more fell into deep distress. We had now to wrestle hard against the powers of darkness. I explained justification by faith. We prayed again and the Lord set three souls at glorious liberty. We went on again and one said her heart was so hard that she did not want and could not have pardon then, and she said it was of no use to pray for her. The conflict was severe; but the Lord applied Ezekiel 36.26, "A new heart also will I give you", etc. One had mentioned that Scripture aloud: another said, "The Lord has sent us that promise". Here faith took hold afresh and rested. She now confessed her heart was softer, prayed and got into liberty. The second who had got into liberty, gave way to unbelief, and sunk again into distress. Prayer was made for her and she again got liberty and rejoiced. Two more got great good and spoke of their interest in Christ with confidence. Glory to the God of all our salvation.

Wednesday morning, prayer meeting at Downley. The Lord was with us. The friends at Downley now counted the number of unconverted persons in the neighbourhood. They then portioned out to each member a share. To those they judged the strongest in grace, they assigned the largest shares. These the members were to pray and believe for and never give them up till they became converted. Tuesday, April 20,1941, the Lord was powerfully with our brethren at Downley and one was set at liberty; and the week following one was saved and two joined. We have added a few people to the old society at Downley.

REG LANGLEY writes:

Chapel Street was a small, plain building, comprising a square chapel which was erected in 1864, with a platform and pulpit, also a schoolroom. Services were informal and the elements in the Communion were brought round to the congregation. My wife and I were the first to be married there after the Church was licensed for weddings in 1943. She was a Primary teacher and the piano she acquired was the envy of the circuit.

I recall pumping the organ - and hoping the organist would not be feeling too enthusiastic! -   also the social evenings, the young people's choir, the harvest auctions and the Sick Fund which filled a real need at that time.   Arthur Hawkins kept the church running until his death in 1962.   One Sunday he became so angry with the preacher for talking politics that he jumped up and told him to be quiet!   After the chapel closed in 1965 it became a furniture showroom, and is now a private dwelling. Along with Ida Langley, Mrs.Hawkins and Mrs.James we transferred to Downley (Sunny Bank) ex-Wesleyan Church.

Connie Webster writes:

        When I was a young woman, Roger Smith invited me to Chapel Street to help in the Sunday School.   (Later he left because of his Spiritualist views.)   My "little pickles" came mainly from the poorer houses.   I helped pioneer teachers' training classes there.

RADNAGE (1865)

HORACE HOOK writes:

        The chapel was built in 1865 in Green End Road.   The Primitive Methodist Magazine records that a missionary meeting was held on 7th February 1866 when "the chairman was our worthy circuit steward, Mr.Thomas Pierce, and the following persons

addressed the meeting: Revs.J.Phillips (London), W.Birks and
W.J.Bullivant   and   Mr.Thomas   Anderson."   There   were   three
services every Sunday and a 1904 programme names the preacher as
John Gomm who later became Mayor of High Wycombe.   Preachers who
came by horse and trap could use the stables next to the chapel.
The "Bucks Free Press" mentions a children's concert that was
held in Radnage at Christmas 1913:   "'Dirty boys' were severely
chastised by their fellow scholars and given a public wash by
their tormentors!"

Mrs.Atkins and Mrs.Dean recall the great Sunday School
Anniversaries which were always held on Whit Sunday.   Ernest
Dormer conducted the singing and long recitations had to be
memorised: reading from a paper was not allowed in those days!
Next day a grand tea was held - outside, weather permitting.   I
came to Radnage in 1958 and helped teach the 80 scholars.   Often
for Anniversary services parents and other villagers had to
stand outside.   The ladies too loved singing and at one time the
Women's Meeting used to go round to other chapels, rendering
their "services of song".

The work of Harry Butler and his wife in the Sunday School
is commemorated by the altar table which was dedicated in 1932.
All the 15 men listed on the chapel roll of honour who gave
their lives in the two World Wars passed through the Sunday
School.   The stables were replaced in 1957 by a new vestry and
kitchen which were built by Ernest Maunder, the society steward.
New windows were put into the chapel, including the stained
glass windows on either side of the pulpit which were donated by
Mrs.Ruth Dormer and Miss Mary Holland.   We remember with
gratitude people like Mrs.Holland, Mrs.Quantick, Miss Bird and
Mrs.Coker who faithfully performed the Lord's work here which we
endeavour to carry on.

GREAT MISSENDEN (1866)

The Primitive Methodist chapel in Church Street was opened
in 1866 at a cost of £200 (one-third of which had already been
raised).   Rev.William Birks at a meeting at Great Kingshill
(Cryers Hill) on 31st December 1865 remarked that the "Prims."
had been preaching for more than 20 years at Missenden but until
then had not been able to purchase any land.   The "Bucks Free
Press" reported a large gathering on Christmas Day 1862 when
addresses were given by Rev.J.Toulson, Mr.J.Worley, Mr.Thomas

Pierce (of High Wycombe), Mr. J. Nash (Kingshill) and Mr. G. Loosley
(Lee Common). The Primitive Methodist Magazine spoke of good
congregations in 1866: "Our society is prosperous numerically
and financially; and we have succeeded in forming a Sunday
School".

The church has the unhappy distinction of being the only
one in the High Wycombe Methodist Circuit to close in the period
between its formation in 1934 and the closure of White Hart
Street in 1951. The chapel became a garage in 1938 and the
members transferred to Prestwood where Annie Gibbs recalls that
she sometimes took her small son to Great Missenden because they
didn't mind small children running round during the service!
(Or listening in the open air to five sermons on Christmas Day?)

STOKENCHURCH (1868)

ELLA BATES writes:

Primitive Methodists at first held cottage meetings at
Parrs Common, Kingston Hill, but later used a building in Thomas
Towerton's wood-mill yard, near the present-day "King's Arms"
car park and the chemist's shop. The "Bucks Free Press"
reported in 1863: "On Tuesday 10th March to commemorate the
wedding of the Prince and Princess of Wales, pupils of the two
Sabbath Schools at Stokenchurch (Primitive and Congregational)
joined in a grand procession, cheering, waving and singing, to
the Primitive Methodist chapel for a tea, followed by a service,
addressed by Revs. V. James and E. Hancock." A piece of ground,
measuring 38 feet by 20 feet, was purchased in 1868 for £100
from Mary Burgess of Wycombe. The chapel built here - behind
the "Royal Oak" - was vacated in 1896 since when it has been
used for various purposes, including a car repair shop.

The present site by the Common was purchased at an auction
for £235 by William Britnell and the church was built by George
Syred for £915 of which £580 had to be borrowed (at 3½%
interest). It was opened in 1896. The organ was installed in
1915 at a cost of £183. In the inter-war years the Church
flourished: There was a strong choir - each member paid an
entry fee of 3d. [1p.] - which sang at the three Sunday services.
Once a year the Sunday School scholars paraded with their banner
round the village, headed by the Stokenchurch Brass Band, before
enjoying their sports in Cooper's Court meadow. Other

organisations were a thrift club, Band of Hope and Methodist Guild. Concerts were held to celebrate Chapel Anniversaries and High Wycombe Male Voice Choir was one of several visiting groups.

S.SHERRATT 1987   STOKENCHURCH

Since the 1939-45 War many neighbouring Methodist Churches have closed, including Ibstone in 1958 and Beacons Bottom in 1970. Together with Stokenchurch they joined the new High Wycombe Circuit from the Chinnor Primitive Methodist Circuit in 1934. By 1976 Stokenchurch too was in considerable difficulty. Extensive alterations were carried out, including the conversion of the church, which was much too large for the small congregations now attending, into two halls - the larger for general meetings and the smaller as a worship area, seating 60 people. Much of the work was carried out by our own members and the money raised from many efforts, including the provision of teas for visitors to the nearby Chilterns woodlands. The chapel's distinguished Italian-style front was retained. During this time services were held at the Church of Saints Peter and Paul, where the body of Hannah Ball, who lived part of her early life in the village, lies buried. The Methodist Church was reopened in 1977. Only one Sunday service is now held (at 11 a.m.) and there is also a weekly Women's Bright Hour. The

Sunday School, though small, continues. The hall is in great demand by the community and accommodates – among others – the Camera Club, Women's Institute, and ballet classes. Roman Catholics meet for worship on Saturday evenings. So we continue to try and serve God and the village.

BEACONS BOTTOM (1868)

Opened in 1868, the Primitive Church joined the High Wycombe Methodist Circuit from the Chinnor Primitive Methodist Circuit along with Stokenchurch and Ibstone in 1934. It was a flourishing Church in the 1930's. The Butler family helped run it for many years. It was famous for its pantomimes in one of which the ex-Mayor of High Wycombe, Mrs.Betty Barratt, played a fairy! The audience used to overflow from the small chapel on to the road outside. The church did a great work among young people but many of the village's young men were killed at Calais (France) in the Second World War and the Church never seemed to recover. In its last days there were sometimes only three people in the congregation and two of them would be sharing the platform with the preacher, one playing the organ and the other pumping it! It closed in 1970, was sold in 1972 for £3750, then converted into a house and resold in 1975 for £27,950. The last trustees were: George Lee, Gwendoline Butler, Eliza Newell, Frederick Webb, Florence Butler, Jean Butler, Harold Butler and Edward Bates.

BRYANTS BOTTOM (1871)

EDWIN RIDGLEY writes:

Village tradition is that the Methodists built their first meeting place where there is now a garden. Its foundations are still to be found, the present owner claims, whenever he tries to dig it! There were once eight pairs of brick and flint cottages some of which survive to this day. The population in the early years of the last century was about 50, mostly children, and the village was divided between three parishes: Hughenden, Prestwood and Great Hampden. People had to go to the "correct" parish church for christenings etc.! Most of the men worked in the brick-field or dug for the sandstone, some of which went to Windsor Castle and some for the cobbled streets in nearby towns. Why did they want to build a church? Perhaps they saw in the beauty of the earth and the strength of the hills a Being on Whom they relied and Who was worthy of their thanks. So they built that first House of God. The present Primitive Methodist chapel was built in 1871 - with no grants or outside help.

In my young days Mr.Allen, a painter and decorator who carried his Bible in his lunch basket during the week, started his Sunday with a visit to a sick woman to whom he read a passage of Scripture before saying a prayer. After that he led the Sunday School and then at the afternoon and evening services did his steward's duties and played the organ. Preachers came many miles. The Randalls, father and son, and Mr. Bignell rode from Lee Common on their bikes; Mr.Rogers walked from Aston Clinton, singing most of the way; Fred Rixon came from Lacey Green; three Sargeants, three Goodearls and Harry Jarrett (for Sunday School Anniversaries) walked from Wycombe (and back in the dark sometimes). All were saints of God. The first Minister I can remember was Rev.F.G.Saville, and one of the most recent was Rev.Ruth Orton - who preached more than 100 sermons at Bryants Bottom.

The "Bucks Free Press" records that on Boxing Day 1913 an entertainment was laid on at Bryants Bottom. Rev.A.W.Pay of Speen was the chairman. This was a few months before the outbreak of the Great War in which the village lost six of its young men and this left a gap in the chapel too. Will Smith later became Sunday School superintendent and steward, also a local preacher, and so the work continued. In the 1960's we were busy with garden parties and other efforts, to raise over £2000 towards the cost of repairs and alterations to the chapel. On 26th January 1974 Lady Nancy Hall, wife of Sir John Hall M.P., attended the opening ceremony and service of dedication which was conducted by Rev.A.Kingsley Turner, Chairman of the District, assisted by Rev.Frank Watts, the Minister. The little "tin tabernacle" at Terriers had closed in 1970 and as some of my family were involved, members were invited to join Bryants Bottom. They still form a welcome part of our afternoon congregation. Mrs. Meeks loved to come and worship until she grew too old, after which we went with Rev.Ruth to her home and took Communion with her. What a wonderful gift memory is! Now we have our modernised little chapel with its new porch, kitchen, toilets and meeting room. It does not take many to fill it. There are now many new houses in the village. We shall need new people if the Church is to have a future. God bless Bryants Bottom!

SLATER STREET - NORTH TOWN (1873)

When the new Primitive chapel in North Town opened in 1873, the Borough of Chepping Wycombe was confined to 126 acres with a population of 5000. It was surrounded by another 5000 who lived in the parish in groups of dwellings which were almost cut off from the town proper. These included North Town which had grown up on the other side of the railway and to which access was difficult until the subway was made in 1890. An attempt to amalgamate borough and parish at the time of the chapel's opening was a failure. The church became known as "Slater Street" but the post office in Totteridge Road retains the "North Town" title to this day.

CHRISTMAS BAZAAR (1874)

On Saturday last at North Town (Slater Street) Primitive Methodist Church a bazaar was held for church funds. The Chinese primroses and cinerarias were presented by Mr.Harman of Duke Street. Stalls were by Mesdames Connell, Cox, Tibbles and Hunt. A meeting in the chapel followed, opened by the Worshipful the Mayor, Thomas Wheeler. Rev.R.R.Connell invoked the divine blessing. The speaker was Rev.J.Woodhouse and the chairman was Mr.Joseph Worley.

"BUCKS FREE PRESS"

DEATH OF MRS.J.SARGEANT (1922)

In the death of Mrs.Sargeant our society at Slater Street has sustained a severe loss. Her family had been associated with Methodism for generations and our sister was worthy of her godly heritage. As a child she gave her heart to Christ and commencing to teach in the Sunday School at the age of 14, she continued until she passed to her reward. She was leader of Junior Christian Endeavour and an active worker in the Senior Endeavour. Not only was she the great inspirer of her husband and son (both of whom are local preachers) but to the last her heart yearned with tender compassion over the young whom she had "mothered" into the church by her gracious ministrations.

UNA LLOYD PAGE

A WARM WELCOME (1931)

When Nick and I arrived from Winnipeg (Canada) where our Church had congregations of over 1000, we found Slater Street very small by comparison. But the welcome we received from Miss Ivy Hester, Mrs.Evelyn Bunce and others, was so warm that we soon realised the fellowship of the Church is the same, whatever the numbers. My sister was the Deaconess at Slater Street and our intention had been, after visiting her, to return to our home in Durham. Well, I am still here - with plenty of time these days to "stand and stare"! I often think about those good Methodists who obeyed the words of Jesus: "A new commandment I give you, that you love one another".

MABS TAYLOR

"CHRISTMAS DAY IN THE WORKHOUSE"? (1945)

I envied the characters in the famous monologue! Sitting with my sleeping Grampy Saunders in Auntie Edie's "top" kitchen (that is, the room which was never heated the rest of the year) and trying to let Uncle Jack win at Draughts, I watched the two lonely lumps of coal in the open grate struggling to keep themselves warm, and the mist rising from the river. George Street was hardly visible. It was almost dark, but Mum's mild suggestion that her sister might like to light the gas, had been sharply turned down. Auntie Ada, Jack's wife, suddenly came to life, teasing me with, "Now don't you go marrying any of them Zion girls!" I was only 14 but resolved immediately, although I had no actual person in mind at the time, to ignore her advice, as I always did.

It was nearly 3 o'clock on Christmas Day 1945 and time to switch on the electric radio (powered by an illegal connection from the house next door) for the King's speech. I glumly thought of the rest of the world celebrating the first peacetime Christmas since 1938, when Dad emerged from the twilight. He had been trying to sort out the warring couple who ran the antique shop on the other side. (The pub opposite was too handy for their good.) Dad disliked Christmas at West Wycombe Road as much as I did but he'd been coming here ever since he started going out with Mum before the Great War, and was the sort of man who would do anything "to keep the peace". His regular Christmas morning service at Slater Street had been on that theme - not that those warm, gentle, happy folk seemed to need such exhortation.

After tea Mum's convenient headache released us, and as we walked home through the dimly lit streets we said, as we always did: "That service was the best part of the day!" (A pity it was not possible to take advantage of the Hesters' annual invitation to spend Christmas with them!) Actually it was to be the last Christmas Day spent like that. Grampy died the following July and Mum decided it was best for Auntie Edie to come up to us. But Dad continued to conduct the morning

service at Slater Street until the chapel's closure and his own
ill health combined to bring the happy arrangement to an end.
Some of my most treasured Christmas memories are tied up with
Slater Street.

D.C.C.

HEZEKIAH DIMMOCK'S NOTEBOOK (1948)

Born in 1870, Hezekiah Dimmock was Sunday School secretary
from 1886 until 1948 when he was 78 years of age. He was blind
for the last seven years of his life and died in 1966 at the age
of 96. He recalls how the Vicar used to come once a month to
the National School (in White Hart Street), to give the children
a Scripture lesson. A book was given to the best boy in the
class so "Kiah" (as he was generally known) decided to make a
special effort and in fact came top of the class. But finding
that Kiah went to Slater Street - and not the Church School -
the Vicar said he could not have the book and gave it to another
boy. When only 13 years of age, he was running the Provident
Club and in the first year collected £120 which was paid out at
Christmas. At the age of 26 he married Rhoda, the oldest
daughter of Mr.G.Seymour, a local preacher. He declares that he
had the "best of mothers and the best of wives". He spent so
much time at the chapel as "keeper" that his wife once suggested
he might as well take his bed down there! Gems from the minute-
book which he kept include the following:

"Moved that we adjourn till fortnight last night";
"Moved that we have tea at 6 o'clock and that we ask the female
teachers to beg the tea";
"Moved that the male teachers pay 1s.[5p.], females 6d.[2½p.]
for tea";
"Moved that the children be rewarded the same as last year and
those that have not enough marks for a 4d.[1½p.] book, can pay
the money up to 4d., the money to be paid before ordering the
book; failing that, the marks be left till next year";
"Moved that we thank Mr.H.Dimmock for disposing of Christmas
cards for the benefit of the School Fund, the profits being
£3.15s.6d.[£3.77½p.] and that we give the teachers a social
evening out of the 15s.6d. [77½p.]"

ROY CLARK

CLOSURE (1955)

Slater Street, a building of some historical interest, was opened in 1873 as a part of the White Hart Street Primitive Methodist Circuit and bore great witness to the power of God in that area of the town. The enthusiastic band of workers raised money for the installation of a pipe organ which is being rebuilt for placing in the new St. Mark's Church. In 1918 the Slater Street church was threatened when fire broke out in the schoolroom. The flames were confined to a small area however and the only damage sustained was to the organ. The building which is included in the town development plan and is zoned for industrial purposes, will be converted for use as a factory by R. Tyzack Ltd., furniture manufacturers. Another Methodist Church - London Road - is destined to be sold but for the time being will continue in united worship with Slater Street members. The proceeds realised by the sale of these two churches, together with funds from other sources, will enable the Methodist Circuit to develop even further its work in High Wycombe.

"BUCKS FREE PRESS"

IVY HESTER remembers:

My first memory of Slater Street is not a pleasant one. I was three years old and watching me for a few moments, the Minister's wife exclaimed in horror, "Is that child left-handed?" Well despite that here I am, still a Methodist, 80 years later and owing much to the love shown at Slater Street to my parents and me. Mr. and Mrs. E. Gomme were typical. He was the choir-master and sponsored Sister Miriam Hammel to do a very caring pastoral work at the church. Another member of that family, John, launched an appeal to buy the first X-ray equipment for the hospital which at that time was in Priory Road.

    Slater Street was always a warm church - physically as well
as spiritually. I can never remember it without electricity and
central heating - in the days when most churches managed with
the ubiquitous tortoise stove (fine as long as it was fed
regularly!). But warmest of all was the night when fire spread
from Tyzack's factory through the rear of the chapel, so fierce
that the organ pipes melted.   Another fire was started
deliberately - at a business meeting! After a long-standing
debt had at last been cleared, George Grimsdale brought all the
papers relating to it and burned them in public before the
surprised members! So perhaps it was appropriate that the
chapel should have been used by fire-watchers during both World
Wars! George was a much-loved Bible Class leader who was taken
ill suddenly at a Sunday School Treat and died. We never wanted
to return to Fawley Court after that.

    London Road to which we transferred after the closure of
Slater Street in 1955, was also known as a friendly church -
despite being Wesleyan to our Primitive! In 1957 we processed
from London Road, led by the youthful Rev.Tony Wells, carrying a
rugged tree-trunk to plant as a cross on the site of the new
St.Mark's building in Totteridge Road (formerly an air-raid
shelter). The Slater Street chapel, used for some years by Long
and Hambly's (plastics), was recently demolished.   Its spirit
lives on.

PRIMITIVE METHODIST CHURCHES

MARLOW (1874)

Rev. James Pole, the Primitive Methodist evangelist, conducted a camp meeting at Marlow in 1835. Rain forced them under cover but he says: "A powerful influence prevailed and much good was done. We began to pray and the kingdom of Satan began to shake and seven or eight professed to receive salvation. Young and old are crying for mercy." The church built in 1874 in Chapel Street was part of the Maidenhead Circuit at the time of the "Deed Of Union" (1932). It was bought by Mrs. Liston for the town's use in 1933 when members, including Marjorie Harvey who was to become a local preacher (Mrs. Pike), moved to the Wesleyan Church. Used by the Ministry of Labour for some years, the old chapel now forms part of Liston Hall, the home of the Marlow Community Association.

WHITE HART STREET (1875)

OPENING SERVICES (AUGUST 1875)

Sunday	8th	Rev. W. Rowe
Monday	9th	Meeting and tea. Speakers – Revs. W. Rowe, G. Grigg, J. Rackham, T. Jeffries, W. T. Dyer and R. R. Connell
Wednesday	11th	Rev. H. Varley of London
Sunday	15th	Rev. T. Penrose (10.30 & 6); Rev. D. Evans of Marlow (2.30)
Monday	16th	Rev. T. Penrose
Sunday	22nd	Capt. H. J. McCulloch (10.30 & 6); Rev. T. Davies (2.30)
Monday	23rd	Revs. T. H. Browne, J. Butler, J. Woodhouse, and R. R. Connell

A PREACHER'S REFLECTIONS

White Hart Street is a microcosm of the whole Church. Built of gigantic proportions, its founders whose church at Frogmoor could no longer cope with the torrent of 19th century worshippers, intended it to last! For many years the centre of activity in the heart of the shopping area, by the 1930's it was already showing signs of decline. The "Deed of Union" (1932) sealed its fate. From being the proud leader of all Wycombe's "Prims." it became second to the grander Vesley. After the Second World War fewer people wanted to go to church on Sundays and more comfortable homes and other activities were taking over its social functions in the week. By the time I got to speak there (in 1950 to the Christian Endeavour: "You are the light of the world") the lonely old church was near the end of its life. Some years later I was about to enter those hallowed walls again – to buy some paint – when an old lady accosted me: "I couldn't go shopping in there – and neither should you!" She had to be wrong of course......?

WHITE HART STREET.
S.SHERRATT. 1987.

EARLY SERVICE AND CONCERT

A Watchnight Service was held at the Primitive Methodist Chapel on 31st December 1876. It was conducted by Rev.C.Jupe and Rev.R.Andrews. A Concert is to be held on Tuesday 23rd January 1877. John Youens will conduct the "Messiah". Reserved seats - 2s.[10p.]. Front seats - 1s.[5p.]. Back seats - 6d.[2½p.]. Tickets from Rev.C.Jupe.

"BUCKS FREE PRESS"

CHARLES HUDSON (d.1911)

Charles Hudson died on 21st April 1911 at the age of 69. His childhood and early life were spent in connection with our cause in High Wycombe. He entered the service of the Prudential Company and in all places to which business called him, showed his unwavering attachment to the Church. On his retirement he settled in Ramsgate. Limited as his earthly means were, he was yet a "great heart" and in the disposal of his slender property left £5 for the Station funds.

HAMILTON AND MADELINE HADDOW

Born in Lanarkshire in 1858, Hamilton Haddow was appointed to the staff at Elmfield College, York, as writing-master in 1876. The religious interests of the school were fully attended to and Mr.Haddow threw himself with zeal into this form of service. Sometimes as many as 100 boys would attend a prayer meeting. With other local-preacher members of staff he organised missionary meetings. At Elmfield he met Madeline Kendall, daughter of the York Circuit Superintendent, whom he married in 1888. Being pressed to begin a day school in High Wycombe, the centre of the furniture industry, he made a modest start with seven boys in one of the vestries of our White Hart Street chapel. A night school was added, the curriculum was widened and the number of pupils so greatly increased that a remove had to be made to more commodious premises. It was feared that the formation of the Borough Technical School might be prejudicial to the private school but it served to introduce Mr.Haddow to a wider circle of influence. He was asked to take commercial subjects, English and Mathematics and merged his own classes in the more general work, finally being appointed secretary of technical education in the town. During his 12 years' service membership rose to 700 and on his retirement he was presented with a public testimonial and a purse of gold at a conversazione in the Guildhall. He has also been clerk to the Governors of Wycombe High School and borough auditor. Nor has this public work lessened the activities of Mr.Haddow on behalf of his own church. For 14 years he was the superintendent of White Hart Street Sunday school until ill health forced him to relinquish the position. In 1914 after an interval of eight years he resumed the superintendency. Some of his happiest hours, he says, were spent leading the teachers' training class for the town and district which has had a marked effect in improving Sunday school work generally.

"A RAMBLER" (1914)

Before her marriage Mrs.Haddow, a fragile girl still in her teens, went through the Alford (Lincs.) Circuit with her gospel message, Sunday and weekday alike. Young and old flocked to hear her and there was such an ingathering as has made her name perpetually fragrant in that area. Many who were thus converted are the local preachers and stewards of that Circuit today. In High Wycombe hosts of young people trace their noblest development to her work at White Hart Street as a Sunday school teacher. Many years ago she inaugurated social gatherings on Wednesday afternoons in the winter months in aid of church

funds. She is also vice-president of the Women's Total
Abstinence Union. Among her conspicuous endowments is that of
public prayer and as a public speaker. She spoke in the City
Temple not only with lucidity but with intense force and
passion. The Haddows' home, Mount Pleasant, stands for
hospitality and fulness of life and is a gathering place for all
and sundry. Their countenance has brought sunshine and
substantial help to struggling causes. Their only daughter is
actively engaged in church work, as secretary of Christian
Endeavour, Sunday school teacher and choir member and is in much
demand as soloist and elocutionist.

UNA LLOYD PAGE (1921)

KEN ROLFE sums up:

    Situated in the town centre, the former mother church of
the High Wycombe Primitive Methodist Circuit was prominent for
its many activities and spiritual concern for members and
outsiders alike. The very full noticeboard outside the church
ended with the words: "Open every night". Sundays began with
Sunday School and morning service. In the afternoon there was
school again, also Bible Class for the older ones. Every
Tuesday there was Band of Hope, followed by Christian Endeavour.
On Wednesday, Women's Fellowship in the afternoon would be
followed by evening Bible study in the lecture room. Thursday
saw choir practice, Girl Guides, Boys' Brigade - and Band of
Hope again. On Friday there was the teachers' preparation
class. The Young Men's Institute was open every night. Cricket
and billiards leagues not only kept young men occupied; they
also encouraged inter-denominational links. Reached by outside
stone steps, the church was well maintained and produced a
number of local preachers who also ran the class meetings. One
remembers Messrs.H.Jarrett, W.Bates, J.Holland - and of course
Mr.H. Haddow. White Hart Street had a young ladies' choir and
even produced its own Operatic Society.

    Albert Jones was a society steward during the 1930's and
recalls finding a burglar in the boiler room. What he thought
was worth taking is an exercise in the realms of fantasy, for
the premises reflected the saying, "poor as church mice"!
"Boiler room" is also a misnomer since there was only a furnace
which - reputedly - supplied warm air to the church above.
After the War the church was much too large for the number of
people attending and as there were many other Methodist churches
in the town, it was decided to close down. The last regular
Sunday service was held on 8th April 1951 when Rev.Walter

N.Parnaby, the former Minister, returned. It was a sad coincidence that one of White Hart Street's stalwarts, Mrs.Esther Harris, should have died a few months before the final service in March 1953. She was in her 99th year and had been associated with the church from its beginning in 1875. Treasured memories of their association with White Hart Street were recalled in 1951 by veteran members like 98 year old Mrs.E.Gomme and Mr. and Mrs. Ladyman. They remembered the days when the Sunday School numbered 500, and those notable Whitsuntide processions when Sunday School scholars paraded the streets of High Wycombe, led by a brass band. The red banner of the School was flourished by the girls dressed in white and the blue banner by the boys.

After its closure many of the 89 members transferred to Westbourne Street, while others went to Wesley. The chapel became part of Murray's departmental store, following the recent closure of which extensive redevelopment has taken place. In the mind's eye one can still seem to make out the shape of the old chapel and imagine it brooding over its memories. It is remarkable what a comparatively brief life span the two "cathedrals" of Primitive Methodism had. Frogmoor Gardens and White Hart Street lasted little more than a century (1848 to 1951) between them, whereas the two Wesley churches (St.Mary Street and Priory Road) have existed more than twice as long (from 1779 to the present day).

WESTBOURNE STREET (1878)

ERNIE PULLEN writes:

Situated in a poor working area of High Wycombe, Westbourne Street Primitive Methodist Chapel which opened in 1878, will be remembered as a happy "family" church with a host of activities. It was famous for its music. The organ was installed in memory of those who gave their lives in the First World War. The choir rendered anthems at both Sunday services and an oratorio on Good Friday. From this sprang the Wycombe Orpheus Male Voice Choir under W.Bromage Smith. A bazaar was held at the time of the Wycombe September Fair which took place in a nearby meadow, to direct money away from the pockets of "sinners" to the more worthy church funds! A "Married and Single People's Effort" aroused keen competition and a lot of cash. After the Second World War attitudes to churchgoing changed. A campaign was conducted in 1951 by Herbert Silverwood and its influence can still be seen today in those who preach and serve in many parts of Britain. Gradually the rows of terraced houses disappeared as the population was moved out to the new housing estates. Despite the addition of members from White Hart Street and Newland membership inevitably declined. When the area was designated an "industrial zone", the trustees decided to close. The last service was on 27th August 1961 and most members transferred to the new church at Deeds Grove. The site is now used by Wycombe Self Drive Hire Company.

KEN PEATEY writes:

The chapel opened on to Westbourne Street, the schoolroom to Baker Street and above them was a rabbit-warren of classrooms the largest of which was known as the Institute Room and housed the billiard table. The area was densely populated. A "tin tabernacle" (which later served as Sands Chapel and finished its life in Mr. Aldridge's orchard in Hughenden Valley) was never big enough and gave way at the end of the last century to the galleried church. Most men worked long hours in the many furniture factories around there but they still found time for church. Westbourne Street was famous for its warmth of fellowship and fervency of song. William Line and William Neville walked miles on Sundays to preach in the villages. George Taylor's Friday class had a huge influence on teenagers,

they tell me, about the time of the First World War;
Messrs. Plested, Hunt and Darvill led the 200-strong Sunday
School; Christian Endeavour and Band of Hope flourished; and
Sunday afternoon singing of Sankey's hymns meant little peace
for the neighbourhood. Concerts and plays were of such a high
standard that requests came from many other churches for repeat
performances. The church boasted a football team, two cricket
teams and a billiards team.

Nor were the needy of the area neglected. During December
evenings the sound of carols could be heard in the streets,
followed by: "We are the Westbourne Street carol singers,
singing on behalf of the sick and poor". No collection was made
until Boxing Day morning and the money collected was distributed
over the year to needy people, usually at the rate of half-a-
crown [12½p.] a time. The "Bucks Free Press" reported the
Annual Effort at Christmas 1913 when local Friendly Societies
and the Salvation Army were present with their banners: "On
Monday an 'At Home' was held. The total raised was £18 which is
£5 less than last year due to the labour unrest in the town."
Another social outreach was the Slate and Loan Club to which
people paid a set sum each Friday. They could then have a loan
to help tide them over a period of unemployment or sickness. A
lump sum was payable on death. At Christmas the money left in
the fund was divided equally among the members. This Club
continued some years after the closure of the premises and was
one of the largest in the whole of Methodism. It was widely
known but who can tell of the acts of generosity and sacrifice,
the bearing of one another's burdens, which were never made
public? Many stories could be told of food provided for people
who were penniless, of footwear, clothing or bedding given
without ostentation to very poor families. The "social
conscience" was very much alive in Primitive Methodism and
continued after the days of "Union".

SANDS (1912)

THE SANDS "EXPERIENCE"

Most preachers have happy memories of Sands at the west end
of Wycombe and miss the fellowship there. It was the sort of
church where we often received more than we gave! One can
imagine the Super wondering what to do about Brother X
(depression; poor health; complaints from certain Churches).

Perhaps he should gently "retire" him? Then his brow lightens.
"I'll plan him at Sands!" he cries; "that should buck him up!"
That may be a fiction but the following is fact.

A certain preacher was feeling deeply troubled. He had
lost his job and as a result his reputation and some of his
(business) friends. He felt too ill to preach and in any case
could not face people. Others had stood in for him for several
weeks and now Christmas was approaching when he had a long-
standing invitation to conduct the carol evening at Sands. Of
course he could not go! But this particular steward was
determined he should. "You don't have to preach," she said;
"the lessons will be read for you; and we'll do the singing!
All you've got to do is STAND THERE!"

So he went in great trepidation, accompanied by a colleague
who had instructions what to do if his poor brother collapsed.
He didn't. He sang all the carols. He preached two sermons.
He could face the future again. His family might after all have
a happy Christmas! When he returned to his own church later
that evening, everyone commented on the complete transformation
in his face. They asked him what had happened. "It was their
faces which changed mine!" he replied. (That steward writes the
article below; thanks to the Sands people the preacher is still
preaching.)

EDNA TONKS writes:

An old railway-carriage on the top of a steep slope,
overlooking the Sands area - that's how my chapel started. The
Victorian "Prims." got tired of holding their services in the
open spaces of the cold Sands and bought the carriage in 1897.
A "tin tabernacle" (redundant from use at Westbourne Street)
followed and then in 1912 the present chapel was built in Sands
Road (Chapel Lane). The Methodists used it for 70 years and
then the Seventh Day Adventists took it over.

A warm friendly Church - that's everybody's memory of
Sands. It was the people who made it what it was - like my
parents, Leslie and Doris Goodearl, who took me to the services
when I was a little girl; the musicians (Messrs. Sherwood and
Ing on violins; Edie Cripps on the cello; Mrs. Annie Large or
Mrs. Frances Welters at the organ; Jack West, the genial
conductor; Harold Gibbons and Ken Rackstraw's lovely bass and
tenor voices); the congregation ever-smiling (the Stallwoods,
Berrys, Rackstraws, Larges, Howards, Pococks, Creswells,

Chadwicks and many others);
and old Walter Barefoot who
kept the roads round Sands
clean and tidy during the week
and the preachers up to
scratch on Sundays! I
remember the harvest
auctioneers (Frank Stallwood,
the apple expert; Reg Sears,
rationing the wartime eggs to
one per family); outings to
Park Farm; Bright Hour, Youth
Guild, Women's Guild; the
Sunday School which used to
descend the stairs from
schoolroom to chapel like an
unending invading army; and
the flower shows with a cup on
offer for the best collection
of vegetables. I am sorry we
had to give up our treasured
chapel at Sands in 1982. But
I'm glad I had the opportunity
to go there and meet so many
good Christian people.

†††††† *TODAY'S THOUGHTS FROM WESLEY'S SERMONS* ††††††††

* All the good things God gives us come from His grace.

* Try to be not an "almost" but an "altogether" Christian.

* A wicked man sleeps satisfied with what he has done wrong.

* Not everybody under your care will become a clergyman.

* A "worm" should not ask God why He is so kind to him.

* Don't wait until you are more sincere to be forgiven.

* Religion is not just a matter of having right opinions.

* Once you love God with all your heart you will be perfect.

* Live by the law and fear God; live by grace and love Him.

* A man who thinks he is good is keen to praise himself.

CHAPTER 6

THE WESLEYAN REFORM UNION

Although the secession of the PRIMITIVES from the WESLEYAN METHODIST CHURCH is the best known, it was in fact only one of several.   In Wesley's lifetime George Whitefield had disagreed with his sermon on "Free Grace" in which he had expounded the "Arminian" doctrine of universal   salvation.   Whitefield was a Calvinist who believed that God had predestined only "the elect" for salvation.   As a result in 1741 he held a Conference in Cardiff where the WELSH CALVINISTIC METHODIST CHURCH was established.   The years after Wesley's death make a sad tale of break-ups and new groupings.   Methodist history now becomes so complicated that we have numbered the various sects, to try and make it more understandable.

(1)   In 1796 Alexander Kilham demanded a more democratic constitution which was refused.   So he set up the METHODIST NEW CONNEXION.   (Its most famous member was to be   William Booth, a Superintendent Minister who was refused permission in 1861 to give up his circuit work.   He resigned and established the East London Mission which later came to be known as the "Salvation Army".)

(2)   In 1815 a group of evangelists among the tin-miners of Cornwall, finding the restrictions imposed by Conference very irksome, set up the BIBLE CHRISTIANS movement.

(3)   In 1828 - in protest against the playing of an organ in Brunswick Church, Leeds - the PROTESTANT METHODIST CHURCH was started.

(4)   In 1835 the WESLEYAN METHODIST ASSOCIATION was set up in protest at the founding of the Wesleyan Theological Institution.

(5)   In 1849 the WESLEYAN REFORMERS' ASSOCIATION was established in protest at the refusal of Conference to accept a petition for redress of their grievances.

(6)   In 1857 some of Group (5) joined with Groups (3) and (4) to form the UNITED METHODIST FREE CHURCH.

(7)   In 1858 the remainder of Group (5) became the VESLEYAN
REFORM UNION.

(8)   In 1907 Groups (1) and (2) joined with Group (6) to form
the UNITED METHODIST CHURCH.

(9)   Throughout this period - and indeed to the present day -
the INDEPENDENT METHODISTS have stayed true to their name!

The most significant of the smaller breakaway movements
from the Wesleyan Methodist Church in the last century was that
of the (7) VESLEYAN REFORM UNION. Its independence of mind and
emphasis on the freedom of the individual church to run its own
affairs, have been over the years a cause of both envy and
annoyance to the rest of Methodism. Many of Wesley's followers
were critical of his 1784 "Deed of Declaration" which gave no
right of appeal against the decisions of the Council of 100
Ministers. A free Conference was demanded in which all matters
would be decided on a majority vote. Individual churches should
have the power to admit or expel members and choose their own
leaders. These   demands were refused although a "Plan of
General Pacification" in 1795 did grant certain concessions.
However the increasingly arbitrary rule of the Ministers over
the next half-century caused much agitation, followed by
expulsions and - only belatedly - reforms. A commonly heard
demand was that the Church should recognise only the "headship
of Christ over all things and the priesthood of all believers".

The clamour for "Reform" was at fever pitch in 1849 when
Revs.James Everitt, Samuel Dunn and William Griffiths were
expelled from the Manchester Conference. The President refused
to grant them an interview. The Secretary of the Conference,
Rev.Jabez Bunting, backed him up. "The government of the
Church," he said, "belongs to the ordained Ministers; the
Superintendent Minister has supreme rights in his own circuit."
Chapels now began to be lent by sympathisers and the (5)
VESLEYAN REFORMERS' ASSOCIATION was set up.   At their
Conference in 1852 the Association affirmed its independence
from the parent body. A "Declaration of Principle" asserted
that "God's Word is the only rule for faith and practice". The
following year both Churches' Conferences were held in Bradford.
100,000 Wesleyan Methodists had now seceded or been expelled but
in 1857 many threw in their lot with the new (6) UNITED
METHODIST FREE CHURCH. The remainder formed themselves in 1858
into the (7) VESLEYAN REFORM UNION which within two years had
17,000 members. Churches were to be found mainly in the north

of England and the Midlands - and in the High Wycombe area where they became known as "FREE METHODISTS".

Unsuccessful efforts were made in 1907 to persuade them to join the new (8) UNITED METHODIST CHURCH and again in 1932 to participate with the latter, the WESLEYAN and PRIMITIVE METHODIST CHURCHES in the "Deed of Union" from which the METHODIST CHURCH was formed. Despite their smaller resources - in 1970 there were only 24 Ministers and 218 preachers for 150 churches - the (7) VESLEYAN REFORM UNION has remained independent to this day. In 1898 it placed a stained glass window in Wesley's Chapel, City Road, as "an expression of loving remembrance of John Wesley who still holds a high place in our affections".

FORMATION OF THE HIGH WYCOMBE FREE METHODIST CIRCUIT

PREACHING PLACES. (1849-1895)

```
                  11        1         1         1         1    1
                  88        8         8         8         8    8
                  45        6         7         8         9    9
                  90123456789012345678901234567890123456789012345
High Wycombe.
   Oxford Road    S                   B
   Newland                                                A
Beaconsfield      T
Penn              T                              E
Hazlemere                             S B
Wycombe Marsh                         B
Farnham Common    S                     B
Wooburn Green             P
```

A = Acquired from Baptist Church
B = Chapel Built
E = Chapel Extended or Additional Buildings e.g. Schoolroom
P = Transferred from Primitive Church
S = Services
T = Transferred from Wesleyan Church

The first three Churches in the Wycombe area to join the new Wesleyan Reformers' Association (which later became the Vesleyan Reform Union), were originally "ordinary" Methodists -

Penn and Beaconsfield (Wesleyan) in 1849/50 and Wooburn Green (Primitive) in the early 1860's. Although the Oxford Road chapel (1863) was Free Methodist - as the Union has always been known in this district - from the start, the original members who had previously rented a chapel in Crendon Lane, had broken away from the Wesleyans in 1849.

Wycombe Marsh (1865) and Hazlemere (1867) started with new buildings and apparently new societies, but we note that in both areas there had been companies of Methodists meeting before this, and we may suppose that in time they supported the new Free Methodist causes. At Farnham Common the members who built their own chapel in 1867, seem to have been an independent group from its inception in 1845. By now there were enough Churches to form a Circuit - although the Free Methodists have always rather been a federation of independent Churches - and Richard Nicholls was its first Minister. (Farnham Common remained outside for the rest of the century.)

<u>PREACHING PLACES. (1896-1942)</u>

```
           1   1       1       1       1       1 1
           8   9       9       9       9       9 9
           9   0       1       2       3       4 4
           67890123456789012345678901234567890123456789012

High Wycombe.
  Oxford Road     E        R†           †
  Newland                  U
Beaconsfield      B        †            †
Penn                       E†           †
Hazlemere             B    †            † E
Wycombe Marsh   R          †            †       E
Farnham Common             †            †
Wooburn Green              †            †          C
Gerrards Cross        S †     B         † W
Saunderton U.V.            †
```

B = Chapel Built
C = Services Ceased
E = Chapel Extended or Additional Buildings e.g. Schoolroom
R = Rebuilt or New Building to replace
† = Services (from Plans available)
S = Services (from other records)
U = Transferred to the United Methodist Church
V = Transferred to the Wesleyan Church.

In 1880 some of the Oxford Road congregation moved to the
Newland Chapel which had formerly been a Baptist cause, but this
seceded to the United Methodists in 1910 at a time when many of
the Oxford Road people had been returning "home", prior to the
opening of their new chapel in 1911. About this time
evangelists were going out to the Gerrards Cross area and in
1915 a "tin tabernacle" was erected. Because of its distance
from Wycombe the cause was difficult to maintain and in 1931 it
went over to the Wesleyans. The Wooburn Green chapel was
declared unsafe and closed in 1938. In 1970 the Oxford Road
chapel was replaced by a new building at The Pastures (in the
Downley area).

PREACHING PLACES. (1943-1988)

```
          1     1           1           1           1           1
          9     9           9           9           9           9
          4     5           6           7           8           8
          34567890123456789012345678901234567890012345678
```

High Wycombe.						
Oxford Road	†		†		C	
The Pastures					B	†
Beaconsfield	†		†			E †
Penn	†		†			†
Hazlemere	†		†			†
Wycombe Marsh	†		†			E †
Farnham Common	†		†			†

B = Chapel Built
C = Services Ceased
E = Chapel Extended or Additional Buildings e.g. Schoolroom
† = Services (from Plans available)

Today the Circuit still consists of six of its eight
members at the start of the century - Penn, Beaconsfield, The
Pastures (ex-Oxford Road), Wycombe Marsh, Hazlemere and Farnham
Common. Each is still run independently of the rest.

SOME THOUGHTS ON THE FREE METHODISTS

As its title implies, a Free Methodist Church is free to
do what it likes! Although it belongs to a circuit, each runs
its own affairs, chooses its own Minister (if it wants or can
afford one) and books its own preachers. All the local Churches

have been successful in different ways over recent years: The Pastures is the largest and has a wide range of meetings and activities;   Hazlemere has seen a revival, particularly in a growing Sunday School; Penn - traditionally the most independent - appoints its own Minister;   Farnham Common is engaged in evangelical outreach; Beaconsfield has a new extension; and refurbishments at Wycombe Marsh have created a beautiful sanctuary for worship.

It is not necessary for Ministers to have a college training or a Wesleyan Reform background, anointing by the Holy Spirit being regarded as the ultimate test of a man's acceptability. Any suitable person (not just the Minister) is allowed to conduct Holy Communion, baptisms, weddings and funerals. The Wycombe Circuit has a few of its own preachers but there is no set training scheme. Pulpits - where there is no resident Minister - are supplied mainly by preachers from other denominations. The lectionary or service book is rarely used.

Discipline over members is in the hands of each Church and can at times be strictly enforced, the only "rule-book" normally being the Bible. There is no Super to intervene nor can the Circuit Meeting ensure obedience to its wishes. Perhaps the two main disadvantages are: the risk of strong-minded people trying to take matters into their own hands and the lack of circuit resources. Being Free Methodist in difficult times can be a lonely experience! But on the whole the Churches prosper and are as proud of their heritage as any "proper" Methodist!

HIGH WYCOMBE FREE METHODIST CIRCUIT: MINISTERS

MINISTERS OF WHOLE CIRCUIT

1864-70	Richard Nicholls	1870	Joseph Butler
1875	John Packet	1876	George Nuttall
1877-82	George Green	1883-84	J.E.Leuty
1885	I.C.Ablett	1886	Joseph Dennis
1887-89	James Pettinger	1890-95	J.O.Scarborough
1896-98	George O.Parr	1899-02	James Pettinger
1900-02	C.W.Hall	1903-09	E.Dennis
1904-21	William C.Smith	1922-33	S.J.Smith

THE WESLEYAN REFORM UNION

MINISTERS OF OXFORD ROAD/THE PASTURES & HAZLEMERE

1934-38	S.H.Reader	1939-41	A.J.Couling
1945-51	V.T.Burkitt	1951-64	Fred C.Wilson
1964-74	David A.Murray	1974-84	John W.Goulder
1985-	Gregory R.Hargrove		

MINISTERS OF PENN, BEACONSFIELD, FARNHAM COMMON & WYCOMBE MARSH

1934-43	J.S.Wilkinson	1944-48	David A.Murray
1949-50	G.Bellamy		

OTHER MINISTERS (from 1951)

Beaconsfield	Wycombe Marsh	Penn
D.Omand	C.A.Metcalfe	L.F.Harris
W.T.Burkitt		J.Tindal
C.A.Metcalfe		M.Farmery
J.Bradbury		A.J.Barker
		P.Aston

HIGH WYCOMBE FREE METHODIST CIRCUIT: PREACHERS

NAME	ADDRESS	PLANS				
		1911	1927	1945	1956	1987
T.Hearne	Hanwell	*				
G.Edwards	Totteridge Road	*				
T.Rackstraw	Widmer End	*	*			
R.Hazell	Denmark Street	*				
G.Morton	Tylers Green	*				
G.Weston	Bridge Street	*				
H.Tilling	Wycombe Marsh	*	*			
G.Ellis	Kitchener Road	*				
E.Bayliss	Tylers Green	*				
G.Dickety	Wycombe Marsh	*	*			
J.Mealing	Victoria Street	*	*	*		
J.Burrows	Green Street	*	*			
F.Ball	Bridge Street	*	*			
T.Tilbury	Hazlemere	*				
J.Alder	Farnham Royal	*				
R.Cox	Gerrards Cross	*				
T.Cheeseman	East Burnham	*	*	*		
D.Fyffe	Farnham Common	*				
V.Meeks	Wycombe Marsh	*	*			

NAME	ADDRESS	PLANS				
		1911	1927	1945	1956	1987
C.Harman	Desborough Road	*				
W.West	Oakridge Road	*	*			
T.Reed	Desborough Road	*				
C.Lane	Desborough Road	*	*	*	*	
Harding	Beaconsfield	*				
J.Hussey	Desborough Avenue	*				
E.Bonnett	Abercrombie Avenue	*				
H.Hooper	Frogmoor	*				
J.Judd	Slough	*				
H.Perry	Gerrards Cross	*				
J.Bateman	Wycombe Marsh	*				
G.Rolls	Kitchener Road	*				
J.Howard	Mendy Street	*				
E.Hearn	Kitchener Road	*				
H.Hearn	Kitchener Road	*				
W.Burrows	Penn		*			
J.Bryant	West End Street		*			
R.Smith	Hazlemere		*	*	*	
W.Witney	Hazlemere		*	*	*	
M.Wise	Wycombe Marsh		*	*	*	
F.Rolfe	Beaconsfield		*			
Buckle	Hazlemere		*			
F.Hearne	Hazlemere		*	*		
E.Tilbury	Beaconsfield		*			
W.Burrows Jnr.	Wycombe Marsh		*	*	*	
K.Kearley(Miss)	Bridge Street		*			
H.Day	Tylers Green		*			
W.Ludgate	Hedgerley Corner		*			
D.Parsons	Hedgerley Corner			*		
E.Benyon	Beaconsfield				*	
G.Hutt	Hazlemere				*	*
G.Howlett	Park Farm Road				*	*
W.Smith	Hazlemere				*	
P.Dyer	Beaconsfield				*	
W.Crockett	Farnham Common				*	
R.Evans	Hazlemere				*	
E.Lacey (Miss)	London Road				*	*
A.Brooks	Desborough Avenue				*	
K.Burden	Cock Lane				*	*
J.Field	Hazlemere					*
N.Keen	Tenzing Drive					*
D.Lee	Wooburn Green					*

CHAPTER 7
FREE METHODIST CHURCHES

PENN (1850)

NORMAN STRETTON writes:

The oldest existing Methodist chapel in this area was opened in 1808 as a Wesleyan society. In 1850 it joined the Wesleyan Reform Union with which it has been associated ever since. Services were always well attended. The "young men's prayer meeting" arranged one of many missions. Tea meetings were popular and the minute book records: "The secretary is authorised to have 200 tea tickets printed and the Holmer Green String Band shall be asked to give a recital afterwards." Thomas Garland who was a Sunday School teacher in 1851, later became Seaman's Missioner and was renowned for his book, "Leaves from my Log". Our forebears were glad to remind people, "he came from our Penn chapel"! In 1874 the chapel was converted into a schoolroom and the present church was opened in 1876. In 1904 - prior to the purchase of further land from Earl Howe - new trustees included: Frank Perfect, Henry Perfect, Arthur Stretton, William Burrows and John Jefkins. Further extensions are believed to have been opened in 1911. In his centenary report (1908) the secretary records a debt of about £200. (Offerings at the time amounted to £40 a year!) Further building has included: the purchase of the Minister's manse, known as "Chapel Cottage", which adjoins the church and was subsequently extended and modernised; complete refurbishment of the church; erecting a new vestry; and - in 1982 - modernisation of the kitchen and toilets.

The Church has always enjoyed wonderful fellowship and spiritual blessings. Among the many who have ministered here, was Dr.Alexanda White, the Scottish divine who preached his last sermon at Penn with his doctor in attendance. During his last sermon, one of my late relatives recalled, his voice became so weak as to be almost inaudible. In a whisper he announced his final hymn, "The sands of time are sinking". Then as if empowered by the Holy Spirit, he almost shouted: "But the dawn of Heaven breaks!" A few days later he was with his Lord. In recent years the Church has appointed Ministers from outside the Connexion, including L.F.Harris, J.Tindal, M.Farmery, A.J.Barker and P.Aston. I conclude with words from the centenary report: "Let us be steadfast, immoveable .... for as much as we know our labours are not in vain in the Lord (1 Corinthians 15.58)".

BEACONSFIELD (1850)

ROY HOGDON writes:

The first Wesleyan Reform Union Church in Beaconsfield which was Wesleyan Methodist from 1838 to 1850, was situated in Queens Terrace in Windsor End. Later it moved to Factory Yard in Wycombe End and then to its present site in Shepherds Lane in 1900. My own family has been involved in the present church from the beginning. I recall many happy times in the 50 years since I was baptised by Rev. Wilkinson. I then lived in the cottage opposite and at the age of one year went to Mrs.Jessie Child's Sunday School class. During the Second World War Dr. Rupert Kipping managed to find sweets to give us children! Sunday School Anniversaries were always great events, the chapel being full to overflowing. They meant new clothes for us and much practice, learning our recitations. Our earliest outings were to the cricket ground for a "bun fight" or, if we were lucky, a trip to Burnham Beeches. After the war coaches returned and it seemed as if the whole town wanted to accompany

us in a fleet of buses to the seaside. Another highlight was
the annual Scripture Examination and waiting to see if we had
won the shield again with yet another certificate for Mr.Holmes
to find a frame for. Prizegiving was always eagerly anticipated
too: had we won a book this year? Yes, we had - and so had
everybody else!

Over the years we held gift days to raise money for a new
Sunday School building. Everyone brought their jars of coins to
have them counted - "bun-pennies", "ship-halfpennies", even the
rare silver threepenny-bits. We also raised money by giving
concerts in the old schoolroom. George Child built the stage
with trestle-tables or railway sleepers brought up from the
station. Regular "entertainers" included Joan Lawrence giving
monologues, and Ted Benyon playing his one-string fiddle. The
new schoolroom was eventually bought but in recent years it was
demolished so that the land could be sold for building houses
and the money used to build in 1986 a fine new brick hall
adjoining the church. I can remember many local preachers, each
with their own special talents, including dear little Tommy
Cheeseman from Farnham Common; Mr.T.W.Apps who ran a cycle shop
at Pinions in Wycombe and had a special petrol ration for his
car during the Second World War for conveying preachers to their
engagements; the scholarly Dr.Donald Omand; and Mr.W.Meeks (of
Wycombe Marsh). They have now passed to higher service but
their influence has touched many lives. Beaconsfield's
building remains, the faithful attend and with God's help a
revival will surely come.

WOOBURN GREEN (1860)

ANNIE VALKER writes:

My parents, Philip and Anne Buckle, lived at Wooburn Green
in the 1890's and attended the Free Methodist Church in Windsor
Lane. He took a very active part in chapel life and always
encouraged his children to attend. My brother Alfred used to
accompany the singing on his violin, as there was no organ at
that time. The family moved in 1900 - before my birth - to
Hazlemere. I returned to work at Wooburn in 1919 and was
welcomed by Mrs.Sarah Walker who ran the chapel. She was also
president of the circuit at one time. Mr. and Mrs. Taylor, two
of the members, lived in the adjoining cottage and their son

Reginald played the organ. The preacher at the evening service
was always expected to help with the afternoon Sunday School!

The chapel which probably was a Primitive Methodist society
until about 1860, closed in 1938 but services continued for a
while in one of the houses. Rev.S.H.Reader, the Minister of
Oxford Road, sometimes conducted services at Wooburn. At his
farewell he said: "It was a real sorrow to me when the church
at Wooburn Green had to come down. Although there were only
eight or nine present [in the house meetings], we had a real
time of blessing". The proceeds from the sale of the site went
to the Wooburn Trust Fund under the Circuit's control.

OXFORD ROAD (1863)

NORMAN KEEN writes:

In 1849 a number of dissenters from the Wesleyan Methodists
began to hold services in a loft in Barton's Yard in Easton
Street, High Wycombe. Later they were given the use of a former
Congregational chapel in Crendon Lane whose congregation had
built a larger church (now Trinity United Reformed Church). In
1862 the Free Methodists, as they were known locally, began to
plan their own building. The "Bucks Free Press" reported:
"The friends composing this denomination having met for 12 years
in a small rented chapel at the eastern end of the town, and
being unable to obtain a lease of it for any period of years,
have come to the determination to 'rise and build' a more
suitable and convenient place of worship. Contributions have
been made among themselves and efforts put forth to gather from
the benevolent of other congregations, and in pursuance of their
purpose, special services have been held, the most recent of
which we now record.

"On Sunday last 14th December 1862 three discourses were
delivered by M.Berlyn of London, a converted Jew. All the
services, especially that of the evening, were well attended and
the collections amounted to £4.10s.0d.[£4.50]. On Monday 15th
December a public tea meeting was held in the Town Hall, the
materials for which were given by members of the Church and
congregation; about 150 sat down and enjoyed the social meal.
In the evening a public lecture was delivered by M.Berlyn on
'The Manners and Customs of the Jews'. The hall was quite full;
the chair was taken by Thomas Wheeler Esq., the meeting having

been opened by Mr.Lacey of Penn and prayer offered by Mr.Garland of Penn. M.Berlyn expressed the pleasure he felt in endeavouring to assist the progress of the gospel in this neighbourhood. The first part of his lecture dealt with the Jewish ceremonies connected with the observance of the Sabbath day. The lecture occupied two hours and a half in its delivery and was listened to with great interest and attention. Votes of thanks to the lecturer and chairman were cordially agreed to. The meeting closed with the benediction. A collection was made at the close, which amounted to £3.3s.0d.[£3.15]."

In 1863 the new church opened in Oxford Road on the corner of Temple Street. (A model of this church is shown, right.) As the movement prospered, several cottages in Temple Street were purchased and used as classrooms. These were demolished in 1900 and a hall with classrooms on the first floor was erected. Eventually the congregation outgrew the church and several cottages in Remington Terrace, Oxford Road, were bought. Church and  cottages were demolished and a fine church erected which seated 450 people. It was opened for worship in 1911. Later a splendid organ was installed as a memorial to those who died in the First World War. The Church shared the ministries of Rev.W.C.Smith and Rev.S.J.Smith with the rest of the High Wycombe Free Methodist Circuit but in 1934 the arrangement was ended and future Ministers (Rev.S.H.Reader, Rev.A.J.Couling, Rev.W.T.Burkitt, Rev.F.C.Wilson and Rev.D.Murray) were shared with Hazlemere only.

Mention must also be made of lay stalwarts like Charlie Lane, the Sunday School superintendent who - rather like the Pied Piper - seemed to attract children from nowhere, and Mr.W.West, one-time Church president, and the long-lasting musical partnership of Mr.W.Burrows (organist) and Mr.W.Jefkins (choirmaster). A report in the "Bucks Free Press" (1913) said:

"A special service was conducted at Oxford Road Free Methodist
Church on Christmas morning   by Rev.W.C.Smith.   At a special
evening service the choir conducted by Mr.W.Jefkins, sang the
anthem, 'While shepherds watched'.   Mr.W.J.Burrows was at the
organ."   In 1963 the local authority put a compulsory
acquisition order on the church in order to relieve congestion
on the A 40 road, and in 1968 offered an alternative site a mile
away on a hill to the north-west in the middle of a new housing
development.   Plans were drawn up and a builder engaged.   On
17th January 1970 the Minister, Rev.David Murray, formally
unlocked the doors of The Pastures and we entered our splendid
new premises.

WYCOMBE MARSH (1865)

KEN BURDEN writes:

The first Wesleyan Reform (Free Methodist) church in
Wycombe Marsh was built in 1865 at the junction of London Road
and King's Road.   Although small, it had a balcony and was also
used as a day school.   (In recent years before its demolition it
was a Fish and Chip shop.)   The "Bucks Free Press" reported:
"The quiet village of Wycombe Marsh came alive on Monday 8th May
1865 as a very large crowd of people gathered together to
witness the laying of the foundation stone to the new chapel.
The site is at the eastern end of the village on the London
Road.   The building will measure 24 feet long by 15 feet broad,
with an estimated cost of £100.   It is intended to establish a
day school in connexion with the Chapel which will supply a want
that has been felt for a long time.   Mr.Snell of Beaconsfield
opened the ceremony at 3 o'clock by announcing the hymn,   'This
stone to Thee in faith we lay.'   This was followed by prayers
led by Mr.William Holland of High Wycombe.   The Scripture (1
Kings 8) was read by Mr.Wald Taft,   a Wesleyan Reform Home
Missionary.

"The foundation stone was laid by Mr. Thomas Martin of
High Wycombe who spoke a few words appropriate to the occasion.
Mr.Snell and Mr.W.Holland addressed the people, followed by an
address from Mr. Wald Taft, giving an outline of the great
principles on which they, as Wesleyan Reformers, builded.
Contributions were laid on the stone to the amount of
£3.14s.0d.[£3.70] and a hymn having been sung, the congregation
dispersed.   A large number found their way to the schoolroom

connected with the Union Baptist Chapel where a 'comfortable' tea was laid out. In the evening Mr. Taft preached in the schoolroom to a crowded audience from Malachi 4.2. The sum now in hand towards the building fund amounts to £9."

The present church in Abbey Barn Road opened in 1896. The pipe-organ which is still in use, came from Iver Church and was dismantled, transported by horse and cart and reassembled by Watson Tilling and Sidney Burden. For many years the organist was Georgina Timberlake in whose memory two stained glass windows were given, and the secretary/treasurer was Alderman Henry Tilling. He was also a preacher, as were William Meeks, Morgan Wise and William Burrows. For most of its existence the Church has depended on local preachers for pulpit supply, although during and after the Second World War it shared with other churches the services of Revs. James Wilkinson and David Murray. The oak pulpit front, lower platform, Communion table and chairs were given in memory of Norman Malpass who was killed while serving with the Royal Air Force.

Traditionally there were two Anniversary services - in February and July - when we had the help of Mrs. Martin (cello) and Messrs. Dancer and Child (violins). The February Anniversary was followed by a Saturday party and prize-giving, the July services by the Treat at Burnham Beeches. 300 scholars and adults (who paid 2/3d. [11p.] each) travelled in a fleet of lorries, owned by Alfred Ford (coal merchant and Primary leader), Jack Biggs (haulage contractor and Sunday School superintendent) and W.A.Steevens (builders; driven by Albert Bowler). The provisions waggon was always loaded first - with tea urns, crockery, cutlery and very dry madeira cake. On board went the elderly "cutters-up" and away to a good cheer. The afternoon service of the July Anniversary was an outdoor event in King's Square, with chairs and piano brought from the church. The square was packed and the windows of nearby houses were opened as Bert Sargeant began the service. In earlier times, we are told, John Gomm, a former Mayor, was as much welcomed for the £1 he placed in the offering plate, as for his message!

In the 1920's the church was not large enough to cope with the number of children so the former Congregational chapel in Ford Street was rented from the British Legion for use by the Primary. A plot of land in King's Square was purchased and a new schoolroom which had two floors, was opened in 1935. Slowly numbers have dwindled and the building was recently sold for office use, an extension being added in 1981/82 to the rear of the church and a larger vestibule at the front. The Women's Guild, started in 1929 under the presidency of Kate Stonell, has always been an active part of the fellowship, raising considerable sums of money. The Church still bears a loving witness to our Lord. Attendance has decreased considerably in recent years but we continue to pray for the day when God sends others to join us.

HAZLEMERE (1867)

ADA DAY writes:

In 1865 a few people met for Sunday evening services in Mrs.Tilbury's cottage - opposite the present Ford's superstore in Amersham Road. Numbers increased so a small chapel was built in the lane near Putnam's, the undertakers, who sold the site for £8. The foundation stone was laid by Thomas Wheeler on 27th May 1867, followed by special services on 31st May conducted by Miss Stedman. The chapel was finished in August 1867. A Church was formed and a Sunday School and weeknight meetings arranged. The fellowship was keen to have responsible members so applicants were put on three months' trial. At one meeting the secretary asked members to adhere to the rules and said there had been slackness about attending class meetings. The first anniversary in August 1868 was a "thorough good day and collections were good: morning 7/2½ [36p.]; afternoon 7/9 [39p.]; evening 11/4 [56½p.]" On the Monday following the tea and meeting were "joyful, happy and glorious".

In 1900 a complete circuit was formed with the seven other Free Methodist churches. There were two Ministers – Revs. J. Pettinger and C. W. Hall. The Church continued to grow and a larger chapel was needed so fund-raising began: bazaars, teas and entertainments on Monday evenings "as near the full moon as possible". Mr. F. Putnam offered a site in Penn Road for £45, a sum which had already been raised. His father paid £65 for the old chapel which is now a house. On Wednesday 12th September 1906 the door of the old chapel was locked by Mr. T. Rackstraw and the Ministers, Revs. W. C. Smith and E. Dennis, headed a march of members to the new chapel singing, "All hail the power of Jesus' name". On arrival there, the door was unlocked by Mr. O. Bridger. The new chapel was a place of entertainment as well as worship. The Speen Band was asked to come in 1908 "at little expense as possible". When the ladies gave a concert, the men provided refreshments (and vice-versa). But a resolution in 1909 demanded that "we have new milk in our tea"! In 1911 Brother Buckle was asked to put something to prevent the sparrows

getting into the chapel. When making arrangements for one
bazaar, it was passed that Sister P. see Sister B. and tell her
that "we would have no second-hand stall"!

Members always had a care for the needs of others and made
many donations to missions, the sick and needy and a charity
called "Beal's Home". On 14th October 1909 a Band of Hope was
started and many of the village children attended. On 21st
October 1910 a licence for marriages was granted. A "Pleasant
Sunday Afternoon" (P.S.A.) was started when an address was
given - rather than a sermon - and a musical item included. In
1912 when the parish church had a new organ, the Vicar,
Rev.C.H.Clissold, offered the old organ to the chapel. On Whit
Mondays Anglicans and Methodists had a combined fete in the
vicarage meadow, the proceeds being shared. The service at the
war memorial was always a united one. Mr. Clissold and his
successor, Rev.L.Mackney, came to the chapel and Rev.W.C.Smith
went to Holy Trinity. There has always been a happy
relationship between the two Churches. In 1933 Vicar and
Minister made a joint protest about proposed dog-racing in the
village.

In August 1919 it was decided to "give a welcome tea to all
the soldiers and their wives, to any who had been scholars of
the Sunday School, children of the village from the age of four
to fourteen and old people over 70 years of age". As several
former scholars had given their lives in the 1914-18 War "it was
decided to build a memorial schoolroom" - at a cost of over
£1000. The stone-laying took place in September 1927 when the
foundation stone from the old chapel was relaid by Mr.Rackstraw.
The schoolroom was opened in December 1929. During the 1939-45
War soldiers were stationed in Hazlemere Park and some attended
the chapel. They were allowed the use of two small rooms, one
as a rest room. But they had no electricity which was not
installed until 1945, twenty-one years later than gas. Many
alterations and improvements have been made in the postwar
years. No church can carry on however without the loyalty of
its members whose influence is never forgotten. We are a
smaller fellowship now than once we were. But numbers have
started to grow again under the ministry of Rev.Gregory Hargrove
whom - like his predecessors - we share with The Pastures. The
Sunday School, youth club and Women's Meeting are all thriving.
With God's help we anticipate a bright future.

FARNHAM COMMON (1867)

JIM CARGILL writes:

In 1845 Thomas Chamberlain of Thames Street, Windsor, started a class meeting in Farnham Common. By the early 1860's there were enough members to embark on the building of a little chapel. The sum of £5 was paid for the land and a further £100 bought the materials. Working in their free time - but never on a Sunday - the congregation built the chapel with their own hands. Queen Victoria gave her permission for the balcony to be supported by two busts of her head. Even the pews were made by members of the congregation, the timber being hewn from Burnham Beeches, and on 13th October 1867 the chapel was officially opened.

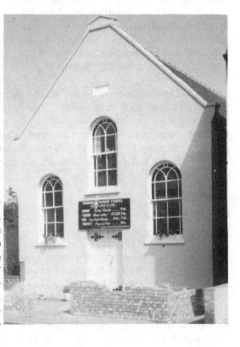

Designated a "Free Methodist Chapel", these early Wesleyan Reformers at last had their own place of worship. The earliest surviving minute of a members' meeting records:
" (1) The Lord's Supper shall be administered once a month.
(2) Baptisms shall be performed on the second Sunday each month.
(3) The following shall be prayer leaders to conduct the prayer meeting on Wednesday evenings: Brothers Earl, Ward, Bird and Carpenter."
The names of Ann Eliza James and Ann Ludgate are listed among the founder members and today distant relatives of these two pioneers still worship with us. An 1887 minute reads:
"The treasurer is authorised to pay the sum of three shillings [15p.] towards horse hire or railway expenses to all preachers from High Wycombe."

The Church joined the High Wycombe Free Methodist Circuit in the early part of this century. Thomas Cheeseman was Church Secretary for some 50 years. There are still people in Farnham Common who fondly remember Tommy and his "portable library" - a bicycle and a bundle of tracts. Preachers recall how he would kneel at the Communion table during the prayers. He was assisted by Will Crockett as treasurer and Mrs.Gilder who "cleaned the chapel so beautifully and never once complained of the children's muddy boots!".

Today we serve the same Master as those early Reformers. The village has changed; the chapel is much altered; but He remains the same. Regarding Thomas Chamberlain the register simply records: "Gone beyond the sea". Which sea, we do not know. Maybe it was the Jasper Sea but one thing is sure: he lit a lamp in Farnham Common which still shines today!

NEWLAND (1880)

As its name suggests, this area of Wycombe which is now the bus-station, had once been the "new land" where the richer folk lived. But by the mid-nineteenth century they had long gone and now it was crowded with tiny working-class dwellings. The cobbled alleyways were full of drunkards, poorly clad children and women taking the clothes to the River Wye to wash. Outside lavatories (privies) were shared one to a number of households, the sewage inevitably finding its way into the river. Drinking water was to be obtained only from the wells which stood next to the privies. It is not surprising that the death rate in Newland was so high and that often typhoid fever was the cause.

Along with the pubs, St.Paul's Mission and the police station stood a little chapel which had long been used by the Strict Baptists. A disagreement had caused many of them to go out to the fields at the edge of the town and build in 1862 a new church (Zion) in Bridge Street. Those who remained struggled on for a time, but in 1880 surrendered their chapel to the Oxford Road Free Methodists who used it as a "chapel of ease". In the early part of this century many of the worshippers returned to Oxford Road, including Mr.G.A.Wood (the well-known gents' outfitter), and in 1910 Newland became a United Methodist Church.

FREE METHODIST CHURCHES

OXFORD ROAD MINUTE BOOK (1880)

22nd March   In the event that we purchase Newland Chapel we lend the trustees (that may be appointed for the same) the £150 that we now have in hand for five years without interest.   That we offer £400 for Newland Chapel on condition a good and correct title be provided.

24th March   The report of the Deputation respecting Newland Chapel was received, Mr.Collins offering the chapel for £450. It was resolved that the Deputation wait again on Mr.Collins to try and arrange matters with him. Try to get the Chapel for £50 less than by him proposed. In case of failure to make an offer up to £425.

31st March   The report of the Deputation received – that after using their best endeavours with Mr.R.Collins, they succeeded in securing Newland Chapel, including all fixtures, cottage etc. for the sum of £425, subject to the consent of the County Court. The following brethren were elected as Trustees for Newland Chapel and Premises – James Woodbridge, Child, Frank Howland, R.Hazell, Robert Howland (Senr.), William Hearn, John Britnell.

5th April That we appoint the Deputation (Bros. F.Howland and Boyles) to secure on behalf of the Church £250 as mortgage on Newland Chapel.

19th April   That the members of Newland Chapel be considered members of this Church.

CHURCH REGISTER (Revised 1894)

Original surviving members (from 1880 at Oxford Road)

James Woodbridge	51 Desborough Road
Frederick & Mary Howland	40 Newland Meadow
James & Eliza Nash	Hughenden Road
Susannah Woodbridge	51 Desborough Road
John & Emma Burrows	192 Desborough Road
Arthur & Constance Wood	232 Desborough Road
Thomas & Harriet Barrett	Newland Meadow
James & Eliza Barlow	5 Vestbourne Street

Transferred from Oxford Road 1894-5

George & Mrs.Mellett   Green Street
Edward & Mrs.Child   Desborough Road
Henry & Mrs.Walls
Charles & Ada Griffin   Desborough Avenue
Walter & Jane Copeland   "Bird in Hand"
William & Caroline Selwyn   Mendy Street
James & Mrs.Pettinger   West Wycombe Road
Miss Beatrice Pettinger   West Wycombe Road

GERRARDS CROSS (1915)

The work began here in 1908 when the High Wycombe Free
Methodist Circuit sent out some evangelists who found a ready
response, especially among the servants at the big houses. Soon
there were seven members and in 1915 a "tin tabernacle" was
opened in Oak End Way at a cost of £200.   In 1931 the Church
joined the Wesleyan Methodists. On the site today stands a fine
new Methodist Church, built in 1958 and part of the Hillingdon
Circuit.

THE PASTURES (1970)

THE PASTURES   S.SHERRATT
1937

NORMAN KEEN writes:

There are seats for 270 people in this church which opened in 1970 after the closure of Oxford Road. It measures 40 feet by 60 feet. The pulpit, Commmunion table and grand piano stand on a platform behind which are the organ pipes . The console is situated in front of the platform. There are also a hall measuring 40 feet by 30 feet, three classrooms, lounge, vestry, vestibule, kitchen, toilets, cloakrooms and an adjoining caretaker's flat. The church has a panoramic view over the west end of Wycombe. That first Sunday morning saw a surge of children into the hall. In subsequent years attendance at Sunday School has dropped, but there are Bible study classes for young people. The premises are used during the week by many groups, including Girls' Brigade (whose founder at Oxford Road, Mrs.L.B.Biggs, has recently retired after 37 years), Cubs and Scouts, Women's Meeting, as well as fellowship meetings, singing groups and young mothers' clubs.

We have always been a "family Church". Mr.G.A.Wood who relaid the 1863 foundation stone of the first chapel at The Pastures in 1969, joined Oxford Road from Newland. One of the "fathers" of the Church, his sons and grandsons still follow in his steps. We are an evangelical Church of 130 members, faithfully served in recent years by our Ministers, Revs. David Murray, John Goulder and Gregory Hargrove. When we were trying by our own will to rebuild in the town centre, God withheld His blessing. When we obeyed His will and came to The Pastures, He opened the floodgates of blessing. Many loved persons have passed away but new, lively, devoted younger people are making sure that the work of the Lord Jesus is carried on. We give God the praise.

MUSIC IN THE PASTURES

In our first year music for worship was provided by the grand piano until the Oxford Road organ could be installed. Since then that instrument, under faithful organists like Brian Wood and Bill Peatey, has added its own richness to the music of the Church. The choir which had been in existence for many years at Oxford Road, continued under George Howlett until 1983. In the late 1970's a new wave of Christian music was being published much of which could be accompanied by guitars and other instruments. It was at this time that a ladies' singing group was formed. First called "Kara" (the Greek word for "joy") and later to become "Pastures Folk" (when it opened its doors to male members), this group was to introduce the congregation to many of these new songs and develop its own ministry in drama, song and worship-dance. New action songs were taught in the morning services and Junior Church, so that the children could participate in worship in a more meaningful way.

In 1980 the Church celebrated its tenth anniversary with a production of mime, drama and song, entitled "The King is Coming". This was followed by "Come Together" and other Christian musicals like "A Grain of Mustard Seed" and "Greater than Gold". The young people's input into the worship has been greatly valued and encouraged, starting in the early days with the Junior Choir, and since then in services led by the Junior Church and youth group, and the formation of the young people's instrumental group. Hosting concerts by many Wycombe societies, well known Christian artistes and the "Youth for Christ" movement, The Pastures was privileged in 1987 to be the venue for the first performance of the Christian rock musical, "The Trumpet Call". So in this variety of ways we have tried to use music to make The Pastures more "green"!

SUE WAKEHAM

Beaconsfield Free
Methodist Church.

CHAPTER 8

THE UNITED METHODIST CHURCH

NEWLAND (1910)

The United Methodist Church was formed in 1907 from a union of the Methodist New Connexion (1796) and Bible Christians (1815) with the United Methodist Free Church (1857) which was itself an amalgamation of other groups. It is interesting to note that the only local representative of this new multi-hued Church was a little cause in the poorest area of Wycombe which had formerly been in the hands of the Strict Baptists and Free Methodists. So in 1910 Newland unfurled its new "United" flag. There were to be no imitators amongst its more orthodox sister-Methodist Churches. But Newland had the last laugh: unlike them, it secured a Minister (and a chapter of this book) all to itself!

MINISTERS

1910-12	C.W.Crump
1913-14	S.R.Strongman
1915-16	R.Dawson
1917-19	A.Urwin
1920-25	E.Genner
1926-27	V.C.Hope
1928-32	V.C.Smith
1933	E.Dennis [Wesleyan]

MOLLY HOPE writes:

When I first came to Newland United Methodist Church in 1929, I felt homesick for Blyth (Northumberland). But Caleb Bridger who owned a shoe shop in Easton Street was waiting for me, and took me to meet the choir up in the gallery and in particular Maud Peddle and Mary Goodchild. (We always sat together after that and were known as "The three M's"!) After the service Beatrice Barrett invited me - a complete stranger! -

to her home. I was so surprised that they'd "taken" to me! This was typical of this friendly, intimate chapel which was always so beautifully kept. The pipe organ was in the gallery which circled the whole chapel, behind the pulpit. Outside there were cobblestones and a tight-knit community of old terraced houses. This was the "real" old Wycombe but without the squalor of the previous century. Inside there were warm-hearted people like Alf and Minnie Cant, Wilf Perfect (who finished up at Deeds Grove), Norman Gardiner (who went to Holmer Green) and Fred Deane.

Frequent jumble sales stick in my memory, for we were a poor Church despite the generosity of the "furniture" families of Howlands, Cartwrights and Barretts. Then there were the operettas we performed, and the billiards room upstairs which my husband Joe enjoyed. When we were told our little chapel had to close in 1955, we were heartbroken. We could have gone to Wesley but most went to Victoria Street because it was smaller and we used to sing "Messiah" with their choir. What an interesting story Newland could have told before it was demolished to make way for the bus station! It started as a Strict Baptist chapel, became Free Methodist in 1880, United Methodist in 1910, Methodist in 1934 after the "Deed of Union"

and after we had gone in 1955, was used by the Jews as a synagogue! Yes, Newland was unique!

Newland 1936.

THE "BUCKS FREE PRESS" SUMS UP (1955)

By the closing of Newland, the claim has been revived that it was the oldest Nonconformist place of worship in the borough. Although the old chapel in St.Mary Street which now forms part of the furniture manufacturing premises of Nicholls and Janes Ltd., is claimed as the birthplace of Wesleyan Methodism in High Wycombe, John Wesley having preached there after its opening in 1779, there is reference in the "South Bucks. Free Press" issue of 18th June 1880 to Newland having been "occupied by a Nonconformist place of worship in connection with the Baptist denomination for nearly 200 years before this present time". Endorsing this newspaper report is the fact that the Superintendent of the High Wycombe Circuit, Rev.F.B.Hudson, has in his possession old deeds relating to the history of Newland from 1694 to 1863. In 1932 when Methodist Union was achieved, Newland became incorporated in the High Wycombe Methodist Circuit. Included in the town development plan, Newland is earmarked for use as a car park.

†††††† *TODAY'S THOUGHTS FROM WESLEY'S SERMONS* †††††††

* Real happiness comes from loving God
                              and obeying His rules.

* Bread and wine have no special power of themselves.

* If we rely on our own resources we shall fail.

* Faith in Christ is not only assent but complete trust.

* The "other world" is not far away; it is all around us.

* Don't walk with empty shadows; God and eternity are real.

* Most see little, guess a lot, and jump to a conclusion.

* If your friends make you offend God, leave them.

* If you are doing God's will
                              don't be afraid to stand alone.

* If ordinary sinners mislead
                              how much more do bad Ministers!

†††

CHAPTER 9

THE METHODIST CHURCH

THE "DEED OF UNION" (1932)

With the 1907 gathering together of the smaller breakaway groups of the previous century (with the exception of the Wesleyan Reform Union) under the wing of the United Methodist Church, the road to reunification of the three existing Churches (Wesleyan, Primitive and United) was now open. Despite Primitive fears that they might lose their spontaneity of worship, and United forebodings of greater ministerial authority, there was a real desire to bring the Union about, so that there could once again be a united Methodist witness. We must not imagine that any of the three Churches particularly needed the others' strength. Each was a viable unit as these 1921 figures show:

	CHURCHES	MEMBERS	MINISTERS	PREACHERS	CHILDREN
WESLEYAN	8533	498,870	2768	19,043	965,950
PRIMITIVE	4442	206,372	1095	14,383	424,452
UNITED	2286	138,921	709	4,828	262,595

The single Methodist Church was finally brought about in 1932 with a "Deed of Union" which declared: "The Methodist Church ever remembers that in the providence of God Methodism was raised up to spread Scriptural holiness throughout the land by the proclamation of the evangelical faith". The Union was blessed in 1933 by the birth of the much-loved Methodist Hymn Book. Although they might not always agree on the finer points of theology, Methodists of all kinds - including the Free Methodists - were eventually singing the same hymns - with their usual enthusiasm! The faith of the Methodist Church was restated at the 1952 Conference. Regarding the individual the statement says: "A Christian is one who believes that God has revealed Himself in Jesus Christ, accepts Jesus Christ as his Lord and Saviour, lives in communion with God and in the power of the Holy Spirit, and takes his place in the fellowship of Christ's Church."

Regarding the Church and its ministry the statement continues: "Wherever Christ is, there is the Church and His presence is shown by the preaching of His Word, the administration of the Sacraments and the living of the Christian faith. Within the one holy, catholic and apostolic Church the Methodist Church is the communion which was brought into being by the Holy Spirit, chiefly through the work of John Wesley, and continues as a witness to the universal grace of God. All persons are welcomed into membership who sincerely desire to be saved from their sins through faith in the Lord Jesus Christ and seek to have fellowship with Christ and his people by taking up the duties and privileges of the Methodist Church. The ministry of the Church is exercised by all those ordained to the caring of souls, the preaching of the Word and the administration of the Sacraments, by those fulfilling particular functions in the ordered life of the Church, and by all members in their worship and service."

HIGH WYCOMBE METHODIST CIRCUIT: THREE-IN-ONE (1934)

Let us imagine five strangers standing one Sunday morning in 1931 by the famous fountain at Frogmoor in High Wycombe. Each asks directions to the nearest church of his denomination. The Anglican is soon on his way to All Saints' Church, the Roman Catholic to St. Augustine's in Castle Street and the Congregationalist to Trinity (now U.R.C.) in Easton Street. The Baptist has a simple choice between Zion Strict Baptist Church in Bridge Street and Union (General) Baptist Church in Easton Street. It is the Methodist who has the real problem! Within a few hundred yards there are four Methodist Churches - each of a different denomination: Wesley (Priory Road) opened in 1866, replacing John Wesley's church in St. Mary Street, and is the head of the Wesleyan Circuit; White Hart Street opened in 1875, replacing Frogmoor Gardens, and is the head of the Primitive Circuit; Newland (on the site of the present bus station) has been the only United Methodist Church since 1910; and Oxford Road (opposite Hull, Loosley and Pearce's shop) started in 1863 and is the head of the Free Methodist Circuit.

Soon the confusion will be less. In 1932 the "Deed of Methodist Union" will bring the Wesleyans, Primitives and Uniteds (but not the Free Methodists) into the one new Methodist Church. In Wycombe it will take two years for the Union to become effective; in some areas 15 years or more! If our stranger returns in October 1934 and asks the same question, he will still have the four choices. But at least three of them will now bear the single title "Methodist". White Hart Street will remain open until 1951; Newland will close in 1955; Oxford Road will be replaced by The Pastures in 1970. In future years the Wycombe area will have new churches which will never have been anything other than "Methodist": Marlow Bottom (1936), Castlefield (1953), St.Mark's (1959), Deeds Grove (1963) and Tylers Green, Coppice Farm (1968) will seem a great distance from that Frogmoor scene!

ALAN GOODEARL reminisces:

"Are you one of us – or one of them?" That was the question often asked me when, with a Note to Preach (an actual Note signed by the Super in those far-off days), I arrived to help in the conducting of worship for the very first time at the various chapels in the High Wycombe Methodist Circuit. The year was 1936, four years after the 1932 union of the Wesleyan, Primitive, United and a few small denominations had officially taken place. At last – one united Methodist Church, with the exception of the Wesleyan Reform or "Free" Methodists who opted out. One united Church – or so it looked on paper as the official "Model Deed" was brought into operation after many years of discussion. But in practice, at least in this circuit, it was a very different story.

The ex-Wesleyan and ex-Primitive circuits were united, together with the Newland United Methodist Church, and one circuit plan was issued, covering no fewer than 36 churches, stretching from Marlow through Wycombe to Chesham and Amersham; and from Stokenchurch to Bourne End. So far, so good – but it was to be several years before the individual chapels were to lose their "ex-Prim." and "ex-Wesleyan" tags; a number of leading members, particularly in the villages, were solidly against the union. Ministers were invited to the circuit according to their "ex-P." or "ex-W." associations for in no way could a former Wesleyan Minister be accepted by a predominantly ex-Primitive section.

For my own part, having been brought up at Wesley (ex-Wesleyan) and transferring from there to Sands (ex-Primitive) when I was 15 years of age, I found myself generally accepted by all but the most cantankerous (and there were a few) officials! One such society steward at one of our village chapels, to show his repulsion at "Union", gave his church's "quarterage"

(allocation) of £1.10s.0d [£1.50] to the local preacher on the
Sunday before the Quarterly Meeting for him to bring back to
Wycombe and take to the home of the circuit steward. A small
task you may think - but the money was in pennies and the
preacher, a man of small stature at that, had six miles to walk
with his load of pennies!

The circuit Quarterly Meetings were quite lively affairs,
often continuing after tea on the Saturday until well into the
evening, following a 2.30 p.m. start. At one of the first ones
which I attended the Super, frustrated after one ex-Prim. worthy
had stubbornly opposed every resolution on the agenda, could
stand it no longer. "You're a natural born 'objectionalist',
Mr. -------- !" he exploded, to which the worthy responded: "Ah
and I be always a-gooing to be, whatever you or that there
Conference might have decided - I'm having none of it!" At
Downley - quite a small village in those days before the new
estates grew up - the two chapels at Sunny Bank (ex-Wesleyan)
and Chapel Street (ex-Primitive) continued to hold separate
services twice each Sunday until after the 1939-45 war, despite
several attempts to unite them. A new generation of worshippers
was to come along before it was brought about.

For the preacher the "united" circuit had its problems when
choosing hymns. In 1933 the Methodist Hymn Book was introduced
but for over 20 years the old books continued to be used in many
of the chapels. The preacher chose his hymns from the M.H.B.,
the Wesleyan Hymn Book, the Primitive Methodist Hymn Book or the
United Methodist Hymnal according to the chapel he was preaching
at. The desire to retain the hymnal on which a worshipper had
been brought up was perhaps understandable, particularly among
the ex-Prims. who objected strongly to the omission from the
M.H.B. of such hymns as "Day is dying in the West". (Today we
see in the circuit a similar reluctance among some churches to
adopt "Hymns and Psalms" for almost identical reasons.)

The Primitive Methodists had much to offer the Church
following Union, bringing with them their evangelical zeal.
This was typified in their camp meetings held in the open air at
such places as Lee Common (each Whit Monday), Booker and the
Wycombe Desborough Recreation Ground. The preachers neither had
nor needed amplifying equipment, their strident powerful voices
carrying well into the crowds which gathered. They may have
lacked education but they possessed something far greater - a
personal knowledge of the unsearchable riches of God. Today we
see a welcome return to the evangelical zeal of our forefathers,
with the introduction in several churches of "house fellowships"

and "prayer and praise gatherings". The choruses of "Mission Praise" have been introduced regularly into the Sunday services at some chapels to the further enrichment of the worship. Eyebrows may be raised by some of the older worshippers at some of the modern methods used in proclaiming the Gospel but today at least we can claim to be a united Methodist Church, with no-one asking the question of a visiting preacher: "Are you one of us - or one of them?"

HIGH WYCOMBE METHODIST CIRCUIT - CHURCHES

```
                1   1 1      1        1        1        1
                9   9 9      9        9        9        9
                3   4 5      6        7        8        8
                4567890  0123456789012345678901234567890012345678
High Wycombe.
  Wesley        W††††††  ††††††††††††††††††††††††††††††††††††††††)
  White Hart St P††††††  †C
  Newland       U††††††  †††††C
  Victoria St.  W††††††  ††††††††††††††††††††††††††††C
  Westbourne St P††††††  ††††††††††C
  Deeds Grove            ††R††††††††††††††††E††††††††††)
  London Road   W††††††  †††††††††C
  Slater Street P††††††  †††††C
  St.Marks               R†††††††††††††††††††††††††††††)
  Terriers      W††††††  ††††††††††††††††††††C
  Castlefield        ††  †††B†††††††††††††R†††††††††††††††††††††)
Marlow          W††††††  †††††††††††††††††††††††††††E††††††††††)
Sands           P††††††  †††††††††††††††††††††††††††††††††C
West Vycombe    W††††††  †††††††††††††††††††††††††††††††††C
Radnage         P††††††  †††††††E†††††††††††††††††††††††††††††††)
Vooburn Green   W††††††  ††††††††††††††††††††††††††††††††††††††)
Lane End        W††††††  †††††††††††††††††††††††††††††E††††††††)
Wheeler End     P††††††  †††††††††††††††††††††††††††††††††††††††C
Chalf. St.Giles   G†††   †G
Vinchmore Hill    G†††   †G
Vinchmore Hill  WC
Amersham Common   G†††   †G
Downley (C.S.)  P††††††  ††††††††††††††††††C
Downley (S.Bk.) W††††††  †††††††††††††††††††††††††††††††††††††††)
Naphill         P††††††  †††††††††††††††††††††††††††††††††††††††)
Lacey Green     P††††††  †††††E††††††††††††††††††††††††††††††††††)
Bryants Bottom  P††††††  †††††††††††††††††††††††††††E††††††††††††)
```

```
                       1    1 1         1         1         1         1
                       9    9 9         9         9         9         9
                       3    4 5         6         7         8         8
                       4567890 0123456789012345678901234567890123456789012345678

Penn/Tylers Gn.  Ptttttt   ttttttttttttttttttRttttttttttttttttttttt>
Amersham (H.St.)Wtttttt   tG
Chesham          Wtttttt   tG
Lee Common       Ptttttt   tG
Great Missenden  PtttC
Flackwell Heath  Wtttttt   ttttttttttttttttttttttttttttttttttttttEttt>
Bourne End       Wtttttt   tttttttttttttttttttttttttttttttttttttttttt>
Bledlow Ridge    Wtttttt   ttttttttttttttEttttttttttttttttttttttttttt>
Holmer Green     WttRttt   tttttttttttttttttEttttttttttttttttttttttt>
Gt.Kingshill/
  Cryers Hill    Ptttttt   ttttttttttttttttttttttttttttEtttttttttEt>
Booker           Wtttttt   tttttttttttttttttttttttttttttttttttttttttt>
Piddington       Wtttttt   ttttttttttttttttttttttttttttttttttttttttC
Prestwood        Vtttttt   tG
Stokenchurch     Ntttttt   tttttttttttttttttttttttttttttttEttttttttttt>
Beacons Bottom   Ntttttt   tttttttttttttttttttttttC
Ibstone          Ntttttt   ttttttttttC
Marlow Bottom    Btttt     ttttttttttttttttttttttttttttttEtttttttttttt>
```

B = Chapel Built
C = Services Ceased
E = Chapel Extended or Additional Buildings e.g. Schoolroom
R = Rebuilt or New Building to replace
G = Transferred from/to Chalfont St.Giles Circuit
N = Transferred from Chinnor Primitive Circuit
P = Transferred from Primitive Circuit
U = Transferred from United Methodist Church
V = Transferred from Wesleyan Circuit
t = Services (from December Plan)

HIGH WYCOMBE METHODIST CIRCUIT — MEMBERSHIP

	1935	1940	1950	1960	1970	1975	1980	1985	1987
Beacons Bottom	13	14	19	13	11	(closed)			
Bledlow Ridge	9	15	13	12	16	12	10	8	7
Booker	29	27	23	19	15	10	9	15	22
Bourne End	20	25	18	32	28	16	9	13	17
Bryants Bottom	10	15	17	20	17	20	22	19	16
Castlefield			20	30	76	69	82	96	102
Cryers Hill	50	51	54	69	76	73	64	47	44
Deeds Grove					99	70	72	66	46
Downley(Chapel St.)	27	27	27	24	(closed)				
Downley(Sunny Bank)	34	33	48	46	58	44	45	35	28
Flackwell Heath	28	29	30	45	57	65	62	66	49
Great Missenden	9(closed)								
Holmer Green	35	48	45	65	113	128	109	97	90
Ibstone	9	6	5	2(closed)					
Lacey Green	33	32	26	37	33	31	28	21	19
Lane End	75	65	70	63	52	36	26	25	21
London Road	20	21	38(closed)						
Marlow	59	52	58	64	68	96	107	127	131
Marlow Bottom		4	6	4	18	23	30	29	57
Naphill	42	38	43	40	50	47	38	33	28
Newland	76	81	53(closed)						
Piddington	12	12	24	26	23	19	16	12	(cl)
Radnage	12	12	22	16	13	15	15	12	16
St.Mark's				71	116	126	89	73	73
Sands	43	60	83	84	68	60	46(closed)		
Slater Street	38	26	27(closed)						
Stokenchurch	55	64	47	45	41	39	33	33	36
Terriers	9	8	5	5	7(closed)				
Tylers Green:									
Church Road	12	25	10	23(closed)					
Coppice Farm					62	79	79	58	41
Victoria Street	141	132	142	186	104	70(closed)			
Wesley	189	206	130	202	230	232	212	182	159
West Wycombe	22	22	27	24	19	15	6(closed)		
Westbourne Street	165	171	166	159(closed)					
Wheeler End	13	16	19	12	10	11	8	8	7
White Hart Street	152	123	89(closed)						
Wooburn Green	17	25	22	14	26	34	35	28	23
Carried forward	1458	1485	1426	1452	1506	1440	1252	1103	1032

<u>1935</u> <u>1940</u> <u>1950</u> <u>1960</u> <u>1970</u> <u>1975</u> <u>1980</u> <u>1985</u> <u>1987</u>

Brought forward 1458 1485 1426 1452 1506 1440 1252 1103 1032

<u>Trans. to Chesham/Chalfont Circuit (1951)</u>

Amersham (High St.)	24	21	28						
Amersham Common		49	63						
Chalfont St.Giles		63	74						
Chesham	72	109	97						
Lee Common	28	23	21						
Prestwood	37	50	39						
Winchmore Hill		26	21						

TOTALS   1619 1826 1769 1452 1506 1440 1252 1103 1032

THE TEN WISE SUPERS

Or 12 to be precise, if we include at the beginning Rev. W.S. Hinchcliffe who was Superintendent Minister of the White Hart Street Circuit until the Union of the Primitive Methodists with the Wesleyans became effective in September 1934, and at the end Rev. Tony Barnard who became "Super" - to use the common, affectionate abbreviation - in September 1987. In those 53 years ten men have ruled the High Wycombe Methodist Circuit. Each has contributed his own particular talents and each has left his own mark. In the following pages we look at the "reigns" of the Ten Wise Supers with the help of the Circuit Plans.

REV. ERNEST DENNIS (1934-37) had already been Super of the Wesleyan Circuit from 1932-34. Of medium build he is said to have "looked the part"! Helped by a charming wife, he moulded the three former circuits (Wesleyan, Primitive and United) into one.

REV. ERNEST G. LOOSLEY (1937-40) was a well-built man who was thoughtful, yet decisive. A man who had fought for peace, he had to cope with the early wartime effects on the circuit.

REV. ARTHUR WALTERS (1940-45) was a tall, slim man whose wife was an authoress. Near retirement age when he arrived, he could often be seen in the war years riding his bicycle around Wycombe. He was the friend of all, especially the children.

REV. BENJAMIN TATTERSALL (1945-49) a man of average build, is remembered for his good sermons and helpful, practical nature. He and his wife were particularly caring towards the elderly.

REV. FRANCIS B. HUDSON (1949-55) was a short, stocky Super who could easily have been a businessman. He had a good sense of humour but was not afraid to speak his mind. His wife took an active role in the circuit.

REV. G. ERIC FIRTH (1955-62) was the only one of the ten to return to Wycombe after his retirement. His wife, who was a gracious asset to him, still lives here. Short and wiry, he was quick-thinking and is remembered best for his common-sense approach to problems.

REV. WILLIAM G.B. REAM (1962-67) was a kindly man in whom it was easy to confide. His was a personal ministry. He loved his people.

REV. R.L.JACK KAYE (1967-74) had a natural presence and - like his wife - was a born leader. He went on later to become Chairman of the District. A regular attender at Council of Churches and Sunday School Union meetings, he encouraged links with other churches.

REV. HAROLD SLATER (1974-82) was probably the smallest of all the Supers but he had a powerful voice. His sermons were an orator's set pieces. Humorous and friendly, he was popular outside the circuit, particularly through his R.A.F. connections. His wife was gifted in craftwork.

REV. A. GEOFFREY JONES (1982-87) was a tall man whose wife was active in Overseas Missions' work. Serene, gentle and a good listener, he guided Wesley's many attempts to obtain planning permission for rebuilding to ultimate success, and also tackled the problems of future strategy in the circuit.

Now we look to each Super's "reign" in more detail.

REV. ERNEST DENNIS (1934-37)

As we have already noted, until October 1934 there were three Methodist circuits in High Wycombe: Wesleyan whose mother

Church was Wesley, Priory Road, under Rev.E.Dennis; Primitive with its mother Church White Hart Street under Rev.W.S. Hinchcliffe; and United whose only Church was Newland, also under Mr.Dennis. Since the "Deed of Union" in 1932 each circuit has made its own Plan but these were printed (by Freer and Hayter) in the one booklet. Now there is one High Wycombe Methodist Circuit which includes not only the three local circuits but also three Churches transferred from the Chinnor Primitive Methodist Circuit: Stokenchurch, Beacons Bottom and Ibstone. The Plan costs 3d.[1p.] per copy, and Mr.Dennis from his Priory Road manse (telephone: H.W. 747) is in charge. Mr.Hinchcliffe at Roberts Road (H.W. 85) now heads the White Hart Street section. No other Minister has a telephone. . One can imagine the unruffled peace at West Wycombe Road (Rev.R.O. Stobbs - Victoria Street), Plumer Road (Rev.F.C.Searle - Westbourne Street), Bellingdon Road, Chesham (Rev.E.W.Eavis - Chesham) and Park Lane, Lane End (Rev.J.H.Cartwright - Stokenchurch)!

The "Super's letter" does not yet feature but there is an appeal for "Hurricane Week"- two months hence! A stern injunction in heavy type warns: "The raising of funds by raffles or similar methods is not permitted under any circumstances"! The Ministers jointly appeal to be told about cases of sickness or other trouble (by telegram?). Mr.W.V.Hearn (Lane End) and Mr.H.T.Turnbull are circuit stewards. Each section too has its own steward, including Mr.O.T.Goodearl in the Victoria Street section. There are 83 preachers of whom 81 are male. But Miss Margaret Darvill is already "on trial" and all set for a "double" (very common in those days) on Young People's Day at Radnage. The Mission Band has 11 members; Westbourne Street has its own. There are 35 churches - plus Piddington (which administratively belongs to West Wycombe) and 1808 members with another 53 "on trial". The Balance Sheet (September 1934) is still in two sections. Both show a "balance due to stewards" - of £78.15s.7d. [£78.78] for White Hart Street and £23.7s.3d. [£23.36] for Wesley, but fortunately "insurance on Ministers" costs only 10/- [50p]! The "new Methodist Hymn Book" is in use at Holmer Green, Victoria Street, Chesham, Flackwell Heath and Marlow; Piddington uses the New People's Hymnary. There is no indication what the rest use. Typical of entries in the directory (before the days of post-codes) is :"J.Barrow, Stokenchurch". Mr.C.W.Rogers and Mr.C.W.Rogers Jnr. at Bledlow Ridge stand out from the rest by having a telephone (Radnage 19).

In 1935 preachers Mr. G. H. Taylor and Mr. H. James have died
and Bryants Bottom has bought each of its 10 members a copy of
the Methodist Hymn Book. Mr. J. Copeland is one of the leaders at
Kingshill (Cryers Hill). The Ministers as a body (still no sign
of the Super) ask support for the visit of the President of the
Conference, Rev. William Younger, a former Primitive Minister, to
Wesley and friends are urged to bring a gift to the Tea Fund.
Rev. N. Renshaw takes up residence at Beaumont Rise, Marlow,
Rev. Ernest Jones replaces Rev. W. S. Hinchcliffe and "exhorters"
have become "helpers". Rev. H. Binks arrives at West Wycombe Road
in 1936, preacher Mr. W. Saunders dies, Mr. D. S. Howard joins the
list and a discreet article in the January Plan over the
initials "E. D." urges praise to the circuit stewards and a quiet
trust in God (in that order). Emboldened by this effort - and
perhaps a rise in stipend to £3 a week! - the Super writes a
much longer note in April in which he mentions the opening of
the new hall at Marlow Bottom - "with most encouraging
congregations". The Local Preachers' Study Circle is suddenly
cancelled however and the last Plan of the year is full of
"Xmas" (sic) services.

In 1937 the fortunate Rev. N. Renshaw moves to Cambridge
House, Marlow but Rev. F. C. Searle is still laid low by a serious
illness. Isaac Brearley, Mr. J. Plested and Mr. E. J. Gray die but
Mr. E. R. Bates and Mr. A. Goodearl come "on trial". Members are
assured "there is no desire to make the Sunday evening prayer
meeting compulsory" and finally the modest Super signs - for the
first time - his last letter with his full name. "The many
problems consequent on amalgamation have been dealt with in the
spirit of good will," he writes, "and it is gratifying to mark
the steady growth of the sense of unity which exists." Special
thanks go to Wesley Church for "setting me free from claims
which might have been made". There is space for only one more
line - just enough for him to say: "P.S. A kind contribution
by Rev. Ernest Jones has been crowded out!"

REV. ERNEST G. LOOSLEY (1937-40)

Rev. Ernest G. Loosley arrives in 1937 at the same time as
the Chalfont St. Giles Circuit whose three members - Amersham
Common and Winchmore Hill complete the trio - have joined the
Wycombe Circuit along with Rev. J. W. V. Owen. Marlow now heads a
new section. There are 40 churches all of whom have two
services each Sunday - except Terriers (eight members) and
Ibstone (seven) who have one service each ; Lee Common (26) has
three! The pulpit at Wesley (200 members) is occupied for the

whole quarter entirely by Ministers. The mind shudders at the thought of the pulpit at tiny Marlow Bottom (with no recorded membership) holding on one occasion three lay brethren (Messrs.C.G.Craft, E.R.Bates and F.Rolls)! Section leaders White Hart Street (148 members), Victoria Street (129) and Westbourne Street (162) are all in good form. So is Newland (77) where Mr.A.Cant is society steward. Every church has a regular weeknight devotional meeting except Ibstone - and Wesley! 10/- [50p.] per member is requested to be sent to Mr.A.E.Steevens on Temperance Sunday. And a solitary exhorter appears - Mr.H.Chapman. The situation is looking good.....

In 1938 Mr.H.Wingrove (Holmer Green) becomes a circuit steward and the Super urges the circuit to evangelise - perhaps starting with visiting preacher Mr.A.Crimes who has only an accommodation address? Evangelism however doesn't save Great Missenden (seven members) from closure. Rev.Walter Yeomans (White Hart Street) and Rev.William Irving (Marlow) arrive at the same time as Rev.G.R.Maland (Westbourne Street) who occupies the new manse in West Wycombe Road, close to his colleague Binks. The Super, facing the unchanging problem of writing his letter several weeks before it appears in the Plan, assumes correctly that the threat of war will have been removed and urges "Christian peace-building by personal contact". The Methodist Hymn Book is now in use in all churches except White Hart Street, Cryers Hill, Downley - Chapel Street ("evenings only"), Wheeler End, Ibstone, Chalfont St. Giles and Amersham Common (Primitive Methodist Hymnal); Terriers and Marlow Bottom ("old Methodist Hymn Book"). Preachers Mr.G. Darvill and Mr.E.Veller have died.

1939 starts with a problem. The evangelical campaign has been so successful that, says the Super, "no fewer than five local preachers have written to ask for no appointments on account of their Sunday School work"! He asks, "What's to do?" (Cancel future evangelical campaigns perhaps?) Matters are not helped by the deaths of three preachers - Mr.G.Castle, Mr.G.Shaw and Mr.A. Savage. But at least the Ministers now have the services of a manse steward, Owen Evans. Worse is to come. In April 1939 the Super writes: "The work of the next three months has been planned at a time when the international situation fills the mind with misgiving". In October with the cry, "We face the work of the winter under conditions of war", he records the change of many evening services to the afternoon but urges people to utilise the "parish lantern" and to that end helpfully appends the phases of the moon! However, trying to look on the bright side, he adds, "There may be Methodists among the London evacuees!" In his distress he has forgotten to welcome Rev.F.Pilkington to Marlow.

In January 1940 the Super reminds society stewards that all windows must be blacked out after dark. Some favoured brethren are to be allowed to preach at Amersham Institution. Sister Sadie Martin, driven out from her work with the Leysian Mission, descends on Castlefield where she starts services in the day-school. Rev.J.W.W.Owen and preacher Mr.G.Seymour die. July 1940 sees a thinner Plan with the directory omitted and Rev. E.G.Loosley writes: "The calling-up of younger men has made it impossible to fill all appointments. Also it may on occasions be impossible for the appointed preacher to reach you. Please arrange for someone to be prepared to take the service in such circumstances, leading the congregation in worship, prayer and Bible reading, even if no sermon is possible". But all is not lost. Lee Common continues to enjoy three services every Sunday and raffles are still definitely prohibited! The wartime man of peace ends his last letter with a plea that everyone should endeavour to keep in contact with those who have been called up and to "commend them constantly to the loving care of the Father".

REV.ARTHUR WALTERS (1940-45)

The Battle of Britain is raging over the skies of London as Rev. Arthur Walters settles into his new parish. He has almost a new staff: Rev. Robert Pearson (Victoria Street), Rev.A.W.Heathcote (Marlow - and a new manse in Oak Tree Avenue), Rev.George Glandfield (Chalfont St. Giles) and Sister Elsie Kitchener (Castlefield). Fortunately old hands Yeomans (White Hart Street section - seven churches), Maland (Westbourne Street - eight) and Pilkington (Chesham - seven) are still here, no doubt cheering on colleague Pearson who has nine churches! The Super remains until the end of the war (1945) and is at least spared many staff changes: Rev.F.Pilkington becomes an Army Chaplain in 1941 and is replaced at Chesham by Rev.F.Bertram Clogg; Rev.Walter N.Parnaby arrives at White Hart Street and Rev.Arthur Baxter at Westbourne Street in 1944. Owen Evans gives up his post as manse steward and is not replaced. Messrs.E.T.Barrington and W.O.Haines become circuit stewards in 1942 and 1944 respectively. In 1943 Mr.H.Lord enters the "on trial" list, a year after a "Mr.K.Peaty"(sic) - a spelling mistake which remains for the rest of the war. (No doubt Mr.Peatey has more important things on his mind at this time but would be very flattered by the title "Mr." which is normally kept for visiting preachers and stewards!   The promotion is cancelled next quarter!)   Preachers George Pratt, Mr.T.Smith, Mr.W.Youens J.P., Mr.J.Shirley, Mr.H.Bignell and Mr.W.Bunce die during this period.   Veterans Mr.T.W.Apps (accredited 1890) and Mr.H.Woodward (1894) and many others are regularly taking 15 appointments or more each quarter.

The war rages on and the Super's letters detail the entry of Japan ("I remember long ago hearing somebody say, 'God help us when Japan breaks loose on the world'"), D-Day ("While they fight, it is ours to do the 'daily round and the common task'") and VE-Day ("As I write, the country prepares for the General Election and each party puts forward its plans.   What miracles they are going to work and how happy everyone is going to be!").

The circuit Plan after becoming thick again with the reappearance of the directory in April 1941, suddenly loses weight a year later - but it's only the substandard paper!   In April 1943 it comes blushing in a startling pink.

But the Super soldiers on, never complaining, always thanking the remaining preachers and apologising for the more and more frequent appearance of the word "Supply", for ever concerned with the prosperity of the churches and in particular the progress of the building fund at Castlefield.   He inherits 40 churches and in five war-years not one is lost.   1914 members have decreased to 1883 but a deficit of £40 has turned into a balance of £66.

Picture a cold wartime Sunday - 18th January 1942.   Imagine the faithful stumbling in late afternoon or evening into unlit lamp-posts in almost total darkness.   Torches are allowed to emit only a faint beam and there are no welcoming outside lights when they arrive at church.   We list below the churches (the head church of each section in CAPITALS) and the names of preachers (Ministers' names in CAPITALS) and stewards.   The times of services, the number of members and the quarterly allocation are also included.

THE METHODIST CHURCH

CHURCH/MEMBERS	TIME	PREACHER	-----STEWARDS------		ASSESSM'T £ s. d.		
WESLEY	10.45	WALTERS	Evans	Fox	93	0	0
(190)	6.00	PEARSON	Lord	Rushbrooke			
Slater Street	10.30	Shirley	Taylor	Miss Hester	8	0	0
(24)	6.00	Apps	Dimmock				
London Road	11.00	Apps	Fry	Curtis	5	5	0
(21)	3.15	Andrews	Pearce	Hughes			
Terriers (8)	3.00	Woodward	Mrs.Lee	Miss Goodall	2	7	6
Castlefield (16)	6.00	Jarvis	Sis.Elsie	Mrs.Dean	1	11	6
WHITE HART ST.	10.45	Rixon	Symes	Worley	41	0	0
(122)	6.00	YEOMANS	Jones	Perfect			
Newland	10.45	Thomas	Cant	Saunders	13	5	0
(71)	3.00	YEOMANS	Lewington	Rolls			
Sands	10.45	Collins	Stallwood	West	19	10	0
(60)	6.00	Pearce	Bailey	Grace			
Holmer Green	10.45	Jupe	Wingrove	Stevens	12	10	0
(48)	6.00	Slade	Parker	Dean			
Cryers Hill	2.30	Parkins	Dean		12	10	0
(52)	6.00	Parkins	Copeland				
Wooburn Green	11.00	Osborne	A.Smith	Slade	7	0	0
(21)	3.00	A.Sargeant	F.Smith	Mrs.Slade			
Penn	2.30	Steevens	Witcher	Mrs.Witcher	4	15	0
(10)	6.00	Steevens	Mrs.West				
VICTORIA STREET	10.45	Clark	Biggs	Haines	40	10	0
(127)	6.00	Lacey	Evans	Lord			
West Wycombe	10.45	PEARSON	North	Sampson	8	0	0
(19)	3.00	Silversides	Robertson	Mrs.North			
Piddington	2.30	Guichard	Lee		2	15	0
(12)	6.00	Guichard					
Naphill	11.00	Greenstreet	Evans	Shaw	15	0	0
(46)	6.00	MALAND	Bristow				
Lacey Green	2.30	Clark	Claydon		8	15	0
(30)	6.00	Clark	Hickman				
Downley-S. Bk.	10.45	Ms Kearley	Stratford	Youens	12	12	6
(35)	3.00	J.Sargeant	Batts	Ford			
Downley-C. S.	10.45	Turnbull	Hawkins	Langley	5	15	0
(30)	6.00	Evans	Mrs.Hawkins				
Bryants Bottom	2.30	WALTERS	Smith		6	15	0
(15)	5.30	WALTERS	Stacey				
Beacons Bottom	2.30	Symes	Stratford		6	0	0
(12)	6.00	Symes	Butler				

CHURCH/MEMBERS	TIME	PREACHER	-----STEWARDS------		ASSESSM'T £ s. d.		
WESTBOURNE ST	10.45	MALAND	Plested	West	46	0	0
(186)	6.00	Coker	Chapman	Barnett			
Lane End	10.45	HEATHCOTE	Thorne	Witney	21	0	0
(64)	3.00	HEATHCOTE	House	Hearn			
Stokenchurch	11.00	CARTWRIGHT	White	Atkins	19	10	0
(60)	3.00	CARTWRIGHT	Drinkwater	Bates			
Booker	11.00	(Supply)	Pearce	Burnham	7	10	0
(27)	2.45	Chilton	Seymour	Murcott			
Wheeler End	2.30	Hearn	Mrs.Webb	Webb	4	15	0
(17)	5.30	HEATHCOTE	Ing				
Radnage	2.30	Dormer	Dormer	Steevens	6	0	0
(15)	5.30	Deane	Mrs.Stratford				
Bledlow Ridge	2.30	Bishop	Rogers	Bowler	3	7	6
(15)	6.00	Bishop	Miss Smith	Rogers Jnr.			
Ibstone (4)	6.00	Thomas	Judge	Geary	1	18	0
CHESHAM	11.00	Burch	Russell	Moore	30	10	0
(107)	6.00	CLOGG	Brooks	Scott			
Amersham Common	11.00	CLOGG	Hall	Plummer	10	0	0
(48)	6.00	Moulster	Beckett	Johnson			
Prestwood	10.45	Ault	Evans	Harding	12	0	0
(52)	3.00	Ault	Chandler	Smith			
Lee Common	10.45	Randall	Barrett	Randall	9	0	0
(22)	2.30	CLOGG	Bignell	Mrs.Holland			
	6.00	Baker	Miss Randall				
Amersham	11.00	Moulster	Hill	Nancarrow	7	0	0
(21)	6.00	Burch	Pratt	Mrs.Stratfull			
Winchmore Hill	2.30	Garlick	Hatch	Mrs.Slade	7	0	0
(26)	6.00	Garlick	Mrs.Hatch				
Chalfont	11.00	GLANDFIELD	Rance	Parr	26	0	0
(62)	3.00	Moulster	Wellings	Lofty			
MARLOW	11.00	Sis.ELSIE	Harvey	Denton	34	10	0
(55)	6.00	Goodchild	Nichols	Miss Wellicome			
Flackwell Heath	11.00	Hawkins	Smith	Howard	11	10	0
(28)	2.45	Hawkins	Saunders	Milne			
Bourne End	11.00	Dron	Goodearl	Gray	5	5	0
(26)	3.00	Fulford	Shirley	Mrs.Shirley			
Marlow Bottom	4.00	Osborne	Osborne		1	0	0
(4)							

We can imagine the smile of relief as Rev. Arthur Walters ends his last letter before he heads off for a well-earned retirement: "You might find time to offer up a prayer for the old Super, that he may never grow old but that if he does, he might not be a bore, a bear or a burden to anyone!" It's a paradox that these years of international turmoil seem to have been the most settled for the Wycombe Circuit!

REV. BENJAMIN TATTERSALL (1945-49)

With the new Super, Rev. Benjamin Tattersall, come Rev. W. A. Cooper (Chalfont St. Giles), Sister Jessie Brine (Castlefield) and Rev. Norman Thomas (Marlow) who quickly sets up a Youth Group. The Marlow manse moves again - to Beaumont Rise.

Rev. F. Bertram Clogg is recalled to Richmond College in the summer of 1946 and is replaced at Chesham by Rev. Eric G. Chapman. The Marlow manse moves to Newtown Road. Later in the year Rev. Cecil F. Guy comes to Victoria Street and Rev. Leslie D. Cox to Marlow; the manse is now in Claremont Gardens. Mr. H. Wingrove (Holmer Green) returns as circuit steward. Preacher Mr. W. W. Coker dies, as does Rev. Ernest Dennis of Aylesbury, the former Super.

More deaths follow in 1947: senior preacher Mr. A. Edwards (accredited 1882), Mr. A. Higgs, Mr. A. Willott and Mr. G. Rolls. The Super urges churches to start Sunday Schools and a weekly fellowship meeting and suggests an annual circuit crusade. The Devil's response to this threat is the hardest winter in living memory and the quarterly meeting can find only enough energy to rejoice, "And are we yet alive?" That autumn Westbourne Street welcomes Rev. Alan L. Whittard and Marlow Rev. Arthur Speed who is well named - because the manse has now moved to Sunny Bank!

The following year two new appointments are made. Mrs. G. B. Lee becomes local secretary for Methodist Homes for the Aged and Alan Goodearl rejoices in his new label: "Migration Secretary"! (He is to keep in touch with young people who leave home.) Rev. J. Henry Cartwright (Lane End) receives a cheque to mark his 60th year in the ministry, Mrs. Jupe (Widmer End) celebrates her 100th birthday - and Mr. Speed is simply thankful that he has managed to keep the manse rooted to the same spot for a whole year!

So the quiet Super ends his term with a lament that membership has fallen to 1851. Preachers Mr. H. O. Bishop, Mr. T. Barnett and Mr. G. W. Darvill have died; the name of veteran preacher Mr. T. W. Apps has simply disappeared. ("He walked with God and was not" - perhaps?) But there are still 72 preachers and another six are "on trial". There are no fewer than 21 helpers who now include Mrs. Greenstreet (Tylers Green), the well-known temperance campaigner. Mr. A. V. West (Golf Links Road, Flackwell Heath and formerly of Westbourne Street) has become circuit steward and the accounts are surely well audited by Mr. D. Christian!

The 40 churches which Rev. E. G. Loosley handed over to Rev. Arthur Walters in 1940, are safely passed on nine years later by Rev. Benjamin Tattersall to his successor. Each church has two services every Sunday - except Terriers, Castlefield, Ibstone and Marlow Bottom who have one. Who would guess in 1949 that within 40 years the number would be halved?

REV. FRANCIS B. HUDSON (1949-55)

Christmas Day 1949 falls on a Sunday. There are the usual two services in the churches. Only Tylers Green and Marlow Bottom have no appointed preacher. The new Super, Rev. Francis B. Hudson, is at Wesley this morning; Rev. Owen M. Collins is at Newland in a united service with White Hart Street; Rev. Deryck N. Howarth is away, recovering perhaps from the effort of keeping pace with the Marlow manse which has now come to rest in Claremont Road; Colin U. Church, one of 33 preachers "from other churches", occupies his usual Christmas morning place in the pulpit at Slater Street. Four Watch Night services the following Saturday will, everyone hopes, herald a time of peace for the world in general and High Wycombe Methodist Circuit in particular. By the time Mr. Hudson leaves in 1955, the circuit will have shrunk from 40 churches to 30 and the membership from 1839 to 1391 - the largest drop in its history. The main reason is the departure of seven churches - Chesham, Amersham, Amersham Common, Prestwood, Lee Common, Winchmore Hill and Chalfont St. Giles - to form the new Chesham and Chalfont (later Amersham) Circuit. But in addition closing services are held in White Hart Street in 1951 and Newland and Slater Street in 1955. Downley (Chapel Street) has no preachers planned for five quarters in 1950-51 and is urged to share "united services" with its neighbour, Sunny Bank. The "blockade" is lifted on 5th April 1951 when normal supplies of preachers start to get through again! On the brighter side the new church hall at Castlefield is opened on 5th September 1953.

THE METHODIST CHURCH

There are many ministerial changes in this period. Rev. George B. Middleton (Victoria Street), Rev. Thomas J. Welch (Chesham), Rev. W. J. Penberthy White (Chalfont St. Giles), Rev. Ernest G. Kitchin (Westbourne Street) and Sister Eva Blyth (Castlefield) all join the staff in 1950. Rev. Redvers G. Cornfield comes to the new Stokenchurch section – and a third manse in West Wycombe Road – in 1951 and is succeeded in 1953 by Rev. P. Guy Stanford who takes up residence in Marlow Road, Stokenchurch. In 1954 Rev. Philip H. Foster comes to the Westbourne Street section and Rev. Kenneth V. Curtis to the Victoria Street section. In 1951 Mr. Middleton, tired of trying to cross the busy West Wycombe Road in order to use colleague Kitchin's phone, finally gets one himself and is no longer able to avoid hearing the pressing problems of his members rich enough to have a phone of their own. The restless Marlow section watches its Minister chase his manse first to Glade Road, then to Institute Road – where it finally gives in and remains until 1966! Mr. C. A. Cole (Amersham), Mr. G. Thorne (Lane End) and Mr. A. E. Steevens become circuit stewards and Mr. W. J. Parkins local preachers' secretary during these years. With the departure of the Chesham Circuit the Plan "proper" (preachers' appointments) goes broadsheet – as in olden times – but is inserted into the familiar booklet form. It is still printed by Freer and Hayter (who have reached "series 61", that is the number of changes since they first printed the Plan in 1932) but nowadays it costs 6d. [2½p.] The kindly Super gives his preachers a well-earned promotion: the men are all awarded the title "Mr."!

It is a trying period but the Super beavers away, chipping off an unwanted bit here, repairing a crumbling part there; but always looking for the opportunity to redevelop elsewhere. "How peaceful it must have been in wartime!" one can imagine him sighing, as he pens :

"What will YOUR church be like in ten years' time?" (January 1950)
"Heavy expenditure lies ahead." (April 1950)
"There is need to understand God's Word better." (October 1950)
Serious losses have occurred in our ranks by death." (April 1951)
"The Wycombe of the future will be vastly different." (Jan. 1955)
"A notable loss is that of Albert Pearce of London Road who would have celebrated his jubilee as a preacher next year." (April 1955)

In his last letter (July 1955) the busy Super looks forward
to a less hectic life in Dunstable ("it has been a strenuous
time in Wycombe in every way!"). He urges his readers to look
ahead too : "The closing of Slater Street and Newland have
caused regret to many hearts, yet the new churches in the new
areas will be ample compensation. We have secured a fine site
in Totteridge Road on which a splendid suite of church property
will be erected. At the other end of Wycombe we are looking for
a suitable site. Also at Hicks Farm we have the option of a
site. Whatever lies in the past, your interest must now be with
the future - looking ahead!"

REV.G.ERIC FIRTH (1955-62)

The next Super, Rev.G.
Eric Firth, briskly greets his
new flock.   On behalf of
himself and his colleagues,
Rev.Arthur H.Freeman (Marlow)
and Rev.Anthony B. Wells
(Stokenchurch), he says: "It
is a joy to come in your
midst, that we may work
together at the many tasks
before us". It is autumn 1955
and he is glad to see how well
the Newland people have
settled in at Victoria Street
and the Slater Street folk at
London Road. Lacey Green has
been open 100 years and new
projects - like the schoolroom
at Cryers Hill and the organ
at Holmer Green - are going
ahead well. This kindly man
of action allows others - such
as   Rev.Leslie   J.M.Timmins,
leader of the Circuit Campaign Council - to write the "Super's
letter" whenever possible.   Another writer is Rev.Philip
H.Foster who in 1956 takes over the new Castlefield section and
moves to a manse in Spearing Road. Victoria Street and
Westbourne Street, formerly both heads of sections, are now in
the same section. Mr.Wells takes over the vacant West Wycombe
Road manse and also the London Road section - to both of which
Mr.Freeman moves in 1957. Sister Freda Young takes charge at
Stokenchurch in 1956 and Rev.W.Rowland Jones at Marlow in 1957.

THE METHODIST CHURCH

These "musical chairs" conclude with Mr.Foster moving to a manse
in Rutland Avenue in 1958 and Mr.Freeman to Lucas Road in 1960.

In 1956 Mr.H.T.Turnbull returns as circuit steward; Walter
Goodearl dies after 50 years' preaching; Mr.W.A.Steevens has
completed 60 years. Councillor H.Fry (London Road) becomes
Mayor the following year and the Wycombe Circuit is now part of
London North-West District under the chairmanship of
Rev.L.O.Brooker. Mr.W.J.Perfect is appointed circuit steward
and is joined two years later by Mr.L.W.Capell. But we must
return to the Super's letters before they are taken from us. In
1957 after upbraiding the moaners ("I have been disappointed to
hear people complain that they are not consulted about decisions
taken: if you do not attend meetings, it is not fair to
criticise") and reminding treasurers to send their contributions
to the Local Preachers' Travelling Fund (on a sliding scale from
£2.2s 0d. [£2.10p.] for a church of 100 or more members, down to
10/6d [52½p.] for one of under 50 members), his voice is
silenced and we must wait four years for his next letter.

The reason is a new style Plan which makes its slim
appearance in 1958 and consists only of a broadsheet of
appointments together with Ministers' and preachers' names and
addresses. It costs 4d [1½p.] The following year it reverts
completely to the style of earlier times. The Ministers are
numbered from 1 to 7; circuit preachers from 8 to 58; and those
from other churches from 101 to 169. Only the numbers are
printed in the actual Plan. Now each church can learn at a
glance its position in the circuit. Oh the joy at seeing a row
of low numbers, the dismay at high numbers. Wesley's aggregate
for Sunday morning services in the first quarter is a mere 344,
giving an average "score" of 26 - the equivalent of having
preacher Mr.F.Collier M.A. who was accredited in 1940, in the
pulpit each Sunday. It would have been 183 (average 14 - Albert
Hester - 1930), had not unfortunate brother 161 intruded one
Sunday in September. Downley (Sunny Bank) on the other hand
amasses a total of 1014, a heavy weight of preachers indeed with
an average of 78 - which is "no man's land" between the helpers
and such as the Baptists! Mistakes must have occurred (the
eagerly awaited 33 turns out via a printing smudge to be the
dreaded 38?) and the Super persuades the circuit to abandon the
scheme two years later. For July 1961 there is no Plan at all,
then Martell Ltd. produces the familiar glossy booklet,
containing everything anyone could possibly want to know about
the circuit, although still with an inset broadsheet Plan
(which in 1962 becomes two normal double pages). The Plan costs
6d.[2½p.] and contains advertisements for the first time.

Butler's are offering the Cameron bedroom suite for £53, while
A.W.Hawkins reproaches us: "There are Methodists who have not
yet paid us a visit!"

During this period the last service at Ibstone (2 members)
is conducted on 5th October 1958 by Mr.M.Brittin and at London
Road (67 members) on 4th October 1959 by Mr.A.Goodearl. But the
latter Church reopens the following week - with three further
members - as St.Mark's in Totteridge Road (preacher -
Mr.H.A.Goodearl). In 1960 Rev.A.E.Glendower Jones comes to
Westbourne Street, Rev.Alan Cox to Castlefield, Rev.Leonard
G.Jones to Marlow and Sister Mary Ferrall to the new Lane End
section. The last service at Westbourne Street (141 members) on
27th August 1961 is followed the next week by the first at Deeds
Grove; Mr.Glendower Jones conducts both. No other churches are
closed during this period so the century-old Ibstone is the only
net loss. In February 1962 Mr. Firth thanks all those "who
battled through the snow and ice the other Sunday. But I am
sorry to hear that some turned up, only to find the service had
been cancelled." However,this does not prevent him sending
Mr.B.Sutcliffe on his first preaching appointment through the
icy wastes to Beacons Bottom! In his final letter after the
last of many appeals for increased circuit giving, the sensible
Super who hates fuss, wishes everyone a happy holiday and
departs without further ado.

REV.WILLIAM G.B.REAM (1962-67)

Rev.A.Kingsley Turner is now Chairman of the District.
Rev.Edward W.Crew comes to St.Mark's at the same time as the new
Super.and takes charge of the Youth Committee (where he is
helped for a time by Mr.A.Kinch, soon to become a Minister
himself). Rev.W.G.B.Ream inherits the difficult mantle of the
High Wycombe Circuit including the lighter load of "performing
rights". In his five years of office he sees the closure (long
expected) of only one church - Downley (Chapel Street) on 25th
April 1965. More than 30 years after the united circuit was set
up, and 14 years after Rev. F.B.Hudson's unsuccessful effort,
this quiet Super persuades its 11 members (ex-Primitive) to take
the short journey across the common to the other Methodist
chapel (ex-Wesleyan) - which out of respect promptly surrenders
its delightful "Sunny Bank" title (to be replaced later by the
more severe "Moor Lane").

Rev. and Mrs. Ream - John - Janet - 1966.

Circuit finances continue to be a problem. A debit balance of £550 in 1962 decreases over the next five years by only £8 (and this thanks to a grant for "fireplace conversion" at 223 West Wycombe Road where the Minister has become "smokeless"). Giving us an idea of the debt in "real terms", the Plan informs us in a table of postage rates that it now costs 4d.[1½p.] to post a letter. A helpful map of the area is also included with verbal instructions how to reach town churches like Wesley ("look for Marks and Spencer's"). Everyone presumably knows where Moor Lane is: the map stops at Chapel Street! Membership actually rises over these five years - from 1415 to 1502. The largest Churches in 1967 are: Wesley (259 members); St. Mark's (134); Victoria Street (115); and Deeds Grove (107). The smallest are: Beacons Bottom (10); Wheeler End (10); Terriers (9); and Marlow Bottom (6). All have two services every Sunday except: Terriers (2.30); Tylers Green (2.30); Beacons Bottom (3.00); Piddington (6.00); Radnage (6.00); Wheeler End (6.00); Booker (6.15); and Marlow Bottom (6.30). The 48 services each Sunday are conducted by some of the six Ministers and a Sister; 49 fully accredited preachers (from senior Mr. G. A. Puzey to junior Mrs. G. Tyler); seven "on trial"; six helpers; and 62 preachers from other circuits and churches.

Sister Sylvia Darwent takes up residence at Roberts Road in
1963 and eventually assumes responsibility for the Cryers Hill
section.   Rev. J. Leslie James comes to Victoria Street in 1964,
Rev. Marcus Pattern to Castlefield and Rev. Haldane R. Adams to
Marlow in 1965 and Rev. Denis Reed to St. Mark's in 1966.
Mr. K. J. Peatey becomes a circuit steward in 1964 and
Mr. R. F. Hester in 1966, inspiring the last move of the Marlow
manse - to Wycombe Road.   One letter serves to typify   the
Super's   graciousness.   He writes in July 1966 of his
colleague's premature retirement: "We wish Mr. and Mrs. Crew a
happy and healthy time in the open spaces of Lincolnshire.   We
have appreciated his preaching, his challenging and wise
contributions at meetings.   St. Mark's and Holmer Green have
valued his hard work; he has given a lot of time to the Tylers
Green scheme; and Wooburn Green and Terriers are grateful for
his faithful oversight.   We shall miss the boys who have been
such a cheerful feature of the landscape.   Our prayers go with
them and all the more naturally as they have made so many
friends here and helped so many individuals in time of need."
(The last words could as easily apply to the writer himself.)

REV. R. L. JACK KAYE (1967-74)

Rev. Jack   Kaye,   like
St. Paul, never rests.   For
ever encouraging the faithful
to greater efforts and urging
on those who have become
dispirited, he is at the same
time deeply spiritual and
extremely practical.   We have
collected a few of his wise
sayings into one "epistle":
"Laymen must be trained to
deal   with   pastoral
problems..... Door   stewards,
take the newcomer to his
seat..... Talk   about   your
faith..... Open   up   your
homes..... Learn about the Holy
Spirit..... Throw out what is
useless..... Look for others to
carry on your work..... Space

which is used for worship on Sunday, may be used for a playgroup
on Tuesday..... Look out of your little 'boxes'..... See that your
church   is   clean   and   free   from   dust..... Touch   the

untouchable....." On the Methodist Conference's call to evangelism he writes: "How much time are we prepared to give to prayer, the Bible, outreach?" Notice his order of priorities! But surely it is a printing error when we are reminded: "You are saved by grave (*sic*) alone"!

At the start of his superintendency he calls on the circuit which now has a debit balance of £1061, to "rationalise itself". In the middle he commends Deeds Grove for their "bi-monthly evening meals"! At the end he outlines the new plans for holding the Circuit Meeting and Church Council Meetings only twice (instead of four times) a year. His mind ever open to links with other churches and the need to deepen his own people's understanding, he encourages them to attend courses at Wycombe College, such as "Christian Education"(1970) and "Bible Theology" (1972). Those who go find the Super already sitting there! On 4th August 1968 Rev. Denis Reed conducts the last service at the old Tylers Green Chapel which later will become a base for writer John Metcalfe. The 28 members are urged to attend the new Coppice Farm Church which opens the following week with services at 10.45 a.m. and 7 p.m. conducted by Rev. W. G. B. Ream, the former Super. Few actually make the transfer. Rev. Francis E. Watts arrives at St. Mark's in 1969. Mr. P. D. Carter (of Loudwater) conducts the last service at Terriers on 25th January 1970. The seven members are asked to transfer to St. Mark's: most go to Bryants Bottom! The little corrugated chapel, quietest of all the churches, is to become a centre for the deaf. Rev. Percy Tucker takes over at Deeds Grove and Rev. Norman Burrows at Castlefield. The last service at Beacons Bottom is conducted by Rev. Marcus Pattern on 8th October 1970. The ten members, few of whom have attended in recent months, are spared any "transfer orders"! The chapel will later become a private house.

Let us now pause in January 1971 and see how the High Wycombe Circuit is currently arranged. There are 1,491 members in 27 Churches - 26 of which can still sing at their annual covenant service, "What conflicts have we passed"! (MHB 709).

CHURCH	MEM.	STEWARDS	ORGANIST	S. SCHOOL
Rev. R. L. J. Kaye	(275 members)			
WESLEY	242	D. Griffith/R. Ing	K. Fox	L. Capell
Piddington	23	G. Lee/J. Martin	Mrs. L. Ing	G. Lee
Wheeler End	10	F. Webb/H. Oxlade	R. Webb	-

CHURCH	MEM.	STEWARDS	ORGANIST	S.SCHOOL

Rev.P.A.Tucker (278)

DEEDS GROVE	92	P.Syson/W.Hook	D.Oxlade	W.Hook
Victoria St.	96	W.Haines/E.Barlow	F.Deane	T.Sampson
Downley	55	A.Styles/R.Langley	H.Ford	Mrs.Langley
West Wycombe	18	Mrs.Busby/Mrs.Holt	L.Vernon	Mrs.V.Holt
Bledlow Ridge	17	C.Rogers/A.Brooks	F.Cross	-

Rev.H.R.Adams (235)

MARLOW	77	J.Denton/E.Plumridge	Mrs.Child	J.Lee
Lane End	51	W.Hearn/D.Lewis	MissTwitchen	A.Foster
Flackwell Hth	55	Mrs.Squibb/K.Wilks	Mrs.Langston	J.Lloyd
Bourne End	22	C.Gray/J.Eaton	-	Mrs.G.Lee
Booker	14	R.Pearce/F.Pearce	Mrs.Pearce	-
Marlow Bottom	16	W.Osborne/Ms.Gilbert	-	M.Gilbert

Rev.F.E.Watts (318)

ST.MARK'S	118	Mrs.Youens/R.Clark	H.Bunce	Mrs.Warkcup
Holmer Green	111	H.Wingrove/W.Parker	Mrs.Hughes	N.Nibloe
Tylers Green	63	C.Sadler/J.Raby	G.Davis	M.Stanyon
Wooburn Green	26	F.Slade/A.Smith	H.Slade	F.Slade

Rev.N.Burrows (211)

CASTLEFIELD	77	P.Chubb/P.Gibbons	Mrs.Goodear	lP.Chubb
Sands	71	N.Chadwick/R.Sears	-	Mrs.Stallwood
Stokenchurch	39	E.Bates/P.Rixon	W.Saunders	Mrs.M.Atkins
Radnage	14	E.Maunder/H.Hook	Mrs.Atkins	E.Maunder
Beacons Bottom	10	Mrs.Butler/H.Butler	(closed)	

Sister M.Smith (174)

CRYERS HILL	73	F.Burrows/J.Copeland	-	R.Dean
Naphill	45	L.Brown/N.Mead	MissLawrence	MissLawrence
Lacey Green	32	J.Claydon/H.Hawes	Mrs.Church	G.May
Bryants Bottom	24	E.Ridgley/Mrs.Hawes	D.Ridgley	E.Ridgley

Later in 1971 Rev.Harold W.Ward arrives at Marlow and
Sister Ruth Orton takes charge of Victoria Street, Sands and
West Wycombe. Mr.D.B.McLean, Mr.L.R.Waller, Mr.C.P.Dyer and
Mr.K.T.Fox are appointed circuit stewards during these years
which end with a revolution: Miss Orton has joined the
previously all-male domain of ordained Ministers! Things can
surely never be the same again.

REV. HAROLD SLATER (1974-82)

Exit King John; enter King Harold! Rev. R. L. Jack Kaye is now Chairman of the London North-West District; Rev. Harold Slater O. B. E. is the ninth Super of one of its components: the struggling High Wycombe Circuit to which it is becoming increasingly difficult to attract new Ministers. He expresses surprise at the warmth of his welcome in 1974. A warmer manse awaits him in 1977 – at 9 Rye View. But after all his own warmest efforts, in his last letter he has to sigh, "This circuit is a very demanding one"! It is the longest "reign" of any of our ten Supers – eight years. Popular inside and outside the Church, he is friend of all and secret counsellor to many troubled individuals. Despite this two more churches are closed: Victoria Street (69 members) – in the heart of an ethnic minority area – on 1st June 1975 and Sands (42 members) on 29th August 1982. Both premises are bought by independent churches. Most of the Victoria Street people transfer to Deeds Grove and some of the Sands members move to Castlefield. The chapel at West Wycombe also is closed in October 1977 and is converted later into offices. Services however are resumed, after a quarter's break, at St. Paul's Church in February 1978. In January 1980 the society of six members becomes a "Wesley class". So we see that at the end of this period there remain 24 churches (including West Wycombe), nine of which have fewer than 20 members. The number of Sunday services has declined from 46 to 41 which are conducted by five Ministers, a Sister, 40 circuit preachers and 35 non-circuit preachers. Membership has dropped from 1,454 to 1,209.

However there is much to enjoy. Rev. Norman Burrows is organising brass band concerts (including the Black Dyke Mills Band at the Parish Church); Wesley Church is off on its family holiday; Sands holds daffodil rallies; Cryers Hill has its traditional cherry-pie suppers; Castlefield celebrates with roses; Booker holds flower shows; Lane End presses on with its modernisation scheme; Marlow opens its new extension; Tylers Green offers "Family Focus"; Dr.Geoffrey Rose is trying to persuade the preachers to "involve the congregation in worship"; Dr.Chris Sworn is commissioned for service with the Methodist Missionary Society in Rhodesia. The list is not finished yet! "The Small Hundredweight" is returning - by popular demand - to the carol festival; the first Circuit Covenant Service is being held at Wesley in 1976; Marlow tries a "teatime" (4.30) service - without the tea; Rev.David Watson is coming to "Celebrate the Faith" in March 1979. And our desire for peace is excited by the announcement: "'Disarmament - is there an alternative?' (Details later)" - the "Big Bang" perhaps?

In 1975 Rev.Wilbert G.Putman takes over a new section (Holmer Green) - and also a new manse (Pheasants Drive); Rev.Douglas Graham receives just the Castlefield section. The same year Rev.Ruth Orton moves to the Old Bakery, Stokenchurch, but is displaced in 1976 by Sister Eileen Rogers who takes over the Stokenchurch section; Miss Orton is now put in charge of the St.Mark's section. Rev.Alan L.Baxter comes to Marlow in 1977, Rev.Keith Phipps to Castlefield in 1980 and Rev.Roy McP.Jackson to St.Mark's in 1981. The last two Ministers are in their first stations. New circuit stewards in these eight years are: Messrs.D.Jackson,   B.Murgatroyd,   H.T.Trigwell,   A.I.Mounteney, P.McNair,   J.Higginbottom,   C.Haddock,   R.Slocombe   and Mrs.P.Maidment (the circuit's first woman steward). Stewards may come, Ministers may go. But one thing goes on for ever - problems with the Plan seem unending! Once again the printers have conspired to prevent the Super from addressing us. Now after a two-year absence Rev.Harold Slater suddenly reappears in the November 1978 Plan with the good news that "the circuit has decided to strike a new contract with the printers, in order that my letter and the diary of events may once again be printed in the Plan". He keeps the bad news to last: the price has had to be doubled to 2/-[10p.]! In this era of inflation prices seem to rise without effort. The thought occurs to us that a little inflation in those membership figures might not be a bad idea!

REV.A.GEOFFREY JONES (1982-87)

Now we have a new Chairman of District, Rev.Stanley K.Chesworth, and our tenth Super, Rev.A.Geoffrey Jones, a big man both in stature and heart. His kindly nature is typified by the inclusion of the preachers' Christian names in the Plan! He faces difficulties at Wesley which loses the use of its schoolroom, including the Hannah Ball Room, through arson attacks, and has several planning applications to rebuild the whole church, turned down. There are difficulties in the circuit too. In 1982 Rev. Mark Booth (conscientious and another probationer) comes to Marlow. In 1984 Rev. Arthur F. Royall, a supernumary Minister, takes the oversight of Bourne End from him; the Lucas Road manse having become the target of vandals, a larger house is bought at Fleet Close, Hughenden Valley; and Sister

Vera Pearson comes to Stokenchurch. Rev. Alf Shannahan is welcomed at Holmer Green in 1985, not least because his senior years will add balance to the staff. But his health gives way and he is replaced by a supernumary Minister, Rev. Harold E. Winter, in 1986. Another supernumary - Rev. G. Eric Firth, the former Super, who has spent his retirement in Wycombe - dies in 1985. A third - Rev. Herbert E. C. Pettet - is still with us but much missed at Wycombe Hospital where he was once a chaplain. New circuit stewards in this period are: Mrs. Joan D. Trigwell, Desmond Kelly, Kenneth D. Freer and Richard Powell.

Three more churches close: the "Wesley class" at West Wycombe (whose five members are transferred to Bledlow Ridge); Piddington (nine members to Wheeler End or Stokenchurch); and Wheeler End (eight members to Lane End). So we have witnessed at the western end of the circuit the collapse - like a line of dominoes - of: Victoria Street (1975); Sands (1982); West Wycombe (1983); Piddington (1986); and Wheeler End (1987). One can imagine Bledlow Ridge (nine members in 1987) and Radnage (16) bracing themselves. There now remain 21 churches with a total membership of 1047. There are 38 services each Sunday - just half the 1949 total. Evening services are poorly attended - perhaps 30 at most in one or two churches, as few as four or five in certain others. United services, especially in the

St.Mark's section, become frequent. Some evening services transfer to the afternoon during the winter. Four staff, including the Super, are leaving in 1987 but Sister Vera is not to be replaced: Rev.Roy Jackson will then have oversight of six churches. A Circuit Policy Committee decides the only solution is to concentrate resources on the 13 churches which seem to have growth potential; the rest should amalgamate with others, where possible.

Reflecting as ever the state of the circuit, the Plan is reduced in size in August 1986, becoming a triple-fold leaflet, printed by Art Lines. It now contains basic information only: the Plan itself and the names and addresses of the Ministers, preachers and circuit stewards. The Super's letter now appears in a new publication, "Circuit News", edited by David Sparks.

However, as always, there is much to be thankful for. Three men are accepted for training as Methodist Ministers: Andrew Barker (Tylers Green); Fred Day (Deeds Grove); and John Lloyd (Flackwell Heath). Another preacher - Gregory Hargrove - becomes the Minister of The Pastures and Hazlemere Free Methodist Churches. There is a surge of new preachers coming "on trial". A new hymn book, "Hymns and Psalms", is published and generally - despite the omission of many favourites - well received. The Super organises many inter-church house groups, some on the subject, "What on earth is the Church for?".

Flackwell Heath and Lacey Green enjoy refurbished premises; Wesley and Wooburn Green look forward to having theirs; Bourne End has a smart new frontage; Marlow will one day have a modern schoolroom; Cryers Hill has a splendid porch; Tylers Green's roof and windows now keep the elements out; Downley's organ is put back into prime condition.

Most churches have a lively Sunday morning service; Marlow is packed. Bourne End and Booker are riding on the crest of the wave, so many new people - albeit mostly senior citizens - have come in. Arrive early at Marlow Bottom (including the preacher) if you want to find a seat!

So we could go on. We conclude our 53-year survey of the High Wycombe Methodist Circuit by looking at the position of each Church in April 1987. (Section Churches in capitals).

THE METHODIST CHURCH

CHURCH	MEM.	SERVCS		*	STEWARD	OWN PREACHERS	
WESLEY	159	10½	6	H	A.Drage	M.Dore	W.Egner
						K.Peatey	G.Tyler
						G.Beard	D.Hunter
Deeds Grove	53	10½	6	H	W.Hook	E.Pullen	
HOLMER GREEN	82	10½	6	H	D.Dickason	G.Rose	M.Brittin
						E.Barnett	A.Singleton
Tylers Green	51	10¾	6	H	E.Jarvis	E.Jarvis	J.Jarvis
						G.Beddard	P.Stevens
						P.Howarth	
Cryers Hill	43	10½	6	M	B.Pearce	B.Sparks	D.Sparks
MARLOW	129	10½	6½	H	T.Dennis	B.Dennis	A.L.Kerr
						J.Smith	
Flackwell Heath	57	11	6½	M	P.Lloyd		
Wooburn Green	26	11	6	M	J.Ash		
Marlow Bottom	47	11	6½	M	M.Gilbert	K.Lewis	M.Mason
Bourne End	13	10¾		H	E.Andrews	S.Sherratt	A.Goodearl
						E.Andrews	
ST.MARK'S	77	10¾	6½	H	T.Widdess	R.Woodbridge	D.Church
						C.Campbell	J.Widdess
						T.Widdess	
Downley	31	10¾	6	M	C.Knapman		
Naphill	32	11	6¼	H	M.Webb	M.Webb	B.Sutcliffe
Lacey Green	20	2½	6	H	R.Spencer		
Bryants Bottom	17	2½	6	H	E.Ridgley		
Bledlow Ridge	9	10½		M	C.Rogers		
CASTLEFIELD	96	10	6	H	H.Goodearl	L.Phipps	P.Howard
						F.Rolls	
Lane End	23	10¾	6	M	D.Lewis	G.Lewis	
Stokenchurch	36	11		H	G.Allen		
Booker	22	3¼		M	R.Stevens		
Radnage	16	6		M	A.Atkins		
Wheeler End	8	3		M	F.Webb		

* Hymn Book: H = Hymns and Psalms; M = Methodist Hymn Book

POSTSCRIPT (1988)

It is New Year's Day (1988) as the new Super, Rev.Tony Barnard, contemplates his far-flung High Wycombe Circuit. He will need his predecessors' wisdom - as well as his own - to solve this jubilee year's problems. He came in September 1987 with two other new Ministers - Rev.Michael Edwards in the Castlefield section and Rev.E.Brian Mason in the Marlow section. The latter will be leaving the Circuit later this month for personal reasons and his four Churches - Marlow, Flackwell Heath, Wooburn Green and Marlow Bottom - allocated to the rest of the staff, including the only other full-time Minister, Rev.Roy Jackson, who is being replaced in September 1988 by a probationer, Rev.Martin Williams.   In the general state of uncertainty a Plan for one month only (February) is to be issued. So what is the current state of the Churches?

WESLEY   Problems with the present building have caused activities to be scattered. A great sense of loyalty holds the members together.   Over 160 children are catered for in the Sunday School and uniformed organisations.   There are tenuous links with Trinity U.R.C.Church.   No members now live in the vicinity. Wesley must provide leadership.   [LES VERNON]

DEEDS GROVE   Work is centred on the young people, although the Sunday School is smaller than it used to be. There is a lack of contact with the neighbouring estate and much effort is needed to maintain the buildings. There are some links with St.John's Church. Good leaders provide hope.   [JOHN ROGERS]

HOLMER GREEN   Times were hard following the departure of Rev.Wilbert Putman and during the illness of Rev.Alf Shannahan. But Rev.Harold Winter has pulled the Church back together. Everyone is willing to "have a go". Communications with those outside could be improved.   There is a Sunday School of 100 and many clubs. New people are coming. There are close links with the Baptist Church and Christ Church.   [COLIN HADDOCK]

TYLERS GREEN This Church has few traditions and is unconventional.   It is widely used by the community. The membership, especially among the young people, needs to increase if the Church is to have a future. House groups are strong. There are links with Hazlemere and Penn Free Methodist Churches.
                                          [DOUG JACKSON]

CRYERS HILL   The Church "jogs along" and is renowned for its happy friendliness, also its choir. The Sunday School is smaller than it used to be. The people are good workers; church and graveyard are well maintained. The main problem is that the church is too hidden away.   [BERYL PEARCE]

MARLOW   The increase in numbers is due to Rev.Mark Booth's popularity with young families. A good team spirit has allowed much money to be raised for the new schoolroom which it is hoped will have a wide community use. The aim now is to build the membership up further. [PHYLLIS SIDDENS]

FLACKWELL HEATH   The people come from a wide range of denominations. Fellowship groups have enabled them to get to know one another. Now there is a need to look outward. John Lloyd's departure has coincided with the loss of many of the young people. There is a strong pastoral (visiting) group. There are close links with Christ Church. Coffee mornings have led on to a work among agoraphobics. [HEATHER HARMAN]

WOOBURN GREEN   After a long delay over plans it is hoped the new building works can soon begin. Extensions could lead to greater community use and the growth of the Church. The Sunday School is now quite small. [SHEILA HILLIARD]

MARLOW BOTTOM   The strength of this Church is the love and friendship - despite differences - between individuals. Drawing its membership from many denominations, it is non-conforming but supportive of Methodist preachers. There is good contact with the village, including St.Mary's Church. [MILDRED WHITE]

BOURNE END   The work is progressing due to the work of Rev.Arthur Royall and the erection of nearby flats. There are three local preachers among the membership. Recent baptisms point the way to the future. [SHEILA JOHNSON]

ST.MARK'S   Its strength is a great family feeling, aided by the minibus - which encourages togetherness! After difficult times in recent years there is a greater readiness to work together. There is a tolerance towards new ideas. The Church might one day become less shy. [JUNE CAMPBELL]

DOWNLEY   The Church (including the Sunday School) is growing with the arrival of new families and those on the fringe are being drawn into closer fellowship. Jobs are well shared. There are close links with St.James' Roman Catholic and Anglican Church, and The Pastures Free Methodist Church. There is definitely a future for the Circuit's oldest Church.
[ANGELA REDDING]

NAPHILL   Church and village are closely linked. The sick are visited and newcomers welcomed. Combined services and other functions are held regularly with St.Michael's Church of England (Hughenden). [JEAN LAWRENCE]

LACEY GREEN   The fellowship is warm and premises and grounds are well maintained. There is a good Sunday School and a faithful congregation. But a "middle line" of younger adults is needed for the work to continue. There are close links with Loosley Row Baptist Church.   [VERA MAY]

BRYANTS BOTTOM The arrival of a young and enthusiastic couple from the new houses has brought fresh hope. More are needed for the chapel to remain an integral part of the village. Each needs the other.   [SYLVIA HAVES]

BLEDLOW RIDGE   The death of Rex Rogers was a severe blow but others have taken over. The Sunday School is growing and the morning adult congregation numbers 12 or more. There are united monthly services with St.Paul's Chuch of England. The future looks bright.   [SHEILA BELL]

CASTLEFIELD   After a barren period the Church has begun to take a new direction. More freedom in worship may be desirable. There should be an outbreak to the (mixed faith) community through the love and compassion which Rev.Keith Phipps showed in practical ways and Rev.Michael Edwards is reinforcing in a teaching ministry. Links with St.Birinus' and Our Lady of Grace Churches continue.   [PETER ANSELL]

LANE END   People on the fringe have been brought in to help with the growing Sunday School which - along with a flourishing Wives' Group - points to a bright future.   A central position is an asset, so is a good spread of ages. The "hymnalong" is a favourite with the community. The Elim Church's move into the village may quicken interest in religion generally.   [PHYLL HEARN]

STOKENCHURCH   The opportunities in this expanding village are immense but the Church lacks young people. The Roman Catholics use the premises for Saturday evening worship and Ss. Peter and Paul's Church has an early morning Sunday School here.   All unite in a village carol service.   [JOHN WEATHERHEAD]

BOOKER   Numbers have increased but the congregation is elderly and transport is a problem.   Ron and Jean Stevens' departure made a large gap. The Sunday School continues with about 12 children. There are links with St.Birinus' Church. The aim must be to build up a balanced Church. "Watch this space!"   [KEN ACTON]

RADNAGE   There is a nucleus of older worshippers which
does not increase.   Both this Church and St.Mary's Church have
made efforts with Sunday School work but the few children are
the same!   Recent work on subsidence of the building revealed
dry rot which will be costly to repair.   But witness in this
area must continue.   [JOHN JONES]

HIGH WYCOMBE METHODIST CIRCUIT MINISTERS

1934-37	Ernest Dennis	1934-35	W.S.Hinchcliffe
1934-39	Ernest W.Eavis	1934-36	R.O.Stobbs
1934-38	F.C.Searle	1935-38	Ernest Jones
1936-40	H.Binks	1936-38	N.Renshaw
1937-40	E.G.Loosley	1937-40	J.W.W.Owen
1938-44	Walter Yeomans	1938-44	G.R.Maland
1938-40	Wm.Irving	1939-41	F.Pilkington
1940-45	Arthur Walters	1940-46	R.Pearson
1940-45	A.Heathcote	1940-45	G.Glandfield
1941-46	F.Bertram Clogg	1944-49	Walter N.Parnaby
1944-47	Arthur Baxter	1945-49	Benjamin Tattersall
1945-46	N.Thomas	1945-48	W.A.Cooper
1946-50	Cecil F.Guy	1946-50	Eric Chapman
1946-47	Leslie Cox	1947-50	A.Whittard
1947-49	A.J.Speed	1949-55	Francis B.Hudson
1949-55	Owen M.Collins	1949-51	D.N.Howarth
1950-54	George B.Middleton	1950-51	Thomas Welch
1950-54	Ernest G.Kitchin	1950-51	W.P.White
1951-53	R.G.Cornfield	1953-55	P.Guy Stanford
1954-60	Philip H.Foster	1954-60	Kenneth W. Curtis
1955-62	G.Eric Firth	1955-62	Arthur H.Freeman
1955-57	Anthony B.Wells	1957-60	W.Rowland Jones
1960-64	A.Glendower Jones	1960-65	Leonard G.Jones
1960-65	Alan Cox	1962-67	William G.B.Ream
1962-66	Edward W.Crew	1964-70	J.Leslie James
1965-71	Haldane R.Adams	1965-70	Marcus A.Pattern
1966-69	Denis Reed	1967-74	R.L.Jack Kaye
1969-76	Francis E.Watts	1970-75	Percy A.Tucker
1970-75	Norman Burrows	1971-77	Harold W.Ward
1974-82	Harold Slater	1974-81	F.M.Ruth Orton
1975-84	Wilbert G.Putman	1975-80	Douglas Graham
1977-82	Alan L.Baxter	1980-87	Keith M.Phipps
1981->	Roy McP.Jackson	1982-87	A.Geoffrey Jones
1982-87	Mark R.Booth	1984-86	Alf Shannahan
1987->	Anthony Barnard	1987->	Michael Edwards
1987-88	E.Brian Mason		

SUPERNUMARY MINISTERS

1934-54 J.H.Cartwright	1934-50 O.J.Griffin
1935-46 W.Hindes	1939-50 R.Robinson
1939-45 C.W.Posnett	1940-41 H.Binks
1944-47 E.W.Smith	1947-48 G.J.Chamberlain
1948-59 A.G.Burnham	1948-49 P.S.May
1954-56 T.Arthur Udy	1957-59 William H.Curtis
1965-81 Harold Hadwen	1967 William Schofield
1968-84 G.Eric Firth	1971 John Jones
1972-> Herbert E.C.Pettit	1983-> Arthur F.Royall
1986-> Alf Shannahan	1986-> Harold E.Winter

WESLEY DEACONESSES

1934 Sis.Miriam Hammel	1934 Sis.Edith
1940 Sis.Sadie Martin	1941-45 Sis.Elsie Kitchener
1945-50 Sis.Jessie Brine	1950-53 Sis.Eva Lyth
1952 Sis.Jessie Brine (R)	1952-71 Sis.Christine Cox (R)
1956-60 Sis.Freda Young	1960-63 Sis.Mary Ferrall
1963-68 Sis.Sylvia Darwent	1968-71 Sis.Margaret Smith
1971-74 Sis.Ruth Orton	1976-78 Sis.Brenda Fuller (R)
1976-83 Sis.Eileen Rogers	1983-87 Sis.Vera Pearson
1976-> Sis.Sylvia Hawes (nee Darwent) (R)	

(R) = Retired.

Walter Goodearl   Rev.Eddie Crew   W.Jack Parkins

Back row. (l. to r.). Rev. E. Dennis, Not Known, T. W. Apps,
S. Goodearl, S. Howard, Rev. A. Whittard, Rev. W. Parnaby, Rev. C. Guy.

Front row. H. Woodward, C. Cutler, F. Rixon, -. Jarvis, D. Sargeant.

HIGH WYCOMBE METHODIST CIRCUIT: ACCREDITED PREACHERS

ACCR	NAME	FROM/TRIAL	PLAN	ADDRESS	LEFT	REASON
1877	William Line	*P	1934	Kitchener Rd	1942	*D
1878	G. Seymour	*W	1934	Totteridge	1940	*D
1881	V. Cook	*W	1934	Lane End	1936	
1882	H. James	*P	1934	Totteridge	1935	*D
1882	A. Edwards	*W	1934	Amersham	1946	*D
1885	G. Darvill	*P	1934	Desborough St	1937	*D
1885	F. Hunt	*P	1934	V Wycombe Rd	1950	*D
1886	Isaac Brearley	*W	1934	Lane End	1936	*D
1888	G. Castle	*P	1936	Oakridge Rd	1939	*D
1889	G. Rance	Chal. St.G	1937	Chal. St.G	1951	Chesham
1890	Thomas Apps	*W	1934	Pinions	1949	Camberley
1891	C. Bunce	*W	1934	Bridge St	1940	*D
1891	G. Taylor	*P	1934	V Wycombe Rd	1934	*D
1892	C. Cutler	*W	1934	Gordon Road	1951	*D
1892	E. Dormer	*P	1934	Radnage	1961	*D
1892	E. Gray	*P	1934	Desborough Rd	1937	*D
1892	J. Plested	*P	1934	West End Rd	1936	*D
1892	G. Shaw	*P	1934	Naphill	1939	*D
1892	V. Youens	*W	1934	Downley	1945	*D
1892	J. Barrow		1938	Stokenchurch	1954	*D
1894	H. Woodward	*W	1934	Green Street	1951	*D
1895	A. Savage	Cleckheaton	1937	Keep Hill Dr	1939	*D
1896	V.A. Steevens	*W	1934	Albert St	1961	*D
1897	James Holland	*P	1934	V Wycombe Rd.	1942	*D
1897	G. Castle	*P	1934	Oakridge Rd	1936	
1897	R. Jupe	*P	1934	Widmer End	1958	*D
1898	A. Higgs	*W	1934	Rickmansworth	1947	*D
1898	A. Purdue	*W	1934	Eaton Avenue	1937	Moved
1898	D. Sargeant	*P	1934	Rutland Av	1951	*D
1898	J. Sargeant	*P	1934	Gordon Road	1945	*D
1900	John Shirley	*W	1934	Bourne End	1945	*D
1901	Reg. Nancarrow	*W	1934	Amersham	1951	Chesham
1902	J. Symes	*P	1934	Hughenden Rd	1955	*D
1903	H. Collins	*W	1934	Flackwell	1952	*D
1903	George Brown	*W	1934	Pinions	1959	*D
1904	V. Markham	*W	1934	Green Street	1938	
1904	J. Lacey	*P	1934	Southfield Rd	1951	*D
1904	A. Sargeant	*P	1934	Vest End Rd	1951	*D

THE METHODIST CHURCH

ACCR	NAME	FROM/TRIAL	PLAN	ADDRESS	LEFT	REASON
1904	F.Berry	*P	1934	Abercrombie	1955	*D
1904	T.Castle	*P	1934	Bassetsbury	1953	*D
1905	T.Weston	*W	1934	Totteridge	1941	Removed
1905	H.Bishop	*W	1934	Southfield Rd	1947	*D
1905	George Pratt	*V	1934	Amersham	1941	*D
1906	Albert Pearce	*W	1934	Gordon Road	1955	*D
1906	V.Hearn	*W	1934	Lane End	1965	*D
1906	Walter Goodearl	*V	1934	V.Wycombe Rd.	1954	*D
1906	G.Stratford		1934	Studley Green	1937	Resigned
1906	J.Barrow		1934	Stokenchurch	1938	
1907	A.Randall	*P	1934	The Lee	1951	Chesham
1907	H.Bignell	*P	1934	Lee Common	1945	*D
1907	P.Hall		1937	Amersham	1951	Chesham
1907	A.Louis	Windsor	1943	Prestwood	1943	Soton
1908	F.Rixon	*P	1934	Lacey Green	1959	*D
1908	S.Goodearl	*P	1934	Kitchener Rd	1963	*D
1909	W.Garlick	*V	1934	Chesham	1951	Chesham
1909	V.Coker	*P	1934	Piddington	1946	*D
1909	H.T.Turnbull	*P	1934	Bassetsbury	1958	*D
1910	H.Jarrett	*P	1934	Priory Road	1962	*D
1910	S.Carr	*V	1934	Lane End	1959	*D
1911	T.Barnett	*P	1934	Oakridge Rd	1947	*D
1912	T.Weatherill	*W	1934	Chesham	1951	Chesham
1913	V.Smith	*P	1934	Booker	1946	
1913	F.Randall	*P	1934	Ballinger	1951	Chesham
1913	G.Puzey	Windsor	1935	Flackwell	1968	*D
1915	V.Saunders	*V	1934	West End Rd	1935	*D
1916	G.Darvill	*P	1934	Slater St	1949	*D
1916	G.Rolls		1934	Kitchener Rd	1947	*D
1919	V.Cooper	*V	1934	Bourne End	1935	Resigned
1920	T.Smith	*V	1934	Abercrombie	1941	*D
1920	E.Weller	*V	1934	Priory Ave	1938	*D
1920	V.Jack Parkins	*V	1934	Manor Gardens	1982	*D
1920	F.Thomas	Christchurch	1943	Priory Ave	1965	*D
1921	Harold Goodearl	*V	1934	Bourne End	1973	Stoke on Trent
1921	William Bates	*P	1934	Abercrombie	1981	*D
1921	C.Cole		1949	Amersham	1951	Chesham
1921	W.Pearcey	Cromer	1959	Hughenden Rd	1968	
1922	Mrs.Sheppard		1934	Stokenchurch	1950	*D
1922	G.Smith		1937	Vinchmore Hl	1950	*D
1922	H.Ault		1940	Coningsby Rd	1941	Moved

ACCR	NAME	FROM/TRIAL	PLAN	ADDRESS	LEFT	REASON
1923	L.Rundle	Cornwall	1960	Medmenham	1969	
1924	H.Rodgers	Oldham	1937	Keep Hill Dr	1952	Moved
1924	F.Taylor		1964	Lacey Green	1967	*D
1925	F.Batts	*W	1934	Downley	1959	*D
1925	Miss Browning		1936	Amersham	1940	
1925	C.Rance	Wembley	1943	London Road	1945	
1925	H.Peters	East Ham	1943	Amersham	1943	Removed
1926	E.Barlow	*P	1934	Oakridge Wood	1959	Windsor
1926	G.Jones	*P	1934	Benjamin Rd	1940	Removed
1926	Miss E.Shipham	*P	1934	Terriers	1935	Moved
1926	E.Castle	*P	1934	Oakridge Rd	1957	Removed
1926	M.Hughes		1937	Bowden Lane	1955	
1926	F.Carter	Shepherd's B	1947		1947	Cliff C.
1926	F.Harcourt -Munning		1954	Brentford	1955	Ealing
1927	A.E.Steevens	*W	1934	Amersham Hill	1973	*D
1927	A.Quenell	Brighton	1935	Wooburn Green	1940	Moved
1927	J.Simpson		1935	Royal Grammar	1937	Scarboro
1928	Miss Bryant		1937	Amersham	1951	Chesham
1930	Albert Hester	*W	1934	Whitelands Rd	1969	*D
1930	F.Collins	*W	1934	Cressex Lane	1963	Resigned
1930	Vilfred Osborne	*W	1934	Marlow	1980	*D
1930	William Smith	*P	1934	Bryants Botm	1985	*D
1930	Stan Sherratt	Macclesfield	1979	Cressex Road	--->	
1931	A.Willott		1938	Keep Hill Dr	1947	*D
1932	V.Bunce	*W	1934	Chairborough	1945	*D
1932	G.Sheppard	*W	1934	Royal Grammar	1961	Orpington
1932	Fred.Howard	*W	1934	Flackwell	1983	Resigned
1932	H.Hudson	St.Austell	1936	Sands	1937	
1932	F.Neville		1937	Chal St.G.	1951	Chesham
1932	Miss F.Dyer	Leighton Buz	1943	Chesham	1951	Chesham
1933	Miss N.Ives	*W	1934	Marlow	1951	
1933	F.Welford	*W	1934	Coningsby Rd	1954	Moved
1933	A.Brake	*P	1934	Booker	1950	
1933	Mrs.Simpson		1935	Amersham	1937	Scarboro
1933	Miss K.Kearley		1940	Eaton Avenue	1961	Sutton
1933	Miss M.Dore		1972	Coningsby Rd	--->	
1935	Miss M.Darvill	1934	1935	Slater St	1982	*D
1935	Mrs.G.Newell (Mason)	1934	1935	Gt.Kingshill	1951	
1935	D.Howard	1934	1935	Dashwood Ave	1974	*D
1935	V.Baker	1934	1935	Chesham	1951	Chesham
1935	Miss H.Smith		1937	Amersham	1951	Chesham

ACCR	NAME	FROM/TRIAL	PLAN	ADDRESS	LEFT	REASON
1935	I.Kemp	Chalf.St.G	1936	L Chalfont	1941	
1935	Reg.Carr	Alton	1937	Beaconsfield	1937	Alton
1936	Len Goodchild	1935	1936	Southfield Rd	1965	*D
1936	Clifford Craft	1936	1936	Plumer Road	1965	Swaffham
1936	Frederick Deane	1935	1936	Abercrombie	1971	Looe
1937	William Egner	S.Shields	1984	Penn	--->	
1938	H.Hewish		1951	Kendalls Cl	1953	
1938	H.Saint		1954	Marlow	1954	*D
1938	Mrs.F.Mann	Kilburn	1962	Uplands Cl	1970	Aylesbury
1939	F.Slade		1939	Wooburn Green	1979	*D
1939	Alan Goodearl	1937	1940	V.Wycombe Rd.	--->	
1939	R.Hearn	1937	1940	Lane End	1947	
1939	D.Christian	1938	1940	London Road	1952	Boston
1939	E. Jarvis	1939	1940	Sands	1958	*D
1940	F.Collier	Coventry	1957	Penn	1961	Coventry
1941	P.Guichard	1940	1941	Desborough Av	1945	Removed
1942	H.Burch	Baptist Ch.	1942	Coleshill	1945	Resigned
1942	H.Guite		1943		1943	Slough
1943	Miss M.Rodgers	1943	1944	Keep Hill Dr	1952	Moved
1943	V.Davis		1944	Chesham	1945	
1943	Miss F.Valters		1959	Harefield	1962	Brentford
1944	Leslie Dron	1942	1944	West End Rd	1961	Faversham
1945	Miss J.Gayler	1943	1945	Amersham	1951	Chesham
1945	D.Gregory	1944	1945	Marlow	1975	
1945	G.Turnwell	East Ham	1946		1947	Bexhill
1945	Miss B.Owen		1949	South Heath	1951	Chesham
1946	Mrs.A.Jones	Scunthorpe	1960	V Wycombe Rd	1964	Sheffield
1946	R.Clarke	Finsbury Pk	1960	Tylers Green	1961	Resigned
1947	R.Craske	Cheam	1952	Southfield Rd	1953	Moved
1947	V.Arthur Dodd		1965	Disraeli Cres	1974	Resigned
1948	E.King	1947	1949	L Chalfont	1951	Chesham
1948	B.Mitchell	1948	1949		1950	Leighton
1948	D.Imrie	Romford	1953	Coningsby Rd	1957	Grantham
1949	Keith Lewis		1951	Marlow	--->	
1949	Dr.G.Rose	Amersham	1963	Holmer Green	--->	
1950	J.Goodwin		1950	Desborough Rd	1964	*D
1950	Mrs.M.Pike					
	(Harvey)	1949	1950	Marlow	1974	Chepstow
1950	Horace Lord	1943	1950	Lane End	1984	Swanage
1950	M.Tweddle	Willesdon	1959	Vestover Rd	1963	Clacton
1951	Kenneth Peatey	1942	1951	Upr.Green St.	--->	
1951	F.Baker	Maidenhead	1954	Chairborough	1965	Hemel H.

ACCR NAME	FROM/TRIAL	PLAN ADDRESS	LEFT REASON
1951 Mrs.M.Ream		1962 Priory Ave	1967 Moved
1951 Mrs.M.Edwards	Redhill	1987 Rutland Ave	--->
1952 Mrs.R.Woodbridge			
(Clarke)	1950	1952 Denmark St	--->
1953 Mrs.H.Adams		1965 Marlow	1971 Banbury
1954 A.Castle	1947	1954 Green Street	1958 Resigned
1955 William Haines	1955	1955 V.Wycombe Rd.	1981 *D
1955 C.Burrell	Bishops Std	1963 Beaconsfield	1968 Newbury
1955 P.Carter	New Zealand	1969 Loudwater	1971
1956 Mrs.M.Ing		1966 Disraeli Cres	1976 Resigned
1956 R.Cleaver		1966 Micklefield	1966 *D
1957 Mrs.M.Wayman		1962 Marlow	1967 Newport (IOW)
1957 Miss J.Anderson	Bedford	1963 Holmer Green	1964 Amersham
1958 Mrs.Vera Holt	1957	1958 V.Wycombe Rd.	1975 Moved
1958 J.Hodgkinson	Rochdale	1961 Marlow	1968 Bolton
1958 Eric Jarvis		1963 Chairborough	--->
1958 J.Best		1966 Marlow Hill	1968 Ilkley
1958 Arthur Cook	Wantage	1974 Sands	1983 Wantage
1958 Mrs.J.Barnard	Driffield	1987 Rye View	--->
1960 Anthony Kinch	1958	1960 Stokenchurch	1963 Ministry
1960 D.Bates	1958	1960 V Wycombe Rd	1963
1960 M.Dick		1964 Medmenham	1968
1960 Mrs.H.Maynard	Australia	1965 Amersham Hill	1967
1960 David Short	Amersham	1968 Knights Hill	1981 Moved
1960 A.I.Mounteney	Peterborough	1971 Hazlemere	1980 Colch'ter
1961 Mrs.A.Cooper	1961	1961 Desborough Av	1978 U.Bapt.
1961 Anthony Cooper	1957	1961 Desborough Av	1978 U.Bapt.
1961 M.Wheeldon	1958	1961 Hughenden Va	1963
1961 M.Brittin	1955	1961 Holmer Green	--->
1961 R.Maynard	Australia	1965 Amersham Hill	1967
1961 Mrs.P.Syson	Portsmouth	1962 Deeds Grove	1971 Harpenden
1961 Peter Syson	Portsmouth	1962 Deeds Grove	1971 Harpenden
1961 Mrs.J.Jarvis		1963 Chairborough Road	--->
1961 Miss F.Cattmull		1965 Penn	1965
1962 David Church	1961	1962 Hobart Close	--->
1962 A.Colling	1961	1962 Tylers Green	1966 Moved
1962 Miss R.Harris	1961	1962 Rupert Ave	1964 Grosall
1962 Miss J.Anstey		1963 Beaconsfield	1967 Tonbridge
1963 Mrs.R.Neville	1963	1964 Cressex Road	1967
1963 Mrs.C.Godwin	Barry	1967 Lane End	1970 Worthing
1963 P.Steare	Uckfield	1967 Speen	1971 U.Bapt.
1963 Ernest Barnett	Yewsley	1967 Hazlemere	--->

ACCR	NAME	FROM/TRIAL	PLAN	ADDRESS	LEFT	REASON
1963	Norman Nibloe	Yewsley	1967	Hazlemere	1973	Tonbridge
1963	G.Alan Bateman		1976	Hazlemere	1987	C.of E.
1964	Ernest Andrews	Baptist Ch.	1964	Wooburn Green	--->	
1965	A.Mahoney	1963	1966	Guinions Rd	1969	Resigned
1966	Barry Sutcliffe	1962	1966	Totteridge	--->	
1967	Mrs.G.Tyler	1965	1967	Queen Street	--->	
1968	Miss.A.Hayter		1970	Bracknell	1971	Resigned
1969	P.Springell	1966	1969	Gayhurst Rd	1970	ChippingN
1969	Andrew Barker	F.M.Church	1983	Tylers Green	1984	Ministry
1970	Miss J.Capell	1968	1971	Rupert Ave	1974	Redhill
1972	Mrs.G.Marks	1971	1972	Marlow	1974	Beverley
1972	Mrs.B.Dennis		1980	Marlow	--->	
1972	Gerald Beddard	Harpenden	1986	Penn	--->	
1973	Jeremy Plummer		1976	The Greenway	1980	Uxbridge
1976	Geoffrey Beard		1978	Totteridge	--->	
1978	Peter Stevens	1978	1978	Tylers Green	--->	
1978	Dr.Chris.Sworn	1973	1979	Harlow Road	1984	Oakham
1979	Mrs.D.Plummer	1976	1979	The Greenway	1980	Uxbridge
1979	Stephen Piper	1978	1979	Baronsmead Rd	1986	C.of E.
1979	Greg.Hargrove	1977	1979	Booker Lane	1984	Pastures
1980	Colin Campbell	1973	1980	Green Hill	1987	*D
1980	Mrs.B.Sparks	1978	1980	Cryers Hill	--->	
1980	Mrs.P.Maidment	1972	1980	Hazlemere	1982	Nantwich
1980	A.Lindsay Kerr	Newcastle/T	1984	Marlow	--->	
1983	David Hunter	1981	1983	Cedar Court	--->	
1983	Jeffrey Orange	Streatham	1987	Holmer Green	--->	
1984	David Sparks	1981	1984	Cryers Hill	--->	
1984	Frederick Day	1981	1984	Deeds Grove	1985	Ministry
1984	Mrs.Briony Seymour (Barkes)	1983	1985	Marlow	1986	Pastures
1985	Jeffrey Smith	1984	1985	Marlow	--->	
1985	Miss S.Jones	1984	1985	Rye View	1985	Harrogate
1985	John Lloyd	1983	1985	Flackwell	1986	Ministry
1986	Mrs.L.Phipps	1983	1986	Rutland Ave	1987	Sunderl'd
1986	Michael Mason	1984	1987	Marlow Bottom	--->	
1987	Mrs.J.Widdess	1984	1987	The Brackens	--->	
1988	Peter Howarth	1978	1988	Mayhew Cres.	--->	

*   D = Deceased
    P = High Wycombe Primitive Methodist Circuit
    W = High Wycombe Wesleyan Circuit

PREACHERS "ON TRIAL" (T) & HELPERS(H) ONLY

FROM
1934	(T)	L.Goodway	W.Myers		
	(H)	W.Chandler	H.Brasier	A.Allen	F.Lee
1935	(H)	A.Thomas	G.Ginger	A.Filby	J.Rackstraw J.Ing
		V.Neville	E.Rose	J.Grace	F.Chilton A.Searle
		F.Slade			
1937	(T)	E.Bates	F.Rolls		
	(H)	E.Drinkwater			
1938	(T)	E.Pullen			
	(H)	H.Chapman	J.Geary	H.Mayo	M.Eke
1939	(H)	E.Judge			
1940	(T)	H.Neville	P.Howland		
1941	(H)	H.Silversides			
1942	(H)	J.Bird	A.Hawkins		
1943	(H)	A.Mayo			
1945	(H)	H.Judge			
1946	(T)	P.Stringer			
	(H)	F.Webster			
1947	(T)	D.Hawkins	R.Bridge		
	(H)	P.Cook	E.King		
1948	(T)	D.Gregory (Mrs.)			
	(H)	Lake (Mrs.)	Greenstreet (Mrs.)		
1949	(H)	C.Cole	W.Jones	G.Mott	
1950	(T)	P.Sims (Miss)			
	(H)	V.Rance	W.Durrant		
1951	(T)	A.Goodearl (Miss)			
	(H)	G.Judge	E.Chilton	J.Gomme	D.Wright D.Gregory(Mrs.)
1952	(T)	C.Chambers			
1953	(T)	J.Hazell			
	(H)	H.Saint	W.Haines		
1954	(T)	A.Chilton	M.Stubbs	W.Parsons (Mrs.)	
	(H)	E.Pullen			
1955	(T)	D.Barlow	M.Ludlow (Mrs.)		
1956	(T)	A.Bowler (Miss)			
1957	(T)	R.Palmer	W.Goddard	K.Lawrence	
	(H)	F.Horne	D.Jackson	N.Thorne	G.Lee
1958	(H)	J.Miller	D.Cross		
1959	(H)	J.Dean			
1960	(H)	W.Richards	F.Goffin (Sis.)		
1961	(T)	R.Bowler	D.Browning	B.Tabner (Miss)	J.Freeman(Miss)
		C.Pemble (Miss)			
	(H)	E.Harewood	H.Falconer	K.Pusey (Miss)	A.Cox (Mrs.)
1962	(T)	B.Cooke			
	(H)	D.Crewe	J.Ward	A.Freeman (Mrs.)	

1963	(T)	K.Pusey (Miss) S.Langley (Miss) J.Anderson (Miss)
	(H)	H.Parr
1964	(T)	L.Dean D.Rance P.Langston
1965	(T)	P.Fox (Miss) J.Rickard (Miss) J.Blackford (Miss)
1966	(T)	R.Clark (Miss) N.Parkinson
1967	(T)	F.Riddle
1974	(H)	H.Pettet (Mrs.)
1975	(T)	R.Slater (Miss)
1977	(T)	D.Hatt H.Graham (Mrs.)
1979	(H)	D.Hatt
1981	(T)	A.Chuck
1982	(T)	J.Bradshaw J.Baxter (Mrs.)
1983	(H)	M.Webb
1984	(T)	S.Gisbey (Miss)
	(H)	F.Rolls
1985	(T)	P.Howard
	(H)	A.Chuck
1986	(T)	G.Lewis T.Widdess K.Newton (Mrs.)
1987	(T)	A.Singleton (Mrs.) P.Fox (Dr.)
1988	(T)	B.Taylor (Mrs.)

TEN FACTS ABOUT PREACHERS

* (1) Those who remained as preachers in the High Wycombe Methodist Circuit which was formed in 1934, until their death, served (in this or earlier circuits) an average of 44 years from the time of their accreditation.

* (2) Preachers in the above category who served the longest time, were:

E.Dormer	69 years	(1892-1961)
W.Line	65 years	(1877-1942)
F.Hunt	65 years	(1885-1950)
W.A.Steevens	65 years	(1896-1961)

* (3) Preachers in the above category who served the shortest time, were:

Colin Campbell	7 years	(1980-1987)
R.Cleaver	10 years	(1956-1966)
V.Bunce	13 years	(1932-1945)

* (4) The average period served by preachers in the Circuit, is 12 years.

* (5) Preachers who served the longest time in the Circuit, (but no longer do so) are:

William Smith 51 years (1934-1985)
Fred Howard   49 years (1934-1983)
William Bates 47 years (1934-1981)
Miss M.Darvill 47 years (1935-1982)

* (6) The preacher who has served in the Circuit for the longest time and continues to serve, is Alan Goodearl: 49 years.

* (7) The preacher who has served another Circuit (Macclesfield) and this Circuit for the longest time, and continues to serve, is Stanley Sherratt: 58 years

* (8) Reasons for preachers ceasing to preach in the Circuit are:

Moved to another circuit	33%
Death	32%
Resigned	5%
Transferred to another Church in Wycombe	3%
Training for the Ministry	2%
Removed from plan	2%
Reason unknown	12%
(Continuing to preach at present time)	(11%)

* (9) The ratio of preachers in the Circuit (1934-1987) has been:

Males	80%
Females	20%

* (10) The ratio of preachers in the Circuit in 1988 is:

Males	74%
Females	26%

AMERSHAM CIRCUIT - CALENDAR

1951 Seven Churches hived off from the High Wycombe Circuit, to form the new Chesham and Chalfont St.Giles Circuit

1959 New Church at Little Chalfont

1960 Amersham Common Church replaced by new St.John's Church, Amersham

1962 Circuit renamed Amersham Circuit

THE METHODIST CHURCH

1966 New Church at Chesham to replace old building

1977 Chalfont St.Giles Methodist and United Reformed Churches joined together into Deanway United Church (Rev.Margaret Lawson, U.R.C. Minister, in charge)

1986 Lee Common Chapel refurbished for "retreat" purposes by Churches of all denominations, while being retained for Sunday Methodist worship

1951-1988 Seven Churches increased to eight; with membership doubled

CHURCHES & MEMBERSHIP

OPEN CHURCH	1951	1963	1975	1987
1839 Lee Common	21	15	7	9
1847 Chalfont St.Giles	69	50	48	85
1860 Winchmore Hill	23	27	18	14
1860 Amersham Common	70	(closed)		
1863 Prestwood	37	33	49	78
1897 Chesham	90	125	127	148
1899 Amersham (High Street)	27	27	19	15
1959 Little Chalfont		52	82	126
1960 Amersham (St.John's)		142	206	193
	----	----	----	----
TOTALS	337	471	556	668
	----	----	----	----

AN AMERSHAM PREACHER comments:

The success of the Amersham Circuit is partly due to its size which has been small enough for people of different churches to know one another's needs. There has been a considerable inflow of Christians from other areas who have

The Methodist Church
QUARTERLY PLAN & DIRECTORY
AMERSHAM CIRCUIT

17th NOVEMBER, 1963 — 9th FEBRUARY, 1964

MINISTERS

Rev. J. HENRY DODDRELL, 139 Woodside Road, Amersham. Tel. 504.
Rev. DAVID S. OWENS, 100 Bellingdon Road, Chesham. Tel. 8537.

* * *

Rev. LAWRANCE O. BROOKER, "Grindleford", Chenies Avenue, Little Chalfont. Tel. 3163.
Rev. ROBERT FLENLEY, Maple Cottage, High Street, Prestwood.

* * *

CIRCUIT STEWARDS

Mr. C. T. Horsefield, 73 Oakington Avenue, Little Chalfont. Tel. 2630.
Mr. E. Woodstock, 42 Chessbury Road, Chesham. Tel. 3435.

SECRETARIES

Quarterly Meeting: Mrs. D. Kingston, " Abri," Woodside Road, Amersham. (1221).
Local Preachers: Dr. D. C. Blackley, 100 Berkeley Avenue, Chesham. (298).
Overseas Missions: Rev. J. H. Doddrell and Mrs. R. Fiddes, Raincliffe, Church Grove, Little Chalfont. (L.C. 2640).
Circuit Trusts: Mr. T. Scott, 126 Broad Street, Chesham. (8251).
Women's Work: Mrs. J. Jackson, Briarfield, Brays Close, Hyde Heath (Chesham 3999).
J.M.A.: Mrs. P. G. Stratfull, Wesley House, Mill Lane, Amersham.
Home Missions: Rev. D. S. Owens.
　　Miss E. N. Smith (Treasurer), Homeland, Stanley Hill, Amersham.
Youth Dept.: Rev. David S. Owens.
　　Miss E. Smith, " Englefield," Chequers Hill, Amersham.
Christian Citizenship: Rev. J. H. Doddrell.
　　Mrs. R. Shaw, 32 Piggotts Orchard, Amersham.
　　Mr. G. L. Dixon, "Kaycee", 10 West View, Chesham. (3973).
Education Secretary: Mr. D. S. Carr, 28 Glenister Road, Chesham. (615).
Women's Fellowship: Mrs. J. M. Gunnell, Merdeka, Beechwood Avenue, Little Chalfont (2596).
Church Membership: Dr. D. C. Blackley, 100 Berkeley Avenue, Chesham. (298).

TREASURERS

Overseas Missions: Mr. J. Jackson, Briarfied, Brays Close, Hyde Heath. (Chesham 3999)
General Chapel Fund: Mr. T. Scott, 126 Broad Street, Chesham. (8251).
Youth Dept.: Mr. H. G. Montey, 52 Oakington Avenue, Little Chalfont. (L.C. 2836).
Ministerial Training: Mr. G. Cook, "Westings", 45 Green Lane, Amersham. (2968).
London Mission and Extension Fund: Mr. J. Rutter, 26 Beechwood Close, Little Chalfont. (L.C. 2835).
Methodist Homes for the Aged: Mrs. D. Kingston, " Abri," Woodside Road, Amersham. (1221).
Minister's Retirement Funds: W/Cmdr. J. Jewell, 10 St. Leonard's Road, Chesham Bois. (A.M. 2065).
Women's Work: Mrs. H. G. Montey, 52 Oakington Avenue, Little Chalfont (L.C. 2836).
L.P.M.A.: Mr. C. A Cole, 11 Lexham Gardens, Amersham (350).
W.F. Treasurer: Mrs. B. Palmer, 17 Victoria Road, Chesham.
Local Preachers' Dept.: Mr. W. E. Garlick, " The Croft ", Bellingdon Road, Chesham. (8493).

THE METHODIST CHURCH

AMERSHAM
HIGH STREET

LEE
COMMON

WINCHMORE
HILL

brought fresh ideas and their own talents. The Circuit has been blessed with vigorous leadership. Many Ministers could be mentioned, including Tony Bullock who did wonders at Prestwood; Leslie Henry who cheered on the Amersham Common/St.John's folk ("they'll come!"); Wallace Heaton who inspired the Little Chalfont project; and Guy Stanford who had great charisma and a motor-bike nicknamed "Dorcas" ("full of good works!"). Above all there has been a dependence on the Holy Spirit for the necessary vision.

AMERSHAM METHODIST CIRCUIT: MINISTERS

1951-56	Wallace Heaton	1951-55	Thomas Welch
1955-59	Gordon Poole	1956-61	Leslie Henry
1959-65	David S.Owens	1961-62	A.Kingsley-Turner
1962-67	J.Henry Doddrell	1965-71	Alan Stafford
1967-71	Herbert W.Carlisle	1971-79	J.Wallace C.Jenkins
1971-78	Tony Bullock	1977-->	Margaret Lawson (URC)
1978-84	Marjorie Hopp	1979-86	P.Guy Stanford
1984-86	Michael Sheard	1986-->	F.Barrie Heafford
1986-->	James E.Cooper		

AMERSHAM METHODIST CIRCUIT: PREACHERS

DATE.	NAME	ADDRESS
1889	G.Rance	Chalfont St.Giles
1901	Reginald Nancarrow	Amersham
1907	A.Randall	The Lee
1907	P.Hall	Amersham
1909	W.E.Garlick	Amersham
1912	T.H.Weatherill	Chesham/Chalfont St.Giles
1914	F.Randall	Ballinger/Lee Common
1916	J.Wilson	Tylers Green
1921	C.A.Cole	Amersham
1922	Major A.E.Dennis	Amersham Common
1928	Miss W.M.Bryant	Amersham
1932	F.Neville	Chalfont St.Giles
1932	Miss F.Dyer	Chesham
1934	Miss Helen M.Smith	Amersham
1935	W.P.Baker	Chesham

THE METHODIST CHURCH

DATE.	NAME	ADDRESS
1936	L. Paul Cleminson	Lee Common
1939	G. D. I. Hayton	Little Chalfont
1944	Mrs. G. P. Stratfull	Amersham
1945	Miss J. Gayler	Amersham
1945	Miss B. Owen	South Heath
1948	Mrs. J. W. C. Jenkins	Amersham
1948	E. King	Little Chalfont
1948	W. J. Stephens	Prestwood
1949	Dr. G. A. Rose	Great Kingshill
1949	Dr. F. J. Long	Beaconsfield
1949	Mrs. W. M. Doddrell	Amersham
1949	M. A. Cleaver	Pinner
1953	Mrs. Gwen Taylor-Jones	Chalfont St. Giles
1953	Dr. D. C. Blackley	Chesham
1953	F. G. Reeves	South Heath
1953	E. Cliffe	Chesham Bois
1956	J. Stirling	Amersham
1957	Miss J. M. Anderson	Holmer Green/Great Missenden
1958	William Presley	Amersham
1960	G. L. Dixon	Chesham
1960	S. T. Cato	Jordans
1960	I. Parry	Chesham
1961	K. Eckstein	Beaconsfield
1962	Mrs. M. Spoone	Amersham/Chalfont St. Giles
1962	J. R. Poston	Chesham
1962	R. Daykin	Prestwood
1962	B. J. Mifflin	Chesham Bois
1962	J. K. Jackson	Chesham
1963	Mrs. M. Chalkley	Little Chalfont
1965	Mrs. R. Truscott	Chesham
1966	D. Vinton	Amersham
1966	G. Mills	Chesham
1966	M. Campion	Amersham
1966	Miss J. E. Anderson	Holmer Green/Great Missenden
1966	J. Yunnie	Amersham
1966	Mrs. M. Brice	Chesham
1966	D. Brice	Chesham
1966	Major P. L. Hills	Beaconsfield
1967	E. Leigh	Chesham
1967	David Rigby	Chalfont St. Giles
1968	Miss C. Hesslegrave	Chalfont St. Peter
1971	P. Muff	Chesham
1972	C. T. Horsefield	Little Chalfont
1973	Mrs. J. P. Martin	Lee Common
1974	Mrs. J. Jackson	Hyde Heath

DATE.	NAME	ADDRESS
1974	Dr.Alan Callow	Prestwood
1977	Mrs.C.White	Chesham
1977	Mrs.J.Lambert	Amersham
1978	M.Gunnell	Little Chalfont
1978	Mrs.M.Callow	Prestwood
1985	Martin Wellings	Chalfont St.Giles

† † † † † † *TODAY'S THOUGHTS FROM WESLEY'S SERMONS* † † † † † † †

* An angel is anyone who does the whole will of God.

* Fasting must affect one's soul as well as one's body.

* A man must provide life's necessities for his family.

* Care for the future is no excuse for neglecting today.

* Don't dwell on your neighbour's faults; attend to yours.

* Give God no rest until you awake one day in His likeness.

* Wait on God in prayer and then do the best you can.

* Learn to "hang naked" on the Cross of Christ.

* A good Christian will try to be a good citizen.

* The doctor must first convince the patient he is sick.

CHAPTER 10

METHODIST CHURCHES

(**Note**: Churches which existed before 1934 are listed in earlier chapters on Wesleyan, Primitive or United Methodist Churches.)

MARLOW BOTTOM (1936)

THE FIRST METHODIST CHURCH

Marlow Bottom was the first Methodist (as opposed to ex-Wesleyan or ex-Primitive) Church to join the High Wycombe Circuit. Built without outside assistance, it was for some time administered jointly with Marlow Methodist Church. In its early days few of those who attended - and who had mostly come from non-Methodist churches - were willing to become members or take ordered responsibility. The Church has always been of an independent nature and delights in hearty and informal worship, disliking the more formal features of organised Methodism. Although it has one of the smallest chapels, the morning congregation is large and includes a good number of children. Despite choosing most of its preachers until recently, in latter years it has used its own leaders to conduct the first part of the morning service. One Minister found it more difficult than most to cope with this "chapel in the valley".

Rev. Leonard Jones was Minister of Marlow (70 members), Flackwell Heath (55), Booker (17). Wooburn Green (16) and Bourne End (30) in addition to Marlow Bottom (10) in 1963 when he suffered a breakdown in health. In November he told the Circuit that with his return to reasonably good health he was ready to take all his former duties on again - except Marlow Bottom (which at this time was leading a vigorous campaign against the establishment of a public house in the village). Some thought the best solution might be to close the Church as a Methodist cause and rent the premises back to the congregation as an undenominational mission. In fact Marlow Bottom remained in the Circuit under the pastoral charge of the dynamic Rev. Edward W. Crew (who was already coping with 266 members at St. Mark's,

Holmer Green, Naphill, Lacey Green, Tylers Green and Terriers).
Mr.Jones resumed responsibility for one quarter in 1965 before
the arrival of Rev.Haldane R.Adams.   They and other Ministers
have come and gone; Marlow Bottom remains - a delight to many, a
challenge to all!

S. SHERRATT. 1985.   MARLOW BOTTOM

MIKE GILBERT writes:

From its earliest days Marlow Bottom Chapel has seen its
main task as bringing the good news of Jesus Christ to the
neighbourhood.   In this long valley there were once four farms,
two of which still exist.   Land on the others was sold off for
individual housing development in the late 1920's - at £1 per
foot of frontage.   The resulting "do-it-yourself" buildings
caused the disapproving Marlow townsfolk to nickname the valley
"Tintown"!   In the autumn of 1932 Billy Hunt, a baker's
roundsman who had noticed all the youngsters running about in
the valley, stood up in the morning service at Marlow Methodist
Church, to ask if others would join him that afternoon in
holding an open-air Sunday School at Marlow Bottom.   Among those
who responded to the call was Wilfred Osborne, a printer from
East Anglia who had recently secured employment with the "Bucks
Free Press".   It was a work Wilf was to continue faithfully for
the next 45 years.   As winter drew on someone's front room had
to be used, but numbers were too great and a disused shed by the

side of a chalkpit was utilised. Later Mr. van Petegem, an East London school teacher who came to the valley at weekends, provided a site for a chapel. The High Wycombe Methodist Circuit was unable to support the project because it was already committed to developing a new church at Castlefield. Undeterred, Osborne and Petegem used their own labour and what help they could gather from the valley residents.

In November 1936 the new chapel was opened and remained little changed for the next 33 years. One service was held each Sunday evening with the Sunday School using the chapel in the afternoon. Wilf became the "father of the chapel" (union secretary) at his work but he was the "father of our chapel" too! Through the war years he kept things going almost single-handed - with his wife, Marjorie, at the harmonium. He pedalled all around the area on his bicycle to preach in other churches too. The chapel became part of the Wycombe Circuit officially in 1959. The sum of £250 was paid for the land and building. At first a rental of 5s. [25p.] per week was charged but this was later waived and the premises were now on free loan. Mr. Petegem used his share of the money to help start new churches in other places. The first Minister was Rev. Leonard Jones, followed by Rev. Haldane Adams, Rev. Harold Ward, Rev. Alan Baxter and Rev. Mark Booth. Keith Lewis who had moved to Marlow in 1951, often visited the chapel as a preacher and became a trustee. He and his wife, Doreen, transferred their membership from Marlow in 1970. I myself became treasurer in 1962 and recall that the total income for the first year came to only £100. The work among young people started to grow again with the population expansion and new families came in to help. A porch was added in 1970 and a new hall was built in 1973. The link-block of kitchen and toilets erected in 1974 was followed by the extension and refurbishment of the church in 1975. Morning services now commenced. The first Holiday Club was held in 1976 and these days attracts about 100 children. The preacher now sits in a vestry before the service instead of in a busy corridor!

The 50-year history of our chapel has spanned the life of Marlow Bottom as a growing community. Our membership in the last decade has tripled to 45 with 35 children in the Sunday School. Many others come to the Mother and Toddler Group, Sunshine Corner, Monday Gang, Turning Teens, Bible classes, After Eight Fellowship, morning and evening study groups, the Women's Meeting and the Saturday and midweek prayer meetings. Counselling those in trouble - sometimes using our links with the Marlow Pastoral Foundation - and general caring work are a strong feature. Many people are involved but more remain to be reached with the message which has always been our motto, "Jesus Christ is Lord!" 1961 saw the opening of St. Mary's Church with whom we have close ties, as together we try to extend the Christian witness in this valley. We thank God for the past, praise Him for present blessings and trust Him for the future. May the seed which has been sown, muliply a hundredfold!

CASTLEFIELD (1953)

SONG OF DELIGHT

Written by a preacher on waking up early one Sunday morning and remembering he was planned at Castlefield.
Tune: "Marching through Georgia".

C ome into the morning light
A t Castlefield so fair!
S hare the happy fellowship
T hat strengthens us with prayer.
L eave your cares and fears behind –
E nough that God is here! –
F or we are going up higher!
I n Jesus Christ
E njoyment there will be!
L ook up, look round –
D elightful sanctuary!

M ay the open vestibule
E ncourage passers-by;
T urn them from earth into ....
H EAVEN!

HILDERIC GOODEARL writes:

Castlefield Methodist Church was started by a group of devoted people who had a great faith in God. They were helped by the closure of other High Wycombe Churches (White Hart Street, Newland, Westbourne Street, Victoria Street and Sands) from which members were transferred. House groups began in 1939 under the leadership of Sister Sadie Martin, an American. Taking an active part were Mrs. Dean, Mr. and Mrs. Meeks,

Mrs. North, Mr. Carter, Mr. and Mrs. Warren, Mr. and Mrs. H. Campbell and many others. At the outbreak of the Second World War Sister Sadie had to leave (under defence regulations) and Mr. and Mrs. F. Hughes arrived. Sister Elsie Kitchener formed a Men's and Women's Fellowship which met in members' homes. Guides, Brownies, Scouts, Cubs and a Sunday School were also started. Sunday services - and later the Women's Fellowship - were held in the day school. Helpers from other churches included: Mr. E. E. Soons (the first Sunday School superintendent), Mr. L. Goodchild, Miss Margaret Darvill, Miss Haddow, Mr. D. S. Howard, Mr. A. Goodearl, Miss Connie Bunce and Mr. Hudson. During Sister Jessie Brine's ministry Sunday collections were averaging 13/6d. [67½p.] and the quarterly assessment was £2. Sister Eva Lyth worked very hard for a church hall to be built on land in Rutland Avenue given by Messrs. H. T. Turnbull and A. White.

During the stay of our first Minister, Rev. E. G. Kitchin (1950-55), the stonelaying for the church hall took place. At a thanksgiving service on 11th April 1953 the speakers were Rev. Robinson Whittaker (London Mission) and Rev. L. O. Brooker (District Chairman) and the chairman was Mr. H. Wingrove. The first society stewards were Mr. F. Hughes, Mrs. N. Dean and Mrs. M. North and in 1954 Mr. H. C. Goodearl became chapel steward and treasurer. The official opening on 5th September 1953 was performed by Owen Haines and the dedication service was conducted by Rev. Kingsley A. Turner (District Chairman). The morning service on 6th September was preceded by a procession of

witness from the day school and both services that day were
conducted by Rev.E.C.Urwin. Rev.P.H.Foster (1955-60) was able
to move to a new manse in Rutland Avenue. During the ministry
of Rev.Alan Cox (1960-65) it became evident that the hall was
not large enough to cope with the increasing number of
activities, so plans for a church to be built on the adjoining
ground were drawn up. Our next Minister was Rev.Marcus
A.Pattern (1965-70). On 11th December 1965 the stonelaying
ceremony for the new church was held, 25 stones being laid -
one for each complete year of witness in Castlefield. The
estimated cost of the building was £19,000. The opening and
dedication took place on 10th September 1966 when a plaque was
unveiled by Paul Bartlett Lang and a ceremony conducted by
Rev.Edward Rogers. A hymn was composed for the occasion and
sung to the tune "Castlefield":

> "The One Who names each star
> And spins the planets round,
> Is God, the Lover of each soul,
> The Father of mankind.
> The God Who made the heavens
> And earth with day and night;
> 'Tis He Who seeks the straying lamb
> And heals the broken heart.

> "For Love came here to dwell
> And in a manger lie;
> Love suffered in the garden dark
> And on the cross did die.
> But Love, strong unto death,
> Was mightier than the grave;
> Christ lives - His Spirit still we have,
> Almighty, strong to save!

> "Such love let all repeat -
> It knows no bound nor end;
> For God has shown Himself to be
> Our Everlasting Friend.
> This God let us adore;
> Our hearts to Him we give;
> In humble self-subjection serve
> And take Christ's power - and live!"

The new church was packed to capacity that Christmas when
over 300 people attended the first candlelight service. Carols
were sung by the Junior and Senior Choirs, conducted by Ivan
Goodearl and Peter Gibbons. Morning family services were also

well attended with the children taking an active part. But in 1969 the Sunday School began to spend less time in church. Rev. Norman Burrows (1970-75) arranged a mission to the Castlefield area with help from students at London Bible College. The area was canvassed by people working in pairs, and a charismatic influence began to be felt in the Church. During the ministry of Rev. Douglas Graham (1975-80) the car park was built and enclosed by a wall and garden. So at last the buildings were complete. Our most recent Minister was Rev. Keith Phipps (1980-87) who came straight from college. We shared three happy occasions with him - his marriage to Lynda and the births of David and Rebecca. Under his pastoral care the Church progressed. The vestibule and lounge were carpeted and new heating was installed in the church and ancillary rooms. The Women's Fellowship which has always been an influence in the life of the Church, suffered a great loss in the death of its leader, Mrs. Dorothy Hughes. Castlefield has been greatly blessed by its Ministers (including our present Minister, Rev. Michael Edwards) and the laity who by their witness and pastoral concern - and not least, the preaching of God's Word - have led us over nearly half a century. Thanks be to God!

LITTLE CHALFONT (1959)

KATHLEEN MONTEY writes:

In 1952 a small group of people, living in Little Chalfont and attending the old Woodside Road Methodist Chapel in Amersham, met in the home of Mr. and Mrs. Eric King, to discuss the commencement of a Sunday School in the new village hall. As a result leaflets were distributed and on the first Sunday afternoon in October 1952 16 children attended. A month later an evening service was started. Within a year the Sunday School had outgrown the village hall and a works' canteen was hired to accommodate the younger children. The time was also changed to mornings which increased the attendance further. Youth activities were held one evening a week; Women's Fellowship and other meetings were held in people's homes. The need for a church was very evident and huge fetes, which became quite a feature of village life, were organised to raise money.

In 1954 a plot of land in Chalfont Avenue was purchased for £862. The foundation stone of the new church was laid on 22nd November 1958 when Rev. F. Leslie Henry, the Superintendent Minister, conducted the ceremony. Ten of the original 12 people

who had formed the Church six years previously were present,
including Mr. and Mrs.F.King who had come from Wolverhampton. A
group of people had raised £1000 and an anonymous donor had
given another £1000.   The London Mission Committee had
contributed £10,000. On 2nd May 1959 the first stage of the new
building was opened by Mrs.Dennis, wife of Major A.E.Dennis, a
steward of the society, who received the key from the architect
of the building, Mr.Alick.   Also present was Mr.Stanley Comben
of Comben and Wakeling, the builders. The opening was in July
1959.   It was a dual purpose building with a sanctuary at one
end and a stage at the other. The sanctuary could be screened
off with sliding panels and the seating reversed for concerts
and plays. A classroom, vestry, kitchen and toilets were also
included.   It was soon apparent that the classroom was
inadequate and within two years it had been doubled in size.
The Church suffered a great loss in 1964 in the death of Mrs.
Doris Brooker whose "loving, radiant spirit," wrote Rev.David
S.Owens, "remains an inspiration to us all".

      As Little Chalfont grew, new families were visited by
members and students from Richmond College.   The adult
membership grew slowly, while many people of other denominations
attended services, as there were few other churches in the
locality. A Christian Stewardship campaign was organised in
1967; a Men's Fellowship Meeting was started in 1972, to

encourage links among men and provide service for the community; and in 1974 more house groups were formed. The Sunday School grew rapidly and by 1970 numbered 120 children. In 1976 a large hall was built at the rear of the church and named "Newstead Hall" in memory of George and Ethel Newstead. This enabled the Sunday School, now the Junior Church, to hold their service simultaneously with morning worship. Rev. Wallace Jenkins wrote at the time: "What a joy to see the lovely Newstead Hall opened on 24th January and to have the church itself refurbished with 90 fine chairs! And to have most of the debt on the £30,000 scheme cleared off! We pay tribute to Mr. and Mrs. D. Colville and Mr. David Gane for their time, skill and care in guiding the project through. The local doctor has come out of retirement to provide a limited medical service to the area by using two of our rooms for a surgery and waiting-room."

By 1978 Church membership had reached 133 and more seating was required. A bequest from Miss Eleanor Hill enabled the stage to be removed, new seats for the whole church purchased and a covered link-way built between the church and Newstead Hall. The central heating system was modernised and a new boiler room incorporated in the link-way. The next improvement was the installation of a splendid pipe organ, specially designed for the church and this, together with the rearrangement of the sanctuary, has greatly enhanced the building and its worship. The premises at present are used by: the Junior Church; Youth Fellowship; Rangers, Guides and Brownies; Women's Fellowship; Monday Club; Men's Social Club; Wesley Guild; ecumenical fellowship meetings; choir practice; nursery school; baby clinics; committees; circuit rallies; bazaars and fetes. In 1987 the membership - after a number of deaths - stood at 126 with an average attendance of 60 in the Junior Church.

A VISIT TO THE GUILD

We wanted to learn more about the Church we knew least, and fortunately chose the Wednesday on which the Guild met. The Minister, Rev. F. Barrie Heafford, spoke about the faith of Moses' parents. There were 30 present and future meetings would include talks about hospital chaplaincy, the work of a magistrate and the Thames towpath. A working day was to be held the following Saturday. Nearly everyone spoke to us. The senior steward, Cyril Vincent, showed us round the workmanlike Newstead Hall and the delightfully simple church which we were rebuked for calling "the chapel"! The Church works closely with St. George's Church and was currently sharing a series on loneliness, suffering, ageing, marriage and separation, parents and children and adolescence. The notice-board was appealing for help with a parcel to Poland.

Our brief visit gave us a strong impression of a working Christian fellowship, very much looking outward and forward. This church in the Amersham Circuit with an underground railway station "next door" seemed a far cry from many of the village causes mentioned elsewhere in this book. But as we drove away in the late autumn drizzle, we praised God for all our brothers and sisters in Christ – Church or chapel!

ST. MARK'S (1959)

J.SHERANT 1987 — ST.MARK.

THE FORECAST (1955)

The new church in Totteridge Road, High Wycombe, to be known as St. Mark's, will seat about 250 people and be equipped with classrooms and other useful facilities, including a large hall. Another useful innovation will be a spacious car park situated at the rear of the building. "BUCKS FREE PRESS"

THE STONELAYING (1958)

On 15th November the first stone was laid on behalf of the society by Councillor L. Brain (Mayor of High Wycombe). The estimated cost is £28,000 of which £25,000 is coming as a grant from Methodist Connexional funds. The ceremony which raised £1500 towards the balance outstanding, was conducted by Rev. Arthur H. Freeman, the

Minister, in the presence of John Hall M.P. and Rev.L.O.Brooker (Chairman of London North-West District). A tea followed at Wesley Methodist Church where the evening meeting was conducted by Mr.E.Gomme. Items were sung by the Circuit Choir.

"BUCKS FREE PRESS"

THE OPENING (1959)

The new church was opened on 24th October by Councillor W.O.Haines (Mayor of High Wycombe). The service of dedication was conducted by Dr.Eric W.Baker, President of the Methodist Conference, and the lesson was read by Rev.Arthur H.Freeman, the Minister. Greetings were brought by John Hall M.P., Rev.A.L.Evan Hopkins (Vicar of High Wycombe), Rev.Douglas Watt (President of the Free Church Federal Council) and Keith Hawke (President of Wycombe and District Council of Churches). Rev.G.Eric Firth, the Superintendent Minister, was also present.

"BUCKS FREE PRESS"

MYRTLE CHURCH writes:

The opening in Totteridge Road, High Wycombe, of St.Mark's (formed from the closure of the Slater Street and London Road Churches) brought a message of hope to the large Bowerdean area.

The building cost £28,000 and could seat 250 in the main hall which was dual-purpose with a sanctuary at one end and one of the largest stages in Wycombe at that time at the other. Rev. Arthur Freeman and his wife worked hard, drawing together the members who had been transferred, and also attracting many newcomers. Their loving ministry prepared the way for the energetic Rev. Eddie Crew who came to St. Mark's in 1962 with his wife Freda and their three sons. Eddie was tireless in his efforts to bring people into the Church, which at that time had a flourishing youth club, Inters-Guild, Young Wives' Group, Women's Meeting and Men's Fellowship. The Sunday School had over 150 children on roll. Church Birthdays were great occasions. Many will remember shows like "Mark 10", "Showboat" and "London Pride" which were inspired by Hazel Clark, assisted by Beryl Barnes, Margaret Sutcliffe and many others. The smiling face of Brian Williams was a typical feature of this era. When he died suddenly at the age of 20 in 1966, there was great sadness and bewilderment. The same year Eddie resigned from the ministry because of ill health. He died in 1977 at the age of 46. He will always be remembered with great affection as a true servant of God who "preached to us JESUS". The exchange visit of Rev. Edgar Hammersla also took place in 1966. He came from Maryland, U.S.A. Ed and his wife, Lib, were a delightful couple and although they were with us for only six weeks, friendships formed then have been maintained to the present day. They have had many St. Mark's people to stay with them, including my own son, Brian.

Rev. Denis Reed and his wife, Dorothy, came in November 1966 straight from Burma where they were the last European missionaries. They had few possessions and it was very difficult for them to settle in England. But they gave us an ecumenical vision and we came to appreciate their worth and dedication to their Lord. They left St. Mark's in 1970. Difficult years followed but Rev. Francis Watts will be remembered for his friendliness. He and his wife, Mildred, were very musical, she conducting the choir and he singing songs, especially from "Sound of Music". Probably Frank's most difficult task was conducting the funeral of one of the "pillars" of the Church, Alderman Harry Fry, whose special talent for welcoming people is commemorated by the plaque of hands on the vestibule wall. Frank left in 1976 and his successor was the first woman Minister in the Wycombe Circuit. Rev. Ruth Orton will be especially remembered by the elderly and housebound whom she visited regularly. She gave loyal service to St. Mark's and I owe my own more active role in Church work to her encouragement.

ALDERMAN HARRY FRY

Servant of God - Leader of Men - Friend of ALL
who extended the hand of friendship to all who
entered here.

ST MARKS.   S.J HERRATT 1987

When Rev. Roy Jackson arrived in 1981, straight from Wesley House, Cambridge, he brought new ideas and infectious enthusiasm. The Ordinands' Testimony Service (for himself and Rev. Mark Booth from the Marlow Section) took place at St. Mark's in 1983. Holidays in Bridport, outings in the minibus (which has proved a boon in bringing elderly people to Sunday services and the Women's Meeting), concerts of modern Christian music for young people and challenging sermons have brought a new spirit to St. Mark's. Despite the deaths of many stalwarts like Mrs. Evelyn Bunce, Ernie Chilton and Mrs. Lena White, the church from its hilly position still sends out the message of the illuminated red cross over the Bowerdean valley. High Wycombe probably knows our church best for the Gilbert and Sullivan operettas which the Savoy Opera Company performs to several full houses in the autumn. (When their Patrons, the Prime Minister

Harold Wilson, and his wife Mary, visited them it caused huge
security problems.) But Roy has shown us our main task, that
filled with God's love, we should carry out Jesus' command to
"go into all the world and teach all nations", remembering His
promise, "I am with you always, even to the end of the world".
Perhaps the day may come when we shall be able to leave the
small chapel where most services are now held, and return to the
big hall.......

SOME HIGHLIGHTS

8-11-1959 First baptism (Carol Freeman)

1962-1965 Packed morning services; largest Sunday School in High
Wycombe

1966   Civic Service, conducted by Rev. Eddie Crew, Mayor's
Chaplain. Exchange visit of Rev. Edgar Hammersla of
Washington, U.S.A.

1969   10th Birthday. "Mark 10" Musical Revue

1972   Circuit Sports won by Sunday School - "Batting Cup"

1975   Youth Club at M.A.Y.C. Rally (Albert Hall): "Story of
Albert Green"

1976   "Evening in Old Vienna"; 18th Birthday: "Come
Dancing"; visits to Westminster Theatre: "Ride!
Ride!" (musical)

1979   David Watson's "Mission to Wycombe"

1982   Coach to Aldersgate Street - open-air service
(Rev. John Newton); visit of "New Beginnings"
(mission to High Wycombe schools)

1983   "Everyday Christianity" (David Mitchell)

1984   "Mission England": Billy Graham (Bristol); Luis
Palau (Queens Park Rangers)

1985   Concerts by Paul Field, Garth Hewitt and Adrian Snell

1986   Sermon on the Mount: a spiritual "blitz"!

1987   28th Birthday: "The Land of Faraway" (pantomime)

THE FUTURE

Our Church has much to offer but how can we really get it going? The lady at Lyndale Products had the answer. We didn't know which sort of floor polish we wanted, and she advised us: "Have the 'Vision'!"

AMERSHAM - ST.JOHN'S (1960)

HELEN SMITH writes:

From the London Blitz in 1940 came new people to the old chapel at Amersham Common. They had a dream that one day there would be a large new church up the road, standing in the centre of the Amersham-to-be. And so it was that Cecil Cole, driven out of London by the German bombers, put down a deposit and secured the land in Woodside Road, Amersham-on-the-Hill. The foundation stone was laid in 1959 and a fine new church opened in 1960. What had been destroyed in St.John's Square, Clerkenwell, was resurrected as St.John's, Amersham.

"BUCKS EXAMINER"

St.John's was developed in two stages with the first turf being cut by Mr.Percy Hall, one of the trustees of the Amersham Church, on 6th April 1959. The church hall was scheduled as the first stage of the £41,800 project and this was formally opened by Mrs.C.A.Cole, wife of the circuit steward, on 10th October 1959, the architect Mr.Alistair McDonald presenting her with the key. On the same day Rev.L.O.Brooker, Chairman of the London North-Western District of the Methodist Church, launched the second stage of the project when he laid the foundation stone of the church. St.John's was formally opened on 2nd April 1960 by Mrs.S.A.Comben, wife of the builder of the complex. Again the architect was on hand to present the key at the ceremony. The church is of strikingly modern design and has seating for 250 worshippers, while the hall can accommodate around 300. Amongst the other accommodation are vestries for the Minister, stewards and choir, a primary room, a church parlour, cloakrooms and a kitchen. Most of the money for the project came from outside donations, and it was a proud moment for the trustees of the Church in the Amersham Circuit when they were able to announce in December 1963, that the outstanding debt on the building had been cleared.

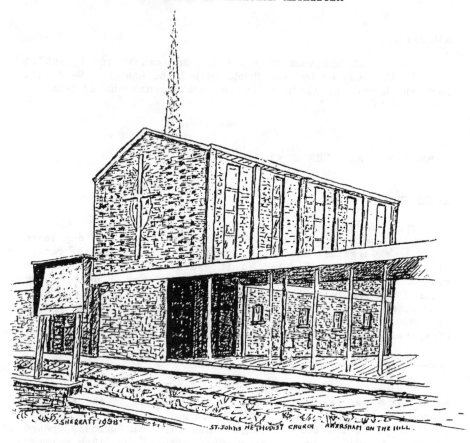

ST.Johns METHODIST CHURCH AMERSHAM ON THE HILL.

SOME EVENTS

1962   Spring Campaign (Richmond Students)

1967   "People Next Door" Campaign
        "Doctrine of the Spirit"   (Rev. Dr. John H. Chamberlayne)
        - "Circuit support disappointing"

1972   Spring Stewardship Campaign

1973   Regular services and visitation   at old   people's
        home;   car rota to take mothers to clinic;   monthly
        coffee mornings bringing more than 30 people into
        fuller fellowship; "fine congregations and worship
        enriched by growing choir" (Circuit plan)

1974   "When someone has reached the landmark of 40 years as an accredited local preacher, it is a cause for celebration. This special honour has come to Miss Helen Smith and the whole Circuit joins to thank and congratulate her for the years of sterling service as a 'servant of the Word'". (Rev. Wallace Jenkins)

1975   Eight house groups formed during Lent bringing more than 100 people together to share in the study of Christ's life

1977   Pageant of the Passion presented on Good Friday in the forecourt of Anglican church in main shopping-street

HELEN SMITH concludes:

The years have rushed by and we are long past our coming-of-age. We have seen our membership rise from around 40 at the foot of Woodside Road to nearly 200 at the top. St. John's overflows with young people and we are striving to build them a new youth hall at a cost of £54,000. Our thermometer of contributions will need to stretch out into the road! The full story is yet to be told. But the text in the old chapel remains true for the new: "The love of Christ constraineth us".

DEEDS GROVE (1963)

PREPARATION (1956)

A campaign - "This we Believe" - is being organised in High Wycombe during August 1956 in connection with the new site for a Methodist church in Desborough Avenue. In October an exhibition will be mounted in the Guildhall, entitled "This is Methodism". It is hoped to visit 3000 houses. The campaign is being run by Revs. Ernest W. Odell and Leslie J. M. Timmins (London) and Revs. G. Eric Firth, P. H. Foster and K. W. Curtis (High Wycombe).

                                     "BUCKS FREE PRESS"

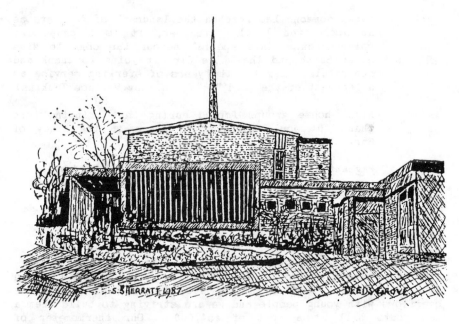

ERNIE PULLEN writes:

Like "a city set on a hill which cannot be hid", Deeds Grove is one of our most striking churches. It was designed to take advantage of the steeply sloping site and has a tall slender spire of light steel and copper sheet. Its members have one of three origins. Some - like myself - came from Westbourne Street which closed on 27th August 1961, a week before the first service at Deeds Grove. Others joined us from Victoria Street which closed on 1st June 1975. The rest are the "new" folk - from the nearby large housing estates or other churches. From that time the various elements have gradually merged into a single unit with the sole aim of serving God and the community. Apart from Sunday services we have a large Sunday School and cater for the Women's Fellowship, playgroup. toddlers' groups, youth activities, clinics and many other groups and meetings.

Services at first were held in a large wooden hut because of delays in building the new church. The members brought paraffin lamps and heaters from their homes. The stone-laying ceremony eventually took place on 26th May 1962 and the official opening was on Saturday 29th June 1963 when Mrs. Nancy Hall, wife of the local M.P., was given the silver key to open the door. A Dedicatory Service at 3.30 p.m. was conducted by Rev. L.O. Brooker

and the sermon was preached by Rev.D.Lee (of Worcester). A
Thanksgiving Service followed at 6.30 p.m., conducted by Dr.Paul
Binks with a sermon by Rev.Donald Lee. The following day a
procession was led by our Minister, Rev.A.E.Glendower Jones,
from Westbourne Street to Deeds Grove where the service was
conducted by Rev.Thomas Earis, a former member of the old
chapel. So we had moved from a town chapel in a clearance area
to an imposing church on a hillside. Sadly one of the first
services was the funeral of Mr.Stephen H.Goodearl on 1st July
1963. He had been a preacher "on full plan" for 55 years. On
9th September 1978 the Sunday School extension was dedicated by
Rev.R.L.Jack Kaye, Chairman of the District, assisted by
Rev.Harold Slater, the Superintendent Minister, and Rev.Douglas
Graham, our own Minister.

DEDICATION OF EXTENSION (1978)

We dedicate this building

To the glory of God the Father Who has called us by His grace,
And of His Son Who loved us and gave Himself for us,
And of the Holy Spirit Who illuminates and sanctifies us.

For the worship of God in prayer and praise,
For the teaching of the Everlasting Gospel,
For the teaching of Christian truths and values.
For the hallowing of family life,
For teaching and guiding the young,
For the provision of healthy recreation.

For the conversion of sinners,
For the promotion of righteousness,
For the extension of the Kingdom of God.
For the unity of the Faith
In the bonds of Christian fellowship
In love and goodwill to all.

In gratitude for the labours of all who have served Jesus,
In loving remembrance of those who have finished their course,
In the hope of a blessed immortality through Jesus Christ our
Lord -

We dedicate this building

POSTSCRIPT (1988): Ernie Pullen has now removed to Cornwall.
The other 'keepers' are maintaining this "lighthouse".

TYLERS GREEN - COPPICE FARM ROAD (1968)

MARION HOWARTH writes:

The land for this newest church in the High Wycombe Circuit
was given by Stanley A.Comben of Comben and Wakeling who built
Deer Park Estate. It was originally part of a larger piece of
land but some was sold for houses. The car park was added to
the original plot so that access could be made to Chilton
Close. The church was built by W.L.Harrison Ltd. with funds
raised locally and generous gifts from the Joseph Rank
Benevolent Fund, the London Mission Fund, the General Chapel
Fund and the White Hart Street Fund. The site was dedicated on
11th November 1967 and more than 100 people watched Harry
Wingrove, one of the oldest members at Holmer Green, lay the
first stone on 20th January 1968. The opening was on Saturday
10th August 1968 when the architect, Mr.D.C.Hewitt, handed the
key to Mr.Comben. Rev.R.L.J.Kaye, the Superintendent Minister,
conducted the Service of Dedication at which Mrs.James presented
a Bible to Rev.Denis Reed, the Minister, and John Hall M.P. read
the lesson. Rev.W.G.B.Ream, the former Super, took the prayers
and the sermon was preached by Rev.D.W.Thompson, former
President of Conference. The congregation numbered 300 and as
the church seats only 95, the overflow used the schoolroom and
other rooms. There was a pre-opening lunch for the special
guests at the home of the Misses Gibson. In later years the
kitchen was enlarged. Marjorie Gibson gave the lectern in
memory of her sister Kathleen and their nephew gave the Bible
stand which is on the Communion table, in memory of Marjorie.
The annexe was designed by Clive Lane and built by voluntary
labour (and still stands!). The original congregation was made
up of people mainly from the old chapel, Wesley and St.Mark's.

A Sunday School was started and the Ladies' Fellowship met on Tuesday afternoons. An evening Wives' Group was formed with about 50 members, also house groups which - after several reorganisations - still meet. Also continuing are the Sunday bread, soup and cheese lunches (with a collection for Christian Aid), which started in 1971. Soon the Sunday School was "bursting at the seams" and the large room was proving very useful for social events. There was also a flourishing Youth Fellowship.

For the tenth anniversary in 1978 a grand reunion was organised and most of those who had moved away, came back for the weekend. This highlighted the rapid turnover of people in this area. For some years on the Sunday of the Church Anniversary we have joined together for a shared lunch in a member's garden. The sun always seems to shine on us, but it rains on buildings! We have had to have a new roof and windows, again with much financial help.

Every day some part of the church is used by the community, including a playgroup, nursery school, ballet classes and an ante-natal clinic. All in all, we who now worship and socialize at Coppice Farm Road, are very grateful to our God and all who have contributed in any way to our very pleasant buildings.

IMPRESSIONS (1)

The building is splendidly modern. The first impression is of wood - not the all-enveloping dark variety of the 19th century village chapel - but the polished lighter shades of floors, seats, sanctuary, pulpit and organ. It is a holy, undecorated place of stillness and almost an emptiness, the nearest we have in Chiltern Methodism to a Friends' meeting house. One instinctively moves and speaks with care. We glance at the hymn numbers in their meagre frame, then at the many teachers and preachers present, as the preacher hands the collection plates (wooden, light shade) to the stewards. It is a Church with a conscience. At a training conference once, one of their many Peters said they explored "what everyone should be doing in God's service - and found that almost without exception each was in the wrong job!" They are friendly, not least the young people. But one wonders how one of the old chapel's Anniversary services (a "Mrs.Greenstreet Spectacular") would have gone here........?

IMPRESSIONS (2)

My first impression of Tylers Green was of a beautiful church - simple, plain and modern. My second was of my reverberating feet and voice. My third was a real alarm that old people coming up to the Communion rail might slip on the wooden floor. Carpeting seemed essential.

(Rev.) ALF SHANNAHAN

†††††† *TODAY'S THOUGHTS FROM WESLEY'S SERMONS* ††††††

* Think of pleasure and wealth as bubbles on water.

* Never think you can force people into God's ways.

* Only God can cast out the Devil.

* Allow others the freedom of thought
                    you expect for yourself.

* Christians are never completely free from temptation.

* Blood moving irregularly in the brain
                    stops normal thoughts.

* If you have only one talent, use it.

* Religion is a thankful compliance with the will of God.

* The sinner declares, "I do not need to be born again".

* Ignorance of the Bible causes mental darkness.

††

CHAPTER 11.

CHURCH LIFE AND WITNESS

MEMORIES

We all have our favourite memories of the people we have known, the events we have taken part in, or the chapels where many of them happened. Was there a Sunday School which did not go to "the (Burnham) Beeches" for its annual Treat? Was there a Sunday School Anniversary where the congregation didn't overflow halfway to the next church? (Nowadays sadly we can often seat the entire Junior Church in the front two rows and Hughenden Park is quite far enough to go to play a few games.) As for people - most of them seemed more saintly than ourselves but even they could have their lapses or memorable peculiarities as we shall see. Some of the contributors have expressed doubts about the authenticity of their stories. We leave the reader to judge. But at least they make history come alive!

SOME INTERESTING EVENTS

* Rev.Frank Searle in a 1935 leaflet invited people to the 7.30 Sunday morning prayer meeting at Lane End. Asking members to join one of the fellowship meetings, he said: "None of us is as good as he might be; all of us find that following Jesus requires all our powers".

* Our choir was giving a concert one winter's night in wartime at Naphill. We were plodding our way across Downley Common in the dark when there was a muffled scream. Somebody had walked into the side of a very muddy horse. The rest of us were in a hilarious state by the time we reached Naphill. I don't know how we managed to sing. [Connie Webster: Downley, Sunny Bank]

* My father used to sell ham teas for 9d.[4p.] outside the chapel when the Wanderers had a big match. But the official caterers stopped him. [Charlotte Bulling: White Hart Street]

*   Jolly "Uncle Tom" Barrett used to say, "Children will be conveyed to the park in clean white pinafores in the coal carts!" Once there, we visited the cave where it was said that if you put a penny on the floor and danced round three times, you would see the Devil. We never did (see him).

[Doris Lewis: Newland]

*   It was pouring with rain as our Women's Meeting went on its annual mystery tour. Our destination was Guildford Cathedral and I asked the driver if he could take us for a ride round afterwards (instead of going to Bird World), if the rain kept on. Mrs. Price overheard and said, "It won't rain: God will look after us". Soon afterwards the driver asked me to look to the right: there was the cathedral, bathed in sunshine! The driver's face was a picture.   [June Little: St. Mark's]

*   As their contribution to Lacey Green Village Day in 1985 the chapel had a display of writings and books relating to 130 years of Methodism in the village. Local artists exhibited a collection of drawings and paintings and there were beautiful flower arrangements. The occasion was featured by Radio Oxford, following a report on the Methodist Conference. From the highest to the lowest perhaps? [Kathleen Church: Lacey Green]

*   A puzzled preacher at Lane End Sunday School Anniversary had been rebuked by one of the mothers for suggesting the children might think of their dinner, while he had a brief word with the adults. A helpful bystander explained that he should have said "lunch".

*   We used to love going to Temple Street, to listen to the Oxford Road orchestra.   [Doris Lewis: Newland]

*   It was early wartime when we took the children to Bourne End on the train - the first ride on a train for most of them. Then we walked by the river to Marlow where we had tea, and caught the bus back to Wycombe. But the last Downley bus had gone. The children were tired. I remember Arthur Youens who was home on leave from the army, carrying one little child on his shoulders. The only bus was a "fast" relief to Booker so with a prayer in our hearts, we got on that. At Booker a Thames Valley inspector was standing at the bus-stop. It was my mother's cousin! I quickly got off and said, "Harry, there are 30 dead-tired children on this bus. Can you make it go to Downley?" And he did!

[Connie Webster: Downley, Chapel Street]

*   Ralph Stevens used to accompany the carol singers on his fiddle.   [Margaret Morris: Holmer Green]

*   I married my first husband at Bledlow Ridge Church. People from the chapel which at that time was not solemnised for marriages, formed a guard of honour outside. My second marriage (to Harry) was at the chapel. People asked why somebody who had lived in Wycombe for so long should want to go to Bledlow Ridge for her wedding. The answer is that I've always regarded that as MY chapel.   [Molly Fry: Bledlow Ridge]

SOME INTERESTING PEOPLE

*   An old lady when asked how she was, replied that for her age (84) she was quite well. "My father-in-law's not so good though," she added.

*   Mr.Apps once told us children that if we learned the hymn "Saviour, while my heart is tender", he would give us sixpence [2½p.] if we recited it the next time he came to preach.   I learned the hymn but Mr.Apps forgot to ask us to recite.
                              [Horace Wright: Holmer Green]

*   The preacher at Lacey Green, looking out of the schoolroom window, remarked that the mist had cleared. He was surprised to learn that it was generally reckoned to be a bad sign if you could see Bledlow Ridge ......

*   A violinist called Elijah used to help out with the music. When the preacher announced his text, "What doest thou here, Elijah?" he replied, "I came to play the violin!"
                              [John Lisley: Cryers Hill]

*   During the Great War I worked in the Rations Office.   It was a great thrill when Rev.Terry Coppin walked in one day - and spoke to me. (I was only a young girl.)
                              [Dorothy Lawrence: Wesley]

*   A centenarian remarked that if he'd known how he'd be feeling at 100, he would have taken better care of himself.

*   The young Minister from Marlow came to our house for dinner. He was still laughing at the memory of the two teachers standing at either end of the gallery, keeping watch over the children, like a couple of policemen.
                              [Connie Webster: Downley, Sunny Bank]

* When I asked Rev.Fred Wilson about the merits of "Methodist" and "Baptist" baptism, he replied, "It's not the amount of water that counts, but the feeling behind it".

[Nancy Field: Hazlemere]

* Mr.F.H.Slade at Wooburn Green used to say to the preacher, "Say the Lord's Prayer slowly and finish the service by 11.55". (The bus left at 12.00.)

* I always made sure I'd brushed the back of my hair when I was preaching at Oxford Road. The choir used to sit above and behind you.

* A drunkard would never accompany his wife to Newland Chapel. One Monday she put a little dinner in front of him with the words, "There you are, Will; it's the best I can do". The words haunted him and the next Sunday he accompanied his wife to chapel and was converted by the hymn, "He breaks the power of cancelled sin; He sets the prisoner free". I know this is a true story because I heard him tell it at Cryers Hill where he was the preacher. [Ralph Stevens (1888-1987): Holmer Green]

* My husband Joe liked Rev.Arthur Freeman because he used to say, "Been up to the Ground recently?"

[Molly Hope: St.Mark's]

* William Line used to walk to his services, shouting "Hallelujah!" as he went. I always think of him when I sing, "O happy day that fixed my choice". His face beamed and I think it was the first time it "registered" for me.

[Horace Wright: Holmer Green]

* The "Prim." was lamenting how badly her church was doing. Then she cheered up: "Anyway the Wesleyans aren't doing any better!" [Jean Cotton: St.Mark's]

* My husband Nick was very absent-minded. When he returned home from evening service I asked him how he'd got on. He replied, "OK but I couldn't read the notices." (He'd left his glasses at home.) [Mabs Taylor: Slater Street]

* Frank Hearne who was a very gentle person, caught some boys altering the memorial stones of the new schoolroom. He asked them not to do it again. But Miss Ethel Rackstraw advanced on them with her umbrella. "If I catch you doing that again," she cried, "you'll feel this across your backsides!"

[Nancy Field: Hazlemere]

* Mrs.Greenstreet who ran the old Tylers Green Chapel, would call up to the preacher from the congregation, "You can start now; we're all here!" (even if there were still five minutes to go).

* "Toffee" Sheldon (of Macclesfield) used to boast that he didn't prepare sermons but left the Lord to put the words into his mouth. A hopeless preacher? Well, on one occasion he was the means of the conversion of myself and seven others.
[Stan Sherratt: Bourne End]

* The preacher from the pulpit could see a man working in his garden next to the chapel. He was struggling to pull out some Brussels sprouts, when he fell over. "I knew he would!" exclaimed the delighted preacher to the puzzled congregation.
[John Lisley: Cryers Hill]

* When I was a boy, all the men teachers seemed to have beards. Mr.Darvill had a handsome ginger one - with hair to match of course. [Reg Langley: Downley, Chapel Street]

* I was always tickled by the 1878 Chinnor plan which hung in the vestry. It gave Isaac Mott's address as "Heaven".
[Mrs.M.Atkins: Stokenchurch]

* One local preacher came to Winchmore Hill in a horse and trap. The horse was put in a nearby stable. When the preacher got to his "one last point" in the sermon, my father went out to harness the horse to the trap and waited outside the chapel. The "one last point" lasted half an hour and as it was a cold winter's night, neither my Dad nor the horse was very pleased.
[Horace Wright: Holmer Green]

* My father, William Neville, was converted at a Christian Endeavour open-air meeting on the steps of White Hart Street Chapel. [Charlotte Bulling: White Hart Street]

* Wilf Osborne began to feel rather inferior as he saw all the new preachers coming on to the plan with letters after their names. His good spirits revived however when he realised that he too was a "B.A." - "Born Again"!
[Alan Goodearl: Castlefield]

* Mr.Hunt of Beamond End couldn't read or write. He used to close Sunday School with these words: "Yonder's my Home, my portion fair; my treasure and my heart are there - and my abiding home". [Ralph Stevens: Holmer Green]

*   Someone sympathised with an old man after the service:
"Dreadful cough you have!"   "That wasn't a cough," he replied.
"Them was time-signals!"   [Eileen Monk: Oxford Road]

*   Dad said the Marlow organist must have Jewish connections
because she always took her shoes off.

*   Charlie Lane, the old Oxford Road superintendent, was a
real Christian gentleman. He always invited my two sisters and
me (we were orphans) down from Naphill, to walk behind the
Salvation Army Band up to Daws Hill Park for the sports.   He
cared about others.   [Reg Aldridge: Oxford Road]

THE GOODEARL FAMILY

IVAN (my brother) - member at Wesley, Castlefield
MARGARET (wife of Ivan) - organist at Castlefield
ALAN (brother) - local preacher, member at Bourne End
LESLIE (brother) - member at Wesley, Sands, St.Mark's
EDNA TONKS (niece) - member at Sands, Castlefield
NORA DEAN (sister) - member at Wesley, Castlefield
JOE (brother) - member at Wesley, The Pastures
BESSIE (sister) - member at Wesley
MONNIE HOWARD (sister) - member at Wesley, Sands, Castlefield
STAN HOWARD (brother-in-law) - local preacher, member at Sands
PETER HOWARD (nephew) - local preacher, member at Castlefield;
WALTER (father) - local preacher, member at Wesley
SARAH (mother) - member at Wesley
MRS.CANT   (aunt)   -   member   of   Newland,   Victoria   Street,
Castlefield
TOM (uncle) - member at Victoria Street, St.Mark's
STEVE (uncle) - local preacher, member at Westbourne Street
HAROLD (uncle) - local preacher, member at Bourne End
BEN (uncle) - member at Victoria Street
J.E. & family - members at Wesley
LEN & family - members at Wesley
VIC CARTWRIGHT (aunt's husband) - organist at Newland, Victoria
Street
RICHARD (uncle) - local preacher, member at Wesley

                                   .... to name but a few!

.... and I (HILDERIC) - member at Wesley, Castlefield (where I
am steward).

THE EDGERLEY FAMILY

I believe the pews in Wesley were provided by Jim Edgerley who owned one of the first furniture factories in High Wycombe. His family were Wesleyans. Grandmother Craft worshipped at White Hart Street Primitive Methodist Church where my uncle Bert Edgerley was steward and member of the cricket team. (When White Hart Street closed, he and his wife Edith moved to Victoria Street.) My grandmother used to meet me from morning Sunday School and take me into the morning service. Being deaf, she always sat in the front and I was terrified as Rev. W.S. Hinchcliffe, who had a loud voice, leaned over the pulpit to make a point! The Crafts also worshipped at Westbourne Street Primitive Methodist Church. George, who lived in Desborough Road next to Plumridge's Saw Mill, owned a chair adzing and seating business. His son was Cliff. He was organist and choir master for many years. Through my preaching I am glad to keep up my connections with the Methodist Church - and Uncle Bert!

GEORGE EDGERLEY

MEETINGS

THE CLASS MEETING

A prized possession of many Methodists is the ticket of membership issued annually to members. The history of the class ticket and meeting is found in early accounts of the Society meetings held at the New Room in Bristol in 1742. Wesley had urged his followers to meet for "prayer, Bible study and conversation". These meetings were being held in a small room and the need for larger premises arose. Members were asked for fund-raising ideas. A certain Captain Foy suggested that members should be divided into classes of 11 people and a class leader appointed to lead the weekly meeting and collect a donation of one penny per person each week for the building fund. These meetings gave members the opportunity to share blessings received, give their testimonies and sometimes confess their sins. The leader would visit the sick and absentees and in time class money was used to help the sick and poor.

From Bristol the class system spread rapidly throughout Methodism. It is still the custom for church members to be placed in the care of a class leader, even when no meetings are

-331-

held. The class system has been a part of Chiltern Methodism
since its early days. Although it declined in the early 1800's
- due perhaps to the popularity of the preaching service - the
tradition continued. One of our local preachers has happy
memories of being a junior class member in the early 1930's and
recalls the announcing of four or five class meetings at Wesley
Church at that time. These were always held on church premises.
Perhaps the Second World War - with members away in the Forces
or busy with war-work - is the cause of some of our members not
being able to recall classes since that time. But in some
churches meetings did continue. In recent years the trend has
been for them to be held in members' homes - and in Methsocs in
our colleges and universities - often nowadays being called
"house groups" or "fellowships". I have shared in the
fellowship of three different classes locally over the past 30
years as part of the life of the Church. Although meetings are
held in various houses, they enrich the whole life of the
Church, as they did in Bristol. The penny donation is no longer
collected but fellowship, prayer and Bible study are still the
aim of the meeting, whatever its title.

DAVE FREEMAN

a short guide to church membership

All those who confess Jesus Christ
as Lord and Saviour and accept the obligation to serve Him
in the life of the Church and the world
are welcome as full members of the Methodist Church.

IN THE CHURCH

Members are committed to Worship, Holy Communion,
Fellowship and Service, Prayer and Bible Study, and Responsible Giving.

IN THE WORLD

Members are committed to the working out of their faith
in daily life, the offering of personal service in the community,
the Christian use of their resources, and
the support of the Church in its total world mission.

God chose what the world looks down on and despises, and thinks is nothing,
in order to destroy what the world thinks is important. This means that no one
can boast in God's presence.

I Corinthians 1. 28-29

Member................. SUSAN CHURCH ....

Minister...

CHURCH LIFE AND WITNESS

THE WESLEY GUILD

Wesley Guild, according to Dr.Frank Cumbers, is "the largest and most effective spiritual fellowship in Methodism. All over the land there are Guilds and to this day you may find men and women taking their first steps in public speaking in the inspiration of its meetings." Formed at the end of the last century to combat the enormous loss of young people from the Church, it grew rapidly until in 1909 there were 2200 Guilds and 152,000 Guilders. The Methodist Youth Department became responsible for the Guild in 1943 and gave it a new Charter:

IN LIFE	DEVOTED
IN CHURCH	A FAMILY
IN PERSON	FIT
IN FAITH	EQUIPPED
IN SERVICE	A WORLD CITIZEN

It is to the older Methodists nowadays perhaps that the movement mainly appeals, but in the Guild Holiday Homes all ages share fun and fellowship. In High Wycombe we have a large and active Guild Meeting at our Wesley Church. Subjects and ages cover a wide range and we would be glad to welcome new members. Little Chalfont also has a strong Guild.

NELLIE DYER

OTHER MEETINGS

A glance at circuit plans in the 1930's to 1950's reveals that almost every Church had a weeknight devotional meeting - a Christian Endeavour, Bible Study or Prayer and Preaching Service. Children were catered for in the Junior C.E. or Band of Hope (where they were encouraged to "sign the pledge" - of total abstinence from alcohol - at an early age). Inters Guild, youth club or billiards room provided recreational facilities. Church-based uniformed organisations used the premises two or three times a week and usually had long waiting-lists. Sunday Schools met morning and afternoon and the constant cry was for more teachers.

Strangely today many of our churches are used as extensively as ever but now mainly by the community - for Keep Fit or ballet classes, playgroups, clinics and the ever-popular jumble sales - and in some cases the only time the neighbourhood sees Church members using their own buildings is for Sunday morning worship and the occasional business meeting. (There are of course exceptions - like Marlow Bottom whose Sunshine Corner, Monday Gang and Turning Teens illustrate what imaginative new names, if nothing else, can do!) Fellowship and Wives' (the "young" has mostly disappeared) Groups usually meet in members' homes. In today's smaller Sunday Schools - or Junior Church - teachers sometimes seem almost to outnumber children. The uniformed organisations however, maintaining their traditional disciplined rigidity, continue in some strength but links with the local Church are now often tenuous. Much effort and money go into the maintenance of a building which is used by the Church itself for perhaps only one Sunday service and the weekday Women's Meeting - which refuses to go away!

Why has this change come about? Without too much thought we might blame the influence of television (people unwilling to miss "Coronation Street" or "Eastenders") or the fear of violence on the streets. But when we look at the large number of people who go, for example, to evening classes or the numerous cars in which most children are ferried around, we realise this argument is false. It may be nearer the truth to say that houses were once rather cheerless, especially in the winter, and at the end of a day's work there was nothing much to do there anyway so the Church was the centre of most people's leisure activities. Nowadays the position is reversed: the house is warm and comfortable; the church may be cold and the seats hard.

This reasoning, though more plausible. is probably no nearer the truth than the former. It is all a matter of motivation. We no longer feel the necessity to give as much time to the public worship of God, cultivate our fellowship with other Christians or make a regular commitment to the running of youth activities. Children may be more resistant to being sent to Church, however interesting the activities, by parents who anyway cannot see much real purpose in it themselves. The picture however is not totally gloomy. Coffee mornings may provide the fellowship (if not spiritual quality) which once Christian Endeavour did; "Greenbelt" and "Spring Harvest" Christian festivals attract teenagers and young adults in vast numbers; children's holiday clubs are popular; and some Churches provide nurture groups and other activities. If the best friends are Christian friends, perhaps we should use our buildings as much as our parents did.

CHRISTIAN BOOKSHOPS have become ecumenical meeting places. Started in 1957 by Mrs.Zettie Clark, St.Andrew's in Great Missenden has been run since 1974 by Ernie Barnett.

CHURCH LIFE AND WITNESS

PREACHING

PAST, PRESENT & FUTURE

We have already seen Methodism's heavy dependence on local
preachers. Sadly, to a few they have always been an undesirable
necessity, mere fillers of otherwise empty pulpits, Second
Division people to be kept away from First Division pitches as
far as possible. To such folk the ideal would be to have a
fully ordained Minister in every pulpit at every service.
Thankfully, others regard preachers as a bonus, providing a
variety of worship which no one Minister, however talented,
could possibly provide. Right from Wesley's time the wonder has
always been that God could use ordinary people, some uneducated
and others with many letters after their names, in quite
startling ways. The one condition is that the preacher must
know his or her calling, and the congregation be willing to
support him or her in prayer. This of course is not in any way
to underestimate the important professional service which the
ordained Ministers provide, (in any case they too are primarily
"preachers"), but under the Methodist itinerant system they
invariably move on after a few years, while most preachers
remain in the same circuit for much longer, some all their
lives, and so develop a unique knowledge of all the churches.

We hear much about the hardships which preachers endured
in the past. John Wesley had a horse; most of his followers
didn't. Having heard God's call and filled with a strong
conviction that without a Saviour men would perish eternally,
they went out, usually on foot, the fortunate in the circuit
pony and trap. The coming of the railways – and buses too later
on – was a boon, as long as one's appointment was somewhere "up
the line"! But how some of them must have agonised as to
whether they should use the labours of other men on the Sabbath
Day, so that they might travel in greater comfort! We asked
Mrs.Phyllis Hawke how her father (Rev.W.C.Smith) coped with
his large "parish" before the days of telephone and car. "Did
he ever have a bike?" we asked. "Oh no!" she replied, then
correcting herself, "Well, he did towards the end – when his
health was giving way!"

When we turn to the present day, our first thought is that
we've all gone soft! If the car is out of action, we 'phone for
a lift; if our voice is faltering, we beg an extra microphone.
The length of the service has shrunk by a third, Family Services
by a half. Woe betide the brother (surely never a sister?) who

makes his sixth point as the parish clock strikes the hour! Yet we still believe that we have a call from God and although much of the urgency has gone, that we must point people to Jesus, the only "Way" to everlasting happiness. (If we don't, what are we doing in the pulpit?) We may try dividing the congregation into small discussion groups, filling the hour with singing or showing a film. But we are convinced that most people who come still want a sermon, (but not too long!) and those who don't, aren't likely to be impressed by the alternatives. Some preachers use the lectionary which at least gives an important continuity in such a diverse ministry as ours; others still rely on inspiration - or perspiration!

What then of the future? Men and women will still need Jesus and as far as we can see, someone to tell them so. But will they still meet in a building or simply plug into a computer terminal at home? Perhaps teaching will displace preaching (as it already has in some of the newer or charismatic churches), the house fellowship the evening service, or the screen monitor the reading of the lesson. Wesley used his unaided voice; the preacher on the beach has his megaphone; we check our loudspeaker systems. Maybe the preacher of the future will lose not only his old-sounding title but his pulpit too. (The average "box" is already far less comfortable than the padded "throne" we used to enjoy!) But God's Word will still be relevant and somehow that Word must be passed on. It seems to us that the human voice will for many years still be the best instrument for this purpose. Ministers may come and go. Preachers may not, like "Old Father Thames", keep for ever "rolling along". But in the Wycombe and Amersham areas at least redundancy does not seem imminent!

PREACHING IN 1839

I often think, as I drive my 1984 Vauxhall Cavalier with its 1600 c.c. engine, that I am following in the footsteps of the preachers of old. Turning out of Chorley Road and into Bottom Road on my way to the little chapel at Radnage, or nipping down the relief road into Marlow on a Sunday morning, I am often aware that I am continuing the work of so many saints of bygone years. The message in the Book on the back seat is the same. It tells of the love of God, the saving grace of Jesus and the power and guidance of the Holy Spirit. The needs of those whom I go to meet are much the same - the desire to worship; the hunger for faith; the search for hope and peace and a sense of purpose for living. The chapel standing in the lovely setting of our beautiful Chiltern countryside, is often the one that has stood and witnessed for a hundred years or more in surroundings where nature proclaims, as it has for countless years: "Yes, God is good!" Yet there are differences between me and my predecessors, between the congregation and the old society. The world we live in has changed. The nature of our Church has changed. I am conscious as I drive that what I'm doing is only one aspect of my life. My world is far more busy than the old one; there is so much more to do, so many more interests and opportunities.

When Mr.Sammons went to Bledlow Ridge on 14th April 1839, how did he go? Did he walk? It was a long haul up West Wycombe Road, past West Wycombe Chapel in Church Lane and on round the hill with the Golden Ball on top, heading up the valley to the right of Chorley Farm and then, having put in a good hour on the road, having to face the hill up on to the Ridge. He was used to it - had done it for a good many years - but at 57 one gets a bit puffed! Now it was plain sailing, just along the road for a mile or so. But what of the Society when he got there? Bledlow Ridge Chapel had been opened in 1834. We don't know how many people had had the vision to buy the land and build a chapel, but we do know that the membership in 1837 was only seven and by 1840 none is recorded! So how many were in the congregation on that April Sunday? We don't know, but to walk all that way, to prepare two services, doubtless to visit some homes and talk of God's goodness between the two - and then to make the return journey down to the town, makes me feel ashamed that my preaching costs me so little. My ten minute run in the car; my service prepared in great haste; my dislike of "doubles" - not that we have many these days; and my feeling low because of the small congregation - do not compare with the dedication of preachers like Mr.Sammons.

I chose Mr.Sammons at random and then looked at one or two more. It's surprising how different the conditions were then. There was a membership of about 550 - half the size of the 1988 Circuit; there were only two Ministers; 664 Sunday appointments had to be filled - apart from the weeknight preaching services or the classes to be "examined" (it was a four month Plan, equivalent to 480 services a quarter); and there were 29 preachers including six "on trial". Mr.Overton, the second Minister, had three services every Sunday, except that for some reason he had no afternoon service on 24th March (his "day" off?). He also had four weeknight preaching meetings most

weeks. Listed below are the planned appointments for three of
the local preachers on the Plan, March to June 1839:

Date	MR. SAMMONS of High Wycombe (Aged 57)	AARON COCK of Little Missenden (Aged about 40)	JOSEPH HAWKINS of West Wycombe (Aged about 25)
March 3	Holmer Green (2)	Little Missenden	Wesley & W. Wycombe
10	-	Bradenham	Lane End (2)
17	Little Missenden	Holmer Green	Radnage (2)
24	-	-	Marlow (3)
31	Lacey Green (2)	Little Missenden	Downley (2)
April 7	Flackwell Hth (2)	-	Bradenham (2)
14	Bledlow Ridge (2)	Little Missenden	Amersham
21	Little Missenden	-	Bledlow Ridge (2)
28	Winchmore Hill (2)	-	Penn (2)
May 5	Holmer Green (2)	Little Missenden	Radnage (2)
12	Radnage (2)	Winchmore Hill (2)	Saunderton Lee
19	-	-	West Wycombe
26	-	-	Downley (2)
June 2	Flackwell Hth (2)	Little Missenden	Bledlow Ridge (2)
9	-	Holmer Green	Lacey Green (2)
16	Bradenham	-	West Wycombe (2)
23	Downley (2)	-	Beaconsfield (2)
30	Lacey Green (2)	-	Radnage
TOTAL (4 months)	23	10	33
= PER QUARTER	17	7	24

B.P.S.

PREACHING IN 1913

If you were a preacher in the early part of this
century, you needed not only a good voice but a strong pair of
legs also! Before the days of the motor car, you might have had
a pony and trap, if you were wealthy (we hired one once from a
firm in Richardson Street for 7/6d. [37½p.] for the day), or
even a bicycle. But if you were struggling to bring up a young
family on £100 per year (with no house provided), as my father
was, it was leg-power - or else! Rev. William Charles Smith was
a Minister in the Wesleyan Reform Union and apart from his

CHURCH LIFE AND WITNESS

duties at the Oxford Road, Newland and Wycombe Marsh Free
Methodist Churches he travelled regularly - for weeknight as
well as Sunday services - as far afield as Gerrards Cross or
Wooburn Green. Hazlemere or Penn meant a walk through King's
Wood but Beaconsfield was "luxury": a ride on the train! I
sometimes accompanied him there and then walked with him along
the lonely road to Farnham Common (near Burnham Beeches). I
think he was glad of my company when it was dark. Certainly we
were glad to get past Dorney Bottom which was quite eerie and
supposed to be haunted!

          When he was on his own, he was sometimes asked in to
tea with Lord Burnham at Hall Barn. But such exalted company
apart, he was always welcomed into people's homes for a meal and
a rest. I can never remember his having to carry food or drink
with him. People were hospitable in those days, especially to
the parson or preacher whom they respected as the "man of God".
My mother often entertained preachers at our house in West
Wycombe Road and in fact always prepared more food than we would
eat at meals - in case anyone called. (They usually did!) I
also knew many preachers who went out regularly from Wycombe to
Stokenchurch, Marlow, Bourne End or Amersham to conduct
services, usually singing as they went. Most churches had two
or three services each Sunday, usually conducted by the same
preacher, and the chapel would generally be full. He would have
to be "entertained" so he got to know people quite well by the
end of the day. A normal service was an hour and a half long
and the sermon would last 45 minutes at least - except at the
"Pleasant Sunday Afternoons" (P.S.A.), like those we had at
Hazlemere (where I have lived most of my married life). Then it
was a bit shorter.

          How some of the preachers scared us with the threat of
Hell-fire! My father was a happy, loving man and I hated
hearing him preach on: "It is appointed unto man once to die",
followed by "the Judgement". I much preferred hearing him talk
about the Resurrection and Heaven (apart from those harps!).
Every sermon in those days was based on the Scriptures and even
the children's address invariably started with a Bible story.
Those preachers always had a sense of urgency which sometimes
seems lacking today - although we still have some fine preachers
with a definite "message from the Lord". "God's love" seems to
have replaced "God's anger" but that's no bad thing, although I
do still like to hear a sermon start with a text! We always
listened to the preachers carefully and never argued or doubted
their word. Of course there were no women Ministers and hardly

any women preachers. I don't imagine they could have coped with the long lonely journeys.

But those hard times had their advantages. There were no 'phones to drive you scatty. If anyone wanted hymn numbers, he had to write but if it was local, he'd probably get them the same day! Then there were the choirs - one in almost every chapel, however small. Men didn't get home from work until 7 o'clock (on foot of course) but wouldn't think of missing choir practice. The anthem in a service was almost compulsory but at least it gave the preacher a bit of a breather! Nowadays he often seems to be leading the singing almost solo! My father would sometimes get to a midweek service at Hazlemere before anyone else and attend to lighting the lamps and stoking the stove. I like to shut my eyes sometimes and think of him and all those other "labourers", most of them poor working men with little education, struggling many miles through the rain or snow, just so that they could "light the lamp" in somebody's heart and point him to Jesus. They were serious men - but none the worse for that - who gave up all their comfort to work for the Lord. Things are easier now, thank goodness, but we who have inherited so much, must pass on the same treasures of the Gospel to the present generation.

PHYLLIS HAWKE

PREACHING IN CHANGING TIMES

What used to be the collection, is now the offering;
What used to be the notices, is now the announcements;
What used to be the reading, is now the lesson;
What used to be the long prayer, is now the intercessions;
What used to be the address, is now the sermon (again);
What used to be the Benediction, is now the Grace;
What used to be the children's talk, is now: "Just a brief word - if you must!"

Thank goodness JESUS remains the same (Hebrews 13.8)!

PREACHING IN 1988

I resisted the call to preach for a long time. The excuses were endless - the children were too small; I was needed as a Sunday School teacher; I was working part-time - but the feeling that this was what the Lord wanted kept niggling below the surface, like a toothache. I argued: "Not me, Lord! I'm

not clever enough; I'm too nervous; I don't think I want to do
it! Couldn't you call someone else?" The call came again –
strongly and impossible to ignore. This time I simply said,
"Yes, Lord!" – and began the training which the Methodist Church
requires its preachers to undertake. I quickly discovered that
a lot of commitment was needed. There are four exams. to pass –
Worship and Preaching; Old Testament; New Testament; Christian
Doctrine – and services to be prepared and conducted. Add to
that the oral examination at the Local Preachers' Meeting and it
can seem a daunting task. Only the love and encouragement of my
family and Church, added to a strong conviction that the Lord
was with me, saw me through.

Preaching and the conduct of worship cover a wide range
of understanding. The preacher needs an inside knowledge of
each church. Where can you sing choruses? Where is the
traditional form of service more acceptable? How can you reach
the uncommitted with the good news of Jesus and convince them
that His saving grace can make all the difference to their
lives? Then there are the "specials" –' Sunday School
Anniversary, youth service, family service, Harvest Festival.
There's a great temptation to "jazz it up" in an attempt to
reach those who don't normally come, or worse, to water the
message down in an effort to make it more acceptable. St.Paul
says, "Woe to me if I do not preach the gospel!". As we preach
our social, political, theological or comfortable gospel, are we
neglecting the real Gospel of "Christ and Him crucified"?

At his commissioning service a Methodist local preacher
promises to stand by the doctrinal standards of the Methodist
Church and preach the "Gospel of Redemption". The recurring
theme in Wesley's sermons is: "By grace you are saved through
faith and that not of yourselves; it is the gift of God"
(Ephesians 2.8). The ability to preach is a gift from God. He
reminds us, "It is no small thing to speak words, as if from the
living God", and we must be true to the Gospel, if we are to be
true to our calling. Preaching nowadays is a great challenge.
The world has moved far and fast from Christian standards and
yet the Word of God can speak as powerfully today as it did in
the past. The responsibility of the preacher – to present the
old message in today's language – is an awesome one. But we do
not stand alone: we are empowered by God's Holy Spirit in
study, preparation and preaching. Opening my life to that power
has meant, I believe, that God has used "even me" to speak His
message for His glory.

JANET WIDDESS

PREACHING IN 2038(?)

Peter stretched in the summer sun. He was sitting outside so that he could feel the breeze but after ten minutes he was already beginning to feel the effects of the unfiltered air; he decided to move back into the precisely controlled environment of his house. His computer diary gently murmured as he passed. Peter stopped, rather surprised. "Nothing on today?" he mused. He confronted the view screen and registered his face and voice patterns to gain access. "PREPARE FOR SERVICE 28th JULY",the screen announced. It was his turn to lead worship in two weeks! Peter sat down at the view consul and asked for the Bible, the lectionary and advisory notes to be screened. Obligingly the computer displayed them, each on a different section of the two-metre screen.

"I'm rather rusty," he thought. "Suppose it is lack of practice." He fell to reflecting on the new (five years old) circuit video network. Gone were the days when he would prepare for an individual church. "It was easier then!" he considered. In those days he could view the notes and profile on the church and prepare the video specifically for that fellowship. "Seems so impersonal now." Still he did understand the advantages of a circuit video network: fewer Ministers and local preachers were needed, no plan to prepare and far less work for the Super - now he had to preview only one tape instead of four (one for each circuit church). Peter brought up one of the sermons from the 1988 "Sermons for Special Occasions" data bank. "Always some good points to glean from these!" he ruminated. He sat back and his couch automatically adjusted, massaging his neck. He contemplated those days back in the 1980's. How did they cope? Not only were there more churches (although they were fast reducing them), they even had TWO services in some places! On top of all that, the services were often as long as 60 minutes! The thought of having actually to travel to the church (which was a separate building in those days - not a group of computer-linked homes) and stand before real people, made him feel quite nervous.

With an effort Peter got back to his preparation. His old skill soon returned and he carefully matched his chosen text, "Then He sent them out to preach the kingdom of God" (Luke 9.2), to the computer graphics sequences. Next he over-dubbed his sermon and recorded his computer image as if he were in a large church, standing high up in a pulpit. He almost forgot the advertisements and notices but did remember to programme the remote screens to request credit card insertion at the right time. He was never sure whether he liked the sequence which displayed how much each of the viewing congregation gave, but then it did at least make people register. Peter finalised his 30-minute video and switched the three-dimensional display to an outer hologram so that the Super's image actually came into the viewer's room. He reflected again on how it used to be, person to person contact (he shuddered at the very thought), actually travelling about rather than contact by holoramphone, then felt himself challenged by the thought that Jesus was "available" to everybody, even in those days before video networks. He wondered how people managed to communicate back in the 1980's when there were no empathy detectors, no holoramphones and power was limited (it was before the sun had been tapped); yet the people mostly stayed at home even then. A wave of love and praise came over him as he realised that God was at work among people even in those days and it was He who provided the love and power that people needed, just as He was doing today.

PETER HOWARTH

Vesley Guild at West Wycombe c.1935.
Can you name them? Answers on a postcard, please.

CHAPTER 12.

THE PRESENT AND FUTURE CHURCH

THE INFLUENCE OF METHODISM

When the child John Wesley was rescued from the blazing
rectory, his mother Susanna declared that he was a "brand
plucked from the burning". A century later (1809) there were
110,000 members of the Wesleyan Methodist and New Connexion
Churches. The spread of the new faith had been as rapid in its
way as the spread of the fire which nearly killed the man who
inspired it. In assessing the historical influence of
Methodism, we must look at other events in Britain and Europe at
the time. Methodism began when Britain was still an
agricultural economy, but during the 18th and 19th centuries the
country was transformed into an industrial nation by the process
known as the Industrial Revolution. The years 1811 to 1816 saw
the Luddite movement - textile workers who rioted and organised
machine breaking; the Peterloo Massacre in Manchester in 1819
when a radical meeting was broken up by a cavalry charge
resulting in 500 injuries and 11 deaths; and the Chartist
movement (1838-48) which sought electoral and Parliamentary
reforms. Abroad, the anticlerical and republican French
Revolution is dated from 1789 to 1799 when Napoleon seized
power, followed by the Napoleonic Wars (1799-1815) fought by
France under Napoleon Bonaparte and England, Prussia, Russia and
Austria.

With unrest at home and abroad it is surprising that
Britain did not go the same way as France and have a revolution.
Many historians point to John Wesley as the reason we did not:
while the French had a revolution, the English had Methodism.
Methodist ideals, with an emphasis on an orderly life and a zeal
for self-improvement, transformed the Industrial Revolution so
that the workers' response to the new discipline of manufacture
was not to revolt but to pray. Where historians disagree, is on
whether or not the Methodist influence was an advantage. Some
would have preferred a revolution and others would not. The
pro-revolution group states that Methodism was used by the
Capitalist factory owners and the Establishment to transform a
previously undisciplined agricultural labour force into a body

of men who would accept rigid time-keeping, work regulated by machines and the discipline of paid labour. The Methodists recruited those who would otherwise have led a revolutionary movement - leaving the workers without leaders - and fixed the minds of the people on the promise of life after death, rather than on the terrible living and working conditions they were forced to endure. The opposing group points out that in industrial areas drunkenness was the usual reaction to bad work and housing conditions, with terrible consequences for the families. In teaching sobriety the Methodists introduced self-respect where there had previously been misery. And far from fixing the minds of people solely on the hereafter, the Methodist churches provided a sense of community for the many thousands who had left rural communities to seek work in the new industrial towns and cities. Most importantly, the Methodist churches through their Sunday Schools provided an opportunity for education - the chance to read and write - for the children of the industrial working classes.

It is as the birthplace of the Sunday School movement that High Wycombe has an honoured place in the history of Methodism. John Wesley had made Wycombe one of his regular preaching places, visiting the town at least 34 times between 1739 and 1789. One of his followers, Hannah Ball, opened a Sunday School with herself and her sister Ann as the first teachers. Later Hannah Ball's ideas were developed and organised by Robert Raikes in Gloucester in 1780. The work begun two centuries ago still bears fruit today throughout the world. Through such agencies as Scripture Union, the National Christian Education Council and the Methodist Church's own Education and Youth Departments Christian teaching material is made available and used in Sunday Schools. The problems we face today are very different from those which faced Hannah Ball. While the early Sunday Schools fought against the problems of poverty - poor housing, lack of health care, few educational opportunities - we have to cope with the problems of affluence - children "too busy" to come to Sunday School, indifferent because of a sophisticated diet of other activities and entertainment. Against the same background the Methodist Church as a whole seeks to witness, ever mindful that while some cope with the problems of affluence, many others - particularly abroad - know the problems of poverty all too well.

Locally Methodists play an active role in the work of charities such as the Save the Children Fund and Christian Aid. We have our own National Children's Home and Methodist Homes for the Aged. We support missionary work and at a recent One World

Week rally in London Methodists from this area were well represented. Some seek to promote economic worldwide justice through the Traidcraft organisation; others are active to promote world peace and disarmament. These are just some of the ways in which Methodists continue to put John Wesley's teachings about Jesus into practice. We have inherited a tremendous tradition of faith, service, preaching and teaching, one which stretches back through wars, social upheaval and more recently a technological revolution to a small boy rescued from a burning house. The "brand plucked from the burning" has set the world alight!

SHEILA TORDOFF

METHODISM TODAY

A WORLDWIDE INCREASE

"The world is my parish!" declared John Wesley and while we may lament the decline of Methodism in this country, the global picture is much brighter. As early as 1747 Methodism was spreading in Ireland. The first Conference in America was held in 1773 at Philadelphia. In 1784 Thomas Coke was sent out as Superintendent Minister and - to Wesley's annoyance - took the title of "Bishop". The result was the Methodist Episcopal Church from which the Methodist Episcopal Church (South) broke away in 1844 on the issue of slavery. The membership figures for 1958 were 4,000,000 and 2,500,000 respectively. There were 17 other secessions. Methodist churches were established in many other countries too. In 1881 the Methodist Church overseas had about 5,000,000 members. By 1940 there were nearly 12,000,000 members in 96,000 churches with 76,000 Sunday Schools. There were 54,000 Ministers, 83,000 local preachers, 820,000 teachers and 7,500,000 children.

The figures of Methodist membership in 1977 in 97 countries throughout the six continents show the continuing advance:

North America	14,500,000	(including 13,000,000 in 40,000 churches in U.S.A. and 1,000,000 in Canada)
Asia	2,500,000	
Africa	1,300,000	
Europe	800,000	(including 500,000 in U.K.)
Australasia	700,000	
South America	200,000	

So we see a total world membership of 20,000,000 with a community roll of as many again. Worldwide Methodism continues to grow!

DECLINE IN THE UNITED KINGDOM

Sadly the story in this country, the home of Methodism, over recent years has been one of steady decline. The figures speak for themselves:

	CHURCHES	MEMBERS	MINI-STERS	PREACHERS	CHILDREN
1921 (Wesleyan Prim.,United)	15,261	844,163	4572	38,254	1,652,997
1954 (Methodist)	14,497	999,705	4871	28,008	843,287
1974 (Methodist)	10,000	557,249	3865	16,962	237,989

So we see that from 1921 to 1974 while there was a net loss of approximately one third of Methodist churches and members, the loss of their "pastors" (Ministers and preachers together) was over a half. The fall in Sunday School membership is even more startling: in 1974 there were little more than 14% of the 1921 number. As someone remarked at the time: "Fewer shepherds means more lost sheep; fewer lambs means ultimately no sheep at all!" Over the last decade the number of members has continued to decline. In 1986 there were 450,406 members of Methodist churches in this country. In these dark clouds however two shafts of light have recently appeared. The rate of membership loss and church closures has begun to slow down. Secondly, the number of Methodist Ministers and local preachers in training has greatly improved.

THE SEARCH FOR UNITY

Sir Winston Churchill's wartime words, "United we stand; divided we fall", would have met no response among Victorian Methodists. The more schisms there were, the more the whole Church - not just the new movement but the parent body also - seemed to thrive. "Methodists we were born and Methodists we shall die!" seemed to be the general attitude. Our forefathers were as determined to remain Methodist as other groups were to keep their own identity. But this century's decline has set the alarm bells ringing. If the rate of membership loss since 1954 should continue, there would be no members left at all early next century! Revival apart - and indeed many individual circuits and churches are doing very well indeed - union with other denominations seems to be the only solution. Just as the Primitive and United Methodist Churches were bound to come back to the mother Wesleyan Church in time, should not we now expect to be reunited with the Church of England from which we broke away in John Wesley's time? (By the same logic some look further ahead to an ultimate reunion with the Roman Catholic Church.) But to our surprise nobody so far has taken the proffered Methodist hand.

Talks on union with the Church of England went on from 1964 to 1969. The Methodist Church voted in favour. But the Anglo-Catholics who saw it as a hindrance to a more desirable union with Rome, were not keen nor were many of the parish clergy. Methodists were happy to recognise the validity of the Anglican ministry but Methodist Ministers would have to be re-ordained because, it was said, the apostolic succession - the laying-on of hands by Bishops on newly ordained clergy - had been broken. The Church of England finally rejected the scheme in 1972, just as a new Church came into existence - the United Reformed Church, which was an amalgamation of the former Congregational and Presbyterian Churches.

Many Methodists now believed that a link with the U.R.C. was the best way forward and in fact many local schemes of union, mostly involving the Methodist and U.R.C. Churches but sometimes others also, started to appear. The Churches' Unity Commission now looked at the possibility of a union between the Church of England, the U.R.C., the Methodist Church, the Moravian Church and the Churches of Christ. (The Baptist Church, at first interested, later withdrew; the Roman Catholic Church sent observers.) Again it was the Anglicans who rejected the scheme - in 1981.

In 1986 inter-denominational house-fellowships all over the country met to discuss "What on earth is the Church for?" It received wide publicity and radio coverage. Christians of all denominations found that they, agreed on nearly all the main issues and would like to worship together regularly. The overwhelming desire, expressed in the completed questionnaires, was for union between the Churches as soon as possible. The chief driving-force was not a fear of growing weakness (a feeling not restricted to Methodists, by the way!) but an open-eyed love. But almost equally strong was the proviso: "Union - but not uniformity!"

METHODISM IN THE CHILTERNS TODAY

By the end of the last century Methodism had spread so
rapidly that almost every village seemed to have its own chapel
- sometimes two! How different is the situation today! But let
us examine the figures. In 1947 the High Wycombe Methodist
Circuit (which included the present Amersham Circuit) had 40
churches and 1835 members. There were seven Ministers and a
Sister and 78 fully accredited preachers. Each Sunday there
were 76 services. The corresponding figures for 1987 (including
the Amersham Circuit) were: 29 churches, 1708 members, eight
Ministers, 45 preachers and 52 services. We notice that whilst
the number of churches decreased by 27% and services by 32%,
membership went down by only 7%, the number of Ministers being
virtually the same. The problem is that half the membership is
found in only six churches (St. John's, Chesham and Little
Chalfont in the Amersham Circuit; Wesley, Marlow and Castlefield
in the High Wycombe Circuit). On the other hand only seven
churches have fewer than 20 members. There are definite signs
of revival - and not only in the larger churches. For example
Booker and Bourne End have seen their congregations treble over
a decade; Sunday Schools at Lane End and Hazlemere almost
vanished but now number about 30 and 50 children respectively.

Methodist witness, at least in the Wycombe area (and most
notably the western end), has without doubt declined in recent
years. But Christian worship generally has gone on growing,
especially in the evangelical and "house" fellowships. "Small"
often seems "beautiful" in the Chilterns. Co-operation between
churches of different denominations is quite common but physical
union is a rarity: Chalfont St. Giles is the only jointly-run
Methodist church (with the U.R.C.). Our sister churches in the
Wesleyan Reform Union value their "Free Methodist" status. But
the coin of freedom is two-sided. On one hand it can mean
building up one's own church without reference to outside
authority. On the other it can mean a lonely struggle without
the resources of a circuit. Anyway we have to note their
determination to survive and greater dependence on the laity
than is the case in Methodism. Nor have any of the Amersham
Churches which were transferred from the High Wycombe Circuit in
1951 disappeared, (except Amersham Common which was replaced by
St.John's). In fact with the opening of Little Chalfont they
have increased by one! Perhaps a smaller circuit is able to
build up its weaker parts more successfully. In the same period
the High Wycombe Circuit has closed 15 churches, although there
have been three new ones: St. Mark's, Deeds Grove and Tylers
Green (Coppice Farm). Replacing an old building with a new one

(perhaps in a different area) or amalgamating two neighbouring societies is good: closing the only Christian witness in villages like Beacons Bottom, Piddington and Wheeler End is sad indeed.

As we have looked back over two centuries, the same pattern has kept appearing. A group of Methodists meets in a spare room or a farmer's barn. They build a little chapel, improve it and watch it grow until almost the whole neighbourhood attends at some time. Then people die, families move away and the church falls on hard times - as common an experience in the inter-war years as now! (Some of our newer churches may have this experience yet to come!) At this point one of three things seems to happen: despair and ultimate closure, or a determination to hold on whatever the cost, or a vision to take God's work out to a different area. Clearly the vision, if it is from God and acted on, will be blessed. But we have noticed that determination - in its more limited way - can have its own success too. New people finally come - probably older than if the church had moved on to a new housing estate - and the church thrives again. The resolution of the Wesley Church to overcome all the planning refusals in order to rebuild the interior of their building, and maintain a Methodist witness in the centre of High Wycombe, is very laudable.

So we must not despair. But is it defeatist to give up some of our present buildings? To rent a village hall or convert a bus for mobile services? To withdraw from expensive premises to the place where we started - our own homes? We may continue as an independent denomination or work more closely with - or within - another. But God's work in the Chilterns must go on, whatever our "label"! Let Lee Common lead the way. As recently as the Second World War it was still holding three services every Sunday. Then numbers fell away until there were only nine members left. It could easily have closed but instead - with considerable outside help - it has opened its doors to the Church and community at large, while maintaining its distinctive Methodist witness.

CIRCUIT POLICY REPORT (1985)

In an effort to face up to the present difficulties a committee, comprising the High Wycombe Methodist Circuit staff and stewards, was formed in 1984 to consider the limitation of manpower, the increasing financial burden and a future policy for mission. They found that total membership had been declining for some years by an average of 32 per year and half the Churches now had fewer than 32 members each. Sister Vera Pearson, who was leaving in 1987 could not be replaced, and with only five staff to cover 23 Churches use of local preachers, including from outside the Circuit, would have to increase. "Local arrangements" were thought to be undesirable. Administrative duties were decreasing the Ministers' scope for pastoral care, thus reducing membership growth, and were a hindrance to attracting new Ministers.

The committee therefore recommended that the Circuit should be divided into "Key Churches" which had scope for growth, and on which ministerial manpower would be concentrated, and others which would receive only limited attention. Among the latter Piddington and Wheeler End should amalgamate with Lane End, Bledlow Ridge should consider its future and Lacey Green was urged to consult with Princes Risborough (in the Aylesbury Circuit).

It was felt that Marlow Bottom could profit from closer co-operation with Marlow; Wooburn Green and Bourne End with Flackwell Heath; Booker with Castlefield; Radnage with Stokenchurch; Lacey Green and Bryants Bottom with Naphill; and Downley with St. Mark's. Generally Churches within a Minister's section should look towards joint services and Church Councils.

"Key Churches" would be: Wesley and Deeds Grove (where the Superintendent Minister might be helped by a Lay Pastoral Assistant), Marlow, Flackwell Heath, Wooburn Green, Holmer Green, Tylers Green, Cryers Hill, Castlefield, Lane End, Stokenchurch, Naphill and St. Mark's.

The report attracted much discussion. An alternative report by Keith Lewis, one of the senior local preachers, put forward a strategy for mission. Other Churches were increasing both in membership and financial resources. Closer co-operation with them, greater use of the laity and more emphasis on a teaching ministry, he said, would ensure Methodist growth. Generally however the Circuit Policy report was thought to be reasonable and it was accepted at a special Circuit Meeting on 13th November 1985.

THE FUTURE OF METHODISM

Rev. ROY JACKSON writes:

"The best lack all conviction,
While the worst are full of a passionate intensity."
(W.B.Yeats)

Many people think that England today has a post-Christian
culture. Christian values are no longer accepted as normal in
our society. Agnosticism is the new orthodoxy even within much
of the Church. "But it isn't that simple," we are told. If
"faith is being sure of what we hope for, and certain of what we
do not see," what future is there for the Christian faith when
it is considered wrong to be certain of anything? How can we
proclaim the truth of Christ when we are told that what may be
true for you, is not necessarily true for me? At present the
Methodist Church, along with other mainstream denominations, is
experiencing numerical decline. There are pockets of growth but
it is not yet clear that they are anything more than minor
interruptions to the general trend. Those branches of the
Christian Church which are growing, are those which offer
certainties to counter life's uncertainties. Often the growing
churches seem to those in the more established churches as
little more than slick estate agencies, offering low mortgage
rates on beautiful all mod-con developments built on sand. But
then we are no longer sure of the rock upon which we have built.
What does the future hold for us?

Of course the rate of decline of membership will decrease
as the number of members decreases, and we should eventually be
left with a rump of diehards, of whom we might suspect that the
chief motive for membership was the desire or need to be
something peculiar. Many Methodists however would rather that
we ceased to exist than that we continued in that fashion. In
contrast to the pervasive feeling within the Methodist Church
that decline is inevitable, there are good grounds for our
expecting not merely to arrest the decline but to grow. Science
has been found not to have all the answers. (Science truly
never pretended to have all the answers but it was fashionable
amongst the unscientific to pretend that it did.) Materialism
which is the addiction of our society, has given some people a
few good trips but has not increased human happiness. The
increase of human potential has brought as many problems as it
has solutions. People are looking for something which deals
more adequately with problems of good, evil, human power,

responsibility and our place within the universe and its meaning. We see this in the increased interest in religions, the occult and astrology. Those who seriously explore Christianity, will find that it can more than adequately answer the demands they make of it. Morally no better way of life has been found than living by faith in God, the Father of our Lord Jesus Christ; like the idolatry of the past the modern decline of Christian faith has been the necessary counterpart to an increase in selfishness. Now however we are beginning to find that in selfishness we have bred a monster that loves to eat the hand that fed it. Only Christianity which talks of being saved by the complete unselfishness of our Creator in His self-sacrifice in Jesus, has got anything which can effectively overcome this monster.

Around the world Christianity is growing; it is only in the West that it is declining. If Christianity is true, we should expect it to be growing. Our faith as Christians is not in ourselves; rather it rests upon a God Who acts upon our behalf for our good, not because we deserve it or demand it nor because we engineer it, but because He is Love and He loves us. Since from a Christian viewpoint we live in a society which is deeply in need of salvation (for example, from its lack of compassion for the world's poor and oppressed) and in which there are many individuals who in many ways need salvation, Christians should be expecting God to act as He has done in similar situations (for example, in the Methodist revival of the 18th century).

The future for Christianity is therefore bright. But what of Methodism? Revival has always been rather careless about human denominations and traditions. If we expect the Holy Spirit to work, we cannot expect Him to confine Himself to our Church. Sadly it has often been those who have had most influence on the structures of the Christian Church, who have been slowest to recognise the finger of God. Can we expect those whom we allow to be weighed down with the burdens of our church administration, also to be alert for the breath of God?

John Wesley's aim, his calling, was not to start Methodism but to spread Scriptural holiness throughout the land, to stir up all parties (both Christian and heathen) to worship God in spirit and in truth. The emphases of his ministry - personal holiness and social responsibility - are still essential and inseparable values in the heart of Christianity. Also while we should be wary of overburdening ourselves with bureaucracy, we do need organisation if we are to be future channels of God's grace, and organisation is one of the hallmarks of Methodism.

THE PRESENT AND FUTURE CHURCH

Therefore whether or not the Methodist Church continues to
exist, we shall still need methodists!

If we think of the High Wycombe Circuit and Methodism in
the Chilterns generally, the factors considered in the large
scale are relevant here. We face decline as the population and
its attitudes change. We have hope. The number of preaching
places will continue to decrease and it is becoming increasingly
expensive to build new churches in new areas of population. In
future therefore a circuit will probably consist of a few big
churches with a large number of localised class meetings or
house groups meeting in people's homes. However if we are to
grow, we must set ourselves the worthy task of learning to look
to God and we must stick to it, no matter what. Then we shall
discover we have a future, God-given and God-guaranteed.

EPILOGUE

So we come to the end of our story of "250 years of
Chiltern Methodism". We hope our efforts will help whoever
writes the story of the next 250 years - of Christianity, if not
Methodism! We shall be glad to hear from our readers,
especially if they have further information they can give us.
We hope that some will be inspired to write the story of their
own churches - at greater length than space has allowed us in
this book. In the last century the only common physical ground
locally between the different denominations seems at times to
have been Saunderton Workhouse! Wesleyans, Primitives, Free
Methodists (and others) conducted services for the destitute
who were made to work hard for their pittance of food from the
"Union". It was a common place for aged parents to spend their
last wretched days. Into this grim place came the Methodist
message of a loving Saviour and the promise of a "house of many
mansions". The Workhouse has long gone but perhaps the duty of
the modern Church is basically the same: to take the Gospel
into the needy parts of the world. In so doing, we shall build
up fellowship with other Christians, strengthen our own churches
and serve the God Who inspired John Wesley.

NOTES

Use this page to keep your own record of Circuit History.

As we go to Press the mystery of Moore's Town (p.164) has been solved for us. Mr.Ridgley tells us it is the original name of Bryants Bottom (p.206).

APPENDIX 1

MEMORIALS

AMERSHAM (HIGH ST.)

WESLEYAN METHODIST 1899

1. Mrs. B. Goodearl   2. Mrs. B. North
3. C. W. Deacon J.P. (Mayor of High Wycombe)
4. C. Swann & F. Free Jun.   5. Mr. J. T. Toovey
6. A. W. Edwards   7. Mr. Samuel Sibley
8. Rev. W. Earl   9. T. Thomas Esq.
10. Mr. B. Hornby   11. Mrs. J. Elliott
12. Mrs. H. Goodearl
13. Mr. C. E. Moxham (Architect - Wycombe) & F. P. Williams (Builder - Amersham)

****

AMERSHAM (ST. JOHN'S)

1. Rev. L. O. Brooker (Chairman of District) - 10th Oct. 1959
2. Methodist Church, St. John's Square, Clerkenwell, destroyed during Second World War
3. Children of Sunday School, Woodside Road Methodist Church - 10th Oct. 1959

****

BEACONSFIELD

1900 WESLEYAN REFORM CHAPEL

1. J. Thomas J.P., C.C. - 6th Sep. 1899
2. W. Dean - 6th Sep. 1899
3. Sir Edmund Lawson Bart. - 6th Sep. 1899
4. The local preachers - 6th Sep. 1899

BLEDLOW RIDGE

WESLEYAN METHODIST CHURCH

1. Defaced....
2. Subscription Stone laid by T.WHEELER Esq. J.P. - May 1887
3. W.GOODEARL   4. R.WHITE
5. S.WELLER   6. S.STEEVENS
7. R.GOODEARL
8. Local Preachers Stone laid by MR.JAMES HUSSEY   May 1887
9. J.R.(?)DRING   10. C....Defaced
11. (?) HARRIS   12. Defaced
13. K.SEYMOUR   14. P.LANE
15. C.E.MOXHAM Architect
16. SUNDAY SCHOOL STONE laid by MR.HENRY GOODEARL (Date illegible)
17. J.BURNHAM
18. Stones with initials only: G.S. H.J.P.

Inside

19. WESLEYAN - Erected Nov.30th 1834.
20. Sacred to the memory of CHARLES WESLEY ROGERS for 50 years Member and Society Steward of this Church, Died Jan.19th 1942 aged 84.   -   Esteemed & Loved by all "Blessed are the pure in heart: for they shall see God".
21. This pulpit is made from Sycamore grown locally by his grandfather, CHARLES WESLEY ROGERS 1857-1942. Was given in loving memory of CHARLES STAINTON REX ROGERS Died Oct. 19th 1958 aged 22.
22. The central cross was given in loving memory of ARTHUR BOWLER Died Aug.9th 1937 aged 21.

‡‡
BOOKER

WESLEYAN METHODIST CHURCH

1. Subscription stone laid by R.WALKER Esq. April 27th 1886
2. B.NORTH   3. Mrs.S.WELLER
4. S.WELLER   5. J.HAWKINS
6. R.WHITE   7. W.GOODEARL
8. G.SEY.... (Covered by buttress, believed to be G.SEYMOUR)
9. GOLDSWAIN   10. J.BROOKER
11. D.R.DRING   12. T.WHEELER Esq
13. J.ELLIOTT   14. W.BARTLETT
15. W.PIERCEY   16. J.SHERWOOD

17. E.SHERWOOD   18. G.SHERWOOD
19. G.W.CROOK   20. H.CROOK
21. J.CROOK   22. W.GILES
23. Bricks with initials only:-   E.G.   G.P.   E.B.   E.P.   C.F.
    M.B.   A.P.   C.P.   R.A.B.   D.S.   E.C.   C.S.   E.S.   G.G.   E.G.
    J.P.   M.T.

Inside

24. WESLEYAN CHAPEL 1847.
25. In loving memory of MARGARET DARVILL for services rendered
    to this church.   1909 - 1983.
26. In loving memory of Lce.Cpl. WILLIAM C.PEARCE Bucks.Batt: Ox
    & Bucks. L.I.   Killed in action at "Aubers Ridge" France
    July 19th 1916.   Greater love hath no man than this, that a
    man lay down his life for his friends.
27. These doors are in memory of ETHEL PEARCE   1908 - 1984.
    Donated by family and friends.   Enter these doors with
    praise and thanksgiving.

Sunday School

28. BOOKER WESLEYAN SUNDAY SCHOOL REBUILT 1907.
29. This stone was laid by MR.JOSEPH DORSETT July 15 1907
30. Circuit Sunday School stone laid by MRS.EDWIN WELLER
31. MR.OWEN EVANS   32. S.G.LONG
33. S.J.SHERWOOD   34. C.W.PEARCE
35. MISS.J.M.SILVEY   36. MRS.SMITH
37. J.BROOKER
38. Bricks with initials only:-   J.P.   G.W.P.   L.D.S.   O.B.
    A.B.   J.W.S.   C.W.C.   G.E.B.   M.M.S.   A.P.   W.S.   S.S.   K.D.
    J.H.C.   A.F.   F.P.   E.S.   C.S.   B.P.   F.F.B.

Notice Board

39. In memory of Mr.G.W.PEARCE 1904-1981

##
BOURNE END

VESLEYAN CHURCH 1910

1. This stone was laid by: SIR ALFRED CRIPPS M.P.   March 28th
   1910
2. This stone was laid by: M.SCOTT NORMAN
3. This stone was laid by: MISS CRIPPS of PARMOOR
4. R.GOODEARL Esq. J.P.

5. C.W.EARLY Esq. J.P. of WITNEY
6. MRS.JOSEPH WOODBRIDGE on behalf of BOURNE END Society of Friends
7. MR. H. COLLINS the FLACKWELL HEATH Society of Friends.
8. C.H.G.   9. E.& D.W.

##
BRYANTS BOTTOM

PRIMITIVE METHODIST 30th May 1871

1. Miss E.A.Coates   2. Rev.P.Coates (Minister)
3. Mrs.Joseph Worley   4. Rev.J.Spooner (Minister)

##
CASTLEFIELD

METHODIST

1. This plaque commemorates the stonelaying of this Church Hall on Saturday 11th April 1953 when 26 stones and 152 bricks were laid.
2. This plaque commemorates the opening of this Church Hall on Saturday 5th September 1953 by Owen Haines J.P., Freeman of this Borough.
3. To commemorate the stonelaying ceremony on 11th December 1965 and the opening and dedication of this Church on 10th September 1966.
4. (Under the clock in the back room) In memory of Dorothy Hughes.

##
CHALFONT ST.GILES

PRIMITIVE METHODIST MILTON CHAPEL - A.D. 1866

1. Porch: Erected 1900
2. J.Thomas J.P. - 25th July 1905
3. W.Key (trustees & Charles Dunham, Minister) - 25th July 1905
4. G.J.Robertson - 25th July 1905

##
CHESHAM

1. Joseph Rank Benevolent Fund
2. Members of this Church & Circuit - 1965

APPENDICES

CRYERS HILL

1. PRIMITIVE METHODIST CHAPEL 1852 - WE PREACH CHRIST CRUCIFIED
2. In remembrance of Lilian A.Turnbull 18th May 1879 - 25th August 1954
3. In memory of Arthur C.Dean - an old scholar
4. This stone was laid by four old scholars of this school - S.Ridgley, R.Chilton, W.Ridgley, L.Copeland
5. This stone was laid by Rev.F.E.Yeomans on behalf of the trustees
6. This stone was laid on behalf of the Sunday School by S.Ridgley, Superintendent, 1930
7. This stone was laid by Mrs.C.Jupe and family in memory of the late Rev.C.Jupe, Superintendent Minister 1877-9 & 1896-9
8. From the Women's Own and in memory of Mrs.S.Ridgley, the first President
9. To the memory of Richard Evans, Sunday School Superintendent 1869-1894
10. In memory of William Page and Rebecca Bailey, old scholars
11. In memory of John Lacey, lifelong member of this chapel
12. Laid on behalf of the Women's Own - to the glory of God
13. R.Saunders, secretary, and R.Jupe, treasurer
14. In memory of Elizabeth Ambler, an old scholar
15. To the memory of John Anderson and family
16. H.T.Turnbull and O.Evans
17. W.& P.Saunders, daughter Anthea
18. Annie Copeland for family
19. T.Mason, an old teacher
20. Mr.G.T.Castle and family
21. Joseph Lisley and family
22. John Lisley and family
23. Margaret and John Lisley
24. Mabel Evans
25. The young people
26. David Andrew Warne
27. Annie and Gilbert Ridgley
28. A.Rixon
29. F.Hunt
30. Mrs.B.F.Crosfield
31. Mr.and Mrs.J.R.Biggs
32. Mrs.A.Rixon - the Sunday School - 1955
33. K.Lawrence
34. James Holland
35. E.J.Montague
36. Barry and Janice King
37. Copeland Family
38. The Choir
39. Michael Brittin
40. Jane Brittin
41. Trevor Dean
42. Mrs.R.Peedle
43. Florence Binder
44. Gwen and Fred Pearce

Inside

45. This tablet was erected by the scholars of this Sunday School to the memory of JOHN BRISTOW who died December 9th 1923 Aged 84 years. For many years a teacher in this Sunday School.
46. To the Glory of God and in memory of Rev.CHARLES JUPE twice minister in charge of this church. Also in remembrance of his wife. This window is given by members of their family.
47. Chair. In memory of Mr.& Mrs.J.BIGGS October,1978.
48. Cross. In memory of Tom Barrett. Presented by his widow. [This cross is believed to have come from Westbourne Street when that Chapel closed].
49. Clock. In grateful remembrance of WILFRED HENRY TURNBULL 1908-1962.
50. Photograph. Presented by Scholars & Teachers in memory of our late Superintendent Mr.S.RIDGLEY Teacher and Superintendent for 50 years.
51. This Porch was built by members and friends of the Church and dedicated to the Glory of God on August 31st, 1986.
52. Table. Made and presented by JIM COPELAND September,1986.

##
DEEDS GROVE

METHODIST CHURCH 1962

1. This stone was laid to the Glory of God by JOHN HALL O.B.E. Member of Parliament for the Wycombe Division Bucks. Deeds Grove Methodist Church 26th May 1962.
2. Lest we forget Harry K.Collins, William C.Lord, Norman J.Peatey, Cyril A.Peatey who made the supreme sacrifice in the world war of 1939-1945 in memory of whom their parents have provided this garden and its walls. Greater love hath no man than this.

##
DOWNLEY SUNNY BANK

1924 WESLEYAN

1. In memoriam SARAH GOODCHILD DARVIL died 1922
2. These served. GEORGE EDEN D.1910 MARGARET (BURROWS) EDEN D.1920 JOSEPH BRISTOW D.1916 MARGARET (EDEN) BRISTOW D.1925
3. In Memory of FREDERICK and EMELINE BARLOW F.H.B.

4. Laid by Mr.JOHN JACKSON for the Trustees and Society.
5. Laid by Mr.W.YOUENS J.P. Mr.G.J.BATTS Sunday School Superintendents.
6. Centenary (1924) Memorial. This stone was laid by ARTHUR FAIRFAX Esq. of Banbury July 10th 1926. Circuit Ministers Rev.E.J.B.RICHARDS Rev.H.J.IVENS
7. Laid by the family of Mr.& Mrs.JOSEPH EVANS who were connected here for many years.
8. Bricks with initials only:- B.L. B.S. C.P.S. E.S. L.S. T.S. G.T.J. F.S. A.A.S. F.S. L.S. A.H. G.S. W.S. L.B. M.P. J.H. A.S. W.C. R.S. A.B.P. H.F.C. H.E.C. E.A.C. L.E.C. G.H. H.K.S. F.S.-H.S. L.A.B. P.METHt D.C. M.K.B. K.D.B. M.Y. W.E.N. E.C.C. W.J.C. S.A.B. C.L. C.G. K.Y. M.J. M.J.H. L.R.H. H.T.S. L.S. P.S. D.E.D. C.T.K. E.B.D.

Inside

9. To the Glory of God and in memory of JOSEPH BRISTOW Died Dec.14th 1916. Aged 63 years. For a time a Trustee, he was connected for the whole period of his life with this Society. A Sunday School Teacher for 46 years. General Secretary, Treasurer, Band of Hope Leader and Distributor of Tracts. "By their works ye shall know them".
In memory of MARGARET BRISTOW.
10. This tablet was erected by the widow and family in loving remembrance of HENRY COLLINS who departed this life very suddenly at St.Pancras Station London January 29th 1877 aged 44 years. He was a member of this Society about 23 years. At the time of his death he was Circuit Steward, Trustee for several chapels in the Circuit, Local Preacher, Class Leader and Superintendent of the Sunday School. Also Chairman of the West Wycombe School Board and a Director of the Wycombe Savings Bank. He was Interred in West Wycombe Churchyard February 3rd in the presence of a large number of his brothers and neighbours and a funeral sermon was preached by Mr.James Hussey from Psalm XII v1 "Help Lord for the godly man ceaseth: for the faithful fail from among the children of men".
11. To the Glory of God and in memory of FREDERICK BARLOW who died 31 October 1922 aged 82 years. For 76 years connected with this Sunday School and 63 years a member of Society. He attended his whole life to the work of God in this Church serving as Society Steward, Chapel Steward. Organist and Choirmaster, also 44 years Sunday School Superintendent. "Blessed are the dead which die in the Lord".

12. (Two Communion Chairs) Presented by the family in memory of Mr.and Mrs.G.STYLES, November 1958.

13. (Communion Table). Presented by the Women's Own and in memory of Mr.FRED.STYLES, August 1939.

14. In memory of PERCY STRATFORD Society Steward, Superintendent, Trustee and Chairman. Called Home 27th June 1952.

15. In memory of GEORGE JAMES BATTS who died 17th February, 1935 aged 63. 59 years connexion with this School and Church. Scholar, Teacher, Secretary, Superintendent, Class Leader and Trustee. - Loved by the children -

16. To the Glory of God and in remembrance of JAMES DARVELL died May 5th 1930 also of MARY his wife died March 22nd 1931 for 40 years members of this Chapel. "By grace are ye saved".

17. In memory of JAMES GOODCHILD who died 12th September 1911 aged 75 years. He was 50 years a member of this Church, a Class Leader 46 years and also Superintendent of the Sunday School.

In the Schoolroom

18. In memory of Alderman ALECK STACEY of Plomer Hill House who died April 6th 1935. In his early years a scholar of this Sunday School. Member of the Bucks County Council. A generous supporter of our School and Church.

19. (Framed Certificates). To JOHN WILLIAM YOUENS In grateful recognition of 50 years faithful service as Secretary of the Downley Sunny Bank Methodist Sunday School. 1894 - 1944. Previously teacher and scholar. May 1944.

20. (Plaque underneath). In memoriam JOHN WILLIAM YOUENS Died 21st January,1946. Erected by Family and Sunday School.

21. (Framed Certificate). Downley Sunny Bank Methodist Sunday School to LAURA ANN BLATCHFORD in grateful appreciation of 42 years of earnest service 1903 - 1945. Senior Teacher; Missionary Secretary; Temperance Secretary; Collector for National Children's Home and Orphanage and numerous other charitable purposes. November 1945.

22. (Plaque underneath). In memory of LAURA ANN BLATCHFORD Died 22nd September 1959.

23. Children's Harvest Festival Sept.30th 1938. We hold in affectionate remembrance our Teacher THOMAS MOORE who was called to the Heavenly Harvest 13th October. Presented by JOHN.W.YOUENS Esq. Secretary.

APPENDICES

FLACKWELL HEATH

WESLEYAN

1. This stone was laid by: MRS.WRIGHT September 8th 1865
2. MRS.J.DORSETT of   3. MR.G.JONES of HANDY CROSS

(Extension)

4. These Memorial Stones were laid October 1. 1883 by
5. J.UNITE Esq.   6. MR.J.HUSSEY of
7. MRS.S.VELLER of   8. MR.R.GOODEARL of

Church Hall

9. These stones were laid to the Glory of God July 7th 1923
   MR.G.BURNHAM
10. MR.J.SHIRLEY for the Trustees
11. MR.J.PYM for the Congregation
12. MR.H.BEASLEY for the Sunday School
13. MRS.H.COLLINS   14. MR.& MRS.J.PYM
15. MRS.J.SHIRLEY

****
HAZLEMERE

FREE METHODIST (WRU.)

1. Mr. A.W.Nash Architect 4/6/06
2. In memory Elijah Stone   3. Emily & Ethel Rackstraw
4. W.Dean   5. G.Rackstraw
6. Mrs.J.Putnam   7. Mr.J.Roberts
8. Mr.G.Tilbury   9. Mr.H.Gripps
10. Miss R.Tilbury   11. Mr.D.Lidgley
12. Wm.Holland 1 Peter 1v25 13. Mr.G.Bridger 4/6/1906
14. President of Circuit. I.W.Wilffier Esq. May 27th 1867
    Relaid Thomas Rackstraw September 14th 1927
15. 1914-1918 War. In memory laid by Mrs.H.T.Cadbury September
    14th 1927
16. Wesley Reform Union President Rev,A.Worley
    September 14th 1927   17. Philip Bristow
18. Wm.Burrows   19. John Putnam
20. W.J.Meeks   21. John Putnam died 1-9-1911
22. Edith Putnam died11-11-1918 23. George Page died 4-10-1918
24. Mr,and Mrs.R.T.Walker   25. P.A.Buckle
26. Mrs.P.Buckle   27. Miss C.Buckle
28. Eileen and H. Cripps   29. Arthur Burnham 25-9-1915

30. Leonard Burnham 20-9-1917
31. Walter Hearne 12th. R.B. Loos Killed 25-9-1915 Age 20 years
32. P.A.Randall
33. W.S.Toms
34. Walter Stanley Collins   1/5th. D.C.L.I. Missing 12-4-1918
    Age 18 years
35. Mrs. Hunt in memory of Mr. Hunt
36. Mr. and Mrs. Putnam
37. Women's Own   14-9-1927
38. David Sturgess O.B.L.I.   Killed   22-8-1917
39. Mary Sturgess died 2-6-1926
40. Choir "Sing to the Lord"   14-9-1927
41. Harold S.Toovey
42. F.Putnam Jnr.
43. Mr.P.Buckle, S.S. 14-9-1927
44. Mr. and Mrs. F.R.Putnam
45. Mr. T.Cheeseman   President of Circuit
46. Christian Endeavour   14-9-1927
47. Laid for Trustees by J.Burrows 14-9-1927
48. Mr. T.Rackstraw in memory of Mrs. Rackstraw

###

HOLMER GREEN

METHODIST CHURCH 1937.

1. STANLEY CHILTON,   CISSIE CHILTON.
2. MR.& MRS. DARVILL in memory of RANDALL BOND FAMILY 1841-
   1937
3. In memory of MICHAEL PURSEY
4. MR.& MRS. S. HADDOCK
5. MR. & MRS. V. PURSEY AND FAMILY
6. ALFRED WINGROVE   7. EVA WINGROVE
8. F. LANCASTER in memory of MRS. F. LANCASTER
9. MR. & MRS. W. CHILTON   10. MR. & MRS. H. WINGROVE
11. In memory of MR. T. BOND
12. Laid on behalf of THE LOCAL PREACHERS
13. MR. & MRS. R STEVENS AND FAMILY
14. MRS. E. GOMME   15. ERIC AND ALAN TILBURY
16. In memory of MR. F. DEANEY 17. MRS. BOSTON
18. In memory of MR. & MRS. J. JAMES
19. MR. & MRS. HUBERT WRIGHT AND FAMILY
20. In memory of ALBERT WRIGHT
21. MISS H. WRIGHT. MISS M. WRIGHT
22. ALDERMAN C. F. LORD of HIGH WYCOMBE
23. MRS. G. SAUNDERS
24. Laid on behalf of "YOUNG METHODISM"

25. MR. & MRS. G. DEAN AND FAMILY
26. MRS. A. JAMES   27. MR. W. V. HEARN
28. DENNIS WILLIAM PARKER
29. WESLEY GUILD HOLMER GREEN (with the Guild symbol).
30. In memory of MR. L. JAMES   31. MR. & MRS. J. GRACE
32. In memory of ALBERT KEEN
33. MR.& MRS. G. STEVENS AND FAMILY
34. MRS.T. J. RUSHBROOKE
35. MR. & MRS. S. WARE AND FAMILY
36. MR. & MRS. V. M. MILLBOURN
37. ERIC DEANEY   PEARL DEANEY   CECIL DEANEY
38. W. YOUENS J.P.
39. A Thank Offering from R. AND T. WINTER
40. MR. C. BUNCE   41. WESLEY GUILD   PRESTWOOD
42. MRS. E. DOWLING   43. In memory of ADELAIDE FOX
44. MR. AND MRS. F. WELFORD   45. WESLEY GUILD   CHESHAM
46. In memory of MR.& MRS.D.DARVILL
47. In memory of MR. O. PALMER
48. In memory of THOMAS BOND by members of the family
49. MR.& MRS. DARVIL
50. Bricks with initials only: M.J.T. L.G.D. A.P. K.J. L.H.
    M.H.   C.H.   G.B.P.   L.A.G.   K.F.   G.F.S.   D.L.S.   C.W.
    C.W.S.   A.J. T.J.   M.S.   R.H.   L.A.B.   D.J.   J.A.J.   E.L.
    O.C.P.   J.E.C. (The following are not so clearly defined)
    T.B.   S.W.   C.T.   J.B.   S.R.   J.+.S.   ?.W.

Schoolroom

51. R.GOODEARL Esq. J.P.   28th May 1912.
52. MRS. G. AND MRS. M. SAUNDERS
53. Bricks with initials only: D.T. L.T. W.K. A.C. F.T.

In Vestry

54. WESLEYAN CHAPEL   ERECTED 1841.   REBUILT 1859.
55. WESLEY GUILD (with the Guild symbol)
56. MR. & MRS. PURSEY
57. MR. & MRS. STEVENS   R. AND M. STEVENS
58. MR. & MRS. WRIGHT

In The Backroom

59. C.F.LORD of CH.WYCOMBE   60. H. WINGROVE   C. LANCASTER
61. MRS. RANDALL   62. MR. J. STEEVENS
63. MR. & MRS. J. JAMES   64. RONALD D NICHOLLS

LACEY GREEN

PRIMITIVE METHODIST CHAPEL 1855

1. These memorial gates were erected in unfading memory of former scholars in this Sunday School who gave their lives for humanity in the Great War. Their names are inscribed opposite.
2.

RUPERT GINGER	WALTER GINGER	FRED HARVEY
FREDERICK W. JANES	ALFRED J. JANES	CECIL TAYLOR
OWEN ADAMS	OWEN BAREFOOT	GEORGE PARSLOW
CHARLIE CURRELL	ALFRED JANES	

****

LANE END

WESLEYAN METHODIST

1. T.W.P.Esq. 1863   [T.W.POCOCK of Virginia Water]

Inside

2. In Grateful Remembrance of the Members of our School and Church who made the Supreme Sacrifice in the Great War. ALFRED BIRD, HARRY BIRD, RALPH BISHOP, RICHARD DEAN, FRANK GRAY, ARTHUR HARRIS, BERT HARRIS, ERNEST HAWKINS, THOMAS PIERCEY, HORACE STEVENS, WALTER SMITH, FRED THORNE, 1914-1919 (Sic) "Lest we Forget".
3. This Tablet is erected in Loving Memory of JAMES ELLIOTT Late of Barmoor Farm who was for many years connected with this place of worship. Who peacefully fell asleep Aug.28th 1905 aged 82 years. "Peace Perfect Peace".
4. On the Organ. To the Glory of God and in Loving Memory of LLEWELLYN GEORGE PIERCEY who for twentyfive years was devoted organist of this Church. Called to Higher Service April 13th,1949.
5. 1939-1945. In Grateful Remembrance of the Members of our School and Church who made the Supreme Sacrifice in the Second World War. AUBREY GIBBS, FRED KING, STANLEY JOHNSON, WILLIAM THORNE. "Lest We Forget".
6. This Vestry was erected in Loving Remembrance of ELIZABETH ANN, the Beloved Wife of JAMES ELLIOTT of Barmoor who fell asleep in Jesus March 11th 1895 aged 67years.
7. Two Pulpit Lamps. (a) Erected in memory of G.E.PLUMRIDGE called home 10th June 1902. (b) "Blessed are the pure in heart for they shall see God".

8. Two Vases.   In loving memory of GEORGE and REBECCA ELLIS
    1940.
9. The Clock.   In Grateful Remembrance of ETHEL BEESON a
    devoted member of this Church 1898 - 1979.

****
LEE COMMON.

PRIMITIVE METHODIST CHAPEL 1839

****
LITTLE CHALFONT

1. Major A.Dennis (Society)
2. Mrs.E.Bennett (Women's Fellowship)
3. Jennifer Crayford & Roger Wingrove (Sunday School)

Inside

4. In Memory of Miss.Eleanor Hill - 28th Oct.1978.

****
LONDON ROAD

WESLEYAN METHODIST 1893

1. Mr.& Mrs.W.J.Cook & fam.
2. Miss Alice Youers for Circuit & S.S.
3. Harold Barfield Esq. (Banbury)
4. Coun.F.Joynson J.P.for Prim./Utd.Church
5. Charles W.Early Esq.. J.P. (Witney)

****
MARLOW

PRIMITIVE METHODIST 1874 (LISTON HALL)

1. Rev.C.Smith & C.Spoon (Ministers)
2. Mrs.I.Jones   3. J.Wilson
4. H.Roberts   5. M.S.Carson
6. R.Wellicome   7. J.S.Carson
8. William Sellman & family

MARLOW

WESLEYAN METHODIST CHAPEL 1900

1. Mrs.DOSETT   2. Mrs.DAVIS
3. Mrs.J.THOMAS
4. H.GOODEARL Esq For Circuit Sunday Schools
5. Mrs.NORTH   6. Mr.A.HARRIS
7. Revd.W.EARL Sup.Minister   8. R.GOODEARL Esq J.P.
9. C.W.DEACON Esq J.P. Mayor of Wycombe
10. Mr.B.BURTON   11. Mrs.Jas.CRESSWELL
12. Bricks with initials:- A.L.T. J.B.W.
13. A single stone with
    initials as shown   R.E.
                              E.M. V ?.D.
                                   \ | /
                              A.D. -|- W.C.
                                   \ | /
                              E.F. -|- A.R.
                                   \ | /
                              E.F. -|- E.C.
                                   \ | /
                              M.C. -|- E.P.
                              ------W------

Inside

14. In loving memory of the Members of this Church and Sunday
    School who fell in the Great War 1914 - 1918.
    W.H.BEAVER   F.H.GOLDING
    R.G.BUCKELL   G.HARRIS
    A.F.BRUNSDEN   A.MOODY
    A.J.CARTER   W.F.STROUD
    C.COOPER   F.SWADLING
    T.COOPER   W.C.WELLICOME
    H.EDWARDS   E.C.WELLICOME
15. This clock was given in loving memory of Mr.JACK UNSWORTH
    1902 - 1970.
16. 1937 This organ was presented by the Trustees of the ex
    Primitive Methodist Church in commemoration of the union of
    the two churches with funds derived from the sale of the
    P.M. church. Rebuilt 1969.
17. On the small organ in the back Schoolroom:- Donated by
    Friends of this Church in Memory of JOHN LEE in appreciation
    of his work in the Church and Sunday School.

Schoolroom

18. This stone was laid by ALICE, RUPERT and WINIFRED WELLICOME in loving memory of their sister AGNES Born June 29th, 1879 Died March 30th, 1884.
19. In Memory of HERBERT CORRINGE
20. Mrs.J.DORSETT
21. ?(Defaced Initials) DUKES
22. T.WELLICOME
23. Mrs.J.CRESSWELL
24. Mr.W.PLUMRIDGE
25. Mr.G.KEMPSTER
26. Mrs.G.KEMPSTER
27. Mr. J.PLUMRIDGE
28. Mr. J.BUSBY
29. Bricks with initials only:- A.W. A.E. S.T. A.H.H. E.B. E.S. S.P.F. M.B.W. P.C.W. A.E.S.W. G.W.W. T.B.W. A.W.D. R.A. J.D. E.C. C.D. M.N.A.L. E.G.L. A.S. M.M. C.M.M. R.B. E.W. F.L. ?.W. M.L. H.H. D.G. M.P. W.D. M.J.F. T.S.E. F.G. J.W. A.M.W. W.W. F.W. A.W. E.W.

###

NAPHILL

1. Primitive Methodist Chapel. 1851. We preach Christ Crucified.
2. OWEN JOYNSON
3. WOMENS COMMITTEE
4. This stone was laid by CONINGSBY DISRAELI J.P. D.L.
5. THE LOCAL PREACHERS
6. These doors were donated by family and friends to the memory of JACK TAPPING 1907 - 1983. 50 years member of this church. Enter these doors with thanksgiving.
7. Mr. and Mrs. J. HOLLAND
8. FREDERICK JOYNSON J.P.
9. Laid on behalf of the TRUSTEES
10. Laid by Mrs.KING in memory of her father and mother Mr. & Mrs. T. LEE
11. Mrs.TURNELL in memory of Dad and Daughter
12. GEO.GINGER
13. Councillor J.WILLIAMS
14. Laid on behalf of OLD SCHOLARS
15. Mrs. C.SHRIMPTON
16. MARGARET MARTIN
17. CHRISTIAN ENDEAVOUR
18. R.GOODEARL
19. FREDK.HUNT
20. In memory of ALFRED & ELIZA HUNT
21. S.RIDGLEY
22. G.B.LACEY in memory of his wife
23. This stone was laid by ERIC H.MILNER
24. In memory of WILLIAM & ELLEN SHAW G.S.
25. R.DORMER
26. J.GRACE
27. E.H.STALLWOOD

Inside

28. Clock. Presented by Sunday School Members to commemorate the centenary of the original Church. 1851 - 1951.
29. Font. In loving memory of LESLIE BROWN 1902 - 1980.
30. Sunday School Shield. Trophy held by the Sunday School for the year.
31. Over the door to Schoolroom. Plaque of Royal Air Force Strike Command.

****
PENN

FREE METHODIST

1. This stone was laid by THOs.CHAMBERLAIN Esquire. August 4th 1875
2. County Fire Badge.
3. In loving memory of a dear husband & father FRANK KING died April 20th 1976 Aged 72 years.
4. In loving memory of a dear wife & mother EDITH MARY KING who died on 26th May 1982.
5. EVELYN PERFECT 1925 - 1984.

****
PRESTWOOD

WESLEYAN CHAPEL

1. Thomas Wheeler   2. O.Glenister - 1872

****
RADNAGE

PRIMITIVE METHODIST CHURCH 1865.

1. This stone was laid by: J.HUNT Esq. May 18th 1865.
2. This stone was laid by: D. CLARKE Esq. May 18th 1865

Schoolroom

3. Laid on behalf of the Sunday School 6th April 1957.
4. Mr.and Mrs.E.J.DORMER.
5. In Remembrance of FREDERICK MAUNDER.
6. In Remembrance of Mr.and Mrs.J.DORMER, ELIZA DORMER and AMY DORMER/CHILTON.
7. In Remembrance of Mr. and Mrs.W.STRATFORD.

8. Mr.and Mrs.W.E.HANCOCK.
9. Bricks with initials only: C.W.   C.S.   R.J.   C.A.   A.D.
   V.D.   M.H.   L.A.   J.R.   M.G.   J.C.   R.G.   K.S.   M.G.   C.D.
   M.P.   G.P.   M.D.   K.A.   J.A.

Inside

10. Remembering the men of Radnage who gave their lives in the
    two world wars
                 1914 - 1918
    ERNEST ASHBY   PHILIP STRATFORD
    WALLACE ASHBY   GEORGE TURNER
    HARRY BALWIN
    SIDNEY BIRD   1939 - 1945
    WILFRED EGGLETON
    STEPHEN LANE   FRED ASHBY
    JOSEPH LAY   JOSEPH BALFE
    ERNEST PITCHER   ROY BAYNES
    FRANK STONE   THOMAS DORSETT
    [Note. All the men of this village who gave their lives had
    been on the roll of the Methodist Sunday School.]

##
ST.MARK'S METHODIST

METHODIST CHURCH 24th Oct. 1959

 1. Mr.& Mrs.G.Bunce   2. Mr.W.A.Steevens
 3. George & Mary Smith (Wooburn)
 4. In memory of Geoffrey [Chilton]
 5. Coun. & Mrs.H.V.Fry   6. Miss A.A.Youers
 7. 5th H.W.Wolf Cub Pack   8. Youth Club
 9. Women's Meeting   10. Sunday School
11. The Society   12. H.W.Dimmock
13. Stones with initials only: J.C.   R.C.Q.   S.H.G.   I.H.& L.H.
    G.M.R.   M.C.C.   E.F.   F.C.& C.K.   A.& A.P.   E.M.J.
    [The Notice Board has no plate but was given in memory of
    Ernest Chilton, whose lifetime of selfless service was a
    blessing to all who knew him.]

Inside

14. The Font. In loving memory of Miss Alice Youers
15. Vase.   In Happy Memory of Rose C. Quarrendon. Died 25th
    Novr.1952.

16. Brass Bowl and Stand. In loving memory of Margaret Ann Sutcliffe (1937-1979). "God make my life a little flower that giveth joy to all".
17. Candlesticks. In happy memory of Carolyn Trew. May 1967.
18. Offertory Plate. In loving memory of Brian Williams, 1939-1963, from Mum, Dad, family and relations.
19. Alderman Harry Fry. Servant of God - Leader of Men - Friend of All who extended the hand of friendship to all who entered here.
20. Pulpit Bible and Tune Books. In loving memory of Evelyn Bunce. Nov.1984
21. Bibles. In memory of Colin Campbell 1922-1987.

###

SANDS

PRIMITIVE METHODIST

1. This stone was laid by the most Hon.the Marquis of Lincolnshire on August 14th 1912.
2. This stone was laid by LINDA MILNER in memory of her mother Mrs.G.H.TAYLOR
3. E.L.TOMPKINS
4. In loving memory of HARRY HARVEY. E.H. O.H. E.B.
5. This stone was laid for Mr.& Mrs.P.W.LOWE by C...R...th LOWE
6. This stone was laid on behalf of the Methodist Church Wesley Circuit.
7. This stone was laid on behalf of the Circuit by Mrs.W.S.HINCHLIFFE
8. This stone was laid by BRIAN EDWIN MILNER
9. In sacred memory of ANN MARTIN this stone was laid by her daughter Mrs.J.Grace
10. This stone was laid by A.FRIEND
11. This stone was laid by R.HOLLAND WILLIAMS in memory of the late ETHEL MAY HOLLAND
12. Ministers Revd.J.C.G.CUSHING Revd.D.DUNN Builders R.H.HARRIS & Co. Architect A.W.NASH
13. This stone was laid by Master E.R.GIBSON MILNER
14. Mr.A.E.HOOK
15. Miss E.E.ABRAM in memory of Mr.HENRY ABRAM of Stockwell JY
16. To the.memory of Mrs.FLORA NUTHALL of Bottom Farm this stone was laid by her daughter May.
17. This stone was laid by Mr.M.CROXFORD
18. This stone was laid by ALBERT GLENISTER Esq. CC
19. This stone was laid by Mr.W.HOWARD
20. Mr.J.HOLLAND and family FW
21. This stone was laid by SIR ALFRED CRIPPS K.C. M.P.

22. Mr.F JOYNSON Senr.
23. E.STALLWOOD and family in memory of Mrs.E.STALLWOOD FW..S
24. This stone was laid by Mr.JAS.BAILEY
25. Miss A.GRACE   26. Miss.E.REDFERN
27. Mr.& Mrs.BURNHAM   28. Mr.& Mrs.JUDGE
29. Miss J.FLOYD   30. Mr.FRED HUNT
31. Mr. C.STRATTON   32. Sunday School HP HP ES
33. Mr.H.PILGRAM
34. This stone was laid by the Mayor & Mayoress Councillor and
    Mrs.V.S.TOMS
35. This stone was laid on behalf of the Trustees by
    Mrs.S.VALPOLE
36. This stone was laid for Mr.& Mrs.FRANK STALLWOOD by KATHLEEN
    STALLWOOD
37. This stone was laid on behalf of the Mens Own JG JW
38. This stone was laid by Teachers & Scholars HP Supt.HLH Secty
39. The Primary Class
40. This stone was laid by BRIDGEWATER SPRIGGS
41. This stone was laid by W.J. & H.S. BRAZELL
42. This stone was laid by the Womens Own MN BES
43. The Girls League   44. Mr.A.E.EAST
45. Mr.& Mrs.V.J.LARGE   46. Mr.& Mrs.G.STRATFORD
47. This stone was laid by JAMES BAILEY
48. Small stones with initials only:-   W.B.C. E.C.-J.C. A.G.-
    D.G. F.E.G. M.E.H. A.R.H. R.R.H. H.F.I. E.R.J. C.C.L.
    H.M.L. E.R.L. D.M.P. H.PEARCE E.F.P. G.C.N. R.V.N.
    FRED HUNT P.P.-M.P. C.P.-K.P. D.P.-S.P. I.G.R. K.V.J.R.
    J.E.R. F.W. K.W. F.J.W. L.B. A.S. A.S. H.B. H.W.
    H.L. A.S.C. R.L. R.L.Jnr. G.H. J.S. A.H. E.G. K.S.
    W.S. F.G.N. B.W. W.S. J.S.-G.S. D.H.S. S.S. M.M.S.
    M.E.S. I.S.-M.S. F.V.S. H.A.S. K.D.S. S.A.D. A.J.B.
    R.V.B. C.F.B. N.R.B. M.E.B. V.B. M.B. E.B. V.R.B.
    G.V. A.J.M. G.M. I.A.H. F.E.H. R.T.A. A.K.H. R.D.H.
    J.A. V.A. K.R.T. G.P. F.G.B. I.G.B. A.W. A.G.H.

****
STOKENCHURCH

PRIMITIVE METHODIST 1896

1. MR.J.BRITNELL AND FAMILY.   2. MR.J.LARNER AND FAMILY
3. MR.J.WHITE AND FAMILY   4. MR.H.SIMMONS AND FAMILY
5. MR.S.BARNEY AND FAMILY   6. MR.JAS.POOLE AND FAMILY
7. MR.J.BARTLETT AND FAMILY, NORTHEND
8. MR.J.BIRD AND FAMILY
9. This stone was laid on behalf of the P.M.Choir by
   MR.V.BRITNELL

10. MRS.D.BATES	11. MR.JOS.JUDGE
12. MR.& MRS.H.PALMER	13. MR.& MRS.W.JUDGE
14. MRS.W.BRITNELL	15. MR.W.BRITNELL
16. MR.G.AVERY	17. MRS.J.A.HARDING of Slough

18. MR.M.CROXFORD of Chalgrove
19. Bricks with initials only: H.J. T.J. E.H. E.J. H.R.
    J.F. M.B. W.S.C.C. S.A.L.

****
THE PASTURES

FREE METHODIST CHURCH (W.R.U.) 1969

1. Removed from the Oxford Road Church & relaid by George A.
    Wood on April 19th 1969. This stone was laid by
    T.Chamberlain Esquire March 31st 1863. Relaid June 5th 1911
    by the Revd. W.G.Smith Minister.

****
TYLERS GREEN - COPPICE FARM

H.Wingrove (Holmer Green) - 20th January 1968

****
WESLEY

WESLEYAN - 1866

Inside

1. To the Glory of God and in honoured memory of Hannah Ball,
    the friend and correspondent of John Wesley, who founded in
    this town in the year 1769 the first Sunday-School. Born
    1733 - Died 1792.
2. Sacred to the memory of Mary, the beloved wife of Edmund
    Hutchinson, of St.Mary Street, High Wycombe, who died May
    28th 1877 in the 81st year of her age.
3. In loving memory of Lieut.John Fox Harper (son of the
    Rev.Richard Harper, Wesleyan Minister), Imperial Yeomanry
    and formerly a member of this Choir, who was killed in
    action before Ladysmith Cape Colony on September 10th 1900,
    aged 24 years.
        "Whate'er his duty may have been,
        His humble task was dignified;
        He served his Country and his Queen,
        And serving - Died."
    This tablet is erected by his sorrowing parents.

4. Also of the above named Edmund Hutchinson who died June 2nd
   1879 in the 81st year of his age.   "The memory of the just
   is blessed."   Proverbs x.7
5. Sacred to the memory of John Bowden, Henry Collings,
   Frederick Copeland, Herbert W.Easden, William Gardner,
   George Litchfield, James Morris, Norman Nash, Albert Newell,
   Arthur Watkins, Albert Worley, Joseph Worley, Joseph
   L.Worley who gave their lives during the Great War, 1914-
   1918. "Faithful unto Death."
6. In memory of those who fell in The World War, 1939-1945:
   Ivor Green, John A.Hughes, Albert F.Lawrence, Henry J.Mudge,
   Leslie W.Sharp.
7. "This organ was erected to the Glory of God and in memory of
   those who fell in the Great War, 1914-1918.

George J.Ball	Arthur J.Bass
Frederick J.Coombes	Frank W.Elliott
Henry Eccles	Clifford J.P.Goodearl
Joseph B.Eccles	Rupert V.Goodearl
William C.Harman	Eric Hodgkinson
Stanley W.Powell	C.Frederick Rose
Walter J.Smith	F.Harry Turner
Joseph H.Varney	George W.Venables"

8. "In gratitude to God for the life of ETHEL ROSE HAINES this
   organ was restored in 1978. Born in this town,
   schoolteacher, Christian leader of women, a Mayoress of the
   Borough, closely connected with the chair trade, in life
   she was serene and gentle, yet a most determined person.
   She died 4th May 1976, aged 74, and at death was sorely
   missed by her husband, two daughters, their families and an
   exceptional company of friends."

****
WEST WYCOMBE

ORIGINAL CHAPEL 1815

   [The Chapel is the first on the left in CHURCH LANE. It is
the original Wesleyan Chapel built in West Wycombe and is now
used as a Christadelphian Church. The following inscriptions are
all etched into the red building bricks and with the exception
of the Mason's brick are all running down the right hand corner
of the building.]

1. J.BIGG Mason 1815   2. J.P. 1815
3. D.BIDMEAD 1815   4. T.R.
5. (All on the same brick) J.H. E.H. H.H. S.H. M.H. J.H.
   B.H.& W.   6. HOBSON

WEST WYCOMBE

WESLEYAN CHAPEL 1894

1. JOHN THOMAS Esq. J.P.C.C.   2. Mr.A.HARRIS
3. This stone was laid by Viscount Curzon M.P. August 8th 1894
4. Mr.& Mrs.B.NORTH   5. Mr.S.WELLER Senr.
6. This stone was laid by Mr.HENRY RACKSTRAW on behalf of the
   Sunday Schools of the circuit.
7. Mr.DORSETT   8. D.CLARKE Esq. C.A.
9. Messrs. C.E.MOXHAM and son Architects Wycombe
10. Mr.S.WELLER Jnr.   11. Mr.J.N.HARRIS
12. Mr.W.MEAD   13. Mr.Jas.BATES
14. Mr.A.CUTLER   15. Mr.C.V.DEACON
16. Mr.Jos.VARNEY   17. Rev.H.MUNTON
18. Mrs.NASH   19. Mr.B.CARTWRIGHT

###
WHEELER END

PRIMITIVE METHODIST CHAPEL 1861

1. This stone was laid by: J.WHEELER Esq. June 24th 1861.
   Rev.MURRAY WILSON Superintendent Minister.

###
WINCHMORE HILL

PRIMITIVE METHODIST JUBILEE CHAPEL 1860

1. T.Wheeler - 21st August 1860
2. In the service of youth - 1953
3. Centenary 1960 - Rev.Murray Wilson (Superintendent Minister)

Interior

4. In Memory of Joseph Cox (Sunday School Superintendent) -
   d.19th November 1916
5. In Memory of John Wright - d.1922
6. In Memory of Arthur Pursey - d.1977
7. In Memory of Olive Pursey - d.1963
8. In Memory of Elizabeth Hatch - d.1967
9. In Memory of Arthur Hatch - d.1971
10. In Memory of those who have served 1860-1960

APPENDICES

WOOBURN GREEN

WESLEYAN

1. T.W. 1872.

Schoolroom

2. This stone was laid by W.ECCLES on May 3rd 1905
3. This stone was laid by J.THOMAS J.P.on May 3rd 1905
4. This stone was laid by MRS.W.ECCLES on May 3rd 1905
5. This stone was laid on behalf of the Ladies Sewing Meeting
    on May 3rd 1905
6. This stone was laid by B.R.WELLICOME on May 3rd 1905
7. A.NORMAN   8. M.S.NORMAN
9. J.DORSETT J.P.   10. J.ECCLES
11. A.ECCLES   12. J.STEEVENS
13. G.NICHOLS   14. M.A.ECCLES
15. G.NASH   16. J.B.ECCLES
17. A.W.LAWRENCE   18. W.P.ECCLES
19. W.F.WHITE   20. H.ECCLES
21. Bricks with initials only as follows:-   E.S.   J.W.   M.S.
    G.S.   W.M.   E.L.   D.R.G.   N.J.G.   A.H.S.   G.B.   E.H.   H.S.

‡‡‡
WYCOMBE MARSH

FREE METHODIST (WRU)

1. This stone was laid by Mr.D.ANDREWS   July 21st 1896
2. MR.W.SIMMONDS   3. W.WOODBRIDGE
4. Relaid 1896.   This stone was laid by THOMAS MARTIN May 8th
    1865.
5. J.BOND Builder.   6. J.N.
7. MR.J.ALDRIDGE
8. This stone was laid by MRS J.HOLLAND   July 21st 1896
9. This stone was laid by J.THOMAS Esq J.P.   July 21st 1896
10. W.HOLLAND   11. H.TILLING .... (unclear)
12. C.PEARCE   13. LOCAL PREACHERS
14. Laid by Miss (?) BALL / The Children
15. HELIOTROPE BRINKWORTH / VIOLET BRINKWORTH
16. THE TEACHERS
17. This stone was laid by MRS.G.EDWARDS   July 21st 1896

TABLE OF CHURCHES

CHURCH	D	MEET	CHPL	EXT	CHPL	EXT	TRANS	LAST
Amersham (High St.)	W	1818	1899				1934(M)	->
Amersham (St.John's)	M		1960					->
Amersham Common	P		1860		1924		1934(M)	1960
Beacons Bottom	P		1868				1934(M)	1970
Beaconsfield	W	1837	1838		1900		19861850(F)	->
Beaconsfield	P	1856						?
Bledlow Ridge	W		1834		1887		19641934(M)	->
Bledlow Ridge	P	1835						?
Booker	W	1845	1847		1886		19071934(M)	->
Bourne End	W		1910				1934(M)	->
Bradenham	W	1837						1856
Bryants Bottom	P		1871	1974			1934(M)	->
Cadmore End	W	1844						1845
Castlefield (HW)	M	1939	1953		1966			->
Chalfont St.Giles	P	1832	1847		1866		19051934(M)	->
Chesham	W	1895	1897			1933/66	1934(M)	->
Chorley Wood	P	1867						?
Cryers Hill(Gt.Kings)	W	1822						?
Cryers Hill(Gt.Kings)	P	1835	1852		1866	1977/86	1934(M)	->
Deeds Grove (HW)	M	1961	1963	1978				->
Downley (Chapel St.)	P	1835	1864				1934(M)	1965
Downley (Sunny Bank)	W	1818	1824	1838/47/50	1924		1934(M)	->
Farnham Common	F	1845	1867					->
Flackwell Heath	W	1822	1865	1884/	1923		19841934(M)	->
Flackwell Heath	P		1848					1877
Frogmoor Gardens	P	1835	1848	1860				1875
Fulmer	P	1867						?
Gerrards Cross	F	1908	1915		1958		1931(V)/34(M)	->
Great Missenden	P	1846	1866				1934(M)	1938
Handy Cross	W	1846						?
Hazlemere	W	1844						?
Hazlemere	P	1835						?
Hazlemere	F	1865	1867		1906	1929		->
Holmer Green	W	1822	1841/59	1912	1937		19671934(M)	->
Ibstone	P		1862				1934(M)	1958

CHURCH	D	MEET	CHPL	EXT	CHPL	EXT	TRANS	LAST
Knotty Green	W	1822						?
Lacey Green	W	1837						?
Lacey Green	P	1835	1855	1955			19871934(M)	->
Lane End	W	1818	1834	1841	1866		19811934(M)	->
Lee Common	P		1839	1962			19861934(M)	->
Little Chalfont	M	1952	1959	1976				->
Little Hampden	W	1874						?
Little Hampden	P	1877						?
Little Missenden	W	1838						1844
Littleworth Common	P		1832					?
London Road (HW)	W	1891	1893	1929			1934(M)	1959
Marlow	W		1810			1900	19781934(M)	->
Marlow	P	1835	1874					1933
Marlow Bottom	M	1932	19361970-75					->
Moor's Town	P	1866						?
Naphill	P	1841	1851			1930	1934(M)	->
Newland (HW)	F	1880					1910(U)/34(M)	1955
Oxford Road (HW)	F	1849	1863	1900	1911			1970
Penn	W	1805	1808	1876			19111850(F)	->
Penn (Tylers Green)	P	1835	1843				1934(M)	1968
Penn Street	P	1835						?
Piddington	W	1904	1906				1934(M)	1986
Prestwood	W	1861	18631872/1926/73/77				1934(M)	->
Radnage	W	1822						1855
Radnage	P		1865	1957			1934(M)	->
St.Mark's (HW)	M		1959					->
St.Mary Street	W	1766	1779					1866
Sands (HW)	P	1897	1912				1934(M)	1982
Saunderton (Workhouse)	W/P/F	1822						?
Scrubwood	P	1877						?
Seer Green	P	1840						?
Slater Street (HW)	P		1873				1934(M)	1955
Speen	P	1835						?
Stokenchurch	W	1818						?
Stokenchurch	P	1863	1868			1896	19771934(M)	->

CHURCH	D	MEET	CHPL	EXT	CHPL	EXT	TRANS	LAST
Terriers (HW)	W		1895				1934(M)	1970
The Pastures (HW)	F		1970					->
Tylers Grn.(Coppice F)	M		1968					->
Victoria Street (HW)	W		1878	1904			1934(M)	1975
Walters Ash	W	1822						?
Wesley (HV)	W		1866	1893			1934(M)	->
West Hyde	P	1867						?
West Wycombe	W		1815		1894		1934(M)	1983
Westbourne Street(HW)	P		1878				1934(M)	1961
Wheeler End	P		1861				1934(M)	1987
White Hart Street (HW)	P		1875				1934(M)	1951
Winchmore Hill	W	1818	1861					1934
Winchmore Hill	P	1856	1860		1953	1966	1934(M)	->
Wooburn Green	W		1811		1873	1905	1934(M)	->
Wooburn Green	P		1832				1860(F)	1938
Wooburn Moor	P	1866						?
Wycombe Marsh	W	1865						?
Wycombe Marsh	F		1865			1896	1935/82	->

KEY

HV = High Wycombe
D = Denomination (M=Methodist; F=Free; P=Primitive; U=United; W=Wesleyan)
MEET = First recorded meeting or service
CHPL = Chapel/church built
EXT = Extension or extensive alterations
LAST = Date of closure; ? = date not known

INDEX OF CHURCHES

(see also tables; * = main reference)

CHURCH   Page Nos.

Amersham (High St.)   21, 25, 39, 49-60, *131-2, 268, 297
                                              *299, 357
Amersham (St.John's)   194, 296-7, 300, *317-319, 350, 357
Amersham Common   132, 172, *193-4, 261-2, 268, 296-7
                                              299, 300, 350
Beacons Bottom   61, 199, 204, *205, 260, 272-5, 351
Beaconsfield (F.M.)   6, 23, 39, *98, 226-8, *232-3,*246
                                              339 357
Beaconsfield (Prim.)   *164
Bledlow Ridge   23, 39, 50-2, 60, *96-8, 109, 279
                                              284, 327, 337, 352, 358
Bledlow Ridge (Prim.)   *163, 191
Booker   23, 38, 50, *101-9, 254, 273, 278-80
                                              284, 350-2, 358-9
Bourne End   25, 51-5, *135-7, 279-80, 283
                                              350-2, 359-60
Bradenham   23, *85
Bryants Bottom   128, 141, 186-8, *206-7, 260, 275
                                              284, 352, 360
Cadmore End   23, 38, *85
Castlefield (H.W.)   253, 262-4, 268, 278, 284, 305
                                              *306-9, 350-2, 360
Chalfont St.Giles (M/URC) *170-3, 261-2, 268, 297, 350, 360
Chesham   9-10, 25, 39, 53-60, *128-30, 147
                                              260, 268, 297, 350, 360
Chorley Wood   *165, 172
Cryers Hill (Wesleyan)   23, *85
Cryers Hill   140, *188-90, 202, 261-2, 270, 277
                                              280-2, 352, 361-2
Deeds Grove (H.W.)   125, 218, 248, 253, 272-7, 282
                                              *319-21, 350-2, 362
Downley (Chapel St.)   86-8, 140-4, 184-5, *199-201, 254
                                              262, 268, 272, 326
Downley (Sunny Bank)   21, 49-52, 60, *85-9, 201, 254, 268
                                              271-2, 280, 283, 327, 352, 362-4
Farnham Common (F.M.)   226-8, *241-2, 339
Flackwell Heath   23, 50-8, *113-5, 260, 280-3
                                              352, 365
Flackwell Heath (Prim.)   *173
Frogmoor Gardens (H.W.) 140-1, 150, *174-84, 213, 217, 252

Fulmer   *165
Gerrards Cross   227, *244, 339
Great Missenden   112, 141, 169, 189, *202-3, 262
Handy Cross   23,*38-9, 85
Hazlemere (Wesleyan)   23, 38-9, *85
Hazlemere (Primitive)   146, *163
Hazlemere (F.M.)   226-8, 235, *238-40, 280-2, 328, 339
                                                       350, 365-6
Holmer Green   23, 38, 50-2, 58-60, *98-101, 248
                               260, 270, 274, 282, 352, 366-7
Ibstone   8, 61, 153, *199, 204-5, 260-2, 268, 272
Knotty Green   23, 38, *85
Lacey Green (Wesl.)   23, *85
Lacey Green   140-5, 153, 188, *190-3, 270, 280
                                          284, 326-7, 352, 368
Lane End   21, 38, 49-52, 59, *89-95, 109
                               278-9, 284, 325-6, 350-2, 368-9
Lee Common   140, 153, *165-9, 189, 254, 261-2
                               268, 297, *299, 351, 369
Little Chalfont   296-7, 300, *309-12, 333, 350, 369
Little Hampden (Wesl.)   23, *85
Little Hampden (Prim.)   *165
Little Missenden   23, 38, *85
Littleworth Common   140, 144, *161-2
London Road (H.W.)   25, 51-60, *125-7, 211-2, 270-2, 369
Marlow   20, 49, 55, 60,*75-8, 260-1, 278-82
                               304, 330, 336, 350-2, 369-71
Marlow (Primitive)   60, 76, 144, *213
Marlow Bottom   59, 253, 261-2, 268, 273, 280-3
                                          *303-6, 334, 352
Moor's Town   *164-5, 356
Naphill   140-2, 153, *184-8, 199, 283, 325, 352, 371
Newland (H.W.)   60, 124, 218, 227,*242-4, 245, *247-50
                          252-3, 260-2, 268-70, 306,328, 339
Oxford Road (F.M.)   23, 226-7, *234-6, 242-5, 252-3
                                               326-30, 339
Penn (F.M.)   20, 23, 39, *75, 226-8, *231-2
                                          282, 339, 372
Penn/Tylers Green (Prim.)   140-5, 153, *169-70, 268
                                               273, 329
Penn Street   143-6, *162-3
Piddington   25, *132-5, 196, 260, 273, 279, 351
Prestwood   23, 50-9, 109, *111-3, 169, 203
                               268, 297, 300, 372
Radnage (Wesleyan)   23, 39, *85
Radnage   23, 141, 153, *201-2, 260, 273, 279
                                          285, 336, 352, 372-3

St.Mark's (HW)   126-8, 211-2, 253, 272-5, 283, *312-7
                                             322, 350-2, 373
St.Mary Street (HW)   5, 11-20, 23, *63-74, 115-6
                                            120, 174,217, 249, 252
Sands (HW)   141, *219-221, 253, 277-9, 306, 373-5
Saunderton (Workhouse)   23, *85, 355
Scrubwood   *165
Seer Green   *163
Slater Street (HW)   126, 141, *207-12, 268-70
Speen   140, 145, *162
Stokenchurch (Wesl.)   21, 61, *85
Stokenchurch   115, 199, *203-5, 260, 279
                                             284, 352, 375
Terriers (HW)   25, 51-5, *127-8, 207, 261-2
                                             268, 273-5
The Pastures (F.M.)   227-8, 236, 240, *244-6, 253, 280
                                             283, 375
Tylers Green (Coppice Farm)   170, 253, 274-5, 278-82
                                          *322-4, 350-2, 375
Victoria Street (H.W.)   25, 49-57, 109, *124-5, 248
                             260-2, 270, 273, 277-9, 306, 331
Walters Ash   23, 39, *85
Wesley (H.W.)   23, 49-60, 109, *115-123, 214, 217
                              248, 252-3, 259-62, 268, 271-3
                                  277-82, 322-3, 350-2, 376-7
West Hyde   *165
West Wycombe   20, 25, 38-9, 49, 57-60, *81-4, 133
                                     260, 277-9, 337, 377
Westbourne St.(H.W.)   141, 153, *217-9, 220, 260-2
                                     272, 306, 321, 331
Wheeler End   133, 141, 153, *196-8, 262, 273
                                          279, 351, 378
White Hart St. (H.W.)   141, 174, 203, *213-7, 218, 252-3
                                  260-2, 268, 306, 322, 329-31
Winchmore Hill (Wesl.)   21, 39, 49-60, *110-1, 329
Winchmore Hill   172, *194-6, 261, 268, 297, *299, 378
Wooburn Green   ,20, 49-58, *78-80, 274, 280-3
                                          328, 352, 378-9
Wooburn Green (F.M.)   140, 145, *161, 226-7, *233-4, 339
Wooburn Moor   *164
Wycombe Marsh (Wesl.)   23, 40, *85
Wycombe Marsh (F.M.)   226-8, *236-8, 339, 379

INDEX OF PEOPLE

(Numbers are page numbers; tables & lists are not indexed)

Accult J.	14	Barrow J.	260
Acton K.	109,284	Batchlor E.	167
R.	109	Bates D.	84
Adams H.	77,274,304-5	E.	203-5,261-2
Addison L.	112	P.	197
Adey G.	166	V.	216,296
Ager C.	109	Batson V.	103
Aldridge	218	Batting J.	5,16,64
R.	330	Batts	60
Alick	310	G.	87,190
Allen	206	Baxter A.	77,263,278,305
Anderson E.	188	Bayliss C.	100
H.	20,38	N.	100
J.	70	Beard	60
T.	202	Beasley S.	101
Andrews E.	184,214	Beck	38-9
Ansell P.	284	Beckley C.	194
Apps T.	233,264,268,327	Beeson	167
Ash J.	78	Bell S.	84,284
Ashley R.	78	Belson	81
Aston P.	232	Bendle	176
Atkins	202	Bennett-Richards E.	112
M.	329	Benyon E.(T.)	233
Axe	173	Berlyn	234-5
		Berry	220
Bailey J.	198	Biggs J.	238
Baker E.	313	L.	245
Ball A.	13,346	Bignell	207
E.	178	H.	263
H.	3,12-18,64,187,204,346	Bilbey	195
Barefoot V.	221	Binks H.	261-2
Barker A.	232,280	P.	321
Barnard A.J.	258,281	Bird	81,93,202,241
Barnes	82	J.	89
B.	314	T.	91
Barnett E.	334	Birkenhead J.	75
T.	268	Birks W.	152,164-9,173,181-2
Barr J.	81		192,196,202
Barratt B.	205	Bishop	176
Barrett	248	E.	192
B.	247	H.	268
T.	326	Blackwell J.	103
Barrington E.	263	Blyth E.	269

Bolton-King	83	Bunce C.	124,307
Booth M.	77,279,282,305,315	E.	208,315
W.	223	W.	263,295
Bourne H.	139,153,166	Bunting J.	224
Bovington E.	39,110,163,195	Bunyan J.	104
Bowler A.	238	Burden K.	236
Boyles	243	S.	237
Bradbury G.	199	Burgess M.	203
Bradford J.	14	Burkitt W.	235
Brain L.	312	Burnham	109
Bramwell W.	70	A.	58,114
Brearley I.	261	G.	58,114
Brenton Dr.	86	J.	114
Bridger C.	247	Lord	339
O.	239	Burr L.	197
Bridgnell J.	70	Burrows F.	190
W.	70	N.	134,275-7,309
Briggs	176	W.	231,237
Brine J.	267,307	W.J.	235-6
Bristow I.	190	Butcher	39,110
Britnell J.	243	Butler F.	205
W.	203	G.	205
Brittin G.	190	H.	202,205
M.	272	J.	205,213
Brooker D.	310	W.	178
J.	124		
L.	97,271,307,313,317	Cambridge D.	123
	320	Campbell	75
M.	124	C.	295
Brown	136	H.	307
J.	75	J.	283
T.	181	Cant A.	124,248,262
Browne J.	108	M.	248
T.	189,213	Capell L.	271
Brunsdon A.	76	Carden	173
Bryant G.	114	Cargill J.	241
W.	194	Carpenter	241
Buckingham E.	191	Carrington C.	182
Buckland	176	Lord	50,96,115-6
Buckle	239	Carter	172,307
A.	233	P.	275
P.	233	Cartwright	248
Buckley G.	116	J.	260,267
Bulling C.	325,329	W.	111
Bullivant W.	173,196,202	Cassham	176
Bullock G.	52-54	Castle G.	262
T.	113,300	Cato L. and S.	173

Chadwick	221	Comben S.	132,310,317,322
Chamberlain T.	241-2	Connell	182
Chamberlayne J.	318	R.	208,213
Chapman E.	267	Cook W.	55
H.	262	Cooper W.	267
Chappel W.	70	Copeland J.	190,261
Cheeseman T.	233,242	Coppin W.	53,75,92,119-21,128
Chesworth S.	278		327
Child	237,243	Coppock A.	100
G.	233	Cordery	135
J.	232	Cornfield R.	269
Chilton E.	315	Cotton J.	328
F.	84	Couling A.	235
Christian C.	129	Cook W.	55
D.	268	A.	272,308
Church B.	314	L.	267
C.U.	268	Craft C.	262,331
G.	129	G.	331
K.	326	Creswell	220
M.	69,313	Crew E.	272-4,303,314-6
Clark H.	314	F.	314
R.	210	Crimes A.	262
Z.	334	Cripps E.	220
Clarke D.	146,181-2	Crockett W.	242
F.	113	Crook H.	108,121
J.	183	J.	108
Claydon D.	190	W.	121-3
Clayton A.	61	Cross D.	89
Cleaver R.	295	F.	97
Clissold C.	240	Crouch M.	90
Clogg B.	263,267	Cumbers F.	333
Clowes W.	139,154	Curtis A.	125
Clulow W.	72-3	K.	269,319
Cock A.	38,338	Cutler M.	83
Coke T.	2,71,347		
Coker	202	Dancer	237
W.	267	Darke E.	165
Cole C.	269,317	Darvill	219,329
J.	15,65	G.	262,268
Collier F.	271	M.	260,296,307
M.	127	Darwent S.	274
Collins H.	39,86	Dashwood G.	181
L.	114	Daveney J.	38,69
O.	268	Davey M.	89
R.	243	W.	163
S.	105	Davies H.	90
Colville D.	311	T.	213

Davis	76	Fane E.	108
Dawson W.	120	Farmery M.	232
Day A.	238	Feesey	189
F.	280	Ferral M.	272
Daykin R.	113	Field N.	328
Dean	109,136,202	P.	316
A.	88,119-20	Firth G.E.	259,270-2,279,313
N.	306-7		319
Deane F.	248	Flexman W.	162
Dell	191,200	Foizey	175-6,181
Dennis A.	76,310	Folly	186,200
E.	239,258-61,267	S.	185
Denton J.	77	Ford A.	238
Dimmock H.	210	H.	87
Disraeli Major	187	Foster J.	58
Dobinson	176	P.	269-71,308,319
Dormer E.	202,295	Fowler G.	195
R.	202	Fox K.	123,276
Downes	72	P.	120
Dring	50-1,79	Foy Capt.	331
Dukes T.	107	Free G.	186
Dunn S.	224	Freeman A.	270-1,312-4,328
Dunne D.	187	C.	316
Dyer C.	276	D.	332
N.	333	Freer K.	279
V.	213	French E.	198
		Fry H.	125-7,271,314,327
Earis T.	321	M.	327
Earl	241	Fryer J.	101
Eavis E.	129,260	Fuller J.	178,192
Eccles W.	56		
Eden T.	15	Gamble	171
Edge S.	58	Gane D.	311
Edgerley B.	331	Gardiner N.	100,248
E.	331	Garland M.	75
G.	331	T.	231,235
J.	331	Garlick W.	54,130
Edwards A.	267	Ghorst V.	168
M.	12,112	Gibbons H.	220
M.S.	282-4,309	P.	308
Elderton V.	194	Gibbs A.	111,203
Elijah	327	Gibson K. and M.	322
Elliott J.	90	Gilbert M.	304
Evans D.	213	Gilder	242
M.	188	Giles E.	83
O.	262-3	S.	101
Everitt J.	224	W.	83

Gill	182	Haddock C.		100,278,282
Gillie R.	119-20	Haddow		307
Glandfield G.	263	H.		215-6
Glenister	112	M.		215
Goff	136	Haines		55
Goldswain H.	103,107	E.		123
Gomm J.	202,238	O.		124-5,307
Gomme E.	211,217,313	W.O.		111,123-5,187,263
J.	211			313
Goodchild L.	307	Hall C.		239
M.	247	J.		97,207,312-3,322
Goodearl	207,330	N.		207,320
A.	135,253,261,267	P.		317
	272,296,307,329	R.		173
D.	220	Hammel M.		211
E.	124	Hammersla E.		314-6
H.A.	58,272	L.		314
H.C.	306-7,330	Hancock		177
I.	308	E.		169,203
L.	220	Hardwick W.		147
O.T.	56,124,260	Hardy R.		71
R.	53,58,59,112,136	Hargrove G.		240,245,280
	187	Harman		83,208
S.	321	H.		283
W.	89,271	Harmer		4,15
Goulder J.	245	Harper R.		128
Gower	20	Harris		81-2
Graham B.	90,316	E.		217
D.	278,309,321	J.		54
Granville Lord	161	L.		232
Gray	136,185	Harvey		76
E.	261	Hatch E.		196
T.	131	Hauks		16
Green E.	112	Hawes		18,38
R.	119	S.		101,284
Greenstreet	170,268,323,329	Hawke K.		313
Greet K.	79	P.		335,340
Griffiths W.	224	Hawkins A.		201,272
Griffits J.	174	J.		38-9,338
Grigg G.	161,213	Hayden J.		175,181
Grimsdale G.	212	Hazell R.		243
Grover	193	Heafford F.B.		311
Guy C.	267	Hearn		81
J.	161-3,166,175,184,199	P.		284
Gyngell G.	163,185-6	W.		243,260
		Hearne F.		328
		Heathcote A.		263

Heaton W.	300	Howland	40,79,182,248
Hedges I.	166	F.	100,243
Henderson	15	R.	243
Henningham R.	75	Howlett G.	245
Henry L.	300,309	Hudson	307
Herbert	176	C.	214
Herridge	176	F.	250,259,268-72
Hester A.	271	Hughes A.	38,81-3
I.	208-11	D.	83,309
R.	274	E.	39
Hewitt D.	322	F.	307
G.	316	Humphries T.	3,18
Higginbottom J.	278	Hunt	171,188,208,219,329
Higgs A.	267	B.	304
Hildreth B.	112	F.	295
Hill	172	J.	176-7,182
E.	311	R.	75
F.	116	Hussey J.	38-9,109
Hilliard S.	283		
Hinchcliffe V.	258-61,331	Ing	220
Hirst	38	J.	197
Hobling V.	172	L.	132
Hobson J.	176	Irving W.	262
T.	175	Ivens H.	57
Hogdon R.	232	Ives J.	185
Holland J.	216		
M.	202	Jackson	88-9
W.	236	D.	278,282
Holmes	233	R.	88,278-82,315,353
E.	76	T.	140,179
Hook H.	201	James	10,16,63,201,322
Hope J.	248,328	A.	99-100
M.	247,328	E.	241
Hopkins A.	313	H.	260
Horberry J.	170,194	J.	274
Hotston	88	S.	100
W.	89	V.	100,203
Howard	220	Jarrett	168
D.	261,307	H.	207,216
F.	296	Jarvis	82
Howard-Smith	128	Jeffries T.	213
Howarth D.	268	Jefkins J.	231
M.	170,322	V.	235-6
P.	343	Jenkins W.	130,311,319
Howe Baroness	75	Johnson	40
Earl	99,231	S.	283

Jones	182	Lee	83
A.	216,272,321	D.	321
A.G.	259,278-81	E.	76
E.	261	G.	132,205,267
J.	285	J.	76-7
L.	272,303-5	Lewis D.	305,326
Judge T.	199	D.W.	89,185
Junior	38	G.	95
Jupe	172,267	H.	50
C.	190,214	K.	76,305,352
O.	128	Lincolnshire Marquis	96
		Line W.	153-4,168,218,295,328
Kaye R.L.J.	113,173,259,274-7	Lisley J.	327-9
	321-2	Liston	213
Keen N.	234,245	Little J.	119,326
Kelly D.	279	Lloyd J.	280,283
Kendall D.	150,181	Lofty	173
M.	215	Loosley E.	258,261-3,268
Kilham A.	223	G.	203
Kinch A.	272	H.	97
King	188	J.	97
E.	309	Lord D.	57-8
F.	310	H.	263
Kingston H.	174	Ludgate A.	241
Kipping R.	232	Lyth E.	307
Kirby	173		
Kitchener E.	263,307	Mackney L.	240
Kitchin E.	269,307	Macpherson S.	190
		Maidment P.	278
Lacey	235	Maland G.	262-3
G.	187	Malpass N.	237
Ladyman	217	Marsland N.	79
Lane C.	235,322,330	Martin	237
Lang P.	308	S.	262,306
Langley I.	201	T.	236
R.	200,329	Mason B.	282
Large A.	220	E.	190
Laurence J.	283	K.	132
M.	75	Maunder	60
Lawrence D.	327	E.	202
E.	100	May V.	284
J.	233	Maynard E.	125
K.	128	McArthur W.	116
M.	190	McCulloch H.	213
Lawson M.	297	McDonald A.	317
		McLean D.	276
		McNair P.	278

Mead	38	Newton J.	316
N.	188	Nicholls A.	100
V.	81	R.	100,226
Meakes J.	88	Norris W.	181
Meeking	188	North B.	57,83
Meeks	128,207,306	M.	307
W.	233,237		
Mereden	167	Odell E.	319
Metcalfe J.	170,275	Omand D.	233
Middleton G.	269	Orme E.	73
Millbourn V.	58,124	Orton R.	207,276-8,314
Miller	71,81	Osborn Dr.	118
Milton J.	172	Osborne M.	305
Mines D.	89	V.	304-5,329
E.	89	Owen J.	261-2
Mitchell D.	316	Owens D.	310
Monk E.	330		
Monkman R.	164,167,171,180,192	Page U.	208,216
Montey K.	309	Palau L.	316
Moon J	54	Parker J.	105
Moorcock J.	81	W.	100
R.	118	Parkins W.J.	269
Moorcroft S.	163	Parnaby W.	217,263
Morris M.	98,327	Parslow B.	187
Mortimer	72	Pattern M.	274-5,308
Mossop D.	177	Pay A.	207
Mott I.	329	Payne F.	100
Mounteney A.I.	278	Pearce A.	127,269
Moxham C.	131	B.	282
Mules J.	163,179,191	F.	109
Murcott V.	109	G.	187
Murgatroyd B.	278	Pearson R.	263
L.	198	V.	279-80,352
Murlin J.	4,11,65,71-4	Peatey A.	100
Murray D.	235-7,245	B.	245
		K.	218,263,274
Nancarrow R.	59,196	Peddle M.	247
Nash	109,182	Penman J.	58-9
J.	203	Penrose T.	213
Neville W.	170,173,218,329	Perfect F.	231
Newall T.	65	H.	231
Newell C.	55	W.	125,248,271
E.	205	Perks G.	79
K.	190	Pettet H.	279
P.	190	Pettinger J.	239
Newstead E.	311	Pettit R.	115
G.	311	Phillips J.	173,196,202

Phipps D.	309	Rackham J.	172,213
K.	109,278,284,309	Rackstraw E.	328
L.	109,309	J.	153
R.	309	K.	220
Pierce	140,171,174,183	T.	239-40
E.	115,162,178	Raikes R.	13,346
F.	182	Ramsay	89,93
J.	170,177-8	Randall	207
T.	163,170,185,201-3	Raw J.	116,181
Piercey	108-9	Ray R.	118
Pike M.	76,213	Reader C.	123
Pilkington F.	262-3	S.	234-5
Pledge D.	189	Ream W.	259,272-5,322
Plested	219	Redding A.	283
J.	153, 261	Reece S.	57
Plowman A.	53	Reed D.	274-5,314,322
Plumridge B.	89	Renshaw N.	261
H.	77,93-4	Reynolds Dr.	51
J.	89,123	Rhodda	14
S.	196	Rhodes	15
W.	89	Ridgley B.	128
Pocock	220	E.	206
Pole J.	140-7,161-3,169,174	Rixon	168
	184,190,199,213	F.	207
Pope H.	176	Robbins C.	167,176-8
Porson J.	72	Roberts	185
Potter E.	83	W.	72,176
R.	83		
Powell R.	279	Robertson B.	83
Pratt G.	263	Robinson	171
I.	170	T.	165,183
Price W.	326	Rogers	207
Pullen E.	217,320-1	C.W.	260
Purcell	135	J.	153,282
Pursey J.	99	R. (C.W.)	96,260,284
W.	99-100	Rolfe K.	216
Putman W.	278,282	Rolls F.	153,262
Putnam	238	G.	267
E.	190	Rose	177
F.	239	G.	188,278
Puzey G.	273	Rowe G.	75
		W.	213
		Royall A.	137,279,283
Quantick	202	Rumble C.	124
Quilter H.	119-20	Russell B.	90
		Rutty J.	181

Sammons	38,337-8	Smith T.	263
Sanderson	14	W.	207,296
Sargeant	207	W.B.	217
B.	238	W.C.	235-6,239-40,335
J.	208		338-40
Sargent M.	130	Snell	38,236
Satchell W.	39	A.	316
Saunders A.	209	Soons E.	307
B.	10	Sparks D.	280
J.	109	Speed A.	267
W.	121,261	Spooner	9
Savage A.	262	Spry	136
Saville F.	153,207	Stallwood F.	220-1
Searle F.	260-1,325	Stanford P.	269,300
Sears R.	221	Stedman	167,238
Seed W.	55-6	Steevens A.E.	59-61,262,269
Seymour G.	101-9,210,262	W.A.	96,136,238,271
J.	105		295
R.	210	Stephenson W.	59
Shannahan A.	279,282,324	Stevens	79,109
Sharman	177	J.	109,284
Shaw G.	187,190,262	R.	99-100,109,284,327-9
W.	115,118	Stiles	168
Shelburne Lord	10	Stobbs R.	59,260
Shepherd G.	60	Stone	173
Sherratt S.	85,296,329	F.	172
Sherwin F.	54	Stonehill	10
Sherwood	108-9,220	Stonell K.	238
Shirley J.	136,263	Story G.	65
Siddens P.	283	Stratford D.	190
Silverwood H.	199,218	Stratfull G.	195
Silvey	109	J.	131
L.	124	L.	196
Skerratt J.	119	Stretton A.	231
Skull	82,182	N.	231
Slade F.	80,328	Stroud J.	150
Slater H.	259,277-8,321	Sutcliffe B.	272
Slocombe R.	278	M.	314
Smith	12,39,171	Sworn C.	278
D.	101	Symonds	164
G.	118	J.	171,180,188
H.	193,317-9	Syred G.	203
J.	104,181,195		
M.	181	Taft W.	236-7
O.	57	Tapping A.	76
R.	201	J.	89
S.	235	Tattersall B.	259,267-8

Taylor	233	Wakeham S.		246
B.	86	Walker		53-5
G.	218,260	A.		233
M.	209,328	D.		114
N.	328	S.		233
R.	86,234	Walklate		72
Tebbles	81	Waller L.		276
Tebby G.	54	Walsh T.		13,18
Terry W.	81	Walters A.		258,263-8
Thomas J.	119	Wane		103
N.	267	Ward		241
Thompson D.	322	C.		106
Thorne G.	269	H.		77,276,305
Tibbles	208	Warren		307
Tilbury	238	Watson		164,185
Tilling H.	237	D.		278,316
W.	237	Waterhouse J.		81
Timberlake G.	237	Watt D.		313
Timmins L.	270,319	Watts F.		207,275,314
Tindal J.	232	M.		314
Tocock E.	167,178	Weathered		136
Tomkins	191-3,200	Weatherhead J.		284
Tonks E.	220	Webb F.		196,205
Tordoff S.	347	M.		186
Toulson J.	202	R.		197
Towerton T.	203	Webley M.		76
Treacher J.	81,87	Webster C.		87,201,325-7
Trigwell H.	278	Weight		81
J.	279	Welch T.		269
Tripp L.	170,173	Welford F.		109
Tucker P.	275	Weller E.		81-3,119,262
Turnbull H.	260,271,307	S.		50
W.	190	Wellicome C.		75
Turner	39	M.		76
A.	207,272,307	Wellings M.		173
Tyler G.	273	Wells A.		270
		S.		15
Urwin E.	308	T.		127,212
		Welters F.		220
Valton	14,16	Wesley C.		19,90
Van Petegem	305	J.	1-19,25,64,72,90,122	
Varley H.	213		128,139,199,225,249	
Vernon A.	118		252,335,345-7,355	
L.	83,282	S.		1,345
Victoria Queen	241	West		81
Vincent C.	311	A.		186,268
		J.		220

West W.	235	Woodward F.	54
Westerdale T.	59	H.	264
Westminster Duke	114	Worley	171
Westrup	14	J.	202,208
Wharton	124	Wright	56,114
Wheeler T.	79,181,195,208,234	A.	131
	238	H.	100,327-9
V.	109	J.	87
White A.	232,307	Wynne W.	60,129
C.	126,188		
J.	76	Yeomans W.	262-3
L.	126,315	York C.	130
M.	283	Youens A.	326
R.	39	E.	182
W.	269	J.	182,214
Whitefield G.	2,223	M.	89,179,182
Whittaker R.	307	R.	89
Whittard A.	267	W.	87,106,118,263
Whopshott E.	114	Youers A.	127
Widdess J.	341	Young F.	270
Wigley	176	Younger W.	261
Wilkinson J.	232,237		
Willott A.	267		
Williams B.	314		
M.	282		
T.	176		
Wilshaw	176-7		
Wilson F.	235,328		
H. and M.	316		
M.	181,195		
Winch	182		
Wingrove	75		
H.	58,100,262,267		
	307,322		
Winter H.	279,282		
Wise M.	237		
Wolfe	4,14-15		
Wood B.	245		
G.A.	242,245		
Woodbridge	40,109,194-5		
B.	123		
J.	136,243		
Woodhouse J.	208,213		
Woodley	186		
W.	181		
Woodstock E.	128		